ETHNIC IDENTITY

ETHNIC IDENTITY

Problems and Prospects for the Twenty-first Century

Fourth Edition

EDITED BY LOLA ROMANUCCI-ROSS,
GEORGE A. DE VOS, AND TAKEYUKI TSUDA

ALTAMIRA PRESS
A Division of Rowman & Littlefield Publishers, Inc.
Lanham • New York • Toronto • Oxford

AltaMira Press
A Division of Rowman & Littlefield Publishers, Inc.
A wholly owned subsidary of The Rowman & Littlefield Publishing Group, Inc.
4501 Forbes Boulevard, Suite 200
Lanham, MD 20706
www.altamirapress.com

PO Box 317, Oxford, OX2 9RU, UK

British Library Cataloguing in Publication Information Available

Library of Congress Cataloging-in-Publication Data

Ethnic identity : problems and prospects for the twenty-first century / edited by Lola
  Romanucci-Ross, George A. De Vos, and Takeyuki Tsuda.—4th ed.
    p. cm.
  Includes bibliographical references and index.
  ISBN-13: 978-0-7591-0972-8 (cloth : alk. paper)
  ISBN-10: 0-7591-0972-9 (cloth : alk. paper)
  ISBN-13: 978-0-7591-0973-5 (pbk. : alk. paper)
  ISBN-10: 0-7591-0973-7 (pbk. : alk. paper)
  1. Ethnicity. 2. Ethnopsychology. 3. National characteristics. I. Romanucci-Ross,
Lola. II. De Vos, George A. III. Tsuda, Takeyuki.
  GN495.6.E872 2006
  305.8—dc22

                                                                        2005036584

Printed in the United States of America

∞™ The paper used in this publication meets the minimum requirements of American National Standard for Information Sciences—Permanence of Paper for Printed Library Materials, ANSI/NISO Z39.48-1992.

Contents

Preface

THIS IS THE FOURTH, completely revised edition of our study of ethnic identity, first published in 1975 as *Ethnic Identity: Cultural Continuities and Change*, reissued in 1982, and revised in 1995 as *Ethnic Identity: Creation, Conflict and Accommodation*. This present edition, *Ethnic Identity: Problems and Prospects for the Twenty-first Century*, reflects our attempt to keep up our attention to the changes that have occurred worldwide in the thirty-five-year period since our initial attention to ethnicity and ethnic identity from a psychocultural perspective. We first held our Wenner-Gren–sponsored conference on ethnicity at Berg Wartenstein, Austria, in 1970.

In the third, and this, the fourth, edition, we have added and dropped chapters as areas of concern and contemporary salient groups to consider. The topics considered, therefore, have changed during this period. What we deem remarkable is that the original volume in its totality was highly predictive with respect to the greater saliency now given to ethnic problems as being central to many political and economic events of relevance to social scientists generally.

Previous Topics of Concern

There are only four chapters remaining from the original volume. We must assert that the chapters that were produced by the original participants at the Wenner-Gren Conference are still germane to the topic of ethnic identity and remain very worthy of reading. We strongly commend referral to *Ethnic Identity: Cultural Continuities and Change*, the 1975 edition that gave attention to a number of abiding topics carefully examined in their complexity by the author participants of the original conference.

In George Devereux's chapter, "Ethnic Identity: Its Logical Foundations and Its Dysfunctions," he formulated a careful distinction between ethnic identity, ethnic attribution, and ethnic personality as related to actual behavior or external stereotyping. He also delineated both the functionality and dysfunctionality of ethnic groups.

Berreman in his chapter on India, "Bazaar Behavior: Social Identity and Social Interaction in Urban India," pointed up how ethnic identity is a matter of shared perception; the communication of that perception to others; and, most crucially, the response it elicits from others in the form of social interaction. He applied his specific insights to the Indian caste system. He believes that traditional concepts of caste were so narrowly drawn that they were often inapplicable to many facets of ethnic stratification found within Indian society. He examined the use of stereotypes as indicators. Comparing rural and urban settings, he concluded that the traditional use of caste categories was diminishing in importance.

Schwartz, in "Cultural Totemism: Ethnic Identity, Primitive and Modern," constructed a provocative analysis of the use of "totemic" thinking in the development of identity and cited material from a number of disparate native sources. He stressed how ethnicity is decidedly relative to primitive societies when they are not taken as isolates but, as we usually find them, as part of a complex of communities.

Taking on the complexity of what it is to be Chinese, Hsien Rin, in "The Synthesizing Mind in Chinese Ethno-Cultural Adjustment," discussed in detail the subjective meaning of being Chinese, the relationship of the Chinese to their neighbors, how Chinese identity was and is maintained in a foreign setting when a territorial base is lacking, the special problems of overseas Chinese, and conversely the treatment of ethnic minorities in specific Chinese contexts such as Taiwan.

Geoffrey Gorer, in "English Identity over Time and Empire," views the self-sufficient aspect of English identity as dominant since the sixteenth century. Within it are regional self-definitions and the sometimes-excruciating continual awareness of social class differences, whether at home or in various colonial settings, wherein they carefully kept themselves separate from any "native" behavior. Today, British entry into "Europe" is very challenging and problematical.

Religion is a crucial element for many groups in defining their ethnic identity when they do not differ in other respects from neighboring groups. Gananath Obeyesekere, in the chapter "Sinhalese-Buddhist Identity in Ceylon," acquaints us with one such continuing occurrence in Ceylon. Group separation may vary in intensity through time, with shifts occurring in political ascendancy. Home and school may reinforce or conflict and thus bring on internal problems of social identity. For many, being Sinhalese means being Sinhalese-Buddhist and therefore means denying being Sinhalese to those who are not Buddhist.

Social identity can be influenced by psychocultural reactions to external cultural forces that have compelled and continue to compel emulation. Victor Uchendu, in "The Dilemma of Ethnicity and Polity Primacy in Black Africa," illustrates how such forces operate in West Africa. Uchendu sees the search for social identity in black Africa as comprising four sometimes-conflicting alternatives. First is a possible identity with the entire continent, based on postcolonial political independence. Second, some uniting "black" racial identity is used. Third are new, synthetically achieved, arbitrary "national" identities of the new political states. And fourth remains the continuing force of separate local ethnic identities. There are situational shifts in identity saliency related to ongoing political and economic changes.

Both El-Hamamsy ("The Assertion of Egyptian Identity") and Wagatsuma ("Problems of Identity in Modern Japan") illustrate similar problems related to a possible sense of alienation that can selectively attack the elite segments of a society heavily influenced by an outside culture. Outside ethnic ascendancy and pressure toward emulation as a social force is not limited to situations of political dominance by either a majority or a minority elite. It is also found in situations where there is no direct political influence. Egypt and Japan, highly dissimilar in cultural content and history, are both cases where members of the elite segment of a culture have had to face serious dilemmas as a superior technology of another group carried with it an alternative worldview and an implicit moral system that could alienate individuals from past patterns.

Raveau, in "Role of Color in Identification Processes," examines the psychological processes involved in the internal adjustment of black migrants entering a white European society. He discusses the part that body image plays in the psychopathological reaction that an African immigrant sometimes suffers as a response to social rejection.

While these chapters remain valid in their presentation of ethnic concerns, more pressing contemporary changes related to ethnicity have constrained us to turn to new situations now deserving exploration as we enter the twenty-first century.

Organizing Topics of the Fourth Edition

The present volume considers the salient features of ethnicity that continue into the twenty-first century. Throughout the chapters of this volume, one can note a range of considerations, from highly "racialist" definitions of ethnic belonging suggesting genetic heritage in some chapters, to highly situational or expediential definitions characterizing the use of ethnicity in others. The topics chosen also range from forms of enduring persistence to situations of radical change. To further define the topics under consideration, we have found four types of interlinking concerns. The first section, "Changing Ethnic and National Identities" (four chapters), examines the interrelation and relative salience of ethnic versus national identities. The second section, "Migration and Ethnic Minorities" (three chapters), deals with ethnic patterns persisting or newly developing in situations of migration in the current, highly mobile world. Ethnic attributions can be projected by the politically dominant as they define subordinate minorities for political, economic, or social status reasons, and we have grouped four chapters in the third section ("Ethnic Ascription versus Self-Definitions") around how ethnic ascriptions of a politically dominant group distort or reflect the self-identity of members of an ethnic minority. In our last two chapters, forming the fourth section ("Shifting Ethnic Identities: The *Realpolitik* of Cultural Control"), we examine changes in ethnic identification related to radical shifts in political ascendancy and power.

Changing Ethnic and National Identities
First to be considered is how what is termed "national" loyalty interacts in either a positive, negative, or highly complex manner with a personal ethnic identity developed in situations of long, enduring residence of several interactive ethnic groups in a given area.

Introducing this first topic is Lola Romanucci-Ross's chapter, "Matrices of an Italian Identity." She examines historically how a profusion of languages and cultures became the contemporary nation-state of Italy with a new, overarching identity shared in a complex way by its constituent population. To illustrate, she examines the historic vagaries of ethnic identity within the area of Ascoli Piceno in central Italy.

In its historic mixture of languages, religions, and traditions, few places can rival "Vilnius, Lithuania: An Ethnic Agglomerate." Czeslaw Milosz draws for us a compelling historical picture of how the inhabitants of Vilnius have persisted and accommodated themselves through changing national definitions in a continuously changing set of allegiances on the border of Eastern Europe. At one recent period, instruction in the schools was given in Polish, Yiddish, Hebrew, Lithuanian, Byelorussian, and Russian. Inside some families, different identities could be assumed by different family members.

A national identity can be lost. A more troubled pattern of ethnicity used for antagonistic purposes is found in what was once the nation state of Yugoslavia. Firsthand intermittent residence as well as research in Slavonski Brod, now on the border of what has become Bosnia and Croatia, by Mary K. Gilliland illustrates the loss of national loyalty. Her continuous contact from 1981 to the present day has permitted her to document changes in loyalties and the expressions of animosity among residents of this area as well as in the former state in general. In the past, identities were not always primarily associated with ethnicity or nationality. The categories of neighbor, friend, relative, and even fellow citizen had dominance in times of peace over the category of nationality or ethnicity. She has revised for us her chapter in the previous edition, "Ethnogenesis in the Former Yugoslavia," to document the continuing adverse trends in tensions and violence, in "Ethnic Nationality in the Former Yugoslavia." The climate of fear has notably increased. Those married between groups are attempting to find various ways to achieve a social self in the new circumstances. Increased violence has led to further separation.

In some instances, ethnic definitions and nationality cannot be separated. Japan is perhaps unique as an extreme of this situation reinforced by extreme racial definitions of the meaning of Japanese ethnicity. The Japanese attitude toward several million minorities reflects the overriding use of racial uniqueness to define not only one's ethnicity, but also the boundaries of the Japanese national state. As a major industrial state, it has lost any isolation that once insulated it from any identification with other parts of Asia. Recognizing its debt to China for many aspects of its traditional culture, it nevertheless has kept much of its mythology of uniqueness of origin as a people. It cannot digest easily as citizens or "nationals" anyone who has become recognized internally as a minority. It still cannot overcome attitudes of alien origin attributed over the years to a genetically polluted caste known as the Eta. Japanese cannot recognize any racial or historical affinity with neighboring Koreans, nor can they recognize as citizens any others that have occasionally acquired residence. They certainly cannot see as but temporary the many menial workers brought in to overcome the declining birthrate of its majority.

Migration and Ethnic Minorities

Migration as an ordering topic is represented in the following three chapters. Estimates suggest that around the world today there are more than 175 million immigrants and refugees. Societies worldwide are being transformed in remarkable ways as a result of these unprecedented geographic changes in the world population.

Many migratory situations involve children or subadults and their formative adaptation of a social identity in a situation of change. What happens differs from setting to setting. In chapter 5, "Ethnic Identity and Schooling: The Experiences of Haitian Immigrant Youth," Fabienne Doucet and Carola Suárez-Orozco examine how the social identities of youth are developed within school and its peer group influences in the contemporary United States. Typically schools are the first setting of sustained contact with a new culture for immigrant children, and academic outcomes are a powerful barometer of current as well as future psychosocial functioning. American racial definitions still influence the mode and conditions of assimilation in most urban scenes.

Contemporary Europe, with a declining birthrate, is experiencing large-scale waves of new immigrants. Some migrants are more readily assimilated to the present nations than others are, for a variety of racial and cultural differences. Religion is still an important issue in the acceptability of assimilation, or, conversely, the resistance to national or "European" assimilation on the part of an entering minority. Muslim migration into various European settings has become a sensitive social and political issue. Philip Hermans, in "Ethnic Identities of Moroccans in Belgium and the Netherlands," reports on his and others' research being recently addressed to the tensions arising about the assimilability or nonassimilability of Muslims.

In the last of our chapters related to migration, Takeyuki Tsuda ("When Minorities Migrate: The Racialization of Japanese Brazilians in Brazil and Japan") shows how racial identity discussed in the preceding chapter has functioned to preserve Japanese migrants as a separate group after moving to Brazil starting at the beginning of the twentieth century. An obverse dilemma occurs when some Japanese Brazilians remigrate to Japan. They are considered genetically "Japanese," but their Brazilian-learned physical behavior and social attitudes cause them to reconsider themselves more as "Brazilian."

Ethnic Ascription versus Self-Definitions

In "Peasants, Ethnicity, and the Politics of Location," Yos Santasombat describes in Thailand how definitions by national or state authorities of what a minority group should do occupationally come into conflict with the social self-identities of the Lua in northern Thailand. He points out that to-day the struggle between the state and ethnic groups in Southeast Asia is not merely a struggle over forest land, property rights, and territorial integrity. It is also a struggle over the appropriation of symbols, a struggle over how the past and present shall be understood and represented, and a contentious effort to give meaning to local history and ethnic identity.

Early European explorers of East Africa, in their writing or word of mouth, projected onto the Africans they encountered their own values and preoccupations. In "'Beautiful Beasts' and Brave Warriors: The Longevity of a Maasai Stereotype," Lotte Hughes traces the history of how some descriptions were passed on and others were disputed in European attitudes and desires to "change" or "civilize" the Maasai so they would assume the agricultural role that political authorities would like them to practice instead of remaining adamantly the pastoralists they were from their precontact past.

The gypsies, or Rom, found throughout Europe are an interesting case of outside ascription not coinciding with inner definitions of self. Andrea Boscoboinik ("Becoming Rom: Ethnic Development among Roma Communities in Bulgaria and Macedonia") discusses how European nations have a long history of contending with marginal "gypsy" groups now considered derivative of a very early migration from somewhere in India. These groups have been designated by various names, most recently by the collective name "Rom." We find from this chapter that they are not so designated internally, although they have for the most part resisted any assimilation into their host societies. Often the children have no birth registered and are not sent to primary school. They do not assume ordinary occupations but practice various forms of behavior for survival that bring them into conflict with the law and the disapproval of those coming into contact with them. During the Nazi regime of Germany, there was wide-scale extermination of those categorized as Gypsy throughout occupied Europe.

Eugeen Roosens's "Subtle 'Primitives': Ethnic Formation among the Central Yaka of Zaire" brings us to totally different circumstances. The definitions of self given others by an African minority in Zaire are manipulated in the designations of self given to others, depending on the situational social or economic advantages accruing to how one designates oneself. Roosens examines the contextual use of alternative ethnic self-definitions of advantage of people calling themselves Yaka under certain circumstances, but Suku or Luundi under others. It can be a most confusing situation to outsiders.

Shifting Ethnic Identities:
The Realpolitik *of Cultural Control*

The events in South Africa allow us to examine how a radical shift in political power necessitates shifts in self-identity in a national state based on racial division. In his chapter, "The End of Whiteness: The Transformation of White Identity in South Africa," Louis Freedberg discusses how key institutions that were central to the maintenance of Afrikaner identity have essentially collapsed. Younger Afrikaners are now questioning how their parents and grandparents could have been so misguided as to dream up an idea as wildly impractical and immoral as the apartheid state. They are undergoing a period of soul searching and are demanding answers from their elders. These days, it is hard to find a "white" person who acknowledges having supported racial apartheid.

In South Africa, "coloureds" seemed to represent the one ethnic group from which every other group wished to disidentify. In "Mixed Feelings: Spoiled Identities in the New South Africa," Nancy Scheper-Hughes states how she explores relations between the previous apartheid state's official construction of "coloured" as a demographic category of indeterminacy, and now how one continues to find personal narratives of exclusion, marginality, suffering, and spoiled identity as still experienced by "coloured" people in the present transitional state. For a number of those placed in this category, however, there is actually some temporary resolution of the social and psychological conflicts in a paradoxical reassertion of a "coloured" identity.

Conclusions

In our summary chapter, "Ethnic Identity: A Psychocultural Perspective," De Vos and Romanucci-Ross reaffirm how a psychocultural perspective is necessary for examining how ethnic identity influences behavior in every modern society.

In our previous editions' introductions and conclusions, we forwarded several arguments and a general assertion that to understand ethnicity as a vital social force one has to include a psychological level of analysis to consider how subjective feelings are related to group belonging more than to objective cultural criteria. Ethnicity can often be a subjective sense of loyalty based on imagined origins and/or parentage rather than something to be measured by objectively visible present cultural criteria or historical facts.

Contrary to what some would still insist as to the invariant, rational, goal-oriented nature of ethnic striving, social belonging is not based simply on rational, instrumental considerations. Although motives for social advantage are found in some instances, in other instances there are emotional issues involved that at times go counter to the rationally considered benefits of asserting, maintaining, or denying an ethnic allegiance.

Our abiding argument was that ethnic loyalties are a more governing, sometimes irrational, always potentially conflictful, social force, stronger than rationally considered social-class loyalties drawn from one's past or present social and political history. It is evident that espousing the saliency of ethnicity over class loyalty as we did in 1970 is no longer as contentious as it then was. Many who were in the past Marxist theorists have now retreated from a sole preoccupation with conflictful class analysis toward espousal of ethnic problems as sources of social unrest. Anti-imperialism now makes a better rallying cry than banners espousing class warfare.

Our concluding chapter reiterates and again formulates what we consider the complex parameters involved, including the psychocultural dynamics that constitute an ethnic identity.

George A. De Vos

Introduction
Ethnic Pluralism:
Conflict and Accommodation
The Role of Ethnicity in Social History

GEORGE A. DE VOS

A SENSE OF COMMON ORIGIN, of common beliefs and values, and of a common feeling of survival—in brief, a "common cause"—has been important in uniting people into self-defining in-groups. Growing up together in a social unit and sharing a common verbal and gestural language allows humans to develop mutually understood accommodations, which radically diminish situations of possible confrontation and conflict. In mammalian societies generally, ordered systems of individual dominance are a major accommodative device. Given the human capacities for cultural elaboration, we go further. Humans can, on the basis of *group definitions of belonging*, develop complex formal systems of individual and group social stratification. These systems are found in many so-called primitive societies as well as in technologically advanced modern states (see De Vos 1966; De Vos and Suarez-Orozco 1990).

The cultural bases for social groupings in society are varied. Some groupings, such as lineage systems, are defined reciprocally and horizontally. Kinship networks, a major form of grouping, very often operate horizontally as forms of reciprocal marital exchange. Other groupings, such as class and caste, are stratified vertically, with emphasis on the status of an individual or group with respect to other persons or groups. Another form of group separation is found most frequently in composite societies and results from the inclusion of groups from supposedly different cultural, or "ethnic," origins (De Vos and Suarez-Orozco 1990).

Ethnicity can be a source of considerable conflict, since in many instances ethnic groups do not remain in a fixed position within a stratified system. A separate ethnic identity, when it persists in a group, tends to

1

maintain boundaries, to use the perspective of Fredrik Barth (1969, 15). Like Barth, I think that in the study of ethnic relations, one must first understand how and why boundaries are maintained, rather than simply examining the cultural content of the separated group. We both contend that boundaries are basically psychological in nature, not territorial. They are maintained by ascription from within as well as from external sources that designate membership according to evaluative characteristics.

It seems necessary, in discussing ethnicity, to start from a theoretical position that regards some form of *conflict* as a normal or chronic condition in a pluralistic society. Social tensions are manifestly different and less readily soluble in pluralistic societies than they are in stratified societies composed principally of an ethnically homogeneous populace.

Ethnically plural societies have occurred throughout human history, most often involuntarily as a result of imperial conquest. Today, however, ethnicity has become an important issue in modern states because of the ethnic interpenetration that has resulted from increasing social mobility (related to individual achievement) and from increasing geographic mobility (due to shifting labor markets).

We are also witnessing a revolution in the recording of social and cultural history. Today's ethnic minorities are not content to remain mute; they, too, seek to be heard. The defeated and the oppressed, now literate, are themselves contributing their interpretations to the writing, or rewriting, of history, adding their own and, where facts fail, creating or deepening their own sustaining mythologies. Social classes or pariah outcastes that were relatively invisible in earlier unrecorded histories are emerging as figures in a larger history of conflict, or as new subjects in historical approaches that deal more directly with stratification in societies. The Marxist philosophy of history has deepened the perception of modern historians generally, enabling them to recognize the existence of historically oppressed groups. Like Freud's approach to personal history, a conflict approach to social history reveals the continuing influence of repressed forces—forces that do not disappear simply because they have been omitted from the official history written by the politically and socially dominant group.

Another social process is also continually at work: the creation of newly salient identities and group loyalties defined as ethnic in nature but that are actually based on a past that has been only recently fabricated and that comes to justify a presently sought-for, selectively contrastive social belonging. Ethnic identity, as we shall observe in several of the following chapters, is a continually evolving social process, sometimes occurring within a single generation.

Ethnic minorities have been present as long as sovereign political states have existed. However, ethnic conflict has usually been treated from the standpoint of political struggles for territory rather than from the psychocultural viewpoint of what occurs within individuals when they are confronted with the necessity of changing allegiance to a new master, adopting a new religion, or even acquiring a new language in order to participate in a dominant political society that is ethnically alien.[1]

Until recently, social science theorists have paid little attention to enduring ethnic or cultural identity as a primary social force comparable to territorial nationalism or class affiliation. Its role in past and present conflicts within complex societies was often neglected by social scientists, who usually concerned themselves with the relations between ethnically different but politically autonomous groups. Once a group has been conquered or absorbed politically, the assumption seems to have been that its existence in a new political state was of less concern than the state's external relations. From the earliest history of the state, however, many forms of intrasocial tensions have arisen from ethnic diversity. Such conflict has not been limited to empires that acknowledged political hegemony over ethnically heterogeneous groups. It is still apparent in states that seek to extend a uniform culture to all its members.

To maintain its focus, this discussion does not deal with conflict between independent cultures; instead, it is restricted to a preliminary and partial overview of the nature of ethnic conflict in established pluralistic societies. In this introductory chapter, I shall briefly examine how ethnicity can be used both *expressively* and *instrumentally* within a pluralistic society and how it may or may not contribute to social instability.

Certain peoples insist on maintaining symbolic forms of cultural differentiation for centuries, despite a lack of political autonomy or even of a particular territory. Given the present abundance of opportunities to observe groups firsthand, there is no excuse to neglect the question of how ethnic identity functions psychologically as well as socially in a complex, stratified social system.

One cannot fully understand the force of ethnicity without examining in some detail its influence on the personality of minority group members. It is insufficient to examine ethnic group behavior directly, from only the vantage point of social structure or social processes. The discussion of ethnicity and social stratification that follows relates one's conflict over allegiance and belonging not only to one's place in the status system, but also to internal conflicts over the priority to be given to past-, present-, or future-oriented forms of identity in "self"-consciousness.

In a primary sense of belonging, an individual can lean toward one of three orientations: (1) a present-oriented concept of membership as a citizen in a particular state or as a member of a specific occupational group; (2) a future-oriented membership in a transcendent, more universal religious or political sense; or (3) a past-oriented concept of the self as defined by one's ethnic identity—that is, based on ancestry and origin. We contend that the maintenance of this latter form of identity is as powerful a force as a present or future allegiance in shaping human social history. The Marxist theory of class consciousness or class conflict tells us much less about human history than does a historical examination of ethnic consciousness.[2]

Ethnicity Broadly Defined

There is as yet no acceptable single word in English for the phrase "ethnic group," no one word equivalent to "class," "caste," or "family" to describe a group self-consciously united around particular cultural traditions, although French anthropologists have suggested the word *ethne* for technical usage. The term "tribe" is used in some contexts, but it implies pejoratively the primitive in an independent social organization. An ethnic group is a self-perceived inclusion of those who hold in common a set of traditions not shared by others with whom they are in contact. Such traditions typically include "folk" *religious beliefs* and practices, *language*, a sense of *historical continuity*, and *common ancestry* or place of origin. The group's actual history often trails off into legend or mythology, which includes some concept of an unbroken biological-genetic generational continuity, sometimes regarded as giving special inherited characteristics to the group. *Endogamy* is usual, although various patterns for initiating outsiders into the ethnic group are developed in such a way that they do not disrupt the group's essential sense of generational continuity.[3]

Some of the same elements that characterize ethnic membership seem to characterize lineage groups or caste membership in some societies. The subjective definitions differ, however, as do their functions. A lineage group or caste perceives itself as an *interdependent* unit of a society, whereas members of an ethnic group cling to a sense of having been an *independent* people, in origin at least, whatever special role they have collectively come to play in a pluralistic society. Thus, caste definitions explicitly point to a present system of formal stratification, whereas ethnic definitions refer to a past cultural independence. In contrast, groups formed around universalist religious or political ideologies are oriented to a future society with less explicit or more satisfactory forms of status stratification. Individuals presently dissatisfied with the social status accorded to them as members of a minority group may seek to leave their group. They may choose either to adopt a future-oriented religious or political ideology, thereby gaining admission to a new group, or they may emphasize their ethnic past and exert pressure to change the collective relative status of their group. (I shall presently illustrate instances of an attempt to escape caste definitions in India and the United States.) An alternative to any change in collective status is a change in individual status, which may involve "passing," as I shall also discuss later.

"Racial" Uniqueness

Some sense of genetically inherited differences, real or imagined, is part of the ethnic identity of many groups, as well as being one of the characteristics about an ethnic minority held by those dominant groups that wish to prevent assimilation. The relationships between caste, ethnicity, and racial definitions are complex in many pluralistic societies. A willingness to acculturate completely on the part of a racially defined ethnic minority, not only in comportment but also in actual identity, may not be acceptable to the dominant group. A system of stratified exclusion can be better maintained on the basis of genetic heritage, which implies that such backwardness is not to be overcome.

A socially defined racial minority wishes to assimilate but finds that intermarriages or other forms of integration are withheld on the basis of race; the group is forced to select another alternative. It can accept an inferior caste status and a sense of basic inferiority as part of its collective self-definition, or it can define the situation as one of direct political and economic oppression. Another alternative is for it to deliberatively redefine itself symbolically, creating a positive view of its heritage on the basis of cultural and racial distinctions, thereby establishing a sense of collective dignity. This separate in-group ethnic sense can be used in an attempt to escape caste stratification. Thus, an ethnic self-definition by a group in an already ethnically plural society such as the United States can heighten the relative status of a group vis-à-vis other groups also defined in ethnic terms.[4]

Territoriality

Most ethnic groups have a tradition of territorial or political independence, even though the present members have become part of another, or sometimes several, political entities. In comparing ethnic groups, however, one notes highly different patterns related to the possession of territory as a means of maintaining group cohesion. At on extreme are groups such as the Japanese, with their own separate origin myth, occupying an entire nation-state; at the other extreme are minorities such as the Jews who had been without a territory for centuries, but who now again, on the basis of an origin myth, claim the territory of Israel. In numerically large, politically independent groups, ethnic identity tends to be coextensive with national or regional identity. Social and political problems resulting from continual attempts by groups to extend their territory account for much of the world's political history.[5]

Strictly used, nationality is indistinguishable from ethnicity. But in a looser sense, the words *nation* and *nationality* often also encompass diverse groups that have achieved political unification but still consider some territorial base, actual or desired. It can be argued that for many people, national identity and subjective cultural identity cannot be distinguished, especially when ethnic identity and a national territorial identity have been united historically.[6] Otherwise, ethnic identity is either a more specific or a broader identity than national identity. Identity may take on a local territorial flavor, so that a person defines him- or herself as Breton rather than as French, or as Roman rather than as Italian. However, a "German" identity can include Austrians as well as inhabitants of a present-day German state. Local identifications may or may not entail some feeling of continuity with the past.

Some ethnic minorities maintain themselves, at least partially, by sustaining hope for political independence or for the recapturing of lost national territory. Native American groups are designated as nations even though many have lost their territorial base. The most striking example of such thinking has been the Jewish vision of reestablishing Israel. Other groups, such as the Kurds in Iran, consider themselves as a nation and still hope to reassert their special autonomy by recapturing or maintaining a political territorial base. Some such groups inhabit territory that is difficult to penetrate and that therefore enables them to maintain a measure of local autonomy. Tibetans have thus resisted becoming "Chinese" nationals.

Some ethnic minorities have been partially incorporated into larger national units; Scottish and Welch incorporation into Great Britain fall into this category. The Soviet Union was an example of a state with continuing tensions resulting from territorial expansion and the incomplete incorporation of widely divergent groups such as the Latvians and Estonians in Europe and numerous Muslim Turkic groups in Asia. They made very complex usage of distinctions between groups considered ethnic minorities and/or nations. Thus, symbolically or actually, territory may be central to maintaining ethnicity, or it may be minimal or even nonexistent (the Rom, the wandering Gypsies of Europe,[7] are an extreme example). The degree to which some territorial concept is necessary to the maintenance of ethnic identity, symbolically or actually, must be considered in relation to the salient use of nonterritorial definitions of ethnic uniqueness and in relation to economic, religious, linguistic, or other social activities.

Economic Bases

Economic factors contribute in a complex manner to ethnic definitions and identity maintenance. An ethnic minority can be well dispersed within another population and still defend itself from assimilation by maintaining a certain amount of economic autonomy. Specific occupational minorities such as particular Parsis in India, Jews of Europe, and overseas enclaves of Indians and Chinese manage to remain ethnically distinct, at least partially because their community organization has a secure subsistence base anchored in special occupations that they can pursue from one generation to the next. There is, however, a great deal of political ambivalence in some areas about allowing quasi-independent, economically secure ethnic enclaves to persist. The often ambiguous political role of overseas merchant Indians in Africa and Chinese in Southeast Asia are cases in point.

Hagen (1962) finds that a minority group may compensate for a prior downward shift in status by innovative economic activities that lead to a consequent resurgence that benefits the relative status of their members. Such an examination of the relationship between ethnicity and economic power is particularly revealing of the means by which group shifts occur in social position.

Religion

Religious conversion can be a means of abandoning one's ethnic identity by adopting a transcendent worldview, or it can be used to maintain a separate identity. In their studies of revivalist cults among politically subordinate groups, anthropologists have found that religion can be used to mobilize members of a group to deal with a perceived threat to their continuing existence or, more directly, to attain a promised change of status through a religiously oriented social revolution.[8] Folk religion often takes the form of myths about the uniqueness of the group or its genesis. Nativism in medical practices—resistance to scientific definitions of disease and a tenacious clinging to traditional curing practices—is another means of maintaining ethnic identity (Crandon-Malamud 1991; Romanucci-Ross 1977).

A written tradition of sacred texts defining the religious faith can also be a strong force in maintaining a sense of identity in each succeeding generation. The Hellenic *Iliad*, the Bible of the Jews, and the Kojiki of the Japanese are three notable examples. The use of religion to support ethnic identity is clear in the case of folk beliefs and practices. But universalist faiths such as Buddhism, Christianity, and Islam can also contribute to ethnic group cohesion when special sectarian differences become important as a matter of group loyalty and identification in specific contrastive or conflictful social settings, as occurred in Europe and is now continuing in Iraq and Iran and in Sri Lanka.[9]

Religious or ideological conflict in society often has more to do with increasing the power of one's own group than with extending the benefits of one's religion to converts. In fact, throughout history, states have exploited religious differences to enhance their power. For this reason, religions have often been nationalized so as to diminish problems of divided loyalty.[10] For some groups, religious beliefs about their historical origin and past tribulations provide the vital definition of who they are. When a native religion is destroyed by the imposition of a conquering people's beliefs, the group identity, if it survives at all, receives a severe blow. There can be widespread loss of morale. The status role of adult males in particular can be affected by attacks on the indigenous religious system. When sustaining beliefs are undermined by this type of cultural contact, the individual and collective will to survive is weakened, leading to collective anomie.

Members of some groups, such as Native Americans, are unable to believe in themselves because they have lost faith in their own religious system and its symbols of dignity and status. At the same time, they cannot draw sustenance from the religion of their conquerors without giving up their own identity. For many African Americans, the Christian tradition remains a strong integrative force. But the preacher or minister, always a social leader, now finds the requirements of his role shifting from accommodation toward confrontation and protest. And some militant blacks today define Christianity, and sometimes Judaism, as white racist religions. They have turned instead to Islam, which they see as less racially discriminatory. As an African as well as Asian religion, it is not associated with European political oppression, whereas Christianity, in Africa and elsewhere, was introduced during colonial occupations and was used to induce psychological and social accommodation to an oppressed status. To forge a new identity, some African Americans have joined new groups, such as the Black Muslims, or have affiliated directly with an established Arab Muslim sect. Implicit also in this pro-Arab movement is an anti-Jewish feeling based on the ghetto experience of many blacks, who perceive Jewish merchants as using sharp practices to take advantage of them.[11]

Other blacks, though not adopting Islam, find it psychologically easier to identify with their African heritage by simply forgoing Christianity. Their sense of ethnic identity takes precedence over even a universalist definition of Christianity or the secular universalist outlook of Marxism.

Aesthetic Cultural Patterns

Particular cultures afford particular patterns related to aesthetic traditions that are used symbolically as a basis of self and social identity. Tastes in food, dance traditions, styles of clothing, and definitions of physical beauty are ways in which cultures identify themselves by aesthetic patterns. In times of ethnic resurgence, greater emphasis is put on aesthetic features related to communication and social communion. The "soul" concept of African Americans is a case in point. Their patterns of communication form a basis for mutual acceptance and identity and include a vocabulary of gestures and formal language characteristics. A new holiday can be fabricated or new styles of dress can be defined as ethnic to signify an ethnic belonging based on "authentic" African culture. The religious, aesthetic, and linguistic features of ethnic identity are related to questions of artistic creativity examined in psychocultural terms. Modes of ethnic persistence depend on the capacity to maintain art forms distinctive of a group rather than of an individual.

Language

Language is often cited as a major component in the maintenance of a separate ethnic identity, and language undoubtedly constitutes the single most characteristic feature of ethnic identity. But ethnicity is frequently related more to the symbolism of a separate language than to its actual use by all members of a group. The Irish use Gaelic as a symbol of their Celtic ethnicity, as do the Scots, but speaking Gaelic or Scottish is not essential to group membership in either case. Where languages have transcended national frontiers, as English, French, and Spanish have, ethnicity is not necessarily broadened to include all speakers of the language, any more than it encompasses all believers in a common faith or all people with similar lifestyles.

Group identity can even be maintained by minor differences in linguistic patterns and by styles of gesture. There are many ways in which language-patterning fluency or lack of fluency in a second language is related to identity maintenance. Changing patterns within groups are related to the sanctioning, positively or negatively, of specific dialects. Reassertion of local versus central political controls is sometimes symbolically indicated by the degree to which local dialect patterns are maintained. This is apparent in European countries such as Italy, and it has strong influence in such pluralistic states as Indonesia. There is reemphasis, for example, in England on maintaining local speech patterns. Political and economic sanctions against "improper" English have lessened in Britain, so much so that it is no longer necessary to adopt standard speech or intonation to apply for a particular job.[12]

The manipulation of language as a status marker can also be used by individuals aspiring to change how they are defined ethnically. Roosens cites how the Yaka of Zaire drop their traditional language when moving to urban settings so that they will not be seen pejoratively by others.[13]

The Invention of Ethnicity as an Advantageous or Deliberately Marketable Identity

When particular ethnic groups or nationalities are examined historically, one becomes aware that the evolution of ethnic consciousness in many instances was not a slow, crescive one. It does not necessarily develop slowly or spontaneously out of a growing awareness of differences from other contrasting groups of different origins. A new ethnic loyalty can be created as deliberatively as can a fabricated or advanced mythology of origin. Belonging to a specific group with a genuinely unique past, or, if need be, a fabricated one, can become a conscious advantage to be manipulated by at least some members of a social or territorial group.

Some special members can designate themselves as scholars examining the supposed heroic past. An origin myth can be created to justify a contemporary political loyalty or a new sense of contrastive, status-enhancing social identity. Some of the newly added chapters to this book discuss how ethnic identity is fabricated and for what purposes. There are several reasons for invention—notably, consolidation and legitimization of political power, enhanced social status, and economic advantage.

A striking example of fabricated identity is described in detail by the historian Schama (1987). He describes how, in the sixteenth century, certain dedicated Calvinist scholars helped create, for inhabitants of the provinces of the newly independent northern Dutch Republic, a single mythological origin involving a folk hero and his followers who came west from Batavia, a small isle lying between the Rhine and the Waal rivers, to build dikes against the North Sea. This "Batavian" identity helped mark off the Dutch and justified for them a special religious-political-economic destiny that distinguished them from the linguistically related southern, yet captive, provinces of the Netherlands (principally Flanders and Brabant), which remained under the control of Spanish occupation forces. The new capital of the Dutch colonial empire in the Indies was appropriately named Batavia to symbolically mark the administrative seat of their expanding manifest destiny in Asia.

Ethnicity: A Subjective Sense of Continuity in Belonging

In brief, the ethnic identity of a group consists of its *subjective, symbolic,* or *emblematic* use of any aspect of a culture, or a perceived separate origin and continuity, in order to differentiate themselves from other groups. In time, these emblems can be imposed from outside or embraced from within. Ethnic features such as language, clothing, or food can become emblems, for they show others who one is and to what group one's loyalty belongs. A Christian, for example, wears a cross; a Jew, the Star of David.

An extreme case, but useful for illustration, is that of the modern American Jew. There is a considerable body of literature written by Jewish intellectuals throughout their history in Europe and in the United States about what it is to be a Jew, and how one reconciles one's sense of ethnicity with citizenship, power, and social status in a prevailingly Christian society. Some contemporary writers fear that with the attenuation of social discrimination, modern American Jews may soon lose their sense of Jewishness. Already, some individuals who consider themselves Jews have no remaining special linguistic heritage, they no longer adhere to any of the beliefs of Judaism or to any customs peculiar to Jewish culture, and they do not believe that Jews constitute any special or distinct racial group. How, then, can they continue to feel that being Jewish is important to their sense of social self or ethnic identity? Apparently it is a difficult task, for today some Jewish youth, although children of nonpracticing parents, study Hebrew, visit Israel, join an orthodox synagogue, and reinstitute the rituals of the Sabbath in order to "find themselves."

This example illustrates dramatically the need for a psychological or emic[14] approach to the question of ethnic identity. As a subjective sense of belonging, ethnicity cannot be defined by behavioral criteria alone. Ethnicity is determined by what one feels about oneself, not by how one is observed to behave. Defining oneself in social terms is a basic answer to the human need to belong and to survive.

In a simple independent culture, the sense of self is relatively uncomplicated. One's instrumental goals and expressive needs are inseparable. One's sense of belonging and social meaning—past, present, and future—are defined without contradiction in a unified belief system. This unified sense of belonging is disrupted, however, when the state emerges as an institution for governing, when several ethnic groups are coercively unified within a single political framework. Social allegiance is further complicated when future-oriented revolutionary ideologies appear. These are often religious movements that offer a transcendent form of identity more encompassing than currently available definitions.

As indicated earlier, religious movements can appear as revivalist cults or as a newly fabricated ethnicity that reinterprets symbols of the past so as to reestablish the group, using the old patterns to evoke an image of a better future for its members. Ethnicity, therefore, in its narrowest sense, is a feeling of continuity with a real or imagined past, a feeling that is maintained as an essential part of one's self-definition. Ethnicity is also intimately related to the individual need for a collective continuity as a belonging member of some group. The individual senses some degree of threat to his or her own survival if the group or lineage is threatened with extinction. Ethnicity, therefore, includes a sense of personal survival through a historical continuity of belonging that extends beyond the self. For this reason, failure to remain in one's group leads to feelings of guilt. It is a form of killing inflicted on one's progenitors, including one's parents, who still "live" as long as some symbols of their culture are carried forth into the present and future, out of the past. In its deepest psychological level, ethnicity is a sense of affiliative survival. If one's group survives, one is assured of survival, even if not personally.

Transcendental religions or universalistic ideologies offer an alternative form of survival by affording a new identity and a new form of continuity. The reasons for rejecting the old and embracing the new are varied and complex. Entering a new religion or leaving the family are marked by symbols of death and rebirth in many forms of initiation ceremonies, such as baptism. These symbolic rituals testify to a transition in identity and are a source of security about survival, whatever the threat of death may be in relinquishing an old identity. Broadly, universalistic ideologies and ethnically oriented social definitions are contrastive and alternative patterns that introduce conflict in complex societies.

Basic Types of Group Allegiance:
Problems of Priority

In a complex society, the body to which an individual gives greatest commitment depends on whether one is oriented primarily to the past, the present, or the future (see figure 1). With a present orientation, one's primary loyalty can be directed toward a country of residence. Patriotism can become a powerful emotion, making people willing to sacrifice their lives for the "fatherland" or "motherland." Here, survival of the nation is more important than personal survival. Although this strength of emotion can bind citizens together, it may, but does not necessarily, involve a concept of past common origin. The emphasis is on present participation. French citizenship and American citizenship are assimilative legal concepts defining vital and continuing national identities.

A less general and sometimes conflicting form of present-oriented social belonging is identity through participation in an occupation or profession. This identity may conflict with a national identity. When an individual acquires competence in a skill or profession, his or her primary commitment shifts to the mastery of a specific skill, or more generally to the social class of that profession. A person may identify him- or herself by status as a noble or a commoner; or by occupation, as a merchant or a worker; or more specifically as a scientist, a physician, and so on. This identity may be much stronger and more compelling than any national or ethnic allegiance. However, in time of conflict, ethnic or national allegiance may assume priority, as happened with some German and Japanese social scientists who distorted professional knowledge in the direction of ethnic-national ideologies in World War II. Present occupation and past ethnic identity can, in addition, sometimes represent caste allegiances.

Individuals who are dissatisfied with the past and the present may adopt a future orientation, attaining a sense of social belonging by identification with a cause or a revolutionary movement. These movements may be directly generated by a religious or politico-social ideology. Individuals whose sense of social self is related to a perceived exploitative, unjust, or immoral present social system may develop a sense of identity that brings them into political conflict with their society. Unrest on the basis of religious or political beliefs may develop in individuals or in whole social groups. Sometimes an ethnic minority will seem to use a future-oriented movement as a vehicle for protest, but in such cases the actual motivation of participants must be carefully examined. Russians in World War II, for

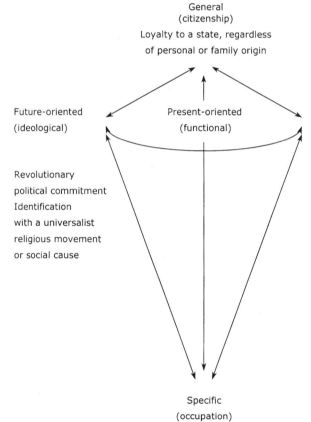

General
(citizenship)
Loyalty to a state, regardless
of personal or family origin

Future-oriented
(ideological)

Present-oriented
(functional)

Past-oriented
(familial-cultural)

Revolutionary
political commitment
Identification
with a universalist
religious movement
or social cause

Past-oriented
commitments
defined by ethnic group
Loyalty to a tradition
based on ancestry
including race
Religion, language,
other cultural traditions

Specific
(occupation)
Loyalty to a profession and/or
to the social status it bestows

Figure 1

example, are reported to have fought more to defend their ethnic homeland than to defend the ideology of international communism.

In contrast to present- or future-oriented sources of social identity, ethnicity is oriented to a special past heritage. It may be congruent with present citizenship in some states or be quite unrelated to citizenship in others. It may overlap with a future-oriented identity when the two are seen as mutually supportive. But ethnicity, as defined here, is primarily a sense of belonging to a particular ancestry and origin and of sharing a specific religion or language. This primary sense of belonging may or may not be related to political or geographical units, and it may or may not bring the individual into conflict with the larger society.

The history of minority peoples and organizations has in general, however, been an unhappy series of conflicts and accommodations arising from the coercive pressures that politically dominant groups exert on their subordinates to gain and maintain loyalty. Some members of subordinate groups may seek to change their assigned or ascribed lower-status positions to more congenial past or future definitions of self and group. This pressure for change causes instability in stratified societies. They often respond with suppressive measures, seeking sometimes to assimilate the group and cause it to disappear rather than according it more autonomy.

Ethnic Pluralism as a Means of Changing Relative Social Status

The conceptual scheme just presented helps explain why social movements based on group belonging take the particular form they do in given cultural-historical situations. The change of status demanded by black Americans from their reluctant white compatriots is a good example of how ethnic membership shapes social movements. Gerald Berreman (1967a, 1967b) and others have advanced cogent arguments defining how caste concepts govern social relationships not only in India but in the United States between blacks and whites. In assessing the status of the Burakumin, the former pariahs of Japan, Wagatsuma and I came to a similar conclusion (1967). Those groups of Native Americans, ethnic Americans, and Japanese who have been treated as members of outcaste or pariah groups show numerous similarities in their collective attempts to overcome the effects of caste.[15] However, the differences are striking and reflect overall differences in cultural history and present social structure. They influence the method taken to change one's status individually and collectively in each instance. The directions taken by their social movements differ depending on the inherent difficulties faced in reconciling class, caste, and ethnic identities. Both caste and class definitions of self are explicitly related to a system of formal stratification, whereas ethnic definitions imply some less explicit hierarchy and hence are more open to change with shifts of economic or political power. Both ethnic and class self-definitions can constitute a challenge to the state, since loyalty to either one may transcend national boundaries. International communism, for example, threatened the state by emphasizing the solidarity of the world's working classes, whereas ethnic groups may threaten by a struggle for political separation.[16] Some of the present caste groups in India were originally non-Hindu tribes, but they cannot draw on this past to change their present relative status. Some of these groups, however, have in recent times reconstructed their history to create, in effect, a myth of a past higher status (Rowe 1960, 1964). Since caste rank is strongly internalized as part of an Indian's identity, freeing oneself from it is very difficult. A socially mobile group in India must, therefore, constrain others to recognize its right to a higher rank, rather than trying to escape from the caste system altogether.

Harijans, or former untouchables, are attempting to escape caste by converting from Hinduism to Buddhism, but with questionable success. A universalistic faith, Buddhism was born in India partially as a revolutionary attempt to overcome caste. When caste-oriented Hinduism prevailed, Buddhism was forced to retreat from India. Now, again, Buddhism is being used for the same revolutionary task that it failed to accomplish in the past. Many Hindus consider Buddhism ethnically alien, just as some Shintoists in Japan have been anti-Buddhist, resenting its universalistic elements. Although Indian state policy has taken steps toward establishing noncaste criteria for social ranking, caste remains the most potent influence on social status. Since ethnicity is not an effective means for changing relative status within Indian society, some territorial-ethnic groups such as the Assamese are seeking political autonomy instead.[17]

The United States, on the other hand, is a mixed class-ethnic society with caste-race features. In order to resolve the caste-related conflict, as well as other social and ideological inconsistencies, the United States is attempting to eliminate caste-race categories in favor of an overall ideology of ethnic pluralism. There is, as a result, a reduced commitment to assimilation and a greater emphasis on religious, cultural, and even linguistic pluralism.[18]

Black Americans are redefining themselves in ethnic terms. Among blacks brought in as slaves, African ethnic traditions only persisted as submerged fragments. Now, however, black Americans are reaching back to a pan-African heritage to create an ethnic tradition of their own, separate from that of Europeans and Asians. They are trying to recreate their identity on the basis of cultural continuities rather than on the simplistic caste-racial criteria used in oppressing them. Blacks are seeking means of amplifying all the criteria constituting ethnicity. Territorial origins in Africa, and territorial and economic strongholds in present American settings; old folk and religious practices; and features of lifestyle, family relationships, and artistic traditions are being scrutinized for their Afro-American flavor.

As with all groups concerned with origins as a source of social meaning, where history is insufficient, myths are created. Some blacks, reversing the pejorative connotations imposed by Europeans, consider "soul" or "negritude" to be biologically inherited and the source of special folk features supposedly shared by all of African heritage but not by Europeans or Asians. The search for origins goes back to a black history that preceded slavery. The slave past is not denied or hidden but is seen as a transitory stage of exploitation of black Africans as a people, not as an occupational class. This ethnic definition is presently more powerful than any occupational or social class as a means of overcoming the disadvantages of caste definitions, since such affinities, where they exist, do not as yet cross the caste barrier among white, European-derived, working-class Americans.

Hence, by using an ethnic definition of themselves to change their relative status, blacks are pursuing a characteristically American path. Ethnic relationships remain as potential sources of identity and of social participation in America. They cut across patterns generated by the various levels of social class positions and occupations that stratify the society economically and socially. It is a way to change relative status that works for the blacks, who have now taken the initiative in defining themselves by means of confrontation and militancy.

Whites of various ethnic backgrounds, especially on the working-class level, are being forced either to fight back or to find some accommodative redefinition that makes sense to them and that they can accept, while still not admitting blacks totally as in-group social participants. Retreating from overt racist positions, some American urban groups are seeking defensive accommodations or are launching counteroffensives on the level of ethnic groupings. Third-generation working-class Jews and Italians in New York and Poles in Pittsburgh, Chicago, and Milwaukee are rekindling a sense of ethnic belonging, thus restoring definitions that had become attenuated by attempts to pass as nonethnic Americans.

A pattern of a dual ethnic-social class identity is found in many so-called hyphenated Americans—for example, Italians, Jews, Irish, Poles, Lithuanians, Armenians, Mexicans, Chinese, Japanese—who are sprinkled throughout various occupational-social class levels in American society and who may or may not maintain overt continuity with their ethnic group as a feature of their social life or as a part of their self-identity. Nathan Glazer and Daniel P. Moynihan, in *Beyond the Melting Pot* (1963), offer many examples of the persistence of such ethnicity despite the American ideology of assimilation.

Much American conformity behavior and concern with loyalty is a reflection of uneasiness over the legitimacy of a claim to be American on the part of second-generation ethnic immigrants. Many ethnics still pass by moving to a suburb. A widespread phenomenon is presently taking place among the third-generation children born in these suburbs. Now attending American universities, they are searching for ways to gain a feeling of some past ethnic identity, which their parents failed to transmit to them. Majority white young people, of various European lower-status origins, seek out some former ethnic identity as a counterpart to the soul espoused by their black classmates. Children of parents who carried little ethnic baggage in their search for upward mobility deeply miss the expressive emotional satisfactions of some form of ethnic belonging.[19]

At this point in American history, past-oriented ethnicity is more appealing to American blacks as a means of reordering their status than is a future orientation, such as a universalist religion or self-definition as a member of an exploited proletarian class. Black workers are aware that emotionally expressive caste attitudes remain a strong part of the spontaneous relationships of the other workers. Many of these white workers are still prejudiced ethnics to some degree. One recognizes that Irish get certain jobs, Poles others, and that they, too, live in special neighborhoods. These American realities are more visible than is any supposed alliance among workers to remove discrimination.

Discussed below, one finds similar caste discrimination in Japan. Despite their Marxist militancy, the former Japanese pariahs get little support from majority-group Japanese workers. Worker unity, emotionally at least, does not seem to cross their caste barrier (Totten and Wagatsuma 1967).

In socially pluralistic America, social primary-group participation is becoming more ethnic oriented, while ways are being sought to eliminate occupational discrimination. The processes occurring in combating the force of caste as a social institution in America are far different from those in India. Out of this use of a new ethnic definition by black Americans is emerging a shared social self-identity that is internally and externally overcoming the negative social definitions that have been internalized by many people in the past.

Ethnicity and Individual Social Mobility

Complex cultures contain differential patterns with respect to how upwardly mobile behavior is learned and how culture is or can be diffused. For example, in Japan until the 1960s, patterns for diffusion of status behavior were related to apprenticeship experiences of men and women, who in their youth had worked several years for individuals or families of higher status. Women from lower-status positions were apprenticed in the houses of upper-status persons and learned patterns of acceptable behavior with which they at least partially identified and that they used to evaluate the behavior of members of their own social class. Such judgments then created internal tensions in lower-status persons, inducing them to acquire the more highly valued traits. Earlier, status emulation was apparent in the diffusion of warrior or samurai traits into the Japanese population at large, especially when the samurai were abolished as an exclusive official class after the restoration of the central status of the emperor in 1868.

With the development of mass-communication media in Japan, these patterns of diffusion have been radically altered. The source of models for emulation is shifting from immediate personal contacts with people of higher status to an extracultural or extranational frame of reference for all segments of the population. The effects of modern mass media on cultural identity should be thoroughly examined for their influence on evaluative patterns related to ethnic behavior and to other forms of social mobility. As the late Hiroshi Wagatsuma suggested in our chapter, much of this behavior is a change of reference group rather than of ethnic identity. Modern Japanese youth are Japanese even though they wear "mod" clothing or sing country-and-western music.

In some instances, there are reverse romanticizations of submerged ethnic minorities; that is, behavioral traits can be borrowed from more active, less rigidified lower-status groups. In California, for example, some Japanese American militant youth in the 1970s, seeking an ethnic pattern of confrontation seemingly lacking in their parental tradition, borrowed the black dialect and its rhetorical inflections directly from members of the black power groups with whom they associated.

Very often, upward mobility weakens ethnic priorities in loyalty and behavior. Maintenance of ethnicity in some societies is obviously more characteristic of non–socially mobile lower-status individuals who have few other sources for self-acceptance to fall back on. Thus, one's ethnic background can be important in proportion to the number of other sources of status (occupational accomplishment, economic success) that are available.

Crises in Alienation

The alienation felt by some successful upwardly mobile individuals may be the result of their having cut so many ties with the past that they have lost a deeper sense of meaning, although the loss may not be apparent to them at the time. The sense of anomie in American society that is commonly attributed to social mobility may often have more to do with the loss of ethnic inheritance than with the simple movement from a lower to a higher class. When occupational success moves a person into an alien group, what is alien is often the change in ethnic behavior required, rather than new status behavior as such.

Jews are an ethnic group that has accommodated well to living within another culture while maintaining internal integrity. Even the resultant psychological problems do not, in the main, interfere with social adaptation. Many occupationally successful Jews have adapted to shifts in social class status without feeling any loss of their ethnic integrity. In fact, Jewish culture looks upon successful individuals as heroic figures. There are many tales of how Jews who were successful in the alien Christian world were able to maintain ethnic integrity and benefit the community, rather than using success for selfish personal reasons. As I shall discuss with respect to patterns of group expulsion as well as passing, other ethnic groups, such as Mexican Americans, have no similar tradition that individual success should benefit the ethnic community, since their culture is so often characterized by deprived social status.

A major source of ethnic identity is found in the cultural traditions related to changes in the life cycle, such as coming of age, marriage, divorce, illness, or death. It is particularly in rites of passage that one finds highly emotional symbolic reinforcement of ethnic patterns. Erik Erikson has delineated well the problem of identity commitment in modern complex societies (1968). Adulthood is particularly problematic for younger members of minority groups because of possible difficulties with what Erikson termed "identity diffusion."

The situations and the time of life in which members of particular ethnic minorities are subject to alienation probably vary from group to group. A Mexican American male child may experience a social crisis involving potential alienation early in his formal school experience when he is torn between the conflicting demands of the school and the peer group. Either he sides with the peer group, which may lead him into a career of social deviance during adolescence, or he chooses to conform to the role of a good pupil. The tensions of minority status are visible in some good students, whose conformity to mainstream expectations may lead to a deep sense of personal alienation.[20] In some minorities, peer group conformity induces one toward a socially deviant career, whereas in other groups, tensions lead to internalized forms of psychopathology that are not visible to the casual observer (De Vos 1965, 328–56).

Patterns of Passing

It is readily observable that in most societies where upward mobility is possible, ethnic minorities continually lose members to the politically, economically, and socially dominant segments. Such mobility not only provides the individual with a means of resolving his or her social and psychological problems, but it also maintains the stability of the society. Individual "evaporation" takes the pressure out of potential social protest movements of dissatisfied groups. When a group is totally blocked in an otherwise mobile society, however, pressure can build to explosive proportions as it has among some racial minority groups in the United States. As we discuss in a following chapter, the Koreans and Burakumin in Japan, who are denied many openings to ordinary careers, are overrepresented in organized as well as in individual criminal activity, similar to what we find for some ethnic minorities in the United States (De Vos and Mizushima 1967, 289–325; De Vos and Wagatsuma 1969; Lee and De Vos 1981).

The term *passing*, used in race relations literature, is usually applied only to situations in which an individual of partial black African ancestry disappears from a black social classification and reappears as white, if appearance permits. By disguising origins, one passes unnoticed, in some forms of participation at least, into white society. Wagatsuma and I (1967) studied this phenomenon in Japan, where members of a former pariah caste cut off all visible contact with family and friends of similar origin as part of individual attempts at social mobility. In this instance, the issue was racial only in that members of this caste are generally but erroneously considered to be biologically, hence racially, different from other Japanese.

Passing is not simply a procedure used for direct social advantage; it also has expressive emotional implications. A variety of intrapsychic as well as external behavioral maneuvers are involved, which can in turn lead to different types of internal tensions related to alternatives in reference groups and alternatives in degree and pattern of partial incorporation of alien elements into the self. In some situations, individuals reidentify with their ethnic origins, having found the alienation and malaise involved in maintaining a new identity too great a strain (De Vos and Wagatsuma 1967).

Since passing is usually effected through self-conscious manipulation of behavior, it requires maintaining a facade. To the degree that the facade is not part of oneself, there is often an internal duality involving a partially pejorative self-image. The self is thought to have been stigmatized by one's parents, in Goffman's sense of the term (1963), with some resulting elements of self-hate or hate of one's progenitors. In psychotherapy, however, the sequence uncovered is often found to be the reverse. *First*, a primary pattern of hate starts within the family, which in turn produces an ambivalence about the self. The individual may *then* seize upon an available pattern of class differences or ethnic pluralism and use social mobility to attempt a resolution of psychological distress.

It is not possible to discuss here the role of conscious and unconscious psychological mechanisms in the original psychosexual identification processes that underlie those later processes that form the total social self-identity, of which ethnicity is a central component. I cannot do more now than introduce the topic of individual passing and its personal motivations as a general phenomenon that cannot be ignored in studying social stratification. Suffice it to say that people often need to escape what is perceived to be a negative social self-identity. Most individuals who pass are, in this sense, prejudiced against their group of origin.

Physical appearance in the direction of favorable stereotypes may provide reinforcement for change. A person whose appearance is not conducive to passing may view his or her appearance as an irremovable stigma passed on by one's group. Obvious physical differences make passing difficult but not always impossible, at least from a subjective standpoint. Some black Americans "become" Hindus. There was a period when some Mexican Americans believed they were socially better off if they passed as Italians. But in any case, the absolute black-white racial distinction is only an extreme among various modes used by class- or race-oriented societies to prevent individuals from passing upward.

Some of the most poignant incidents related to us about the passing among Japanese outcastes were situations in which the individual deliberately exposed his or her stigmatized outcaste origin. We presume this was out of a need to escape the intolerable burden of continual disguise. Many individuals sooner or later find it psychologically more tolerable to drop their facade, to "come in from the cold." Some like to avoid identity ambiguity. Instead of exposing themselves to possible social trauma related to a disguised identity, they use an overt, unmistakable symbol or emblem of identity that signals to others their origins and their continued ethnic or class allegiance. Some militant Korean women, for example, wear Korean dress in Japan (Lee 1981). Such usages resemble what Erving Goffman would consider the flaunting of a stigma. The head scarf among Muslim women in Europe has become an item of political and social tension as discussed in chapter 6 by Hermans.

Withdrawal and Expulsion

Social mobility does not invariably involve passing as we have described it. Much more often, one finds gradual withdrawal from previous social participation. Economically successful upwardly mobile individuals, or members of their family, may no longer feel comfortable with people they know from childhood. New experiences develop social perceptions and needs that move the individual out of the former group. The social alienation is probably mutual in most instances. There may be no shift in identity or disguise of one's past, but rather a shift in acceptable lifestyle.

Sometimes the individual is ostracized by members of his or her own social group. In Mexican American or Native American groups, for example, to be successful economically, or to participate socially with dominant-status whites, is by definition to be a *falso*, a deserter (De Vos 1992). To maintain individual wealth without sharing can be considered a reason for social exclusion.

A social group that has experienced evaporation can be particularly sensitive to the first signs of a member's behavioral emulation of traits of an outside group. From early on, members may be prevented by group sanctioning from taking on other linguistic or social usages. The individual is made well aware of the threat of expulsion; hence, there can be a self-fulfilling prophecy that those who learn Anglo behavior, for example, are not to be trusted.

The child of a mixed union is almost always put into an ambiguous role, a complex topic that cannot be pursued in depth here. Where racial differences in appearance make some social affirmation of identification important, there can still be room for ambiguity in definition of individuals of mixed ancestry. In Brazil, if light-skinned Afro-Brazilians are socially presentable, they are, in a sense, given the choice of passing if they so desire, with passing being treated rather lightly. In the United States, on the other hand, where maintaining the "purity" of the white group has been important, passing is a serious issue for those whites who fear "tainted blood." It is also a serious concern to the black group, which would like to assert sanctions to keep their own members loyal. This is a particular point of tension in contemporary American society, not only from the standpoint of subjective self-inclusion as an American of African ancestry, but also because the word "black" has become symbolic of ethnic membership (as contrasted to the word "Negro," which is seen as indicating excessive accommodation to the culture and viewpoint of the dominant white population). Thus, the role of light-skinned persons of mixed white-black ancestry has become more difficult, especially since the threat of expulsion has increased with attempts to establish a militant black solidarity.

Sanctions of belonging start very early and cannot be separated from the development of the sense of self. The conscious processes involved in the later stages of identity formation are preceded by earlier, automatic processes. The self, as it develops in a human being, is innately social—it is related to the primary community belonging. Experiences in the family develop a sense of self, but peer group experiences in childhood are also important. In some societies, in fact, peer groups are much more important than the family as a principal mediator of social identity. The peer group is certainly a most exacting socializer, which demands continual symbols of allegiance from those participating. Although childhood gangs in many cases are transitory, they are instrumental in setting standards for language usage, and even for modes of thinking, which may in some instances run counter to parental patterns.

In acculturative situations such as those in New York and Chicago in the early twentieth century, primary social identities reflected more the effect of the peer group than of the home in self-definition, especially with regard to language. American-born ethnics of that generation identified themselves as Americans linguistically by refusing to speak the language of their parents, and attitudinally by rejecting many of the expressed values of their parents. Instead, they adopted the values presented by the mass media and the school, as well as by the predominantly American peer group. Social mobility was part of a positively sanctioned American identity. These children accepted without question the characteristics of those who are today viewed with much more ambivalence—the white Anglo-Saxon Protestants who, as many children in New York learned, all came over on the *Mayflower*.

Why was American education so successful in overcoming linguistic pluralism, when other countries encounter so much difficulty in changing the language of minority groups? The explanation may lie in the influence of the peer group at school. Since the school was a meeting ground of peers from different language groups, English became its lingua franca in the early 1900s. No European ethnic minority children could hold out for a language that separated them from the others at school. In other words, the peer groups were broadly American in orientation. The sense of self that developed out of this experience in the sons and daughters of immigrants was of being American rather than of simply remaining Italian—or Jewish, or Irish—in a new setting. Being American was extremely important for the American-born children of immigrant parents at the turn of the twentieth century.

Compared with the experiences of the waves of European immigrants, there seems today to be more difficulty in educating children of Mexican American, Puerto Rican, African American, or Native American background. It is evident, to me at least, that for these children to be amenable to learning majority norms, the counterinfluence of their minority peer groups against such norms must be overcome (De Vos 1992). Threats of expulsion from the ethnic peer group are a strong force against the formal educative processes in the schools. Scattered informal evidence suggests that European schools—for example, in Switzerland, France, or Belgium—are beginning to encounter similar difficulties in educating ethnic minorities, including the children of migrant workers (De Vos and Suarez-Orozco 1990).

For some minority groups, the majority-oriented school cannot provide the means of acquiring occupational mobility. The status of the group as a whole tends to remain depressed, offering no variation in class position or social-occupational models with which members of the group can identify and still retain a sense of belonging. By contrast, some groups, such as Jews and Japanese, severely sanction those who do poorly in school. The conforming attitudes of their peers reinforce in these children the need to learn at school (Caudill and De Vos 1972; De Vos 1973).

Although this topic has more dimensions than it is possible to consider here, we can say that from a social structural standpoint, at least, that early sanctioning to maintain ethnic integrity can cause certain ethnic groups difficulty in changing their status through formal education. Within-group self-perpetuation is a partial cause as much as external social discrimination. In some groups, such as Jews and Japanese, there is sufficient support from within to push those who remain identified with their groups toward occupational mobility, whereas in other groups, such as Native Americans, group identity tends to prevent economic or social mobility.

Accommodation to Minority Status

The notion that externally accommodative behavior on the part of people of subordinate status reflects the true social self-identity of the group's members is not acceptable. Nor is the converse Hobbesian notion that a stratified system that often includes ethnic minorities remains stable simply by the threat of force. Some forms of psychological internalization are found among those forced for any period of time into accommodative behavior.

According to George Herbert Mead, in acquiring a sense of self, one "internalizes a generalized other" (1934). Approaching identity formation from this theory, one would expect a subtle but significant psychological difference between the social internalization of low-status individuals who are members of ethnic groups and those who are not. A lower-status member of a stratified society cannot resist internalizing a negative self-image as a result of the socially prevalent explanations for his or her group's relative occupational and social inferiority. Remaining oriented to a pattern of evaluation originating in one's ethnic group helps an individual avoid the internalization of attitudes toward the self pressed on him or her by outsiders. Nevertheless, ethnic identity is of itself no assurance that a negative self-identity can be avoided, if the negative aspects are continually reinforced by discriminatory social attitudes. Ethnic communities must be examined individually to ascertain how they protect or damage the self-evaluation of their members.

To illustrate briefly, the majority population on the West Coast expected second-generation Japanese Americans to fulfill certain stereotypes: they would become ideal houseboys or gardeners, emulating the lower-status accommodative occupational roles permitted their parents. In California, where the social discrimination was the strongest, there were even attempts to use legal as well as social means to limit the occupational roles open to Japanese. Such social pressures did not prevent the nisei (the American-born generation) from attaining educational and occupational goals defined by their own families and communities rather than by the outside society (Caudill and De Vos 1972). The period of low-status accommodation to social discrimination in the United States has been relatively short. But even more important is that those immigrating to the United States brought with them their own sense of self-respect and cultural attitudes that were useful in overcoming the severe racism of American society.

An estimated 85 percent of Japanese immigrants were from rural areas, but they were not former serfs or peasants in the European sense. In Japan, farmers were a respected class, ranking only after the samurai and ahead of merchants and artisans, regardless of economic fluctuations. The Japanese communities in the United States accorded status to their members that had little or no correspondence to their jobs outside. They did not evaluate themselves on the basis of American attitudes toward them as peasants, or immigrant workers, or "yellow" Asians. Moreover, they brought with them a future orientation, ready to postpone immediate gratification and to endure adversity. Characteristically, a person would submit to an apprenticeship, with the goal of acquiring status through competence (De Vos 1973), just as in a traditional Japanese society one was expected to submit to a long apprenticeship, anticipating status acquired by compliance to a mentor. Japanese also avoided confrontation in working out differences with American discrimination. Direct confrontation was only used as a last resort. In their recent history, governmental authority, both legally and socially, has tended to be paternalistic but responsible, making it possible for them to think of the government as interested in the welfare of the people, rather than hated or feared as exploitative. Compliance was rewarded.

These and other interrelated cultural features help explain the relative lack of confrontation and conflict both in the United States, where West Coast Japanese were put in guarded camps, and in Japan, during several years of postwar occupation. A traditional Japanese does not feel it socially or personally demeaning to be in a subordinate position while he or she is learning. A sense of integrity is not destroyed by adversity. Japanese immigrants to the United States imparted to their nisei children a respect for authority, even the authority of an alien society of which they were to become loyal citizens. This was not inconsistent with Japanese concepts of loyalty to organizations once one becomes a member (Nakane 1971). Children were taught to conform to regulations imposed in school. Improper behavior would bring injury and shame to parents and to Japanese generally. To be Japanese was a matter of deeply felt pride on the part of the immigrant issei, whatever attitudes they met on the outside. They therefore imparted an accommodative but future-oriented concept of success. This pattern is less understood by some third-generation, or sansei, youth who are impatient with what they consider the complacency and conformity with which their parents met social discrimination.

The indirect, nonconfrontational methods of Japanese community leaders in dealing with the racist attitudes of white Americans is illustrated by an incident in Chicago in 1949. The well-known news commentator Drew Pearson learned that cemeteries in Chicago were refusing to bury Japanese, even if they were Christians. He wished to make a public issue of this act of social discrimination, but members of the Japanese community asked him to refrain, saying that they did not want "dirty publicity"—they would find indirect means of resolving the problem.

Given the terrible problems of dislocation of Japanese families in California, our research team failed to find any but a minimal use of public welfare agencies. The Japanese solved their social problems within their own community. The fact that they did well in American schools attests to group consistency with respect to what was expected. Parents were cohesive reinforcers of tightly sanctioned values with regard to education, and the community itself heavily sanctioned conformist behavior in the schools. The Japanese peer group left no alternative to studying hard in the American schools. Conversely, parental pressures to learn Japanese in Japanese language schools were notably unsuccessful. The peer group pressure was in the other direction, toward an American identity. The written Japanese language was not learned. The response of Japanese children in refusing to learn Japanese was in no way different from that of the children of European immigrants who refused to learn Italian or Polish.

The contrast with the ethnic adaptation of Mexican Americans is striking. Since Mexico is directly south of the United States, the continuous immigration encourages the persistence of Mexican ethnicity, including language, a persistence that is not found in those coming from Europe. Nevertheless, the Mexican American ethnic minority, in contrast to the Japanese, manifests a relative lack of cohesiveness, both in the community and in family life. While young Mexican Americans are seeking a positive ethnic identity, the traditions available are sometimes conflictful and nonsupportive with respect to economic and occupational mobility.

The Mexican traditions of status and class are complex (Romanucci-Ross 1986), but in general there are wide status disparities and mutually alienating feelings among Spanish-speaking Americans. Some parts of Mexico have the highest homicide rates in the world because of violence between individuals (Romanucci-Ross 1986, 132–34). American territorial aggrandizement at the expense of Mexico incorporated Mexican minorities into the United States with a variety of internal class and status conflicts that later immigrants have reflected.

The class, racial, and ethnic cleavages are noticeable: those who identify with a Spanish background look down on the Indian culture and people. Others conceive of Mexican ethnicity as membership in *la raza*, a special blend of European and Indian. There has been severe exploitation of peons, a depressed peasantry that has known only a society marked by extremes of poverty and wealth. The history of government authority is suspect (Romanucci-Ross 1986). A Mexican male feels a need to defend himself from being "taken" or penetrated (Paz 1961). Even within his immediate community, he must defend himself against the easily aroused, malevolently perceived envy of neighbors. Social and personal distrust are part of the community life of many. Traditionally, it is difficult to think of the economic success of one person without seeing it as taking something away from others. There is, in fact, a widespread belief in what George Foster terms "the limited good" (1967).

Within the family, one frequently finds distrust between marriage partners. In some lower-status Mexican families, the mother expects the child to take her side against a father who is depicted as drunken, unfaithful, and financially irresponsible (Lewis 1959). The mother pictures herself as keeping the family together for the sake of her children and as lacking rapport with her husband. This contrasts with the Japanese family, where cohesiveness is based on the mutually supportive status that each parent accords the other. Discord within the Mexican family makes it more difficult to inoculate Mexican children against the discriminatory practices and attitudes of the majority group. Thus Mexican youth in many cases are alienated not only from the majority society but from their own parents in such a way that their personal development is debilitated. They find themselves performing inadequately both in school and at work. The peer group for growing boys becomes an escape from family tensions. It is oriented against authority and discipline, and it often takes on a delinquent character. It becomes the principal reference group until marriage, which may, in turn, lead to the repetition of an unhappy domestic pattern.

To make my point, I have stressed the negative aspects of Mexican American ethnicity that contrast in my mind with features of Japanese community and family life. The vast differences in individual and community response of Mexicans and Japanese, both to social discrimination and to occupational opportunity, depend very much on class and ethnic identity, as well as on differential socialization, expected role behavior, and the effect of the reference group. These differences are most graphically seen in patterns of school performance and differential rates of delinquency (De Vos 1992).

Amelioration of the effects of social discrimination against Mexican Americans depends not only on changing the social attitudes and practices of the majority, but on strengthening the positive integrative function of the family and the community. As we have seen, for some Mexican Americans, an ethnic background has not helped maintain a positive social self-identity against majority Anglo attitudes. The Chicano movement is an attempt to develop community pride and cohesiveness in order to give Mexican identity a more positive meaning.

Among Americans of African ancestry, the relative number of individuals suffering from personal debilitation as a result of past as well as present

American racism is considerable. The "mark of oppression," as Kardiner and Ovesey (1962) termed it, is widespread, whether one uses indices of addiction to drugs, brittle and unsatisfactory heterosexual relationships, delinquency and crime, or hospitalization for mental illness. The cases cited by Kardiner and Ovesey or the writings of Malcolm X (Haley 1966) are full of evidence about the psychological problems attendant upon the internalization of a negative self-image. It has been difficult for some black families to provide sufficient psychological and economic security for their young. For too many, racial oppression penetrated into basic child-parent relationships to the degree that a negative self-image was passed on from parent to child, without the child's even having had any direct contact with the outer white society.

Unfortunately for those who seek to change the effects of discrimination by changing laws or social attitudes, a personal sense of failure among some blacks is not due solely to the force of external discrimination but to a generational internalization of traits debilitating to intellectual functioning and to the will to achieve. Malcolm X discusses with great integrity and candor the self-degradation of his generation, of "Negroes" who internalized concepts of physical beauty that flattered the white and degraded the black. It is very often the black man's own mother who "puts him down," causing self-hatred and self-rejection.

In our book, *Japan's Invisible Race* (1967), Wagatsuma and I describe similar processes involving unconscious negative self-images that helped debilitate the former Eta, or pariahs, of Japan and still lead to their relative failure in the economically competitive contemporary Japanese society. These internal processes are never separate from the external forms of discrimination that deepen and intensify the inner difficulties experienced by members of disparaged groups.

Conclusion

I have contended here that ethnicity or ethnic identity is as important as social class or class consciousness in social theory, that a psychocultural approach to social belonging and to defensive or hostile contrastiveness is necessary for understanding social behavior. I have also suggested that a conflict approach to society is more productive in understanding change than one based on formal structure analysis alone.

Change as a result of interethnic conflict is a reality of human history. Seen from one perspective, the history of social life in a culture is a continual rhythm of conflict and accommodation between groups, both external and internal (De Vos and Suarez-Orozco 1990). Stratification allows for some form of accommodation. Those coming to power continually seek a more stabilized allegiance from those subordinate to them. Some theorists who emphasize conflict and coercion in political matters forget, however, to examine the forces of belonging that unify individuals into the groups that then struggle with each other for power. Hobbes, in his discussion of the state, leaves us dissatisfied when he sees coercion as the only force keeping individuals united.

Durkheim, in his *Elementary Forms of the Religious Life* (1947), pointed toward the proper direction for such understanding. He saw humans as social animals who achieve both real and ideal concepts of self partially out of a sense of belonging to a group. In a primitive, occupationally undifferentiated society, there is little tension between a sense of social identity with the political community, with its primary form of citizenship, and the "church," a sacred representation of primal folk ethnicity. The political and the spiritual communities are one. Within such a community, the relatively undifferentiated occupational system affords little basis for divergent concepts of belonging. Hence, it is only in more complex social units—with their occupational divisions and their amalgamation of groups maintaining a sense of diverse origin—that tension develops in the overall sense of belonging. But, depending on the vagaries of their history, not all societies develop chronic tensions resulting from political incorporation. In some instances of recorded as well as unrecorded history, initially separate ethnic groups have indeed disappeared into a unified nation-state, just as nation-states have disappeared by incorporation or dissolution.

In members of simpler communities, one usually finds much less evidence of any form of identity crisis as a part of social maturation. The present widespread existential search for meaning suggests the presence of conflicting alternatives. Modern conceptual systems attempt to relate past cultural traditions to ideological alternatives about the future direction of society and to questions about the degree of allegiance to be paid to the different social units in the system. Those who see individualism as the highest goal sometimes mistakenly assume that individuation or autonomy means a lack of allegiance to any group. They fail to see that individuals today are also searching for meaningful and ultimate units of social belonging and a sense of survival through such belonging.

Problems of choice related to occupation or identity occur only in flexible societies with a great deal of internal social mobility. In rigidly stratified societies, the individual's occupation tends to be predetermined, inculcating early a sense of belonging to a primary occupational group.

Even this situation may not be completely free of conflict, since the state may apply pressure concerning religious and political adherence, leading to conflicts over loyalty.

Seen from this perspective, human history shows numerous combinations of tension, conflict, and accommodation related to conflicts between loyalty to a past ethnicity, a present status, or a future idealized concept of society. Sections of this chapter discussed only a few of the topics related to ethnicity and social stratification, and even they need much more detailed examination than was possible here. Other, complementary approaches to ethnic identity appear in subsequent chapters.

Especially to be noted in what follows is how new ethnic groups are continually created for expedient economic or social reasons, as well as to resolve an inner existential need to belong. The collective fabrication of a mythical past may prove to be as socially efficacious as actual history.

In emphasizing the need for social belonging, perhaps I have not sufficiently pointed up the social and psychological uses of contrastiveness and difference in human interaction. As social animals, we are combative as well as affiliative. Ethnicity can be very negative and destructive in its intent. I may have touched too briefly here on a number of specific psychodynamic reasons for contrastive conflict. The following chapters will, however, illustrate several instances of the destructive use of contrastive ethnicity. Psychodynamically, ethnicity, as with any other form of Otherness, can be an excuse for collective projection of a dehumanizing nature. Such hostile contrastiveness is clearly seen in the chapter by Gilliland describing Serb-Croat-Bosnian relationships in the former Yugoslavia.

There is continual flux in the saliency of an ethnic identity used negatively in response to changing social conditions. Ethnic definitions are projected upon others, who, out of loyalty, cannot escape being partially or wholly identified with their group of origin. A hostile contrastive use of an ethnic definition can be forced upon those whose ethnicity had for them no particular relevance. The sad case of the resurgence of ethnic conflict in the former Yugoslavia points up how the duress of economic stress can rekindle a hostile-defensive ethnic contrastiveness in some, whose abusive acts then provoke a general rupture between the many, who are forced to choose sides again, despite living together in previously harmonious relationships.

Projective dehumanization of another group is a too readily available collective psychological mechanism. If a group allows itself to be susceptible by condoning the irrational acts of any of its members, any past difference can be used as sufficient justification for renewed hostile contrast. The use of anti-Semitic explanations for economic-social malaise has again reappeared as a threatening specter in Eastern Europe despite the now generally acknowledged catastrophic madness of Germany's recent Nazi past. This reappearance should remind us how easy it is to use one's ethnic identity to project negatively onto others. When there is inner need to project or dehumanize, self-righteous ethnicity becomes a potential for mutual destruction.

Finally, for the future, we must seek out some collective transcendence of past ethnicity to achieve present social harmony, as well as savoring the past to give flavor to human experience.

Notes

This revised chapter adds references to my subsequent writings and footnotes that update some issues raised initially by events that have transpired since the first edition. A number of contentions asserting the saliency of potentials for ethnic conflict over those of social class loyalty have been borne out most forcefully since the initial writing.

1. In the past, we have had relatively little concern, for example, with reconstructing the internal crises faced by individual Gauls as they resisted or accepted Roman or Christian influence. Today, however, there is growing interest in those who resisted. It is a sign of the times that the most popular comic book hero in France (from the 1960s to the 1980s) was Asterix, a counterculture Gaul whose Druidic potion gives him superhuman powers to help his tiny band of Celtic warriors resist the establishment Romans.

2. This assertion has been reaffirmed in the last twenty-five years by the collapse of the Soviet Union.

3. See Roosens's discussion in chapter 11 of how this is done among the Lunda of Zaire (now, again, Congo).

4. This is occurring in the self-definitions of a separate ethnicity being adopted by many African Americans.

5. Such is the political history of Serbs in the former Yugoslavia. Gilliland in chapter 3 gives a careful discussion of the interpenetration of meaning between the terms *nationalism* and *ethnicity*.

6. This is most noteworthy in contemporary Eastern Europe.

7. See the discussion in chapter 10.

8. See Schwartz's (1976) extensive discussion of these phenomena and the conflicting theory of Lanternari (1963).

9. Obeyesekere, in our previous edition, provides a severe illustration of this process at work in postcolonial Sri Lanka.

10. In this context, it is interesting to note that until recently, disputes between Marxist-oriented socialist states markedly resembled past sectarian conflicts within Christianity and Islam. Religious adherence on the part of an ethnic group may

also become a symbol of resistance to the dominant group, thereby, regardless of personal belief, reducing religious affiliation to simply being a means of asserting ethnic identity. Thus, many secularized intellectuals in Poland attended church to mark symbolically their allegiance to an independent Poland. (They now no longer find it necessary to do so.)

11. Over the past twenty-five years, there has been an increase in anti-Semitic activities among a number of different black organizations and a curious inability by more moderate African Americans to directly attack such movements, even in university settings.

12. This trend is now apparent on BBC radio and television in the United Kingdom.

13. See chapter 11.

14. An emic approach is an attempt of the scientific observer to understand the conceptual system of the observed and to state one's observations as best as one can within the conceptual framework of the observed. This is opposed to an etic approach, which analyzes an observed situation in terms of the external system of the observer.

15. See further discussion of the adaptation patterns of Japanese minorities in chapter 4.

16. Events since our initial edition demonstrate clearly that ethnic loyalties have prevailed in all instances over any form of class alliance.

17. The Sikhs' seeking of political autonomy has become a serious political movement since our initial writing.

18. This movement is presently producing serious sources of new conflict in universities as well as in American urban settings.

19. These paragraphs, written in 1970, have become even more cogent today. The sense of alienated loneliness found in many youth from so-called old American backgrounds has become even more pronounced.

20. The autobiographical volume, *The Hunger of Memory*, by Richard Rodriguez, exemplifies this process. However, a shift toward acceptance of the successful seems to be moving faster in the Mexican American than in the African American poorer communities.

References

Barth, Fredrik. 1969. *Ethnic groups and boundaries*. Boston: Little, Brown.

Berreman, Gerald. 1967a. Concomitants of caste organization. In *Japan's invisible race: Caste in culture and personality*, ed. George A. De Vos and Hiroshi Wagatsuma, 308–24. Berkeley: University of California Press.

———. 1967b. Structure and function of caste systems. In *Japan's invisible race: Caste in culture and personality*, ed. George A. De Vos and Hiroshi Wagatsuma, 277–307. Berkeley: University of California Press.

Caudill, William, and George A. De Vos. 1972. Achievement, culture and personality, the case of the Japanese Americans. In *Socialization for achievement: The cultural psychology of the Japanese*, ed. George A. De Vos, 220–50. Berkeley: University of California Press.

Crandon-Malamud, Libbet. 1991. Phantoms and physicians: Social change through medical pluralism. In *The anthropology of medicine: From culture to method*, ed. Lola Romanucci-Ross, Daniel E. Moerman, and Lawrence Sancredi, 85–112. New York: Bergin & Garvey.

De Vos, George A. 1965. Transcultural diagnosis of mental health by means of psychological tests. In *Ciba Foundation Symposium on Transcultural Psychiatry*, ed. A. V. S. de Reuck and Ruth Porter, 328–56. London: Churchill.

———. 1966. Conflict, dominance and exploitation in human systems of social segregation: Some theoretical perspectives from the study of personality and culture. In *Conflicts in society*, ed. A. V. S. de Reuck and J. Knight, 60–81. London: Churchill.

———. 1973. *Socialization for achievement: The cultural psychology of the Japanese.* Berkeley: University of California Press.

———. 1992. *Social cohesion and alienation: Minorities in the United States and Japan.* Boulder, CO: Westview Press.

De Vos, George A., and Keiichi Mizushima. 1967. The organization and social functions of Japanese gangs. In *Aspects of social change in modern Japan*, ed. R. P. Dore, 289–326. Princeton, NJ: Princeton University Press.

De Vos, George A., and Marcelo Suarez-Orozco. 1990. *Status inequality: The self in culture.* Newbury Park, CA: Sage Publications.

De Vos, George A., and Hiroshi Wagatsuma. 1967. *Japan's invisible race: Caste in culture and personality.* Berkeley: University of California Press.

———. 1969. Minority status and deviancy in Japan. In *Mental health research in Asia and the Pacific*, ed. William Caudill and Tsing Yi-Lin, 342–57. Honolulu: East-West Center Press.

Durkheim, Emile. 1947. *The elementary forms of the religious life.* Trans. J. W. Swain. Glencoe, IL: Free Press.

Erikson, Erik H. 1968. *Identity, youth and crisis.* New York: Norton.

Foster, George. 1967. Peasant society and the image of limited good. *American Anthropologist* 69:293–315.

Glazer, Nathan, and Daniel P. Moynihan. 1963. *Beyond the melting pot.* Cambridge, MA: MIT Press.

Goffman, Erving. 1963. *Stigma: Notes on the management of spoiled identity.* Englewood Cliffs, NJ: Prentice Hall.

Hagen, Everett E. 1962. *On the theory of social change.* Chicago: Dorsey.

Haley, Alex. 1966. *The autobiography of Malcolm X.* New York: Grove Press.

Kardiner, Abram, and L. Ovesey. 1962. *The mark of oppression.* Part one: The concept of ethnic identity. New York: World.

Lanternari, V. 1963. *The religions of the oppressed: A study of modern messianic cults.* New York: Knopf.

Lee, Changsoo, and George A. De Vos. 1981. *Koreans in Japan: Ethnic conflict and accommodation.* Berkeley: University of California Press.

Lewis, Oscar. 1959. *Five families.* New York: Basic Books.

Mead, George Herbert. 1934. The I and the me. In *Mind, Self and Society*, ed. Charles Morris, 276–92. Chicago: University of Chicago Press.

Nakane, Chie. 1971. *Japanese society.* London: Weidenfeld and Nicolson.

Paz, Octavio. 1961. *The labyrinth of solitude: Life and thought in Mexico.* New York: Grove Press.

Romanucci-Ross, Lola. 1977. The hierarchy of resort in curative practices: The Admiralty Island, Melanesia. *Journal of Health and Social Behavior* 10 (30): 201–10.

———. 1986. *Conflict, violence and morality in a Mexican mestizo village.* Rev. ed. Chicago: University of Chicago Press.

Rowe, William L. 1960. Social and economic mobility in a low-caste North India community. PhD diss., Cornell University.

———. 1964. Myth as social charter: The assignment of status in Hindu caste origin stories. Paper presented at the 63rd Annual Meeting of the American Anthropological Association, Detroit, November 20.

Schama, Simon. 1987. *The embarrassment of riches: An interpretation of Dutch culture in the golden age.* London: Fontana Press.

Schwartz, Theodore. 1976. Cargo cult: A Melanesian type response to culture contact. In *Responses to change: Society, culture and personality*, ed. George A. De Vos, 157–207. New York: D. Van Nostrand Company.

Totten, George, and Hiroshi Wagatsuma. 1967. Emancipation: Growth and transformation of a political movement. In *Japan's invisible race: Caste in culture and personality*, ed. George A. De Vos and Hiroshi Wagatsuma, 33–67. Berkeley: University of California Press.

CHANGING ETHNIC AND NATIONAL IDENTITIES

I

T HE MEDITERRANEAN AREA OF EUROPE has a long history, and knowledge of it, that stretches back in time and fades into prehistory. Richly documented, this continuum was and is illumined by long-established scholarly interests in archaeology and paleontology. Concepts of self-knowledge in such a milieu are linked to a wealth of sources for negotiating and renegotiating a cultural identity. Because Italy is particularly characteristic in this regard, we begin this section with the chapter on Italy to help us define a morphing and metamorphosing of identities. Such generations of cultural-identity transmission lead to reassessments, revealing traits that remain core and others that are amenable to bartering away for various rewards. Like tides rushing in and ebbing, invaders of Italy left cultural as well as genetic traces on the established populations, clashing or blending their traits with those already there. This process has provided mosaics of combinatorial possibilities conserved as a series of successes and failures that were determinants of group survival. Once established as a political entity, a group faces challenges to its survival and finds new sorting devices for cultural identification. In "Matrices of an Italian Identity," Romanucci-Ross considers ethnic personality as a distillate of mythology, adaptation to historical processes, and the aesthetics and strategies that structure as well as define the rules for combining all of these elements. The physical space was small, but historical time was long, and the events that brought about change are numerous. Remembered communal events are commemorated in the names of streets, by statues and plaques, and by feast days and saint's days, but they are also anchored and buttressed by language (especially in the dialects), by kinesics (body language), and by conversational styles and discussions of moral strategies. For even more unassailable statements about identities, one can find them in operas, plays, other theatricals, parades, and ceremonies. Such anchorings are not very adaptive, however, when individuals are forced to live in a foreign culture, such as the United States.

For a long period, invaders or intruders came and went by foot or by boat (although Hannibal's armies crossed the Alps with the aid of thirty-eight elephants during a period of Carthaginian expansion during the Punic Wars). Such movements engendered phenotypic and cultural novelties to be confronted by absorption or rejection, but they are hardly comparable to what can be experienced because of air travel; "culture shock" can arrive within twenty-four hours from anywhere on the planet. In our times, it is not invaders who might come, but more likely persons looking for work offered by entrepreneurs seeking to reduce labor costs. In this, Italy now faces the same challenges to national identity as a number of other European countries. The conglomerations over time that occurred in Italy differ significantly from the case of Vilnius.

Situated between Eastern and Western Europe, Vilnius, capital of Lithuania since 1323, was destined to become an agglomerate constituted of fragments. Vulnerable and flanked by powers and superpowers of its day, its experience can be only very briefly summarized here. Destroyed by the Knights of the Teutonic Order in 1377 and restored by a Polish-Lithuanian Union in 1385, Vilnius enjoyed what its people considered a peaceful hiatus that included development, but it was also punctuated by numerous occurrences of the Plague and devastating fires. In 1656, it was occupied by Russia and later twice by Sweden, only to be occupied once again by Russia, who in 1795 found the city so attractive that it became the seat of the Russian governor-general. However, the majority of the people were Poles, and the second-largest group was Jews. In fact, in the eighteenth century, Vilnius became a center of Rabbinic learning. Occupied by the Germans from 1915 to 1919, it was seized by the Red Army, later occupied by Poland until World War II, but seized once more by the Red Army in 1939 and ceded back to Lithuania that same year. We offer this background by way of introduction to the chapter "Vilnius, Lithuania: An Ethnic Agglomerate" by Milosz, who does not dwell upon its history but rather informs us on what it meant to him to be a lifelong resident of Vilnius. He describes the complexity involved in the identification of self (and how it affects attitudes of others) when one responds to the query, "Who and what are you?" In choosing one language rather than another, one may be exposed or enabled to manipulate a situation to his advantage. The schools in Vilnius offered courses and programs in many different languages, and one selected a school for the language in which he or she wanted to study all subjects, and families did not necessarily choose a school for their children based on the language spoken at home. Choices included Polish, Yiddish, Hebrew, Russian, or Byelorussian. Overlying the linguistic differences were a variety of religions: Roman Catholic, Greek Catholic, Orthodox, and Islam. The Vilnius of Milosz is a showcase of how an agglomerate, born and raised through centuries of violence, has learned to use profound cultural differences to avoid violence. The reader, of course, must draw his or her own conclusions.

Yugoslavia provides a classic example of ethnic belonging competing with the impulse to embrace nationalism, both engendered by a sense of wanting to "belong." These conflicting needs to pledge allegiance are fueled by the interference of greater powers that either fuse or separate ethnic units to suit their own interests. The process can be considered a relic of the often bloody history of Europe. Interestingly, the word "balkanization" in ordinary usage conveys the futility of constant reduction in size of the elements of a conflictful situation, which for questionable reasons does not address the central concern. In 1918, after the end of World War I, the Austro-Hungarian Empire was obliged to relinquish land containing ethnic enclaves, which became the Kingdom of Serbs, Croats, and Slovenes. In 1929, this kingdom officially took the name Yugoslavia. Conflicts and occasionally ethnic hatreds preexisted in the region, however.

In addition to ethnic diversity, Yugoslavia contained a number of religions, including Roman Catholic, Muslim, Greek Orthodox, and Judaism. It was also linguistically diverse and had two alphabets, the Cyrillic and the Latin. All of these elements would seem to augur nothing but conflict. Yet Gilliland, in her chapter, "Ethnic Nationality in the Former Yugoslavia: Ethnogenesis, Ethnic Cleansing, and Present-Day Identities among Croats, Serbs, and Bosniacs," has a different view from the accepted explanations that seek to characterize the violence in the region; she urges the reader to consider that economics and politics were driving forces that cannot be overlooked. She has lived with families during her frequent stays over a twenty-year period, and was fluent in both Serbian and Croatian. Such contact allowed her to learn much about all the microevents that occurred among these groups. She found a great number of ethnic intermarriages between so-called factions, many families containing such cross-marriages for several generations. But the events that brought on dissent and accusations were usually based not on ethnic or linguistic differences, but rather on external events that had either political or economic motivations. Because of certain interventions in the system, usually by outsiders, in later return trips she found a change in the presentation of the self, sometimes changes in religious affiliations, and particularly an increasing "tolerance of difference" that waxed and waned subject to the prevailing ideology that defined acceptable behavior. Desires to present a new "self" were conditioned by newspaper writings or stands taken by leaders of influential countries in Europe and the United States. Saddened and dismayed by the long years of violence, people seemed to become energized by any event reported from outside sources. Of the conflict in the labyrinth of the mid-1990s, one newspaper publisher in the war-weary country said, "This was an artificial war, really produced by television." Yugoslavia seems to have been and remain subject to the renegotiation and regeneration of ethnic identity and belonging for ethnic conflict, including its geographical location within the Balkans that all of these factors have.

In contrast to most regions of Europe, Japan has not been subject to repeated invasions and territorial conflicts between empires and great powers, which has produced much of the dislocation and intermingling of ethnic groups in Europe. This is not merely a result of Japan's geographical isolation as an island nation. The Mongol invaders of the thirteenth century were dispersed and destroyed by a series of fortuitous storms (the origin of the word *kamikaze*—divine wind—which supposedly saved the Japanese nation at the time and was again expected to do so in World War II in the form of suicide pilots). After three hundred years of self-imposed isolation, Japan staved off Western colonial conquest in the late nineteenth century by first opening its ports to foreign trade (in response to American gunboat diplomacy) and then by rapidly modernizing and strengthening itself along Western lines, enabling it to eventually embark on its own colonial conquest of Asia.

Although Japan's population has remained relatively stable and ethnically homogeneous (at least compared to European countries), this does not mean that its history of nation building was smooth and unproblematic. Not only did Japan's political elite after the Meiji Restoration in 1868 have to modernize the country, but they also needed to consolidate the country's disparate local populations and strong regional differences under a single Japanese national identity by invoking an ideology of common racial descent, cultural homogeneity and uniqueness, and the unity of the nation under the emperor. Nonetheless, as George De Vos and Hiroshi Wagatsuma discuss in their chapter, "Cultural Identity and Minority Status in Japan," the considerable Westernization and globalization of Japanese society has influenced not only its popular culture and mass media, but even language and physical aesthetics, problematizing the country's attempts to maintain a distinctive national and cultural identity. Most importantly, about 4.5 percent of Japan's population consists of ethnic minority groups, which has further complicated Japanese ethnonational identity (the notion that the Japanese nation consists of one racially and culturally homogeneous ethnic group).The chapter then focuses on two of Japan's most prominent ethnic minority groups. The first are the Burakumin, an outcaste group who are seen as impure and continue to experience discrimination because of their traditional association with ritually unclean occupations such as leather working, animal butchery, tanning skins, grave digging, and the handling of corpses. Although they are of Japanese descent and thus not physically distinct, they traditionally lived in segregated Buraku communities and maintain some differences in customs and behavior as well as in family and socialization patterns. A long legacy of castelike discrimination and social degradation has produced a number of problems among Burakumin, including negative self-images, deviancy, and negative attitudes toward dominant institutions. In contrast to those Burakumin who politically mobilize on the basis of their minority identities to fight discrimination and improve their socioeconomic status, others attempt to escape their disparaged minority status by leaving their communities, hiding their ethnic backgrounds, and passing to various degrees as mainstream Japanese.

The Koreans migrated to Japan as laborers before and during World War II (many were forcibly relocated) and decided to remain in Japan after the war. Unlike the Burakumin, their stigmatized ethnicity in Japan is not a result of the continued impurity of past occupational status, but the impurity of race. Although most Korean Japanese today have been born and raised in Japan and are culturally assimilated, they continue to be subject to derogation, discrimination, and scapegoating simply because of their Korean descent and negative stereotypes about their supposed cultural differences. As a result, they are not yet *socially* assimilated and continue to suffer from low socioeconomic status, family disruption, defensive ethnic identities that hinder academic achievement, and problems with interethnic marriage. Like the Burakumin, a number of them pass as majority Japanese by hiding their Korean backgrounds, but they do so at the risk of alienating their ethnic peers and forgoing the expressive need for group belonging. It is quite evident that such discrimination and marginalization of ethnic minorities will persist until Japanese society becomes more tolerant toward ethnic diversity (and outsiders in general) and less insistent on a singular ethnonational identity based on a myth of racial and cultural uniqueness.

Lola Romanucci-Ross and Takeyuki Tsuda

Matrices of an Italian Identity: Past as Prologue

1

LOLA ROMANUCCI-ROSS

T HE ITALIAN EXPERIENCE OF GROUP AND PERSONAL IDENTITY is a distillate of millennial fusions of cultural traits in group definitions of "belonging" and occasional fissioning in cultural differentiation. I will focus here on the Piceno as one variant of the historical and cultural processes that could apply to a number of Italian regions. The Piceno is one of the truly ancient regions; others are Apulia, Campania, Latium, Lucania, and Umbria. Until relatively recently (the last century), there was no Italian nation-state, and some Italians like to quip that there really isn't one now. The humor in such remarks barely masks the always more deeply ensconced attachment to regional affiliations, as I will indicate in this chapter.

A profusion of languages and cultures "became" Italy. In prehistory, we can infer only that warrior elements came from central Europe, bearers of the Bell-Beaker culture from Spain, and that here had passed founders of the Terramara culture, and the Villanovan culture which appeared in the Iron Age. The Iron Age also saw the Illyrians cross the Adriatic to join the inhuming Apenine culture to dominate the Picenum (the place and people described in this chapter). Origins are sought in remnants of dialects as well as in archaeological and paleontological discoveries. Italic dialects are described by linguists as a subdivision of Indo-European languages. Only Latin, spoken by a tribe in the lower regions of the Tiber, survived; the rest can be only reconstructed and surmised. Upon this fundamental cultural stratum there came a wave of invasions from all quarters, and we find evidence of these occurring even prior to the Neolithic. Eventually, because of the differing origins of the linguistic groups that invaded or settled, one can determine a definite split between the northern and southern dialects in Italy. These differences were further amplified by the introduction of Slovene speakers in the Udine and Gorzia areas, Albanian speakers in the south-central region, Greek-speaking villages in Calabria, and French Provençal speech in the north.

Etruscans (of Greek origin?) tried but failed to unite the people of Italy. The Romans later succeeded in this for a time, binding groups together through administration and a network of permanent highways. Medieval Italy saw a new period of invasions by Goths and Longobards; the latter brought permanent settlement of Germanic peoples into Italy. Next to cross the Alps were the Franks, with a legacy of cultural features often referred to as Carolingian Italy. Meanwhile, the Arabs had begun the conquest of Sicily in 827 and also began to settle in various places on the mainland. About two hundred years later, the Normans, having come to destroy Byzantine power in the service of the church, were given incentives to begin permanent settlements in Sicily and nearby regions.

In the eleventh century, this welter of cultural overlays began to conform to a new sorting device, that is, to be expressed as "communes," which later became city-states. This geographical fissioning could occur because some Italian towns had reached a level of prosperity and size that allowed development of local self-governments that asserted themselves to rebuff challenges to their authority. Venice, for example, elected its own dukes (*doges*); Amalfi and other cities, their own magistrates. At times, such communes were opposed by the pope (as in the Piceno area). Such polarization of "town and (ecclesiastical) gown" was expressed in conflicts in many city-states and often spread into wider areas under an encompassing leadership for each side, as in the battles between the Guelphs and the Ghibellines. In addition to attaining independence, the city-states, or *comuni*, had two other politico-cultural agendas: to make war upon each other and to conquer and absorb the *contado* (countryside) into their immediate environs; what follows is a discussion of these relationships in the Piceno as a paradigm for other regions of the whole later-to-be nation-state of Italy. The paradigm could apply, for example, to Sicily, where the earliest Indo-European speakers were joined, either through invasion or settlement, by Phoenicians, Greeks, Carthaginians, Romans, Vandals (in the Byzantine period), Arabs, Normans, Spaniards, Savoyards, and Austrians. Markers of these conjoinings in Sicily are found in the dialect, art, architecture, music, historical dress, cuisine, gender relations, family structure, healing and curing rituals, and so on. Regions were characteristic of conglomerates of the many cultural ways of being human.

In Italy, a regional culture can be thought of as an array of elements in a space, which, when configured, characterize and distinguish it from other regional cultures. Invasions came as ocean tides, disturbing the set or array of elements. In the ebbing of the invasion force, either by expulsion or withdrawal, the invaders left their mark. Sometimes they rearranged the elements in the cultural matrix, sometimes they changed the determinants, and sometimes they remained as long-term settlers to become the people they had conquered (Balena 1970; Barzini 1965; Dundes and Falassi 1975; Musa 1964; Petrusewicz 1978; Pulgram 1958; Treggiari 1991).

Relating Time and Space

The city of Ascoli Piceno predates its encounter with the Romans. Not only the city's inhabitants but those in the towns and villages in its province are aware of their long traditions and unique characteristics. Ascoli Piceno lies along the ancient Via Salaria, the Roman "salt road," to the Adriatic Coast, five hundred feet above sea level among the wooded hills of oak and chestnut where the Tronto and Castellano rivers meet. In this chapter, I examine the self-conscious self-perceptions produced by the behavioral strategies the Ascolani developed over long periods of time while interacting with other ethnic groups that came to claim their precious and limited geographical space.

Time and space relations are a crucial element in the creation and preservation of ethnic group identity (Romanucci-Ross 1985, xi). For Europeans who came to many parts of the American continent, space was vast, and historical time in residence was relatively brief. For the English, French, Spanish, and others, "colonization" after several centuries was complete, and an identity (carried from home and slightly modified) was formed. Group identity was based on enduring conquest with accompanying acquisition of land and resources, and an indigenous work force in some cases; it was not interrupted by meaningful historical moments of loss of control. In a nation-state such as Italy, however, the time in residence of ethnic groups reaches back through the millennia (modified though these groups might have been by incursions of some new genes and assimilated cultural traits). Origins of language, "race," and cultural traits disappear in prehistory, and the territory on which all this occurred was relatively small, so that in the long stretch of historical time, ethnic enclaves in Italy produced the diversities that determined group identities. To the outsider, these are readily recognized as broad-stroked *regional* differences; to each *ethne*, the distinctions are finer. But it is recognized that all areas of Italy have shared the historical experience of constant invasions and incursions from political or military representatives of other "countries," even though regionally these were usually not the same specific and particular versions. What was shared was the manner of conquest or persuasion, the occasional revolts, and often the unique feature of the conquerors who came and stayed long enough to blend into the culture and become bearers of the culture they found, even while retaining parts of their own. How did this happen?

Philosophers critical of the school of phenomenology dwell upon the difficulties of reconciling the "internal discourse" (that is, the "I" of solitary discourse; see, for example, Jacques Derrida [1967] or Dilthey [see Hodges 1952], among others, who have written on the history of human consciousness). Such critics feel there is no persuasive model to indicate that a phenomenological (solipsistic?) worldview can ever be shared. Yet, we do have the legacy of George Herbert Mead (1934), which is an attempt to describe the socialization process of the child and the manner in which it becomes a group member. The fieldwork of Margaret Mead (1930, 1975) is an example of an anthropologist recording the process of socialization in the South Seas, in Bali, and in New Guinea, and there have been other commentaries on such a process (Romanucci-Ross 1985). Since we begin with the relationship of time and space coordinates, I suggest at the outset that people who feel part of the Americas model (still exemplified in large portions of the western United States or Argentina) are likely to see themselves more in relation to the *landscape* and less in the view of the Other. People of the Italian model (small space, long time span), on the other hand, have identities more likely to be formed as reflections of the self in the eyes of others.

Accepting Devereux's (1982) definition of ethnic identity as a "sorting device," I describe here the creation and preservation of an ethnic group identity in the nation-state (though many Italians would say "geographical expression") that is Italy and how the notion of group identity is transmitted culturally. Considered, in belonging, are the structure of the family (and the exoticization of romantic love), the mythologized family and other religious symbols, use of language and dialect, conflict resolution strategies, models of behavior, ethics or the creation of ethnic character, aesthetics in the creation of ethnic personality, and how these models are actualized through work and play and the negotiating of exchanges of goods, services, or persons (as in marriage).

The People of the Piceno

The area of the Piceno encompasses the city of Ascoli Piceno and the small towns and villages in the countryside that, circumscribed, constitute the province similarly named; it is all now considered administratively part of the larger region of Le Marche (in central Italy), surrounded by Tuscany, Umbria, Lazio, Abruzzi, and the Adriatic Sea. Much of the province of Ascoli Piceno is agricultural. Its produce consists of cereals, grapes, fruits, vegetables, and products of animal husbandry. However, the area from the city toward the Adriatic to the port city of San Benedetto is becoming increasingly industrialized.

It has long been fashionable to write and think in terms of rural-urban dichotomies and all that implies for behavior and lifestyle, but such a dichotomy is tenuous at best in this locality. In the early nineteenth century, we find remarkable urban-rural homogeneity; 70 percent of those allowed to call themselves Ascolani worked in the countryside (Fabiani 1967, 225–35). From the earliest historical times, there has been a constant movement of individuals and families from the city to the country and from the country to the city. Sometimes temporary, sometimes permanent (at least for several generations), the reasons for these migrations may have been political (refugees from the groups in conflict); economic (inability to live off the land or to survive in the city); or to reestablish family ties (there are villas owned by the well-to-do who have estates outside the city, and there are also small cramped apartments in certain sections of the city for the marginal people who come and go). In the village of "Malva," in which I have conducted many intensive periods of fieldwork over a twenty-year period (Romanucci-Ross 1991), male heads of families (and wives) who work in the city and commute "home" outnumber those who live off only their crops or off their crops and their pensions. Nor is this atypical.

How does an ethnic group interpret and memorialize its own history, and how does the consciousness of it come to be used as an identity marker? Various historical events are remembered in the plan or layout of the city (or piazzas in small towns and villages) and in its streets, buildings, and monuments. Some are recalled in monuments or festivals, some of which call for the dramatization of a period, complete with costumes, food, music, and games of that era. There is also the ongoing artistry and trade of "pictorializing" (on canvas, ceramics, metals, clay, stone, marble, or through photography) ancient bridges, cathedrals, convents, moats and fortresses, churches, monasteries, designs of portals, and house doors. There are also continuous critiques of the originals and of their representations; no one ever seems to tire of any of these activities.

Therefore, the historical events I chose to note have been chosen for me; they are commonly noted, almost universally known and referred to with some frequency by certain segments of the population. As an example, life in *il cinquecento* (the 1500s) is celebrated on the days of the *Quintana* (the *palio* horse-racing event) during the first week of August. This is when much of the city "becomes" sixteenth-century Ascoli, with many citizens joining the parade clad in period costumes. This historical period is very important to the Ascolani as they celebrate annually the transfer of the "keys of the city" from civil magistrates back to the church. The ceremony is conducted in front of the cathedral of Saint Emidio, named after · the city's German-born patron saint; he was Ascoli's first bishop and has protected the city from earthquakes and invasions since his death, or so it is believed.

If you ask the Ascolani or Piceni (the countryside people) about their origins, you will be offered, in a modality that does not distinguish between history and mythology (since to them the word *origin* does not call for that distinction), a set of probable and not necessarily exclusive accounts. The descendants of Peucetios and his friends came from the Aegean seventeen generations before the Trojan War, or perhaps they were those Achaeans (in the *Iliad*) who came as pirates after defeating the Minoans, or the Mycenaeans who emigrated to Italian shores after the destruction of Troy, or those called the Pelasgians. Who knows with certainty? "Certainly it was one or more of these groups. Look it up in the archaeological museum."

They like to tell the story of King Pico, the Italic, and his beloved Pomona, the goddess of gardens and fruit. Circe, jealous of such passion by the king that was not directed toward her, turned him into a woodpecker (*picchio*). In the guise of that transformation, he led the homeless Sabines from upper-central Italy, somewhat south and east of the Ascoli Piceno site. These Sabines were the "chosen" of the *ver sacrum*, also called *primavera Italica*, a ritual moment in which one-tenth of newborns were sacrificed (i.e., selected for a later social death) by a promise their parents had to make that in early adulthood they were to leave for a new land. This is the favored later cultural origin story, considered supplemental to any one of the early Greek migration origin stories (Romanucci-Ross 1991). We know that the Greeks knew of the people of Ascoli, for they referred to them as Askilaioi, and the Etruscans called them Asklaic. Linguistically, it appears that the Piceni were related to the Aegean-Anatolian area peoples by the end of the third millennium BC (Pulgram 1958, 164). There is an oral tradition that passes on a folk explanation of the evolution of language and dialects using bits of archaeology, mythology, and phonology, which in some instances is not too far off the mark from what we know today from scant evidence (Lehman 1993).

In recorded history, Ascoli Piceno was once an ally of Rome and as such was encouraged to fight off the Gauls for Rome. Resenting the nature of such an alliance and the presence of Roman garrisons in their city, the Ascolani severed relations, and by 269 BC they were at war. Losing the war, Ascolani became a vassal state, but being considered a *civitas foederata*, it had the right to bestow military and political honors. By 90 BC, the two cities were at war again, and acorn-shaped missiles with inscribed invectives can still be found in the museum. Any schoolchild knows about these events and will tell you, "We never caved in to Rome" and were "never truly conquered." They further point out that Spartacus and his former slave gladiators defeated Roman soldiers very close to Asculum Picenum (as it was then known). It was on "that very slope" that leads down to the Tronto River, then known as the Truentum, that in 49 BC Julius Caesar himself stopped at the *Castrum Truentum* (camp of the Tronto), and it was there he said, "The die is cast."

The Ascolani may never have been truly conquered for a significant period of time, but their city and its environs became quite Romanized during the long period of nonconquest; the city was considered one of the best organized in Italy. It is not without pride that you will be shown the two ancient Roman bridges (one still in use), the Roman theater, and parts of the Roman wall that once surrounded the city. Ascoli's height of involvement with Christianity occurred in 300 AD, when Saint Emidio was its bishop. In 476 AD—though Rome had fallen—Christianity remained, since it had been (among other things) an anti-Roman sect. This period is memorialized in the baptistery, still standing, and in statues of persons (found in the lower floor of the cathedral of Saint Emidio) who preferred death to renouncing Christianity.

Invaders came from the north: Goths, Franks, Vandals, and Longobards, the latter successful as the others were not in overrunning Ascoli. The Longobards left many marks to which the language, dialect, and remains will attest, and they stayed for centuries, the best example of becoming the people they had conquered. Circa 368 AD, they captured the city already defeated by hunger and disease. Even some personal names (especially those of women, e.g., Isolina) are traceable to this cultural source. One can still find traces of Longobard necropoli in the countryside, and some Longobards are buried in the cathedral of Saint Emidio. During the reign of the Longobards, the papacy became powerful in a political sense, and lands around the city were acquired by the church, often as gifts. Centers of monastic life had already taken root in the hills surrounding the city. These were contemporaneous with other characteristically medieval events, such as sending men off to the crusades; conflicts between noble families, which often symbolized church against state; and attempted invasions of the Adriatic Coast by Turks and others. "Better families" took refuge during these crises, in what are still called "Longobard towers." Everyone knows the names of some of the noble families, whether they sided with Guelph or with Ghibelline, who took turns in power and control, for such names are still found on streets and buildings as well as in the local telephone directory.

These events are recalled as examples of the courage to perdure as a city-state, but so is the establishment of the commune of Ascoli Piceno, first organized legally in 1253. This was an interesting experiment in democratic governance even though it lacked representation for those who had neither property nor money (Fabiani 1957–1959, 1967). But it is important to note, in connection with repulsion of concepts for social reform, that the working class doubled as urban *and* rural workers. They did repair work, ran errands, and transported building materials and all manner of other objects for their employers. Their wives and children helped out with chores, gave gifts (*regalia*) to the patrons (*padroni*) on certain holidays, and even "worked silk" for them in their leisure hours. By the end of the eighteenth century, the army of Napoleon Bonaparte had reached Le Marche, which fell under French "protection." Some Ascolani had become—not knowing what it meant—"Republican." But because of their revolutionary ideals, the French had insulted religion and attacked the class structure by declaring their intent to abolish all titles of nobility, two unfortunate decisions to rich and poor alike in the city and the country.

The Neapolitans, too, under Spanish rule, were beginning to attack nearby ports, and the spectacle of Spanish and French persons wandering in and out of the city brought on a great wariness and deep distrust of all protectors, governors, and governments. This led to a pervasive cynicism that is still the major influence on attitudes toward "the vote," now part of the democratic process. "France or Spain, as long as we eat" is often brought into a conversation on current political choices—meaning that it makes no difference who takes control—if one can only survive. The present "democracy," it is felt by many, merely facilitates corrupt practices and political favoritism.

Brigandage

Even prior to the purchased freedom from the French, this area of Italy shared the pan-Italic experience of brigandage. A locally born man called "Sciabolone" (brigands all had nicknames) hated the Jacobins; he and three hundred men ambushed a group of French soldiers and killed all of them. This ragged band took the city of Ascoli Piceno as they shouted, "Ave Maria." However, the French regained it, this time looting, burning, and killing. Nevertheless, they eventually had to ask for peace from the *briganti*; these were true early guerrilla fighters who took to the hills and attacked constantly. After blows from the guerrillas, together with financial incentives (payments of large sums of money to France after Napoleon's defeat in 1815), the French left the city, helping themselves to precious manuscripts, paintings, sculptures, and other treasures as they left. Ascoli then became once more a papal state, leaving the people with little desire to join the new Italian nation.

In 1849, anti–Roman Republic brigandage was concentrated in Ascoli. In fact, when the Piedmont army (of Italian unification) arrived in a village in the Piceno area on January 28, 1861, they were ambushed by guerrilla fighters. As the Piedmontese army fought with orders to "smash the Sacerdotal Empire" (Balena 1970, 315), many Ascolani took to the woods and hills to fight again for the pope. The poor often joined the brigand leaders in hopes of getting land and rights of which they had been deprived. When combating the Roman Republic, brigands followed their leader, a young mountaineer called Giovanni Piccioni. He was the leader who, with his men, confronted General Pinelli and the troops of Victorio Emanuele II. In every instance, they were inspired and driven to fight foreign governments in the name of the Catholic faith, and Piccioni had a deep hatred for the troops of the future king of Italy, referring to them as "the anti-Christ." Brigands were not always Robin Hoods or primitive rebels, as some would have us think (see Hobsbawm 1959), but often worked for powerful patrons (Davis 1988, 72). These romanticized figures operated with a sociopolitical background of food riots, tax riots, attacks on public officers, cattle rustling, kidnapping, and murder. Many women rode with their men, and some were brigands in their own right. Brigands were common and are remembered in central Italy; *L' albero dei Piccioni*, the tree in which Piccioni and his men hid, still stands and carries his romanticized name.

More accurately, brigands were entrepreneurs who shifted alliances but did not disdain help even from those with more noble motives or from the poor, who from time to time joined the sorties of brigand leaders. Brigand leaders conjured romance in their exploits and took names such as "Crocco" and "Serravalle." Nevertheless, they provided breakthrough occasions for other significant events to co-occur: women as equal partners (if in crime only), the struggle for social justice (even as an epiphenomenal event), and the expulsion of the French (even if for less than purely patriotic motives). Such a period ended by 1865, but the brigands are remembered for driving out the French, although that was not the only reason for the French retreat from the area. The local assessment of the attempted importation of the ideals of the French Revolution was expressed in humorous doggerel verse. Many were not about to abandon the system that made sense to them. After World War II, one heard expressions of pride over a group of young men bayoneted to death on September 12, 1943, a result of the resistance (*i partigiani*), bringing the battle to Ascoli and drawing German troops into the city. These men were thought valiant, but Saint Emidio was given the full credit for sparing the city from German assault and German bombs (presumably meant for Ascoli but dropped by mistake on nearby Macerata). As time went by, these same young men are remembered with pity for their naïveté. How could they not know that it is most important to survive?

Recounting this "historical past remembered" is kept current in the names of the streets or persons, through statues, and in the plan of the city; the architecture of the buildings, too, is a mnemonic device signaling these important identifying events. The city plan is an urban expression of the cosmology of the times, reflecting the ideal "heavenly city." A resident medieval painter, Alemanno, portrayed Ascoli as such. The so-called Longobard towers remind them of the conflict and fractions led by noble families and the intruders from the north who came and stayed and became one people and one culture with them (red-haired, fair, and freckle-faced children often elicit Longobard invasion jokes). The modern buildings, mostly schools and offices, are reminders of the Fascist period, of which only a few ever speak at all, and none with nostalgia (Romanucci-Ross 1991).

A First Reality

Events remembered are the first reality of an identity as a group that has a common experiential past, and part of this rests in the linguistic vein in the local dialect and its uses. Dialect is spoken primarily as an index of intimacy (family or close friends). Between associates, it is a bid for trust, perhaps to establish a deal that can then be negotiated in politics or in business, or in the resolution of a conflictful situation. Shifting to the Italian language during such negotiations means "Are we coethnics or not? You begin to make me wonder."

No one seems to care very much about how the local dialect, "*parlata Piceno*" (Piceno speak), really crystallized. Although, if you ask, you will probably be told by many that it is presumed to be proto-Indo-European bandied about by Italics and Sabines, and maybe by the Volsci, Umbri, and Osci, all later considerably Latinized, as the archaeological evidence would suggest (Pulgram 1958). Interest piques with discussion of Longobard words that entered not only the dialect but the Italian language as well, parts of the vocabulary that deal mostly with the rustic life and a basic existence based on farming and hunting. Longobard words are those for grains, birds, baskets, and mud (*bratta*). The Longobards, who lingered for centuries enriching and diversifying the genetic pool, also left words that described military events, artisan trades, body parts, and animal life (Romanucci-Ross 1991). The strata of cultural incursions are found in an archaeology of added vocabularies, including words they "know" as ancient Greek: the word for "bread bin" or "kneading trough" (*mattera*), or a "snotty-nosed child" (*mierceluse*), and the more recent and familiar Latin words for family members, roads, and the like. More pervasive and behavior determining than vocabulary, however, is the preserved conversational style, accompanied by the kinetics, or body language, regarded by many others in the rest of the world as incomparably eloquent and unique.

Although dialects might be more frequently used in rural areas in other countries, and in rural areas in other parts of Italy, this does not hold in the Piceno area. There it is emitted with ease and comfort in certain contexts, even from city dwellers, the affluent and the poor, the professional and the worker. There is, in fact, a current attempt to dignify and revitalize the dialect by journalists in newspapers, in tourist-attraction brochures, in recordings of songs of the past in the Piceno dialect, and by historical societies and literary groups. The aim is to create a new sense of ethnic belonging and to emphasize a uniqueness to be contrasted with other regions of Italy in a long history of a past rich in artistic and moral splendor and business acumen.

The Family

In contrast to American culture, in the Piceno area, the strongest ties are not within the nuclear family of parents and children. In an emotional sense (and at times in a material way), such ties are fragile in comparison to the attachment to one's stem family. To understand the term *stem* as I have used it in kinship (Romanucci-Ross 1991, 47–48), one has to recognize and give proper weight to the expression *il ceppo*, which is polysemic. It can mean the Christmas log that is meant to never burn out entirely, and from which a new log is lit, which in turn keeps alive the flame for its successor; in fact, *il focolare* (the hearth) is used as a synonym for "family." *Il ceppo* may also refer to the male head of a family (at any point in time) who came to a *place* to begin a line of descendants. The literal meaning of trunk becomes the metaphorical trunk of the family tree. This may not appear extraordinary, except that in this culture the *ceppo* may change over time depending on land ownership changes, or a venture that brings an accumulation of wealth from an unexpected quarter, or acquisition of a title (a remote possibility, but not an inconceivable one). Psychological rather than strict genealogical forces in all such instances can be said to be the motivating principle in defining a new *ceppo* and the reckoning of a lineage. This is not to say that genealogical ties are denied or negated, but simply that in "the telling" or "writing," a person tends to select the *ceppo* of preference within the genealogy from his or her vantage point and to personal advantage.

Gendered spaces (i.e., where women may dwell and play a role) are crucially affected by ethnic belonging. If the groom has a widowed mother, the newlywed bride has a live-in mother-in-law whom she is expected to honor and obey as she does her husband. One does not hear complaints about this from young married women; it is accepted as the way things are and ought to be. Sometimes the eldest son is invited to bring his bride into the paternal home, where, according to local humor, one learns early who is to be in charge. At the wedding, someone (impersonating the groom's mother) will say, "Enter my daughter—at this lintel you will leave all your bad habits and adopt all of mine." The new bride knows she must never make public her husband's faults, but rather she must handle all the public relations aspects so as to hide them and publicize his virtues. She must uphold her husband's family's honor even more than she did her own family's honor before the marriage (homicide for honor's sake was deleted from the Italian penal code as justifiable only in 1981) (Cantarella 1991).

In the parental role, neither parent is ever tempted to "be a friend" to the children. Parent-child bonds are strong, but they are always vertical and are strengthened through discipline and a sense of social place and duty to honor, not friendship. As in Mexico (Romanucci-Ross 1986), mothers seek to bind their sons to them, knowing they will lose their daughters when they "marry out" of the family. This is not as neat and formulaic as it appears, however, for in the Piceno, what married persons do in crucial or crisis moments manifests the very deep loyalties to the stem family of their birth. But even without crises, thoughts, acts, and financial resources are frequently directed toward members of the stem family. Individuals play these roles within the family without too much analysis of them and without the agonistic displays that are sometimes seen in other parts of Italy or in other cultures (Romanucci-Ross 1985). There is an awareness that at times the cost of certain ties is high and that perhaps it does not have to be this way, but if you ask how the people feel about this, you are likely to be told of the advantages rather than the disadvantages of the cultural prescriptions and proscriptions concerning family duties and obligations. It is interesting to observe and analyze how children are reared to become what they must be for their immediate and future family roles (see Romanucci-Ross 1991, 56–63). My purpose here, however, is to indicate briefly that family membership and its expression are part of the ethnic personality within the context of ethnic identity.

Separation rituals (from the family) begin quite early, with baptism and the recognition of a unique soul. This is followed in prepubescence by communion and confirmation for membership in the wider family, that is, the community of the Catholic Church. The marriage rite is a presumed definite (but not always actual) separation from the family of one's birth. Godparenthood is a superimposition of the fictive family, a further affirmation of the parental concept, but with an overlay of the notion that substitution *is* possible should it become necessary. *Comparaggio* (godparenthood) also strengthens bonds between biological and fictive parents, bonds that are often used in business deals, in conflict resolution, or in deciding where one goes for favors.

The Church Family

Immediately beyond the "family in this world" constellation is the apparitional family structure of the administrators of the spiritual realm: the fathers, sisters, mother abbesses, and brothers of the church. These are ideal behavioral models, considered just a bit above the grasp of ordinary persons without vocations. Beyond these, the saints are models of perfection in behavior, symbols of the possibility of transcendence "to real meaning" in worldly existence. Though very few can obtain sainthood, it remains a refulgent transforming goal to a godlike being, in this world and beyond. The local saints are considered of great importance for the young to emulate: there is Santa Rita da Cascia, for example, who lived and died in a fifteenth-century village on the crest of the Apennines. Married to a drunk who was often brutal and was later murdered, she prayed that her two sons would die before they could avenge their father's murder. This they both did, and she, as it is said, "regained her freedom" (De Marchi 1969, 47–49) to join a convent, perform miracles, and become a saint. The lesson for local women? *Amor fati*, love your fate. Think only of pleasing the Lord.

Saint Serafino was so poor he had to work for a *contadino* (a sharecropper who already works for someone else). In Saint Serafino, we find an illiterate who had a calling to preach and spread the faith. Seeking out discomfort and humiliation, badly treated by everyone in his own family, he, like Santa Rita, was eventually revered for his healing miracles. His behavioral model for young men: spurn the pursuit of wealth, for it is harmful to the spirit. Saint Francis preached in Ascoli, arriving in 1226 to establish his order. The church at that time was on one side of the *Piazza del Popolo*, and a thirteenth-century cathedral named after him still stands in that place. Ascoli has a convent of the Poor Claires, founded by his good friend Santa Chiara (Giorgi 1968).

Fathers and sisters of the church offer models for taking vows of poverty and chastity. They, along with the saints, link "good sons and daughters" from secular families to the larger all-embracing spiritual family. The Ascolani have never relinquished that part of their identity that was shaped by the Catholic Church. The urban center of about sixty thousand people has a great (some say inordinate) number of churches and several cathedrals, a fact constantly remarked upon by the residents to visitors and tourists. Without its being viewed as contradictory, even as contrapuntal, you will be shown the statue of Cecco d' Ascoli (Francesco Stabili), the scientist-magician, an original and free thinker who defied the church by lecturing and writing that all could be learned by studying nature and the stars. He was burned alive at the stake in Florence in 1327, along with all his writings. Other naturalist-astronomers such as Cecco are now seen as forerunners of modern science. It has been noted that others who expressed antichurch sentiments were not burned at the stake; but Cecco was arrogant, pouty, and never given to compromise, traits that made him thoroughly Ascolano, the ultimate *scontroso* (a pouting and sulky person). And for that, he is theirs (Crespi 1927).

Time and Identity

In reckoning group identity, time is not only linear and vertical, as in historical remembering or genealogical reckoning; it is also horizontal in the sense that it is cyclical, repetitive, and predictable. From planting to harvesting of vegetables, cereals, and fruits, and from hard work to festivals and joy in the countryside, the shared rhythms of labor and celebration of its rewards are an ever-renewing bond. The men's heavy work of plowing, seeding, and planting in early spring leads to lesser but still demanding work (by men and women) in the fields and gardens. They plant tomatoes, peppers, beans, onions, lettuce, and so on in March and April, and they continue to hoe and weed around the young plants as they grow. During the summer months, fruits and vegetables are ripening while being attended by appropriate rainfall and constant care by the villagers who watch the progress with both apprehension and pride. If nature cooperates, collective expectations lead to the "beautiful" months of harvest.

Harvesting wheat and other cereals in July, gathering vegetables from June on, enjoying the sequence of fruits and berries all summer long, picking grapes in early autumn and shaking chestnuts and olives from the trees around November, along with cutting wood for winter—those who work the land like the repetitive cycle but fear the possible bitter surprises, or even disaster. One keeps an eye on the sky as one walks through the just-about-ready-to-harvest field of hay or wheat that can be ruined by a sudden cruel outburst of hail. An untimely frost can "burn" the tender buds on the fruit trees or young shoots of plants overnight, and one is forced to reseed if one can afford the expense; even ever-elusive money cannot save the crops that will rot if the fields are flooded. The suspense renders the harvest a blessing, and some villages have their village feast day in September, with a procession that begins in the church, led by a statue of the Madonna.

The blossoming of flowers reminds the person of love (in all its varieties, the constancies and the betrayals, the hopes, and the desperate sense of loss). It is said that the appearance of each flower is a specific reminder. There are many feast days in addition to universal Christian holidays; these include a special day to the Madonna, one to a saint to protect the farm animals, and one to the purification period for Mary after the birth of Jesus. Feast days are also perceived as reminders of the need for protection from the unpredictable and for celebration of community.

Community and Conflict

In the community, village or urban, an individual is defined by many recognized hierarchies: occupation, status, gender, age, sex role, and demeanor as to manner of dress, addressing others, and presenting the self.

The urban center also has communities within it—the *sestieri* (sections of the city), which give an even more intimate sense of community. Residents of the various sections run *their* horse and jockey in the *palio*. For the sense of community does not mean equality or a sense of solidarity, and it certainly does not exclude rivalries and conflict in city or country. Patronage systems give rise to factions, and communal land, private landholdings, and collective land use create much to negotiate about—most often not harmoniously. Disputes over collective land use or water use were common historically in central Italy (Davis 1988), and the Piceno area was no exception. Disputes still arise over boundaries of even the smaller plots of land, over a "misplaced" fence line around the house, over seeding, over water use, over firewood, over rights to animal grazing, or even over the question of where and when a neighbor's chickens might wander.

In fact, conflict has the very important function of positioning a family or lineage in the hierarchy of control and respect. In a village I focused upon for countryside ethnography, one conflict over water lasted many decades. It was settled only after the solicited intervention of magistrates and administrators from the *comune* and letters of admonition from a married couple who had gone to live in the United States (a couple that had united the two lineages in marriage). When I expressed relief that there might be peace now, I was told, "Don't count on it. Those two families will always find something to fight over." Clearly that has proven to be the case, since I have found at least half a dozen other conflicts between them: about roads, night lighting, parking, and fences. One of these incidents merited a write-up in an Ascoli city newspaper, referring to the misplaced fence around a house in the village as the "Berlin Wall." Villagers noted that urban conflicts can occasionally be just as trivial, but placing the squabbles of this village in this history-writ-large context became a point for city laughter. As I drove up to the village with an Italian Ascolana friend, she said, "Who shall we visit first—the Guelphs or the Ghibellines?" "They need each other," I replied. "That's how they know who they are."

That appears to be the purpose of conflict; it rarely erupts into violence, murder, or destruction of property. To contain and *maintain* the conflict, to contain one's anger, to use the tort in presenting the self in other contexts demonstrates that one is evolved, civilized, and unlike, for example, the southerners, who are considered emotionally incontinent about all things and in all events. It was actually a strategy at times to allow one's adversary to "win" (by not going to the wall, so to speak) and then to assume a moral stance of "bearing it" without violence or recrimination. Such attitudes toward conflict and conflict resolution allow these people to further contrast their behavior to groups in other regions of Italy and even in other parts of the world, all of them "lesser breeds" without a moral law or knowledge of smart gamesmanship. Other scholars have noted that one very important and neglected area in Italian studies is the working of the criminal courts and criminal law in Italy. I agree with Davis (1988, 87) in noting that *any* knowledge, though not yet systematized, of this area demonstrates how deeply many of the more fundamental institutions of the state were (and are) rooted in the everyday experience of Italian life (Pompeiano, Fazio, and Raffaele 1985).

The Aesthetics of Shaping Ethnic Identity

In the years of Emperor Augustus, the Piceno area was known as the *Provincia Flaminia*. Fruits, cereals, "cooked wines," and stuffed olives were supplied to Rome. Biscuits known in Rome as *panis Picentinum* were singled out by Pliny as notable fare. The ingestion of food, and the manner and timing of it, are linked to health and body image. "Well-upholstered" women and "padded" male bodies were considered healthy. These values were expressed in the context of possible disease states: "The fat ones only grow thin, the thin ones die." Foods are classified as heavy or light, with the designated need for balance. Where foods originate is very important; cultivation within the Piceno area is highly regarded, especially for certain crops such as olives and lentils. But even for other comestibles, there is the problem of how to know what the witches from other parts of Italy will do to their crops if they are thought to be for export.

In certain Italian contexts (illness or malaise), some foods are transformed into medicines. Decoctions or infusions of herbs grown locally are often sought by patients, even those from adjoining provinces who hope to find a cure they did not find at home. They come for this in conjunction with a search for intervention by special saints, both major and minor, who have shrines, monasteries, or churches named after them. There is another long history of events that keeps reinforcing the ethnic bonds in the Piceno in the form of many miraculous cures effected in the area over the centuries. The trajectory of a person's experiences is, always and everywhere, in large part a narrative of experiencing the world as the body allows, does not allow, or "interprets," providing metaphors and nourishing the imagination (Romanucci-Ross 1991, 136).

On beauty: the heavenly city was meant to be filled with beautiful people. Accordingly, the aesthetics of physical beauty include the ideal of Praxitelean symmetry for the body, the facial grace of the Madonnas of

Raphael or Sassoferrato for women, and Michelangelo's paintings and sculpture for men. Skin color should be very light, hair and eye color do not matter, shape of leg is very important, and body contours are crucial. Tall and curvilinear bodies are preferred; *fatt' a pennello* (fashioned by the artist's brush) is the supreme compliment for that. A surprising number of young people can be found who approach this, but the key word is "approach." No sooner is one pronounced *fatt' a pennello* than a moment of silence occurs, followed by rapid critiques. I think of it as the search-and-destroy method of finding minor blemishes and slight asymmetries. What will be recalled of a young person in discussions of beauty (which are quite frequently topics of conversation) is that fraction of that year in which perfection was reached, after which the "sagging" began here and there. The person became *sciupato* (spoiled), like any fruit that is a bit overripe (though a woman's face may reapproach beauty during pregnancy, although perhaps only the first one).

The almost unattainable ideals followed by appraisals and the grading system soon reduce everyone to the same aesthetic rubble, which has the strange effect of converting physical beauty to something of little or no importance. (This is not unlike the "overfixing" of the outcomes of *palio* races, which has the final effect of their not being fixed at all.) If people of other parts of the world find these exercises comic, they are not considered so in the Piceno. It is *important* to know what beauty is in an ideal sense and to strive for it in mating, if nothing else. It is important to think of all the possibilities in a game: both are survival techniques for one's progeny.

Ascolani distinguish themselves aesthetically from their neighbors, near and far. People from a northern province are said to have "crooked legs" (a spite song refers to them as such); a group to the south is said to be "too short" and "too robust," and many other points of differences are noted with other groups. The admonishment not to marry out of your city/countryside is meant also to prevent miscegenation with people from such groups. Yet, at the same time, one hears, "*Non è bello quel ch' e bello, è bello quel che piace*" (Beautiful is not beautiful unless it pleases one). Why? Because true beauty is in gracious behavior. The child is taught to cultivate a pleasant-sounding voice and not to be *sgarbato* (lacking in grace and elegance, politeness, and correctness).

From Childhood to Adulthood

Because it is not believed that one is in control of one's own destiny, it is important that as the child develops, he or she be taught moral strategies.

Ethics and aesthetics therefore appear to be one and the same when socializing and acculturating the child, and they are the source of the meaning
of virtue. The goal of the effort, for parents and child, is to be thought by
others to be a good person and not to "cut a bad figure" (*fare brutta figura*).
(You exist in the gaze of the others, as I indicated earlier.) One must not
lack in graciousness of manner or in dependability. People who don't behave ethically are *brutta gente* (ugly people). One can do much to control
the opinion that others will have of you. It is extremely important to negotiate every encounter, no matter how trivial, with that in mind: how do
you handle the unwelcome caller, reciprocate a gift, and handle a rebuff,
real or imagined? The child must learn to manage small encounters that require "exquisite calibration of boundaries of time, space and affect"
(Romanucci-Ross 1991, 177). Survival, the child is taught, will often be
found to be in correct self-perception and self-correction. This area of development of the ethnic personality is frequently commented upon and
contrasted to analogs in other parts of Italy. To the outsider, such preoccupation with this aspect of child rearing that follows one into adulthood
may appear to be an obsession.

Romantic love is a dangerous game to play, and you will be told that
"most people here" do not marry for "that kind of love." It was that kind
of love that led to the great passions that destroyed Romeo and Juliet, Tris-
tan and Isolde, Paolo and Francesca, and so on. A woman who loves her
husband in *that* way is not to be trusted to handle his affairs, his business,
his reputation. Her personal fantasies about him will render her irrational
and perhaps not even a good mother. Even extramarital affairs are never
discussed in terms of romantic love. This does not mean that romantic love
unions never occur; unquestionably, a number do. What is important,
however, in terms of child rearing and *expectations* is that romantic love is
considered best left to other, less prudent cultures; that is, it is exoticized.
There is constant instancing of bad outcomes that follow romantic love
unions. The pragmatic approach to marriage is counseled: *moglie e buoi dei
paesi tuoi* (wives and bulls should be from your region). There is a complex
volitional interplay among relatives and friends as a young man (or woman)
approaches the choosing of a spouse. Proper social contacts for appraisal are
at times arranged by local priests at church functions, but most often by female relatives of both families that might be affected by such a union.
Mothers of sons are always on the lookout for a suitable daughter-in-law
who will bear their grandchildren. A father is concerned about the type of
man to whom he will be bequeathing a daughter he loves and has reared.
Such practices are very similar to customs in ancient Rome (Treggiari

1991). Thus marriage rules, like food preferences, enjoy a robust cultural continuity in this area.

Ethnic Identity as Theater

Some aspects of ethnic identity exemplify the radiation effect of similar historical events over a wide geographic area. No part of Italy, for example, escaped the reckless but regular intervals of invasions by expansionist groups seeking to extend their boundaries. Some armies, such as the French to the northwest and the Spanish from the south, covered wide regions, at times overlapping in the Piceno area. Arabic invaders from the southeast would hit the coastal area but were concentrated more to the south. All of them left cultural artifacts—material, linguistic, and artistic (visual and musical)—in their wake as the waves of invasions retreated after periods of occupation. Some strategies for cultural survival, then, were pan-Italic and were shared over a large area—among these, how to wait and how to perdure. The manner in which many non-Italian historians write about such strategies, however, shows a lack of understanding. This is exemplified in the Elizabethan period in the perversion of Machiavelli's thought by English writers, turning this astute observer into a master of deceit. In fact, Machiavelli merely recorded his observations about what a wise prince *should* know (about human motivation and political strategies) if he wanted to maintain peace and retain power (Musa 1964); it was also about how to behave in the *polis*. This Elizabethan view of history was exacerbated in recent times by the Italian journalist Luigi Barzini (1965), who found it amusing and profitable to *select* facts to fit his baroque portrait of "the Italians."

Among Piceno pan-Italic characteristics is the acceptance of conflict (perhaps even the necessity of it), the absolute need to contain it, and the strategies with which to accomplish the containment. Theatricalized (perhaps much as the ancient Greek plays were a community catharsis) in a yearly competition, the *Quintana* (or *palio*) of Ascoli Piceno pits the various sections of the city against each other in a horse race. Each of the sections sponsors its own horse and jockey. The winner gets the *palio*, the prized cloth given to the winner and his section to keep for a year (Zeigler 1994). This ritual and ceremonial celebration dates back to the twelfth century. By the fifteenth century, its military aspect in Ascoli was replaced by symbolic combat in games that featured skill and grace within a framework of theatrical elegance. Several Italian cities featured such an event. The tradition in Ascoli is very old, analogous to those of Siena, Asti, and Fermo, the rival city of Ascoli. (Fermo and Ascoli Piceno, neighboring city-states, had sought each other out for occasional small "wars," as was the custom in Italy; Firenze and Pisa and Perugia and Assisi were other examples of "warring pairs" in proclamations of distinctiveness.)

Dundes and Falassi (1975) have described in some detail and with interesting interpretation the *palio* of Siena. In what I consider a particularly insightful description of the preparations, they note that races are said to be "fixed," and also "counterfixed," with innumerable deals and planning. But this, as they note, guarantees that it is so overfixed that it is not fixed at all. Although they drop the argument there, I should like to carry it a bit further, to consider how it would be done in the Piceno context. To the outsider, it may appear to be an exercise in futility, amusing or comic to the extreme, but to the Piceni (and perhaps the Sienese?), it is an important exercise, a honing of skills, a game in which you must try to assess every possible strategy of the other and to know which negotiations might fail, and in what manner. After all, in Ascoli during the horse race, as each jockey races around the track, he *also* "fights" a "Moor" with a lance once during each lap, needing to displace a wooden attachment to score a point. Skills against the Moor are sharpened in the practice of skills against each other.

The same "game theory" aspects can be seen in the strategies of the Italian soccer team. A sports writer for the 1994 International Soccer Competitions described Coach Arrigo Sacchi's changing styles as an affront to the usual way soccer is to be played. For example, he would switch his lineup to 4-4-2, after everyone thought it would be 4-3-3. "They play defensively, just trying not to lose, and then, no one was ever quite sure how, they scored in the winning goal, apparently improvising, making things happen as they went along" (Zeigler 1994). In making inquiries, the sports writer was told, "This is a country of organized chaos. The old way or Italian soccer, called *cantenaccio*, mirrored Italian life" (Zeigler 1994). Sacchi agreed and admitted that Italian culture is not suited to his kind of soccer— to run constantly and always be in control of the ball. But the soccer players do not heed their coach; they decide what to do as they play. Sacchi and the "demigod" forward Baggio argued publicly about how the game should be played before the semifinals. Should they pass more and run less or vice versa? The coach finally exclaimed in desperation, "They ought to run more and talk less" (Zeigler 1994).

In the past thirty-one games, the Azzurri had thirty-one different starting lineups. They won the semifinals and faced Brazil for the World Cup, losing by one point in the postgame penalty-kicking period. One can agree with some game theorists that the only certain way to win is to not know yourself what your next move will be, for then how can anyone strategize from those expectations? It may appear to the outsider as organized chaos, but it may have occurred to the observed that it is good for them that the observer should think that about such strategies.

To the Wall of Unintelligibility

The Piceno person is well adapted to his or her ethnic niche and has learned how to deflect intrusions into the many accommodations needed in daily living. When they go to other parts of Italy, they often encounter many difficulties, and, as Kertzer has noted, problems caused by the presence of a person from another region erase whatever bonds of solidarity may have accrued on the job or in a political party as far as relating to that person is concerned (1980, 169–75). Persons from the Piceno area who immigrated to the United States in the early decades of the twentieth century (during the great waves of European immigration) came to a country where there was one dominant cultural group. Like many other ethnic groups from European countries, they learned that the strategies that worked so well at home had to be redefined and reevaluated. The new standards were the values of the English-speaking dominant culture, whose bearers had found the previous waves of immigrants (German and Irish) not totally to their tastes but more like themselves than the newcomers (Romanucci-Ross 1987). The Piceni, like many groups from Italy, found themselves isolated and burlesqued; they were especially not accustomed to the latter, as they found themselves lumped with Neapolitans, Sicilians, and others. Many Piceni returned home. Those who stayed had to learn that the sorting devices of ethnicity in Italy had to be recalibrated in this new land, yet they did not feel comfortable with the southerners and felt closer to the Tuscans, even though these were thought to be too "cold and unfeeling," not religious enough, and irritating, as they constantly quoted lines from Dante, always noting that *their* dialect had become the tongue of Italy.

There were radically different outcomes in such accommodations, depending on the section of the United States in which the immigrants settled (Rolle 1968). Throughout, all Italians were studied (as though they were homogeneous) to test hypotheses about cultural maladjustment. Most studies stressed lack of mobility and indicated that Italians "huddled" in extended family groups and in certain city neighborhoods. (Contemporary studies show that Mexicans and other recent immigrants also huddle in the same way.) Indeed, as should surprise no one (not even social scientists), those from certain regions of Italy tended to live in proximity to each other in certain neighborhoods, or in certain parts of the United States (Nelli 1970). Still, they all distinguished themselves from the culture of the host country, as well as from the culture of ethnic groups from other regions of Italy. Each group still prefers its own cuisine, its own marriage customs, its own concepts of child rearing. However, culture has recursiveness as one of its major features; the children and grandchildren tend more and more to go to the country and region of their parents—to take vacations, to study, to write, to paint, to compose, and even in some instances to marry. And they often marvel that their parents had survived in America as immigrants without knowledge of language or custom.

But their antecedents did survive. They did so because they shared a view of life as expressed in a play by Pirandello, the Sicilian playwright: life is a series of layers of reality and fiction, and maneuvering in and out of these layers is the only way to get through it relatively intact. In their historic past, such metaknowledge had served them well in the millennia filled with new invaders who culturally had little in common with their invading predecessors. What good to them to spend your life accommodating to details of foreign cultural content? At the same time, if you are in a strange territory (such as the United States), you would be wise to understand that you are not unlike Pirandello's "Six Characters in Search of an Author" and fill in the script accordingly. People from different regions in Italy who came from different *ethnes* were not unaware of the irony of all being labeled "Italian" (or by more indelicate references to mean "Italian" in some instances). But they retained the lessons learned in childhood: see yourself reflected in the eyes of others, and do, or pretend to do, what is necessary for personal and cultural survival. Personal and cultural identity are one, for you cannot lose one without losing the other. Still, they did not hesitate to incorporate new strategies and retain former schemata with modifications in new accommodations. They were able to experience those things that may have required some flexibility but that did not touch the sense of authenticity. At home or school, Italians know that when a situation is different, *they* must be different, as has happened many times over the millennia of their recorded history.

It is still difficult to assess accurately what happened to various ethnic groups in America (those who were already here, those who came of their own will, or those who were brought here against their will) in the relatively brief history of the United States. But the immigrant experiences of the people of the Piceno, those who return or their progeny who return to the old country, have a certain impact on their region. It has been further intensified by the new re-ethnicization of the world, but it had begun years before. There are many attempts within the Piceno area to reaffirm and revitalize ethnic identity. This is done through "celebration" of dialect, historical commemorations, food festivals, promotion of herbal and other alternative folk-healing methods (even by pharmacists), folk music, architectural restorations, and refurbishing of historic buildings and houses.

The Will to Identity

All of the above activities are reminders to group members of how they contrast with other groups. The Piceni did not—and they are adamant about this in prose and print—have an ethnic identity thrust upon them. It is theirs, fashioned by historic events to be sure, but events in which they made choices, or, in other words, "chose to remain free"—free to be a papal state, or free to be a republic city-state (with the countryside villages always at their side), and free to celebrate the events that defined them. Importantly, they also felt free to reject the ideologies that did *not* define them, for instance, the ideals of the French Revolution such as "the tree of liberty" that French soldiers placed in their piazzas along with their ("foolish") ideas about liberty, fraternity, and equality. In the freedom to reject ideologies foreign to them or to accept those to which they feel a congeniality, the references are the matrices, one within the other, of a long and rich historical past and the treasured values within it, of families, worldly and spiritual concerns, and the ever-creating, ever-correcting self.

Epilogue

> *L'uddime chirialë è sembre quillë dë lu preddë. (The last Kyrie Eleison is always that of the priest.)*
>
> —A SAYING IN THE DIALECT

Writing an ethnography while viewing the material as an accepted "insider," but with the critical eye of the outsider, is not one study but many.[1] Such an enterprise might well be constructed employing the stylistics of Italo Calvino's novel *If on a Winter's Night a Traveler* (Calvino 1981), for it is just as amenable to "endless mutations." Like Calvino (p. 61), one could easily have followed "a network of lines that enlace . . . in a network of lines that intersect." However, as better befits the goals of ethnographic writing (regardless of the ethnographer's persuasions), I have confined myself to cross-referencing certain events that lie between the interstices of such enlacings and intersects. The purpose has been to indicate that an event always gathers meaning from its wider contexts and will be viewed in subsequent settings with a multiplicity of meanings. I was fortunate to have been exposed to quite a number of such "meaning sets" in the contexts of my family and friends before my arrival in the field.

To the field I also brought with me some pidginization of the formal (Italian) language—the flow of grammatical correctness being continuing pidginization in the field. This time it occurred with some English words slightly Italianized, a minor and infrequent occasion for laughter. This nicely balanced the amused smiles evoked by my admittedly infrequent expressions that were "certainly correct" but "quaint—sort of nineteenth-century literary ways of saying things." My version of the dialect was less pidginized than theirs, having been hermetically sealed from change in limited family contexts abroad. Deconstructing the "voice" of the engaged analyst (me) was somewhat like a shamanic dream-vision of "seeing" the severing and reassembling of one's body parts. This created a learning situation somewhat more painful than that in my field research in other parts of the world, but understanding came much more quickly as I became involved in festivals, markets, gossip, and conflicts and their resolutions. In searching archives and very old texts in Latin, medieval Italian, and French, I tried to corroborate *their* remembered past with other recorders of it.

There was exhilaration in a method that permitted me to follow events in a culture as an involved observer over a period of nineteen years. The years saw change in both the observer and the observed, but there were also continuities. For example, reaching far into the past was a consciousness of cultural belonging, for me and my parents and several generations before that. In this sense, I learned the intimacies of a culture as expressed in personalities and personal histories long before I visited the Piceno area. In addition, as a child in America, I was given by my parents and significant others minimappings of how to relate to the wider Italian cultural scene. Despite the homogeneous invented Italian character that my father envisioned as his goal of child rearing, I was nonetheless provided with positive and negative role models from selected regions of Italy.

I was told that it was good to emulate the Tuscans in the purity of their pronunciation of the language that Dante froze in print. They were hardworking and determined to succeed, though too materialistic and with more self-confidence than warranted. But the real negatives to be avoided included their acerbic tongues (too readily given to blaspheming) and their emotions, pathologically cold. Also, in the most horrid ways, they knew how to devastate others with cold contempt. For the best in "emotional tone," it was good to be like the southern Italians, but not for their "irrational," excessive, superstitious "perversion" of the Roman Catholic faith. Nor was it admirable to copy their blind loyalty to friends and family as the ultimate morality. Don't follow Southerners in being too "colorful" in every conceivable way.

Such attitudes, unchanged, still provide sorting devices for dealing with group and personal identity, and they withstand all the current media morality programming designed to overcome them (not so much to Italianize a nation as to sell products uniformly throughout it). In the Piceno area, perhaps to a greater degree than in most other places, most of the self is "outside" of one; that is, people are defined to themselves by their reflections in the eyes of others. Such self-conscious self-percepts are produced through successes and failures of strategies for survival over long periods of personal and group historical time. In this study, I have tried to describe in detail such strategies in various facets of cultural expectations and personal responses. In this sense, the "hundred towers" of defense have become bastions of strategies, the goals of which are not to conquer or "to win," but simply to perdure. The goal is to win, but very slowly, an old adage reminds us. Winning slowly still translates (to me) as "not losing." For example, animal models are used as mirrors for unaesthetic behavior or for lack of moral rectitude. A person with a "mean" facial expression is a "camel"; a grasping, greedy person is a "griffin"; a lazy woman is a "cow"; a quiet, scheming woman is a "cat"; and a meddlesome, trivial person is a "monkey." Such labels, once acquired, are difficult to lose and have a long-term effect on how others behave toward an individual. To survive fully, one must have no nicknames—a small but crucial "win."

How the self processes informational inputs shapes identity, and at the same time the processing mechanism itself can be consciously influenced, as indicated in my discussion of approaches to the field. In recent times, national and international forces have encouraged entering the world marketplace and pulling away from the Piceno identity. The moderate success of these forces had engendered a countermovement toward the traditional identity.

I referred to the *Quintana* and described it as a yearly revival of a glorious medieval past. In some neighboring small towns, the idea of recycling and marketing local identification with a culturally rich historical period seems to have caught on. Castel Trosino, just across a gorge on its own small hilltop, now has its yearly identity festival. In late summer, the tourist can purchase tickets to enter the city walls and be greeted by costumed characters of the fifteenth century. Authentic foods of the region as they were prepared during that period are savored. Musicians, entertainers, and the architecture of the town complete the fantasy. Like the *Quintana*, it is a tourist attraction, but one cannot fail to recognize that that is not all it is. The individual adds to himself or herself in such role-playing; also enriched is the communication between and among those in the entire area who resist becoming colorless, one-dimensional persons. Many agree with an ancient lady in Ascoli who regularly proclaims, to all who will hear, "In things that are really important, this so-called 'progress' is actually a regression." (She was especially quoted when the winds blowing from the area of the Chernobyl nuclear accident caused an announcement that all "radioactive" foods must not be consumed for a month, and that children should not go outdoors.)

For the investigator, this particular field encounter was rich in contextual and personal pathways of meaning that gave an almost lyrical quality to the learning experience. Perhaps there was a poetic aspect, too, in the untangling of the n-dimensioned manifolds of group identity in a place where remembered history spans millennia and the geographic area is small. This contrasts dramatically with the four- or five-generation span of remembered history for simple societies, or with the American experience of barely a four-century history. It is my hope that this study can contribute an anthropological understanding of a complex culture in a small area with a long and well-remembered past. The world has much to learn from all types of cultural experiences in the search for a model for conflict resolution on every level.

In the introduction, I stated that studies on the cultures of the world illuminate the many ways of being human. But not every way of being human is maximally effective for survival in situations of radical and rapid culture change. What has been observed about imposed or even voluntary culture change is that it is accomplished neither easily nor quickly. The difficulty lies in learning how to learn an unfamiliar way of doing things. Old solutions may or may not apply to new problems, but without an awareness of "set learning" (learning *how* to learn), it is most often the old, "tried" solutions that are retrieved in confronting new crises. The Piceno people rejected the moral imperative of "liberty, equality, and fraternity" despite all the attempts of the French occupiers. Nor did the Americans, after World War II, succeed in imparting to them and their countrymen what we mean by "the democratic process." It can also be said that the American postscientific culture may not learn soon enough to respect our dependence on our irreplaceable, fragile ecosystem.

Learning how to learn, for all of us, means that we have to know how to analyze and incorporate all we can learn from the many formulaics for achieving desired goals in all the cultures of the world. This is not impossible, for information theory is general and extends to many phenomena. The universe of information includes the cultural as well as the natural world. To understand the implications of this is to be able to achieve a level of discourse in which we find sophistication in peasant or in primitive thought, as well as in our own proliferations of categories. In the Piceno area, the Chernobyl aftermath, in its very personal and frightening effect on daily activities and subsistence, brought home directly (to many if not to all) that survival for all of us is no longer physically or metaphorically "in the towers."

Note
1. Epilogue originally published in Lola Romanucci-Ross, *One Hundred Towers: An Italian Odyssey of Cultural Survival* (Newport, CT: Greenwood Publishing), 181–84, © 1991. Reprinted by permission of the publisher.

References
Aries, Philippe. 1960. *L'enfant et la vie sociale sous L'Ancien Regime*. Paris: Plon.
Balena, Secondo. 1970. *Ascoli nel Piceno*. Ascoli Piceno: G. Cesari.
Barzini, Luigi. 1965. *The Italians: A full length portrait featuring their manners and morals*. New York: Atheneum.
Bateson, Gregory, and Margaret Mead. 1942. *Balinese character: A photographic analysis*. Special publications, vol. 2. New York: New York Academy of Sciences.
Calvino, Italo. 1981. *If on a winter's night a traveler*. Trans. from the Italian by William Weaver. New York: Harcourt Brace Jovanovich.
Cantarella, Eva. 1991. Homicides of honor: The development of Italian adultery law over two millennia. In *The family in Italy from antiquity to the present*, ed. David I. Kertzer and Richard P. Saller, 229–46. New Haven, CT: Yale University Press.
Crespi, A. 1927. *L'Acerba*. Turin: no publisher indicated.
Davis, John A. 1988. *Conflict and control: Law and order in nineteenth century Italy*. New York: McMillan Education.
De Marchi. 1969. *Santa Rita de Cascia*. Bari: Edizioni Paolini.
Derrida, Jacques. 1967. *La voix et le phenomène*. Paris: Plon.
Devereux, George. 1982. Ethnic identity: Its logical foundations and its dysfunctions. In *Ethnic identity: Cultural continuities and change*, ed. George A. De Vos and Lola Romanucci-Ross, 2nd ed., 42–70. Chicago: University of Chicago Press.
De Vos, George A., and Lola Romanucci-Ross, eds. 1982. *Ethnic identity in cultural continuity and change*. 2nd ed. Chicago: University of Chicago Press.
Dundes, Alan, and Alessandro Falassi. 1975. *La Terra in Piazza: An interpretation of the Palio of Siena*. Berkeley: University of California Press.
Fabiani, G. 1957–1959. *Archivio Storico del Comune di Ascoli*. Ascoli Piceno: Società Tipolitografica, 1:9–32.

————. 1967. *Ascoli nel Ottocento*. Ascoli Piceno: Societa Tipolitografica.

Gambino, Richard. 1974. *Blood of my blood: The dilemma of Italian-Americans*. New York: Doubleday.

Giorgi, Raniero. 1968. *Les Clarisse in Ascoli*. Ascoli Piceno: Tipografia Fermo.

Hobsbawm, E. J. 1959. *Primitive rebels: Studies in archaic forms of social movement in the 19th and 20th centuries*. Manchester: Manchester University Press.

Hodges, H. A. 1952. *The philosophy of Wilhelm Dilthey*. London: Routledge and Paul.

Kertzer, David I. 1980. *Comrades and Christians: Religion and political struggle in Communist Italy*. Cambridge: Cambridge University Press.

Lehman, Winfried P. 1993. *Theoretical bases of Indo-European linguistics*. London: Routledge.

Mead, George Herbert. 1934. *Mind, self and society*. Ed. Charles Morris. Chicago: University of Chicago Press.

Mead, Margaret. 1930. *Growing up in New Guinea*. New York: Morrow.

————. 1975. *New lives for old: Cultural transformation-Manus*. New York: Morrow. (Orig. pub. 1956.)

Musa, Mark. 1964. *Machiavelli's "The Prince."* New York: St. Martin's Press.

Nelli, H. S. 1970. *The Italians in Chicago 1880–1930: A study in ethnic mobility*. New York: Oxford University Press.

Petrusewicz, M. 1978. Signori e Briganti: Repressione del Brigantaggio nel Periodo Francese in Calabria Caso Barracco. In *Storia e Cultura del Mezzogiorno: Studi in Memoria di U. Caldora Cosenza*, 333–46. Press unnamed.

Pompeiano, D., I. Fazio, and G. Raffaele. 1985. *Controlto Sociale e Criminalita*. Milan: Mondadori.

Pulgram, Ernest. 1958. *The tongues of Italy: Prehistory and history*. Cambridge, MA: Harvard University Press.

Rolle, Andrew F. 1968. *The immigrant upraised; Italian adventurers and colonists in an expanding America*. Berkeley: University of California Press.

Romanucci-Ross, Lola. 1985. *Mead's other Manus: Phenomenology of the encounter*. South Hadley, MA: Bergin & Garvey.

————. 1986. *Conflict, violence and morality in a Mexican village*. Chicago: University of Chicago Press.

————. 1987. Von ethnologoi: Die Erfahrungen das Einwanderers. In *Die wilde Seele: Zur Ethnopsychoanlyze von Georges Devereux*, ed. Hans Peter Duerr, 383–97. Frankfurt: Suhrkampf Verlarung.

————. 1991. *One hundred towers: An Italian odyssey of cultural survival*. Newport, CT: Greenwood Publishing.

Treggiari, Susan. 1991. *Roman marriage: Iusti Congiuges from the time of Cicero to the time of Ulpian*. Oxford: Clarendon.

Zeigler, Mark. 1994. Baggio scores twice as Italy stops Bulgaria. *San Diego Union*, July 20, D8.

Vilnius, Lithuania: An Ethnic Agglomerate

2

CZESLAW MILOSZ

THIS CHAPTER REPRESENTS THE EXPERIENCE of a man who comes from a very unusual spot in Europe: the city in Lithuania known as Wilno, or Vilnius, which in its mixture of languages, religions, and traditions is rivaled only, and not quite successfully, by Transylvania, Bukovina, or Trieste. My observations were made before World War II, but, as will be seen, the present appears again and again.

Today, if I call this city which is the capital of the Lithuanian Soviet Republic "Vilnius," I give a hint as to my Lithuanian identity. If I call it "Wilno," I present myself to the Lithuanians as probably a Pole or a Russian. Behind the double names lie the complex historical events of several centuries.

Before 1939, this city belonged to Poland, and the languages spoken by its inhabitants were, first, Polish and, second, Yiddish. In the schools, instruction was in Polish, Yiddish, Hebrew, Lithuanian, Byelorussian, and Russian. The question of who was sent to each of these schools has much to do with the problem of ethnic divisions, yet to assume that every ethnic group favored schools in which instruction was given in its own language would be far from the truth. Religious divisions cut across language divisions. Roman Catholicism, Judaism, Greek Catholicism, Orthodoxy, and Islam coexisted, and to these should be added the ethnoreligious group of Karaites, a Judaic sect.

Lithuanians and Poles

The meaning of the statement "I am a Lithuanian" was undergoing a change at the end of the nineteenth and the beginning of the twentieth centuries. Previously it was used by the members of the upper class, the nobility or the petty gentry, whose ancestors had spoken Lithuanian or old Byelorussian, but who no longer used those languages at home. The "Polonization" of the upper classes, a result of the personal union between the Kingdom of Poland and the Grand Duchy of Lithuania in 1385 and of their gradual fusion, was nearly complete by the seventeenth century. Thus, "I am a Lithuanian" was not opposed to "I am a Pole," but meant "I am from here" as opposed to "he is from there," namely, the Kingdom of Poland. The equivalent of such a feeling could perhaps be found in the British Commonwealth where there was opposition of Scottish and Irish to English, but not to British.

In Lathi, which was in that area the language of liturgy; of many legal documents; and, to a large extent, of literature, a "Lithuanian" was defined as a man who was *gente Liihuanus natione Polonus*, while the name of the state, embracing the kingdom and the duchy, was neither Poland nor Lithuania, but Respublica. As to the Lithuanian language, its fate was similar to that of Gaelic. A non-Slavic language, and therefore already handicapped at the moment when, during the Middle Ages, the Grand Duchy of Lithuania absorbed large areas inhabited by Eastern Slavs, it was not used in writing.

Paradoxically, before its union with Poland, the grand duchy adopted an Eastern Slavic dialect (which was to become Byelorussian in the north and Ukrainian in the south) for administrative purposes. Lithuanian, increasingly the language of the peasantry only, remained a low-status idiom. By the sixteenth century, it was used in writing only by those who wanted to descend to the people, in order to convert them to their religious domination. To that end, Protestants and Roman Catholics produced prayer books and catechisms. A Polish-Latin-Lithuanian dictionary, published in 1629, was proof of a Jesuit's zeal. Literature in Lithuanian appeared late and was connected with a revival of national feeling, which challenged the "Lithuanianishness" of the upper classes and made the language spoken at home a distinctive mark.

The Lithuanian national movement, created by the new intelligentsia of peasant origin in the second half of the nineteenth century, regarded the formula *gente Lithuanup natione Polonus* as an unbearable reminder of defeat; the historical Lithuania had lost its upper classes through Polonization. The necessity of choosing between being a Lithuanian and being a Pole seems to be a result of the idea that nationality is defined by language. And, indeed, in the twentieth century, many families had to decide upon their nationality, with the not unusual consequence that one brother called himself Lithuanian, another a Pole, and the third Byelorussian. One has to go back in time in order to explain the strange myth about Lithuania that persists today in Polish cultural patterns.

Lithuania, the last country in Europe to become Christian, was converted in 1386. As a land of primeval forests, abundant wildlife, and pagan deities, it fascinated Polish writers as early as the sixteenth century. This literature contributed to certain stereotypes. The Jesuit Academy of Wilno, founded in 1578, two centuries later became the best Polish university and a hotbed of romanticism. One of its pupils, Adam Mickiewicz (1798–1855) became the most important Polish poet of all time. The most cherished of Mickiewicz's work, a long tale in verse, *Pan Tadeusz*, opens with an invocation not to the muse but to Lithuania: "Lithuania, my native land." Throughout all Mickiewicz's works, nature is Lithuanian. As a sort of emotional puzzle, consider the peasant child in Poland today who has to cope with a poet who called himself Lithuanian. Let us also add that the first history of Lithuania was written and published (nine volumes, 1835–1841) in Polish by another disciple of the University of Wilno, Teodor Narbutt.

A curious game of superiority-inferiority has been played by natives of Lithuania, speaking Polish with their half-compatriots from Poland. "Lithuanians" looked upon themselves as serious, obstinate, persistent, and deep, conceding magnanimously some truth to their being in the eyes of the Poles bearish, uncouth, and miserly. It was assumed that great men of Polish letters could only come from Lithuania, and Mickiewicz's myth was a basic asset in such a contention. But there seems to have been something to the myth, since many eminent personalities come from ethnically Lithuanian families, as did, for instance, a precursor of modern Polish poetry, Cyprian Norwid (1821–1883), whose name in the Lithuanian form was once Narvidas. The question arises as to why a feeling of a separate identity did not express itself in Lithuania as it did in Ireland, where William Butler Yeats and others did not have to use Gaelic in order to be considered Irish patriots. One could go also to Finland, where the intelligentsia had once adopted Swedish, but where the use of Swedish did not exclude one from belonging to the Finnish nation.

That things evolved differently in Lithuania can be ascribed to many causes, but in all probability there is one primary cause underlying all the others. The Polish language was connected with a cultural pattern completely different from the pattern of the Lithuanian peasantry. It would be incorrect to maintain that only the nobility spoke Polish in Lithuania. It was also spoken by the petty gentry who tilled the land themselves and lived practically like peasants. The merchants and tradesmen, if they weren't Jewish, also used Polish at home, as did the non-Jewish artisans and workers in Wilno and in small towns, either because they were descended from the petty gentry or because they were former servants in the manors. All of those people were permeated, however, by the "culture of nobility" and considered their use of Polish a mark of the status that distinguished them from the Lithuanian-speaking boors.

Thus, we observe a class hostility combined with a linguistic conflict. But to make the matter more difficult for investigators, the have-nots could be found on both sides, for rich Lithuanian peasants were often better off than the artisans or the laborers of a neighboring small town. Yet the very idea of an independent Lithuania was greeted by Polonized segments of its population with scorn and hostility. How could the boors pretend to become a nation and impose upon the rest of the people their boorish language? The new Lithuanian intelligentsia that appeared in the second half of the nineteenth century was, with very few exceptions, of purely peasant origin, and since for a peasant family the only possible social advancement was to make one of their sons a Roman Catholic priest, clergymen were largely responsible for the emergence of the national movement.

In the twentieth century, educated members of the higher classes, who for a long time had proclaimed their loyalty to Lithuania for sentimental reasons, realized that they had to choose between Polish and Lithuanian loyalties, that one could no longer be at the same time a Lithuanian and a Pole. In 1918, when an independent Lithuania was being created, some of them opted for the country of their ancestors and started to learn the difficult, non-Slavic language. A very few looked for an intermediate solution, an equivalent of the relationship between English and Gaelic in Ireland. The majority, however, even if they became citizens of the new state, looked upon themselves as Poles. After World War I, the region around Wilno leaned toward independent Poland, and for a short time it was a separate political entity loosely bound to Poland, leaving in history a not very important but an interesting trace in the form of postage stamps, a rarity today. That entity, Middle Lithuania, was absorbed by Poland in 1922 and remained within the Polish borders until 1939.

Relations between Polish-speaking Lithuanians and Poles displayed infinite ambiguities. On the one hand, "Lithuanians" indulged in a certain self-idealization, and on the other, owing to a myth transferred through literature, they were idealized by those outside the country. Self-irony became an increasingly prominent ingredient of that peculiar "Lithuanian" ethnic identity. The difference was disguised as innocent snobbery. Yet it cannot be said that "Lithuanian" ethnic identity belongs completely to the past. "Lithuanians," whether they lived in the region of Wilno or emigrated to ethnic Poland (which occurred en masse after World War II), have been bringing to Polish arts and letters a particular perspective. One may guess that a man who grows up surrounded by people who speak various languages and who belong to various cultures acquires a different personality than does a man brought up in a homogeneous ethnic milieu. Let us add also that "Lithuanians" were much more open to Russian thought and Russian literature than were Poles, This did not make them partisans of Russia, yet it did endow them with some kind of openness to the seriousness of the "Russian phenomenon."

It would be interesting to examine modifications of the "Lithuanian" myth in Polish literature of the last few decades, including the avant-garde literature of the grotesque, the macabre, and the theater of the absurd. In literature in which the aristocratic origin of a character is equated with degeneration and idiocy, a certain mocking respect is shown toward characters from Lithuania. After World War II, Poland became a melting pot of people with different languages and regional backgrounds as a consequence of the shift of its borders from the east to the west. In this new melting pot, "Lithuanians" and Poles have been mixing. Even today, however, among some groups it is considered more dignified to marry within one's own group of immigrants from the East. A relatively small number of the "Lithuanians" who spoke Polish remained in Lithuania. Centered for the most part around Wilno, they represented the artisans and workers who had been inhabitants of that city for many generations.

Lithuanians

Among the peoples of Baltic stock, only the Lithuanians succeeded in creating a state that, in the thirteenth and fourteenth centuries, expanded south and east, mostly thanks to the weakening of the eastern Slavic principalities in the wake of Tartar invasions. The Lithuanian dukes had a strong army, since ethnic Lithuania seemed to be more densely populated than the regions of neighboring Slavs. Moreover, the Baltic Lithuanian ethnic area reached farther east and south than it does today. As a result of the conquest, the Grand Duchy of Lithuania, extending at one point as far south as the Black Sea, counted among its subjects people speaking an eastern Slavic idiom (Ruthenian) and confessing the Orthodox faith, while the ruling Lithuanian ethnic group remained pagan. Penetration of the duke's court by Eastern Orthodoxy, owing to marriages with Christian princesses and the victory of the eastern Slavic vernacular as the administrative language throughout the state, prefigured, so to speak, what happened after the union with Poland in 1386.

At that point, ethnic Lithuania began to convert to Roman Catholicism, the Polish language slowly (though not before the sixteenth century) supplanted the eastern Slavic idiom, and the Latin alphabet replaced the Cyrillic. Lithuanian survived as the language of folk songs of great beauty and antiquity. In some of these songs, called *dainos*, heroes are pagan planetary deities. Protestant and Catholic catechisms and hymns were the only documents of written Lithuanian until the second half of the eighteenth century, when an ethnically Lithuanian Protestant minister in a corner of East Prussia, Kristijonas Donelajtis (1714–1764), wrote his long poem "Four Seasons," depicting the miseries and joys of peasant life. The national revival in the nineteenth century was indebted to partisans of Lithuania who wrote scholarly books in Polish, and to German collectors of Lithuanian folk songs, who were entranced to find in Europe a language still closely related to Sanskrit. But let us imagine the situation of a Lithuanian intellectual (usually a clergyman) in search of his ethnic identity: the glory of the country belonged to the past, for not only was his country a part of the Russian czarist empire, but Lithuania bore a strong Polish imprint; moreover, to be a Lithuanian carried the stigma of a boorish status.

It would not be an exaggeration to say that for such a man the language itself was both his fatherland and his passport. A desperate search went on for the names of illustrious men, which in their Polish spelling preserved Lithuanian vocables. There was also jealous competition with the Poles for the claim to some eminent writers. Thus, since Adam Mickiewicz invoked Lithuania as his muse, he was added to the Lithuanian pantheon. Typical of the Lithuanian language are family name endings in *as* or *ius*. Thus Mickiewicz had to become Mickevicius. An eminent French poet, O. V. de L. Milosz, a relative of the author of this chapter and a Lithuanian by option—in contrast to the other "Lithuanian" members of his family—had his tomb in Fontainebleau engraved with "Milasius." The extremely ambiguous state of ethnic identity among the Polish-Lithuanians often became hostility when confronted with the nationalism of the "boors." This is more understandable if we keep in mind that the word "Lithuania" designated both the grand duchy as a whole and the ethnic area alone.

Many Polonized families, natives of the grand duchy, had nothing to do with the Lithuanian stock, since their ancestors were eastern Slavs who spoke old Byelorussian. Animosity was also exacerbated, especially during

World War I and immediately after, by the Wilno question. Once the capital of Lithuania, Wilno contained by the twentieth century only a small group of people who spoke Lithuanian, a fact that seemed to validate Poland's claim to it. The religious factor introduced an additional complication. Both those who spoke Lithuanian at home and those who spoke Polish were Roman Catholics, and the traditional attachment to the idea of the commonwealth (*Respublica*) was strengthened in the minds of the Polonized by their sensitivity to the danger that menaced their religious faith first from Russian Orthodoxy and then from Communism. The tiny Baltic states created in 1918 were too weak to provide protection. The question of Wilno, which was appropriated by Poland (with the support of its inhabitants), exacerbated the feud between the two groups in the period between the two world wars.

The experience of Poles and Lithuanians as American immigrants forms a marked contrast to their life in Europe. In Lithuania, everything Polish enjoyed prestige, but in America, Poles enjoyed little social status, ranking well below such groups as the Scandinavians or even the Irish. As a consequence of the predominantly upper-class culture in the Polish-Lithuanian *Respublica*, illiterate Poles immigrating to America were particularly helpless in that industrialized nation, since they could rely neither on the status of the "Polish culture" nor on the relatively weak tradition of their own village. In all probability, the Lithuanian ethnic group in America fared a little better. One may guess that the "boor," a Lithuanian peasant, left to himself and rooted in his folkloric tradition, proved to be less vulnerable and somehow in a position closer to that of a Scandinavian, a German, or an Irish plebeian. Moreover, independent Lithuania between 1918 and 1939 produced a whole new educated class, an intelligentsia with peasant backgrounds. Thus every peasant family there wanted to give their children a high school and university education. This ambition affected the Lithuanian immigrants after 1945. Examples abound of rare tenacity and self-sacrifice on the part of Lithuanian parents when they found themselves in America. A typical example is the case of some friends of mine, both with university degrees, who became manual laborers in order to provide higher education for their children.

A kind of cold war between Lithuania, which claimed Wilno as its capital, and Poland, which held it, did not make life easy for the small Lithuanian ethnic group in the years between the two wars. One high school conducted in Lithuanian, some newspapers, and a fraternity of Lithuanian students at the university who steered clear of their Polish-speaking colleagues serve to illustrate the situation of a city where Roman Catholic churches had no Lithuanian sermons and songs—except one, St. Nicholas, where the majority of the faithful was composed of servant women transplanted from their native villages.

Jews

The great number of Jews in the Grand Duchy of Lithuania were for centuries completely separated from the rest of the population by their religion, language (Yiddish), profession (nonagricultural), and even dress. The frozen division between Jews and Christians was a phenomenon typical of several areas and therefore need not be discussed here. What should be mentioned, however, is the place of a nonrural group in a purely rural civilization. They monopolized many branches of handicraft and trade, acting as suppliers of goods to the manor and village, as innkeepers, and as buyers of agricultural products. Their religious communities were closely supervised by their elders so that the contamination of Jews by the Christian milieu and vice versa was minimal. The one exception came toward the end of the sixteenth century, when a radical Protestant movement with an antitrinitarian orientation (Arianism, Polish Brethren, the Minor Church) invoked the authority of the Old Testament against that of the New Testament. This led to friendly theological disputes between the sectarians and Jewish rabbis. In the eighteenth century, a messianic sect founded by Jacob Frank found many followers among the Jews of the grand duchy. Frank, a Jew whose teachings bore a strong Manichean imprint, embraced Catholicism after he had been anathematized by the synagogue, an act that he conceived as a necessary preparation for the advent of a new world. This movement left some marks, since many upper-class families in Lithuania trace their ancestry to Frankists, the Jewish followers of Frank, who had been baptized. In a way, Frank was a precursor of the Jewish rush beyond the confines of the ghetto.

The Enlightenment touched the ghetto at the very end of the eighteenth century and the beginning of the nineteenth century, but here the political predicament of the area made the whole problem of Jewish assimilation a complex one. The entire area, as a consequence of the partitions of the *Respublica*, came under the domination of Russia. Of course, the choice of a language that would supplant Yiddish imposed itself upon the Jews. Polish had preserved throughout some three decades of the nineteenth century with a half-official standing, and the *Haskalah* (Enlightenment) movement among the Wilno Jews turned at first to Polish as the instrument of written expression. The career of an interesting writer, Julian Klaczko

(1825–1906) illustrates this. A native of Wilno, he started to write in He-brew, and he then switched to Polish, only to change his language once again when he immigrated to Paris, where he remained a Polish patriot, though renowned as a contributor in French, to the best Parisian reviews. Not many such instances, however, could be quoted in Lithuania.

After the end of a liberal policy in St. Petersburg, and when the offi-cial language was increasingly imposed upon reluctant subjects of the newly acquired territories, those Jews who were emancipating themselves from the traditional ghetto felt the attraction of a huge area with its uni-fied culture. Things went a different way in other parts of the Polish-Lithuanian *Respublica* after its partition by foreign powers. In central Poland, a considerable number of Jews entered the ranks of the intelli-gentsia, thus becoming Poles of Jewish origin. In the Hapsburg Empire, German and Polish competed for the allegiance of the Jews. The seductive power of Vienna was strong, and the story of Sigmund Freud's family is rather typical. Yet many Polish scholars and writers in Galicia had a Jewish background, especially at the time when the Polish intelligentsia was changing its character and absorbing groups that until that point had been barred from access to higher education (peasants, Jews, and women); that process gathered momentum at the very end of the nineteenth century. The Russian orientation of the Lithuanian Jews produced a large group of the so-called Litvaks, namely those Jews who, instead of Yiddish or Polish, spoke Russian at home.

Antagonism existed between Litvaks and the Jews from central Poland, not to mention the Jews from Galicia, for whom Russian was a completely alien tongue. Since the policy of St. Petersburg in Lithuania consisted of a forceful Russification, especially after the uprising of 1863, the non-Jews regarded Jews as allies of the czarist government by the very fact of their switching to the Russian language and spreading the gospel of great Rus-sian literature. A continuation of this state of affairs was also noticeable in the revolutionary movement, beginning with the 1890s. The movement split into two socialist parties, the Polish Socialist Party and the Social-Democratic Party of the Kingdom of Poland and of Lithuania, with the two parties unequally dividing sympathies of emancipated Jews. Most fa-vored the second party, since it rejected the national aspirations of ethnic groups that had been absorbed by the Russian Empire and it relied upon the All-Russian Revolution which would solve all the problems automat-ically. The socialist Jewish organization *Bund* represented a specific program close to that of the Polish Socialist Party, yet its members were not Litvaks, but Jews clinging to Yiddish.

In the period between the two wars, when Wilno belonged to Poland, the Jewish community was internally divided in a fantastic way. Russian schools in Wilno could count on Jewish pupils only because the number of Russian Christians was exceedingly small. However, Wilno was a strong center of studies in Yiddish and Hebrew. The Jewish Institute of Wilno was to be transferred during World War II to New York. Books and newspapers in Yiddish testified to the vigor of the language, but many young people were also trained in Hebrew and were subsequently instrumental in making Hebrew the official language of Israel. Polish schools did not attract many Jewish pupils, and in this respect the situation was different from that in Central Poland, where Poles whose fathers or grandfathers had used Yiddish were numerous. As to the Lithuanian and the Byelorussian languages, they attracted almost no Jews in the region of Wilno.

Politically, varieties of Zionism competed with socialism and Communism; the latter was rather popular, since in this area it was a direct descendant of the Social Democratic Party of the Kingdom of Poland and Lithuania. The result was anti-Semitic slogans, since the Poles and the Lithuanians only rarely were sympathizers of Russia, in its czarist or its Communist incarnation.

In the region of Wilno, anti-Semitism was not as strong as in central Poland, where there existed a class of non-Jewish small shopkeepers. The right-wing anti-Semitic Polish National Democratic Party (*Narodowa Demokracja*) scored successes primarily at the university, where Jews and non-Jews had separate student unions. The composition of the student body did not, however, correspond to the ethnic composition of the city, since it admitted students from all over Poland, thus representing rather a cross-section of the whole country.

What was characteristic of Wilno was the prevalence of the type of Jew who was quite sure of his ethnic identity, whether he was Litvak or a speaker of Yiddish. If there were some Poles of Jewish extraction, they were mostly imports from Poland proper. In general, survivals of the traditional setup were so strong until 1939, and the economic backwardness of the area was so marked, that it is difficult to guess what the probable course of Jewish assimilation would have been had not the crime of genocide committed by the Nazis put an abrupt end to the centuries-old life of Jewish Wilno.

Byelorussians

To my knowledge, there is practically no literature on this subject free from Polish or Lithuanian bias. It is also doubtful whether those few Byelorussians who wrote about their compatriots in the region of Wilno are any more reliable. The Byelorussian nationality was probably the last to appear in Europe.

As to the identity of those who once used old Byelorussian in writing, the idea of calling themselves Byelorussians would not have occurred to them. If they belonged to the privileged class, they considered themselves for centuries nobles of Lithuania. Like their brethren of ethnic Lithuanian stock, they abandoned their tongue for Polish. For peasants, the concept of nationality was alien up until the 1930s. Upon being asked during a census about nationality, they answered either Catholic or Orthodox, or simply, "I am from here."

That does not mean that the notion of an ethnic identity (of being "from here") was absent. Religious denomination served here as the dividing line. The Orthodox religion distinguished one village from a neighboring village inhabited by Roman Catholics. It also distinguished between the inhabitants of the village and those people in the neighborhood who represented a higher social status—that is, those who spoke Polish—whether they belonged to the petty gentry, owned a manor, were foresters, or were craftsmen. Those people also confessed to Roman Catholicism. It should be mentioned here that peasants of Eastern Orthodox faith were former Greco-Catholics; the Greco-Catholic, or Uniate, Church, created as a consequence of the Union of Brest (1596), which had been engineered by the Polish Jesuits, was administratively destroyed by the czarist government in 1838; in other words, these peasants again became members of the Eastern Orthodox Church.

The Byelorussian peasant remained throughout all the turbulent history of the area the passive object of powers incomprehensible to him. He was gaining silent victories wherever his village neighbored on a Lithuanian village. For complex and little-elucidated reasons, the non-Slavic Baltic element had a tendency to recede territorially. Through intermarriage and gradual adaptation to Byelorussian, a Lithuanian village would melt into a Slavic and Orthodox mass. In such a fashion, the area south and east of Wilno, once Lithuanian, became Byelorussian. Byelorussian villages, however, in the close neighborhood of Wilno, no longer spoke Byelorussian in the twentieth century, but rather a peculiar slang of "people from here," namely, Polish strongly influenced by Byelorussian and to some extent by Lithuanian. This idiom was somehow reminiscent of sixteenth-century documents, many of which preserved a curious mixture of Polish and old Byelorussian, as well as a mixture of two alphabets, Latin and Cyrillic. The ethnic identity on the level of high school or university education was, during the period between the two wars, more or less closely related to Communism.

A young Byelorussian who harbored strong class resentment looked with hostility at the manor and at the Polish administration and looked for his sense of history to the capital of the Soviet Byelorussian Republic, Minsk, with its Byelorussian University, and its press and books published in his native tongue. Stories of purges and persecutions as related by escapees from the Soviet Republic contributed to the effort to create some sort of independent national movement. But the intolerance of the Polish authorities, for whom the Byelorussian nationality was a bizarre invention, strengthened the appeal of Communism.

For other groups, it was very difficult to understand what Byelorussianism was about. Traditionally, the language was considered a folk dialect closer to Polish than, let us say, Provençal is to French. To boost the national morale, the young Byelorussian intelligentsia invoked the official language of the Grand Duchy of Lithuania, claiming it to be their own, although it differed considerably. These young enthusiasts also laid claim to such literary monuments as the first printed translation of the Bible into the vernacular in the Polish-Lithuanian *Respublica*, since that vernacular was not Polish but old Byelorussian (Franciszek Skoryna's Bible, printed 1517–1525). Also, the speeches of lords from Lithuania in the Polish Diet were frequently given in old Byelorussian.

The past, however, was irretrievable, since the dialect had earlier been used by the nobility and by some burghers in the cities, and these classes later switched to Polish. Thus, Byelorussian remained a language suddenly halted in its literary development, revived by nationalists only at the beginning of the twentieth century. Its rich folklore and particularly beautiful folk music have not been matched by literary works of genuine value except by a small number of poems. Perhaps this judgment is unfair, since we should take into account the unenviable conditions of national life that still persist.

Yet this perspective reflects the attitude toward the Byelorussians of all the other groups in the region of Wilno, and it explains why young Byelorussians identified education with training in nationalist-leftist militancy. As I said before, there were instances where in the same family one man heeded "the call of blood" to become a Byelorussian, his brother the same call to become a Lithuanian, and the third to become a Pole. Yet even though we may debate the rank in the social hierarchy of any particular group, it was generally recognized that the lowest place on the scale was for the Byelorussians. This was certainly nothing new—Byelorussian folk songs are heartrending in their melancholy tone and their images of centuries of oppression.

Tartars

Since no native inhabitants of Lithuania would have embraced the Muslim religion, the mosques in Wilno and in some neighboring villages testify to the presence of immigrants who arrived many years ago, mostly in the fourteenth and fifteenth centuries. Lithuanian dukes had gladly used them as soldiers and recompensed them for their services with land. Because of their religion, the Tartar villages preserved their separation from the surroundings. Their status was superior to that of peasant villages because, being settlers from outside, the Tartars were never just serfs of landlords. As to their native tongue, they abandoned it during the seventeenth century, preserving for quite a long time, however, the Arabic alphabet. Some extant religious books are written in a mixture of Polish and old Byelorussian, but in Arabic letters. Being quite energetic, many Tartars acquired estates and titles of nobility. In such a way, the upper class in Lithuania numbered not only people of Lithuanian, eastern Slavic, immigrant-Polish, and immigrant German stock, but also Frankists and Tartars. The social peers of the Frankists and Tartars accepted them, but on different bases. The acceptance of the first was due to their being Christians, while for some strange reasons a noble of Tartar origin was accepted even if he remained a Muslim. Tartar villages, on the other hand, could be cited as a case of religious barriers that led to economic barriers. If certain professions were a distinctive mark for the Jews, something similar applies to the Tartar villages, which in certain districts monopolized the production of leather goods, such as sheepskin coats and gloves.

The ethnic identity of Muslims was well preserved, taking the form of pride in their warrior ancestry. In the 1930s, two periodicals (the *Tartar Yearbook* and *Tartar Life*) appeared in Wilno, both published in Polish. They are interesting by virtue of their catering to the ideal of the "Lithuanian Tartar" (of Polish language) well rooted in his adopted country. Those publications usually traced the history of the deeds of valor performed by the Tartars in the service of the Polish-Lithuanian commonwealth. The upper-class orientation on the part of the Muslims explains their being little attracted by the Lithuanian element or the Byelorussian element, though some Tartar villages spoke Byelorussian rather than Polish. In general, however, Muslims had a tendency to melt into the Polish-speaking intelligentsia of gentry origin.

Karaites (Karaim)

A tiny ethnic and religious group, which in this century numbers barely a few thousand all over the world, the local Karaites were, like the Muslims, a relic of the grand duchy's expansion far to the south, to the shores of the Black Sea. At one time, the Kievan Rus' dealt with the Khazars, an industrious tribe that had converted to Judaism. Karaites, a Judaic sect not recognizing the Talmud and the tradition, was a part of the Khazar scene. The history of the sect in the subsequent centuries is obscure, but no less obscure than the circumstances in which some Karaites settled in Wilno and the surrounding neighborhood during the reign of the Grand Duke Vytautas at the end of the fourteenth century. Karaites created an exotic island, being neither Christians nor Jews. They were distinguished by their physical type and their language, which was incomprehensible to others. They were by tradition cucumber growers. They are mentioned here because their influence in Wilno was quite out of proportion to their small number. The most closed religious-ethnic group, they possessed a temple (*Kenessa*), the head of their religious hierarchy was their spokesman, and they published one periodical in Polish (*Karaite Thought*) and one in the Karaite language.

Conclusion

Wilno, as a city marked by the social transformations of the twentieth century, reflected to a large extent the ethnic differentiation in the countryside. A rural district might feature the following: manors where Polish was spoken; a few gentry villages inhabited by Polish-speaking farmers with titles of nobility though they labored in their fields like ordinary peasants; little towns, Yiddish in their commercial center, Polish in their workers' and craftsmen's outskirts; and villages, either Lithuanian or Byelorussian. Since Wilno lacked villagers, Polish and Yiddish prevailed. The intelligentsia, white-collar workers, and merchants were either of noble origin or of Jewish origin. The local burgher class, although its traditions went back a couple of centuries, had become extremely weak. The core of the Wilno population lived either in the narrow, picturesque streets of the ghetto or were artisans and workers who lived in the village-like outskirts of the city. For the majority of the population in that area, the modern idea of national identity that followed the lines of language and ethnic stock came as a surprise. Yet choices had to be made, and for the most part they were made, thus creating a web of mutual resentments and mutual hostilities.

If one takes a detached view, the tragic fate of that corner of Europe acquires comic and macabre dimensions. Poland and Lithuania could not resolve peacefully the question of Wilno, which remained a bone of contention throughout the two decades between the two wars. The Soviet

Union, in fulfilling the Molotov-Ribbentropp agreement, occupied Wilno in September 1939, only magnanimously to offer it two weeks later to Lithuania. However, already at that time, the fate of all three Baltic states was sealed. They were incorporated into the Soviet Union in 1940. The Nazi offensive in the summer of 1941 reached Lithuania in a couple of days and opened three long years of terror and genocide. The whole Jewish population of Wilno was first closed within the walls of the ghetto and then massacred. After the terror and mass deportations applied by the Soviet Union between 1939 and 1941, Lithuanians and Byelorussians, much like the Ukrainians in the south, for a while attached some hope to the arrival of the Germans. They were soon disillusioned, and the Nazi policy in that part of Europe was exemplary in its folly, though consistent in one respect—scorn for the subhumans, that is, any ethnic group other than German. It is difficult to know if the Germans were responsible for the hostilities that emerged between the ethnic groups, particularly between the Poles (or rather, "Lithuanians") and the Lithuanians, before the Red Army entered Wilno again in 1944. Perhaps the massacres of Polish and Lithuanian guerrilla units by each other in the name of patriotism were the result of old hatreds. The Poles maintained that Wilno should belong to Poland, the Lithuanians that Vilnius had always been and would always be a part of Lithuania. Perhaps those sardines fighting each other in the mouth of a whale are not untypical of the relations between humans when they search for self-assertion through ethnic values magnified into absolutes.

Postscript

In 1992, I returned to Wilno after fifty-two years. It is now officially Vilnius, the capital of independent Lithuania. The three tiny Baltic states—Lithuania, Latvia, and Estonia—succeeded in separating themselves from the Soviet Union, into which they had been incorporated by force in 1940. Yet they bear the scars of a long totalitarian rule.

People who have not had the opportunity of comparing a given place in two different phases of its history may be surprised by a term I use to describe the situation in Vilnius: degradation of reality, or decay of reality. Many buildings bear the scars of the war, and the Jewish quarter, with its medieval narrow streets, was practically razed. Yet it is the progressive decay of houses in the beautiful old town, not renovated for decades, that is responsible for the grayness so typical of the Communist system, and the smell of poverty to which Orwell was so sensitive in his *1984*. Yet the Baltic counties fared much better under that system than did Russia, and for the Russians they were the epitome of the West. Vilnius has grown, and the Lithuanian architects have succeeded in limiting the impact of the barrack-style Soviet prescriptions when designing new buildings.

Perhaps the tensions between national groups, the subject of my chapter, fill the air with an undefinable malaise, or perhaps there are just too many taboos against talking about the past to move in that city with ease. There are no Jews, and the shadows of the assassinated have not been exorcised by bringing to light the role of Lithuanian death squads. The goal of Lithuanian nationalism, recovering the city as a historical capital of Lithuania, has been achieved, but as a result of the pact between Hitler and Stalin that partitioned prewar Poland and deprived Lithuania of its independence for fifty years.

The Polish-speaking population of the city, threatened by mass deportations to Siberia, left in a mass exodus for Poland in 1945. Vilnius, however, is far from being homogeneously Lithuanian. The Polish-speaking inhabitants of the republic, around 8 percent, are concentrated in Vilnius, as are the groups of new arrivals, Russians and Byelorussians. Around 40 percent of the people in Vilnius speak minority languages, which creates a problem somewhat similar to that in Latvia and Estonia, countries with a large Russian minority. Poland makes no claim to the city, and in its conciliatory attitude goes so far that local Poles accuse it of forgetting to defend their interests. Some rightist elements in Poland are inclined to raise the issue of the Polish minority in Lithuania, but they have only a small following. There is no doubt, though, that Vilnius is a part of Polish cultural history, and as such, it attracts many tourists from Poland who visit it as a land of shrine.

Vilnius, in my opinion, has a tremendous potential as a tourist city. Its location, on the banks of two rivers, between pine forests on the hills, enhances the charm of its baroque architecture. It is adorned by some forty churches, mostly from the seventeenth and eighteenth centuries. They have been preserved, as has the university campus, a vestige of the Jesuit Academy founded in 1578. One of the most beautiful cities of northern Europe, Vilnius, at the time of this writing, is struggling with the erratic course of a post-Communist economy.

Ethnic Nationality in the Former Yugoslavia: Ethnogenesis, Ethnic Cleansing, and Present-Day Identities among Croats, Serbs, and Bosniacs

3

MARY KAY GILLILAND

T HE NAMES BOSNIA, SERBIA, CROATIA—once republics of the former Yugoslavia, and now mostly independent nations—are nearly synonymous with terms such as "ethnic cleansing" and "ethnic war." From 1991 to 1995, most of these southern Slav regions were embroiled in brutal wars that were portrayed by outsiders as revivals of deep-seated, historically constructed enmities. Though ethnic-national conflict is certainly a part of the history of the region, the popular characterization of the Balkans in general, and these people in particular, as fractious, divisive, closed groups who have not and will not get along is also extreme. The region provides an important case for examination of ethnicity and nationalism—particularly the notion of "ethnogenesis," or a re-creation of the primacy of ethnic identities, boundaries, and borders.

Background: Ethnic Nationality and "the Balkans"

Ethnic, nationalist, and religious conflict were seen to characterize the region and the personalities and cultures of its peoples; these provided simple (and overly simplistic) explanations of the recent wars and linked them historically with several other periods of intense conflict also generally blamed on nationalism or ethnic hatred. The Serbs and Croats always hated each other and always would, nonspecialists were likely to say. Only heavy-handed oppression kept the peace under Yugoslavia's charismatic socialist leader, Josip Broz, better known as Tito. After Tito's death, these peoples, who could never really get along, were once again in conflict and eventually war. The demise of socialism meant the breakdown of a rigid political system that had kept nationalistic fervor under check for nearly half a century.

In an equally simplistic explanation, the world at large was reminded that these were the Balkans, and Balkan peoples are primitive, wild, and unable to get along. There were reminders of the Balkan wars at the end of the nineteenth century. World War I is said to have begun with the assassination of Archduke Francis Ferdinand, the Hapsburg heir, in Sarajevo, by Bosnian Serbs. It was easy for other Europeans, and the Western World in general, to distance themselves from the conflict; it was inevitable, many said, only a matter of time. This was a "Balkan" problem. It had little to do with larger issues shared beyond the boundaries of the former Yugoslavia.[1]

These simplistic characterizations ignored the long histories of peace throughout the region. They also failed to address the complexity of ethnic-nationality questions within the former Yugoslavia. While outsiders had heard of Croats and Serbs, for example, the situation of Bosnian Muslims, or Bosniacs as they came to be called, wasn't entirely clear. How could a religious community be an ethnicity or a nationality? This problem led some in the West to characterize the war as "religious" rather than "ethnic" or "nationalistic," another wrongheaded and simplistic view.

Even within the former Yugoslavia, however, members of different groups came to create stereotypes of ethnic-national "others." This was not necessarily the case prior to war, but increasingly so as more people experienced the hardship and losses associated with war. For some Serbs (though certainly not all), Croats became *Ustashe* (singular—*Ustasha*, from a verb meaning "uprising"), the fascist Croats of World War II, members of the movement that allied itself with the Nazis. It is worth noting that during World War II this represented a minority of Croats, but they did, for a short time, have some control, and along with the Nazis they slaughtered Serbs, Jews, Roma (Gypsies), and others. Jambresic-Kirin, a Croat ethnologist and war ethnographer, writes that the resurrection of stories of *Ustashe* came to the forefront in Serb political rhetoric, and in Serb *national consciousness* after the election of Milošević and other nationalist leaders in the late 1980s. The stories of civilian and partisan suffering during World War II, sufferings shared by all south Slav peoples, were recast as the national sufferings and victimization of Serbs and "contributed to the process of shaping a *new* collective identity (among the Serbs in all republics of former Yugoslavia.)" (Jambresic-Kirin 1996, 72). To Croats and Bosniacs, Serbs became *Cetnici* (singular—*Cetnik*), who during World War II sought to reestablish Greater Serbia, which would have included parts of Croatia and much of Bosnia. Even the violence of Muslim Turks against Serbs in the fourteenth century, or the belief of some Serbs and Croats that Bosni-acs, or Bosnian Muslims, were really Serbs or Croats who "sold out" under the Ottoman Turks (unlike Serbs in particular who held fast to their iden-tities and Orthodox faith and eventually succeeded in driving the Ot-tomans out of Serbian lands) was brought up in local media and public discourse. A noted Croat ethnologist, Professor Dunja Rhitman-Augustin, objected to the title of a special publication of an American journal, *War among the Yugoslavs*. According to Rhitman-Augustin, there were no Yu-goslavs, only Croats, Serbs, and so forth. Furthermore, this was not a civil war, as the title implies, but a war of aggression of Serbs against Croats (there is no mention in her work of the conflict in Bosnia that involved Croat aggression against Bosniacs).

The former Yugoslavia included six republics. From north to south, these are Slovenia, Croatia, Bosnia-Herzegovina, Serbia, Montenegro, and Macedonia. Within Serbia, there were two politically autonomous regions: the Voyvodine in the north, sharing a border with Hungary, had a large Hungarian ethnic population; Kosovo, to the south, had a large Albanian ethnic population. The other major ethnic or nationality groups through-out the region were Slovenes, Croats, Serbs, and Muslims, or Bosniacs. This essay doesn't concern Slovenes; Slovenia was a relatively homoge-neous and small population. War, which broke out first there, lasted only nine days. People seem to have forgotten that Slovenia had also been a member state of the former Yugoslavia. Of all the former south Slav states, Slovenia is doing quite well economically and will be the first of them ad-mitted to the European Union. People from Montenegro and Macedonia are primarily Serbs, or in Macedonia, Albanian Muslims, though ethnic Serbs from these regions also maintain a sort of separate, regional identity. Indeed, Serbia and Montenegro are now the remaining states included in the Federal Republic of Yugoslavia, but are now only loosely tied, as a kind of confederation, and in 2005 they voted to separate into two distinct countries. Today, though the wars are over, tensions remain in the region. Bosnia is still essentially divided into a Serb half and a Bosniac-Croat half. Kosovo, technically part of what remains of Yugoslavia (Serbia and Mon-tenegro), is under United Nations control. Macedonia still doesn't have a name (other than "Former Yugoslav Republic of Macedonia," which was originally regarded as a temporary name until issues over ownership of the name "Macedonia" could be sorted out with Greece). Croatia struggles economically, though less so than the combined regions of Bosnia and Ser-bia, the latter now much worse off than before the war began. As the war crimes trial of former Serbian president Slobodan Milošević continues in

The Hague, some of his political allies are back in power in Serbian towns and are said to be consolidating key military positions. The wars are finished, but as always, damage, national and personal, physical and otherwise, takes longer to repair.

In this chapter, I take another point of view. I have argued before, and maintain, that the recent Serb-Croat-Bosniac wars (and the slightly later war in Kosovo) and remaining tensions are primarily economic and political, manufactured by old socialists who, in the 1980s, resurrected nationalist ideologies that, until then, lay under the surface of social and political life. This is a more encompassing explanation than those that give primacy to notions of repressed ethno-nationalism or religious conflict resurfacing after Tito's death (see Gilliland 1995; Olsen 1993). Still, reducing ethno-nationalism and war to either materialist *or* ideological explanations over-simplifies complex social, cultural, and psychological phenomena. This chapter addresses the historical; political-economic; and, as much as possible, individual psychological connections between ethnic nationalism and the recent Balkan wars. It approaches ethnicity or nationality as identities that are always subject to change, that are never written in stone, and that are rarely causal in themselves (Fox 1990, 65).[2]

I will examine, primarily, the discourse about nationalism and ethnicity, public and private, among residents of a midsize town, Slavonski Brod, which lies in the Slavonian region of eastern Croatia on the border with Bosnia, about halfway between the Croatian and Serbian capitals of Zagreb and Belgrade. This town is within the old Croatian Military Frontier, lands held by the Austro-Hungarians and abutting those held by Ottoman Turks. The region came to be known in the most recent wars as a part of the *Krajina*, literally "Region," from the old Serbo-Croat *Vojna Krajina*, literally "Military Region." It has been, for the past several hundred years, fairly ethnically mixed. I spent twelve months of ethnographic field research there in 1982 and 1983, when Croatia was still one of the constituent republics of Yugoslavia. Additional research was carried out for six months in 1991, in the summers of 1993 and 1995, and again for six months in 1996 and 1997. During those later periods of research, I also spent considerable time in the Croatian capital of Zagreb and on one of the islands of the Eastern Adriatic, Hvar, and I worked not only with local populations but with displaced Croats and Bosnian refugees during all periods after 1991. Most recently, I have worked with refugees from Bosnia in Tucson, Arizona (mostly Bosniacs, but also some Croats and Serbs). Thus the data include a long-term relationship with residents of Eastern Croatia and broader, comparative material from elsewhere in Croatia and Bosnia.

Slavonski Brod:
Changing Identities from 1981 to 1991

People in the former Yugoslavia perceived themselves to be both different and alike—sharing much in the way of language, culture, and history, and yet different in customs, dialects, religious beliefs, manner, dress, and local histories (Bringa 1993). My own experiences in Slavonski Brod in the 1980s suggest that identities were not always primarily associated with ethnicity or nationality.

The Sava River separates Slavonski Brod from Bosanski Brod in Bosnia. The two towns are old ferry crossings. (*Brod* means "ship," and according to folk etymology, the names of the towns mean Slavonian or Bosnian Ship or Ferry; the names may also be derived from the verb *broditi*, meaning to cross a river—Petrovic and Belic 1970, 15). A bridge made it possible to cross from Croatia to Bosnia in minutes, by car, bicycle, or foot. Many people did so every day, working in one town and republic and living in another. People crossed in both directions for social and other reasons, to go to markets, to the mosque in Bosanski Brod, to films or coffee bars, or to visit relatives or friends.

At the time I lived there, I was aware that it was a border region. I was also aware of the ethnic or nationality mixture. The population of Brod and of Slavonia is dominated by Croats, but there has been, particularly since the Second World War, much ethnic mixing. In 1981, of roughly 170,000 residents in Slavonia, 125,000 were Croats, another 25,000 were Serbs, and a remaining 20,000 were other nationalities, including Hungarians; Czechs; Slovenes; Muslims (including those from Bosnia, who were primarily Slavic, and those from Kosovo, who were Albanian Muslims); and Roma (Gypsies) (*Popis stanovnistva* 1981).

In 1982 and 1983, I did not fully realize that this particular region was much more heterogeneous than other regions in Croatia and Yugoslavia and that it was therefore, like Sarajevo, a special case. The family with which I lived in Brod and the people whose lives I came to share in those years represented a striking ethnic mix. The majority were Croat, but there was a large Serb population (mostly Bosnian Serbs) as well as many people who came from mixed families. The most common mixed marriages were between Croats and Serbs, but I knew of several cases in which either a Croat or a Serb had married a Muslim. Other families included a parent who was Slovene or non-Yugoslav (Hungarian, Czech, German, or Italian).

In the early 1980s, contrary to my own expectations, people rarely spoke of ethnic nationality. That is not necessarily an indication that it was unimportant. In fact, it seems that among some (those who remained concerned with ethnic nationality, perhaps) there was a kind of taboo. I felt, and was sometimes told when I raised it myself, that the topic was inappropriate. I heard similar conversations between others I knew, who stopped each other from discussing ethnic-national differences. Many people, however, seemed to have redefined themselves not as Croats, Serbs, and so on, but as Yugoslavs. In Brod, they seemed attached to the town and the region as much as to ethnic nationality. Croats and Serbs alike expressed this attachment in the sentimental way they talked about the region, and in self-identification as "Slavonians" or "people from Slavonia." They participated in events and activities linked to local culture and history, such as state-sponsored folklore groups. Mixed marriages were not uncommon, though maybe not as common as it seemed to me at the time (Botev and Wagner 1993). I attended five weddings in 1983, and two of these were between a Croat and a Serb. In one case, the bride was Serb and the groom Croat. In a second case, the situation was reversed. People at that time were separated as much by socioeconomic class as by ethnicity (though this was not true for all ethnic groups; I will come to that later).

On my first visit to Brod, at the invitation of a Yugoslav friend, Braco, (whose father was a Serb, originally from Lika, and whose mother was half-Croat and half-Serb, originally from Bosnia), I spent a lazy afternoon eating fried fish with my friend's mother and her sister and later drinking Turkish coffee in a neighbor's garden, perched on a wooden stool under the shade of young willows. I accompanied Braco and members of his established group of friends (*drustvo*) to town in the evening. We walked, making circle after circle, in the town square, the *korzo*, filled in the evenings with young people out for a good time. Friends greeted each other; made comments about clothing, companions, or soccer; gossiped about other people; and talked about plans to go somewhere to listen to music, watch a film, or continue the conversation over a coffee or beer. I learned in the next few days that the groups of relatives, neighbors, and friends whose social gatherings I had shared were not all Croat; some were Serbs, and others identified themselves as Bosnians (they would now also describe themselves as Serbs). Still others, though only a few, were Slovenian or Hungarian. People seemed interested in ethnicity as a part of their total identity, but not centrally so. The topic was first raised tangentially in conversation by my host's neighbor, because her name was "Slovenka," and she in fact came from Slovenia, to the north. I asked about the identities of others present. Everyone there readily discussed their backgrounds and those of other family members not present (husbands or wives), but no one behaved as if this were particularly important.

In the early 1980s, even after Tito's death, there was in Slavonski Brod a lingering cult of Tito. His photograph hung in every place of business and in many homes. His birthday celebration, also known as National Youth Day, was one of the big events of the year. Partisan war films were a regular feature of a state-run television network. These films often reduced my landlady to tears. She was not alone; other middle-aged women in my neighborhood would often cry when they saw photos of Tito. The heroism of the partisans in the Second World War was sometimes mentioned while discussing a television film or a local cultural event connected with socialist history; on these occasions, too, someone would often shed a few tears. A young mother of twenty-five years held her two-year-old daughter up to see a picture of Tito on a neighbor's wall (there was not one at her own house). "That's Tito," she told her daughter, in a very positive and gentle voice. Each night, the television broadcast in Eastern Croatia ended with the chorus of a song: "Comrade Tito, we follow in your ways." This same song and others like it were often sung by groups of young men and women in the coffee bars where they congregated after work.

For some people, the interest in Tito may have been only on the surface. The photos were particularly common in the houses of Communists. In this region, at that particular time, however, it seemed there were more people with Communist sentiments than otherwise. I recall a village family who lived near Brod. On their kitchen wall, a portrait of Tito hung next to a religious calendar. This was one of the few families in which some members professed to be both Communist and Catholic. One of my neighbors held similar views. She did not understand why one could not be both. "If Jesus were alive today," she said, "he would be a Communist." "Sure," replied the grandmother in my household, "but he wouldn't much approve of the church." Those who seemed truly to support Communism and the state believed that their lives were better than those of their parents and grandparents. Many of them also believed that things would continue to improve. Their optimism was centered on the economy, despite growing evidence that all was not well. I will come to that topic shortly.

Anthropologists who have worked in more homogeneous regions of the former Yugoslavia claim that all efforts to foster a Yugoslav national identity were doomed to failure from the start, except among those who were products of mixed marriages (see, especially, Simic 1991). The educational system promoted a Yugoslav and socialist worldview, but in homogeneous regions (for example, on the island of Hvar in the Eastern Adriatic region of Croatia, where I worked in 1991 and later), family, church, and community influences tended to ensure that many regarded themselves as Croats first and Yugoslavs second, if at all.[3] This was undoubtedly true in small towns and homogeneous regions throughout the south Slav region. I remember feeling surprise at anti-Serbian sentiments expressed by two old women in a village on the northern Croatian coast. At the time, I had lived in Brod for nearly eight months and had come to accept the idea that ethnic nationality was relatively unimportant. In a town like Brod, however, there were many who were products of mixed marriages or whose families had migrated from elsewhere. There had been some state-sponsored resettlement of both Serbs and Dalmatians after the Second World War and further migration as a result of army service, marriage, and the search for jobs. Also, there was no obvious advantage to being Croat or Serb. In such situations, ethnicity as a dimension of personal or group identity tends to diminish. (Muslims represented only a very small minority in Brod and were regarded differently by both Croats and Serbs. I address this difference later.) Nina, who lived with her parents and was my neighbor in 1982, reminded me in a recent letter that from her perspective things had been different in the past. "We were Yugoslavs," she wrote. "My generation grew up believing that."

In short, most of the people I knew in the early 1980s were relatively unconcerned about ethnic-national identity and remained so in the late 1980s. The concerns people expressed most often then were economic ones. Shortages, inflation, and lack of jobs or housing were often what people talked about when I lived there, and later what they wrote about in their letters (along with news of people married, babies born, and those who died, and of vacations and other items of interest in their personal lives).

In 1991, when I returned to Croatia, things were different. Throughout Yugoslavia (which until June 25, 1991, remained a single nation), fear, anger, and blame featured in many conversations. Individual Serbs began to be afraid. The grandmother in the household in which I had lived in 1982, herself a Bosnian Catholic, had married a Bosnian Serb in the period between the two world wars. Her children and grandchildren also married across ethnic lines. As a result, some but not all were Serbs. Grandma Ana's husband had been killed at the outbreak of the Second World War by Croatian *Ustashe*. Ana was then twenty-seven years old, had eight children to support, and had a first grade education. When I knew the family in the 1980s, they spoke of Yugoslavs as a united people. Ana's daughter, in whose house I lived, was a member of the Communist Party. Their history was the history of socialist Yugoslavia. But the family also maintained another history: the story of Ana's husband's death at the hands of (or so they believed) *Ustase* (or "*Ustashe*," as the word has been anglicized) persisted as a family legend. This was in spite of the fact that Ana herself was Croat and lived then in Croatia. Killings such as this were part of the history of nearly every family. Who got the blame varied.

Eastern Croatia became a focal region for ethnic-nationalist unrest, along with other places where Serbian enclaves existed within majority Croat surroundings (a similar scenario existed in the region of Kosovo in Serbia, where the majority population is Albanian—see Reineck 1993). Milošević, president of the Serbian Republic and of what remains of Yugoslavia, and Tudjman, then president of the Croatian Republic and now of the new Croatian State, had both come to power. Both were elected on nationalist platforms. In Croatia, new symbols of Croatian nationality were evident in a new flag,[4] in place names,[5] and in the identification of the language as Croatian instead of Serbo-Croatian or Croato-Serbian. There was talk, then, that Croatia might secede from the Socialist Federal Republic (SFR) of Yugoslavia. Tensions were brewing elsewhere at the same time, particularly in Bosnia-Herzegovina, a territory shared by Bosniacs (then still called Muslims), Croats, and Serbs. Slovenes, to the north of Croatia, also spoke of secession from the federal government.

In 1991, I saw old friends presenting themselves differently than they had in the past. Communists had become democrats and Catholics; people once unconcerned about ethnicity or nationality now spoke about it freely, and those who were ethnically mixed or married across ethnic-national and religious lines were confused and apprehensive. Families who had vested interests in socialism were fearful, and those who had secretly longed for change became hopeful. People devoured news and opinions in newspapers and magazines and followed television newscasts more closely than before. Personal, family, and ethnic histories were rewritten; loyalties shifted; and past experiences were reevaluated. Both Croats and Serbs claimed to have been the leading group among the partisans. Tito's life was reexamined, and there was speculation and argument about what he really was. Some Croats said that in the end Serbs controlled him, and that although he was worthy of admiration, he had not, for many years prior to his death in 1980, been able to speak his mind. (Tito was half Croat and half Slovene.) Others (including Croats and others living in Croatia) thought less kindly of Tito and traced the current problems not only to corrupt politicians in recent years but to Tito himself or to his followers. Serbs thought that Tito had pandered to the Croats; Croats saw him as having "sold out" to Serbs. There was talk of atrocities committed by partisan bands, mass graves were uncovered in Croatia, and various scandals were connected to Tito's name (see, for contrast, Denich 1994).

Croats and other ethnic nationalities in Croatia spoke of Serbian un-fairness and exploitation (this within the context of the former Yugoslav nation). According to Croats, there was a disproportionate number of Serbs in high-ranking government and military positions. The federal gov-ernment was physically located in Beograd, which they believed gave Serbs advantages when it came to government hiring and favors (due primarily to the importance of personal connections in obtaining jobs and other benefits). This imbalance, according to Croats, had existed for many years but had, by 1991, become intolerable.

Croatian Serbs voiced different concerns. They feared what might hap-pen to them, their families, their jobs, their homes, and their very lives should Croatia become an independent nation. These fears were aggra-vated by memories of *Ustasha* violence against Serbs during World War II (Croats would quickly point out that most Croats were not members of the *Ustasha* party) and by the resurrection of symbols, such as the checkered flag, associated with that time.

The content of Serb conversations and accusations was similar but re-versed. I was in contact with no one who was Serb and lived within a Ser-bian enclave in Croatia, and my contacts in the Serbian Republic are few (see, for contrast, Milicevic 2003). I did have occasion to travel to Beograd and also to a village in Serbia where the grandmother in my former house-hold had relocated (she lived there with a daughter and the daughter's fam-ily). I also knew a number of Serbs who had lived all their lives in or near Slavonski Brod. Some of these (though mostly not those who lived in Croatia) began to talk about the Croatian fascists, who sent Serbs, along with Jews, Roma (Gypsies), and others to concentration and death camps. According to a variety of sources (print and other media), Serbs in Serbia and elsewhere outside Croatia blamed Croats and Slovenes, but particularly the former, for their own lack of economic development; the Western portion of the former Yugoslavia, they said, had gained at Serbian expense. Croats and Slovenes turned the argument around; they had been support-ing, with the products of their own hard work, the less-developed regions, but worse, they had also been paying for a growing military and a corrupt government bureaucracy heavily dominated by Serbs.

The dominant impression left on me from that time (1991) was a lack of clarity. Everyone seemed confused, and afraid. Almost no one was ready to believe that war would come, yet people *behaved* as if they expected violence to break out around them at any time. The voices in each group (Serb, Croat, or Bosniac) were by no means uniform. Among each of these groups could be found pacifists, others who did not think the secession of any republics a good idea, and some who thought, sadly, that dismemberment was the only feasible solution to the tensions that had grown among the various groups through the past decades. Some continued to assert that ethnic nationality was of no importance, while in other, subtle ways showing renewed interest in nationality issues and religion.

Serb-Croat violence began in February of 1991, not far from Slavonski Brod, in the town of Pakrac, also in Slavonia. I was sitting at my former neighbor Nina's kitchen table, eating a meal with her family, which comprised a Bosnian Serb woman; her husband, a Croat; their son; and the Bosnian woman's daughter (Nina) from a previous marriage to a Bosniac. They all expressed fear that nothing good could come of the current political situation, or of secession, or of war. "If war does come to Croatia," Nina said, "it will be absolutely the worst in Slavonia, because here we are all mixed." Her mother said, "It will be even worse in Bosnia! Who would have thought we would even be talking about this?"

At first, each act of violence was regarded as an isolated incident. People expressed shock and dismay. They denied that this could really be happening; there must be some way to solve political problems peacefully. They suspected that what was shown in the news was not all it seemed to be (or worse, that behind it was some larger conspiracy orchestrated by one or another elite organization). The brutalities, however, were widely publicized and contributed to a growing sense of ethnic nationalism and unrest. The media coverage was, of course, selective. Serb atrocities against Croats were broadcast on Croatian news stations in detail, complete with footage of massacred bodies. Coverage of events in the Serbian Republic was reportedly the other way around.

When I returned to Slavonski Brod at the end of war in 1996, I found it a much sadder place. Houses had been shelled with artillery and rocket grenades. Hundreds had fled the region, leaving behind most of their belongings. Their houses were then sometimes occupied by displaced persons or refugees from towns such as Vukovar, where most buildings had been entirely destroyed. Even the gravestones of Serbs had been toppled (including that of my former landlady, Branka, and her husband Dusko). The bridge between Slavonski Brod and Bosanski Brod had been partly destroyed and was then rebuilt and occupied by UN forces. Ordinary people could no longer cross. People with relatives on the other side had to travel to Hungary, then to Serbia, and then into Bosnia. What had been a several-minute commute turned into a several-day journey. Needless to say, most didn't make it. Even telephone service was unavailable between the regions at the time. Not a small number of people who had once called themselves Yugoslavs felt compelled to redefine themselves along ethnic-nationality lines. These were a minority, overall, but a significant minority in regions such as Eastern Croatia. Even in places such as Zagreb, ethnic-nationality divisions were issues for some, but among better-educated urbanites, the issues often remained more private. Nina told me when I saw her in 1993 that my friendship was more precious than before, because for me, an American, she was not Nina the Croat or Nina the Serb, but simply Nina, my friend. Even now, when I do not answer her letters promptly, she worries that I have turned against her because of her nationality, although she knows this is not a realistic fear.

Nina eventually came to terms with a new sense of who she is. We never talked much about ethnicity before, though she was proud of her "Bosnian" maternal grandmother (*Bosanka*), who turns out to be have been a Serb, not a Bosniac. Nina herself claims that she never thought much about whether her friends were Croat or Serb or Muslim or Catholic; in those days, few people in Brod town were religious, and none of that really "mattered." She recalled a wedding we both attended in 1983. I had been one of the few guests who knew what to do at a Catholic Mass. Nina and her friends had to follow my lead. They were all greatly amused, since it was usually I who did not know what to do in social situations. Now, of course, religion does matter, since to be a Croat is also to be Roman Catholic. Likewise, *Srpstvo*, or "Serbianness," is defined by membership in the Serbian Orthodox Church. Bosniacs are also, to some extent, defined by religious affiliation, in spite of the fact that they are no longer called "Muslim."[6]

Nina's biological father was a Bosniac. That he was from Bosnia, I knew; that he was Muslim (though nonpracticing, like many urban Bosnian Muslims), Nina did not mention until 1993, ten years after I first met her. He abandoned Nina and her mother when Nina was an infant. She had not seen him for fourteen years when I met her in 1982. Nina was raised by a Croat stepfather. She speaks a Croatian dialect; writes in the Roman, not the Cyrillic, script; and dated both Croat and Serb men (though never a Muslim) before marrying her husband, who is Croat. When their children were born, they wrote *Yugoslav* for the children's nationality. Nina wrote to me in August 1991, just after the Croatian declaration of independence, that she would have to change the children's nationality to Croat. Yugoslav was no longer a permissible national category in Croatia.

Economic Factors

"It's an artificial war, really, produced by television," said Milos Vasic, founding editor of *Vreme*, an independent magazine still published in Beograd (quoted in the *New Yorker*, 1993, 4). In Sarajevo, until the war broke out there, television broadcasts could be received from both Beograd and Zagreb. Pajic, a professor of law at the University of Sarajevo, agreed with Vasic:

> On Beograd T.V. the Croats became Ustashas. On Zagreb T.V., all Serbs were Chetniks. These are terms from the Second World War that today are ethnic insults. And then both stations began to play with the notion that Muslims are unreliable, dangerous fundamentalists. You could just watch these stations and know that something really big was rolling behind.

Vasic, the journalist, continued, "It's very easy. First you create fear, then distrust, then panic. Then all you have to do is come every night and distribute submachine guns in every village, and you are ready."

The media and propaganda had an important role to play, but why were they used at all to foster nationalism in these former Yugoslav republics? The production of fear was an important element, to which I return later. But how and why was the conflict begun at all?

In the 1980s in Brod, there was, to borrow the novelist Andric's words, the appearance of peace and progress, an overriding optimism. But under the surface, tensions were evident (1977). These tensions, however, seemed to be economic, not ethnic. One of the hallmarks of Tito's Communism was decentralization of power to the republics (except for the army, foreign policy, and some other areas of national concern). In the early 1980s, there was much talk about Yugoslavia's hard-currency debt. My neighbors in Brod understood that each republic had managed its internal financial matters independently from the others with little coordination. Western nations required repayment of Yugoslavia's large debts, and the lack of hard currency became a serious problem. The dinar had been repeatedly devalued. In 1981, after Tito's death, an austerity program was introduced, designed to limit imports and promote exports. A system of rationing gasoline, coffee, and laundry detergent was instituted in 1982. Restrictions were placed on foreign travel. This was intended to limit the use of hard currency abroad and to restrict black marketeering, particularly in coffee, detergent, and denim and leather clothing.

⚭The average salary then for a family of four was approximately $150 per month. Nina, who had been working for two years as a bookkeeper for a state-run hospitality firm, made only $80 per month. Her stepfather, a clerk, had a monthly salary of $110. My landlady, a bookkeeper with some administrative duties, made just over $100 per month. A loaf of bread cost twenty cents, as did a cup of coffee or a beer in a cafe; rent on a state-subsidized flat was about $10 per month, and a pair of leather shoes was about $20. One could travel from Brod to Zagreb by train or bus (a three-hour ride) for $2 to $3 one way.

⚭ Shortages became increasingly common. Some items, such as coffee and detergent, could only be bought periodically, with ration coupons. The purchase of gasoline, and in other regions, cooking oil and sugar, was also restricted. Other items, including chocolate, toothpaste, and nylon stockings, were available only irregularly and sometimes disappeared from the store shelves for months on end. The random disappearance of consumer goods for unpredictable lengths of time added to the anxiety.

This enhanced an attitude toward government that had existed for a long time. People like the grandmother in my own household distrusted any government. She had seen several governments collapse and had endured the wars that followed. Shortages encouraged people with government jobs, or access to anything in short supply, to steal or to cheat for their friends whenever possible. People in this region had always relied on networks of relatives and friends (*veze*) who provided access to goods, services, jobs, housing, and other needed or desired commodities. These attitudes, and the practice of helping relatives and friends, did not disappear during the Tito era. According to stories I was told, people continued to look out for their self-interests in these ways. Networks, however, became particularly important during difficult times. In Slavonski Brod, one's connections might not necessarily be a member of the same ethnic-national group.

Still, there was optimism. At the time, in a town such as Brod, which was still relatively prosperous compared even to the recent past, and in nearby villages, which were also economically stable (because agriculture provided a reliable source of income), people did not have to worry about basic survival. They did worry, however, particularly about children who remained without housing or jobs. In the 1980s, there was a shortage of housing and jobs (people had to wait on lists for several years after they finished school), but once an apartment or job was acquired, it was impossible to lose. They worried as well about rising costs and the increasing scarcity of some consumer goods. Nonetheless, new houses were being built, young people went out on the town at night, new clothing was purchased, and almost everyone could afford a vacation within Yugoslavia. These were working-class and middle-class people (low-level professionals), among whom the standard of living varied little. There was very little outright poverty in the region, aside from Roma, who were marginalized. There was also little conspicuous wealth, except among local political leaders, who might have foreign cars or weekend houses or other status symbols that ordinary people could not afford. None of these individuals in Brod, however, lived outrageously beyond the potential reach of an ordinary family. It was not unrealistic for people to hope.

The goal of the austerity program was to stabilize the national debt, ironically, by 1991. Even at the end of 1983, however, the people in Brod believed the program would not succeed. By that time, a new system of rationing included electricity. The town was divided into three districts. Each day, one district was without electricity from 2 till 11 p.m. This plan was tolerated at first and was even a source of hilarity. Older folks noticed that it promoted more visiting and talking in the evenings when people couldn't watch television, or people went to another part of town to watch with a relative or friend. In a very short time, however, electricity rationing began to be an irritation. My landlady had purchased a deep freeze with the dollars I paid her for rent. In late summer, we killed and plucked fifty chickens and ten ducks, and she froze them to see her family through the next winter. Of course, the chickens partially thawed every third day, and she feared they would spoil. This represented a large financial investment and an important source of material security. The tolerance for any system of rationing dwindled. Before the end of the year, the system had disappeared. By the time I left Yugoslavia in November of 1983, coffee and other luxury items were once again available in stores, but at much higher prices. People complained; they had not anticipated inflation.

By the time I returned in February of 1991, the dinar had been devalued twice. Then a 2 dinar note (a new note) was worth the same as an older 20,000 dinar note. Pensions and other "fixed" incomes were barely adjusted to accommodate the inflation. Many received their salaries in theory only; at my host institute in Zagreb, there were several pay periods when no one received checks, and several others when people got half the pay they were owed. At other organizations, they heard, workers received envelopes with IOUs inside. Discontent was rising along with prices. People who lived in Zagreb now drove to Graz in Austria (three hours by car) to buy groceries. They did this despite the high cost of gasoline, which was no longer rationed. Trips to Italy or Hungary for clothing and household goods were not uncommon. Inflation, unemployment, and increasing economic instability were evident. This became a source of friction and anxiety in everyday life.

In 1990, there was talk in Croatia of creating a confederacy, or of outright secession from Yugoslavia. My friends and colleagues in Zagreb were angered by the economic muddle. They argued that the wealth of the country was concentrated in the north and the west. The Adriatic coast generated tourist dollars and deutsch marks. They also had mineral resources, industry, and business. Some claimed that as much as 70 percent of the republic's gross income was taken in tax by the federal government. This figure was quoted in newspapers and on television news. The money supposedly went to help the development of poorer regions in the east and south, but many believed that their taxes, their labor, and their wealth were supporting an increasingly corrupt government and a too-large army.

This suspicion was encouraged by Franjo Tudjman, then president of the Croatian Republic. Croatia, under Tudjman, reinstituted many powerful symbols of Croatian nationalism, such as the old checkered Croatian flag, which then began to appear throughout the Croatian Republic. The names of streets, squares, and other public places were changed from those of socialist heroes to Croatian ones. In 1990, for the first time since before the Second World War, Christmas was an official paid holiday in Croatia. There was an increasing desire for self-determination and self-government. This sentiment was not universal among Croats, nor was it uniformly resisted by Serbs and other minority nationals in Croatia. Nevertheless, members of non-Croat nationalities, particularly in places like Brod, began to be apprehensive.

The official Serbian response, and the response of Serbs within Croatia, was not to block independence for its own sake but to protest that Serb enclaves in Croatia had not been guaranteed their rights. The Serbs demanded a clear policy of protection. (Croat commentators pointed out that protection of a Serb minority was also the justification for Serb aggression against Albanians in Kosovo.) Croats, however, claimed that Serb leaders in Beograd were more afraid of losing their jobs than they were of potential Croat violence against Serbs. Serbs within Croatia who voiced objections to an independent Croatia were regarded as extremists. While Croats accused Serbs of promoting ethnic-national self-interest, they maintained that nationalism was not at the heart of their own concerns.

Why did the discontent over economic and political power turn into nationalist violence? The rape of women, violence against children and the elderly, the destruction of cultural monuments, and the killing of intellectuals signal a hatred that goes beyond a desire for political and economic reform. There were economic, political, and social motivations for change in Croatia and in Bosnia, but more than that phenomenon is needed to account for the regeneration of ethnic nationalism.

Nationalism

The terms *ethnicity* and *ethnic group*, like *family* and *household*, are variously defined. Most definitions take the following form: an ethnic group is a "self-perceived group of people who hold in common . . . traditions not shared by others with whom they are in contact." These traditions include religious beliefs and practices, language or dialect, a sense of historical continuity, and common ancestry (De Vos 1975, 5). For such groups, the term *nationality* would be appropriate in the case of the former Yugoslavs, or southern Slavs.[7] In what used to be called the Serbo-Croatian language, now separated as Serbian and Croatian, *narod* translates as "nationality," but it may also be glossed as "people" or "folk." This is the term people use to refer to Serb, Croat, Macedonian, or other groups that we would call ethnic. Each of these groups has a somewhat unique historical identity, associated in most cases with former kingdoms or empires. Almost all of them have been dominated by other, more powerful entities for the better part of modern history (e.g., the Austrian Hapsburgs or the Ottoman Turks), in some cases for more than five hundred years. Each group has a language it considers to be its own, although Serbian and Croatian have been described as a single language with two alphabets and numerous dialects. (Macedonian and Slovenian were recognized as separate languages within the former Yugoslavia.) Each group has a dominant religion and customs it considers to be distinctive.

The case of Bosnian Muslims, or Bosniacs, was a little bit different. Within Yugoslavia, Bosnians of all nationalities were believed, before the war, to share not only a homeland but a history, a language, and a culture in general with Croats and Serbs. The term *Bosanci* was widespread and included all people who lived in Bosnia, emphasizing regional affiliation over ethnic nationality or religion. Muslims were an official *narod*, or nationality, though under socialism, this was patently not a religious identity (Bringa 1993, 70). This was very confusing to outsiders, who, confused by the term *Muslim*, argued that the war was a religious one. In the end, people who identified as Muslim before the start of the war in Bosnia in 1992 became known instead as "Bosniac." This gave primacy to ethnic nationality over religion and distinguished them from Serbs and Croats residing in Bosnia (for more on ethnic nationality and religion, see Bringa 1995; Gladney 1991; Hammel 1993).

Except in places where large ethnic-national minorities resided and mixed marriages were tolerated, nationality and territory tended to coincide. But, in the past fifty years, there has been increased physical mobility. People have moved from villages and small towns to cities, and in border regions like Slavonia, from one republic to the next, because of jobs. For a period, all men were conscripted into the army for one year, and military service was never in the conscript's own republic. This practice was partly responsible for more intermarriage than had been the case earlier. Increased mobility and intermarriage meant that there were (and are) individuals scattered throughout the southern Slav territories who do not "ethnically" belong where they live.

Moreover, even during the worst of the wars, the ethnic-nationality conflict was not clear cut. Not all Serbs in Croatia were against the independence movement. Although I have no reliable numbers, I was told by Croatian colleagues (quoting Croat news sources, which tend to be biased) that of the Serbian ethnic-nationals living in Croatia (approximately 15 percent of the total population), only one-fifth fought with Serbs against Croats. The remaining four-fifths were in favor of an independent Croatian state.

Some, like my one-time neighbor Nina, were against the independence movement at the start. Later, although she is Serb, she has come to feel that her current situation can largely be blamed on Serbian aggression in Croatia. Serbian gunfire left scars on her parents' house. No one was seriously hurt, but Nina became afraid for the safety of her children. Her husband had been working in Rijeka. He urged her to leave Brod and to bring the children to live with him in a worker's camp. Nina became convinced, eventually, that the federal government (that is, the Serbs) was to blame for the war.

Braco, my former landlady's son, had been at one time a true believer in Communism and Yugoslavia. He is Serb (another child from two generations of mixed marriages, who had until recently been a Yugoslav). His wife is Croat. He openly sided with the movement for Croatian independence. He had his son baptized Roman Catholic. He hoped there would be a future for his family in an independent Croatia. By the end of 1991, however, he became completely disillusioned; he took his family and a few possessions, abandoned their house and remaining property, and fled to Italy, where he was able to find work teaching karate to children. One of his Bosnian Serb cousins in Bihac went to war there on the side of Serbs. Another cousin remained in Serbia and was convinced that Serb economic woes were the fault of Croats and Bosniacs. Braco's wife's family, Croats who remained in Brod, lived for several years with the fear of Serbian artillery, and they struggle still with economic hardship as they rebuild their lives. Braco, meanwhile, immigrated to the United States with the help of another, more distant cousin in Minnesota.

In the same way, not all Croats, Slovenes, or Bosniacs were clearly for secession of their territories. Some, including my original Slavonian contacts, as well as Croats, Bosniacs, and Slovenes I met later, claim they would have preferred some political compromise to independence.

There is much confusion about the role that ethnic nationalism played and whether it was rekindled or entirely reinvented, not only among scholars, but among citizens who lived with the fear and horrors of war. Anthropological work carried out in ethnically homogeneous villages and towns throughout the former Yugoslavia (including my own field research) indicates that for some people a conscious ethnic-national identity persisted throughout the Tito years, while for others, ethnic nationalism was subconscious or unconscious. For what I now see to have been a minority, Yugoslav citizenship replaced ethnic nationality. My data indicate that these were usually people who had no clear *narod*. During and after the recent wars, these people had to choose the ethnic nationality of either their mother or their father.

Plejic, a Croatian ethnologist, collected life histories and war narratives from displaced citizens of Vukovar and Mirkovci in eastern Croatia. Vukovar and Mirkovci are also in Slavonia, and in them both, the population was a mixture of ethnic-national groups. The interviewees, according to Plejic, struggled in the course of their stories to clarify events of the war. They couldn't believe that such violence was possible among people who had once lived together peacefully. The changes in relations between neighbors were highlighted in many of the narratives. She writes, "The categories of neighbor, friend, relative, even fellow citizen, had dominance, in times of peace, over the category of nationality" (1992, 233). This is reflected in the perplexity expressed by informants, all displaced persons as a result of war in eastern Slavonia, in Croatia. "With people who sat at your table and drank with you yesterday. . . . He wants to slaughter you," said one informant, identified only as Ivan from Vukovar, referring to former Serb neighbors. Ivan is a Croat. Another Croat, Ema, from Mirkovci, tells of a Serb who came to warn them that trouble was brewing in the region. "We really had good relations, and really, we never had any bad experience with Serbs," she said. That Serbs could simultaneously be good neighbors and brutal aggressors was difficult for her to comprehend. Ema, like many others, began to distinguish between local Serbs, whose sins were only of not standing up for their Croat neighbors, from "outside" Serbs, who were the real villains in the war (Plejic 1992). I heard similar stories from former neighbors in Slavonski Brod, as well as from displaced persons and refugees from Croatia and Bosnia who came to live temporarily in refugee centers on the Croatian island of Hvar (Gilliland, Spoljar-Vrzina, and Rudan 1995). Other anthropologists reported similar conversations, similar struggling among Croats, Bosniacs, and Serbs to make sense of the unthinkable—neighbor turning against neighbor, people brutalizing each other in the name of nationality.

These narratives expressed a lack of conscious interest in ethnic nationality. At the same time, individuals were at least aware of nationality differences and commented on "the lack of trouble" with ethnic others; if there had truly been a total lack of concern with ethnicity or nationality, a person's *narod* might not even be known to others. In just these fragments, we can also see the ways in which people begin to personalize the violence. Serbs as a group were regarded as neighbors, or friends, or at least "not a problem"; suddenly, individual Serbs, people who had *taken food and drink at your own table*, turned against you. This brings the war symbolically into one's own home. For many of these interviewees, the war has been experienced and is real. Their actual homes had been destroyed, their neighbors and relatives killed. These near or actual experiences of violence change people's thinking (Bailey 1988, 13–20).

No single factor can explain the resurgence of nationalism in the Balkans, but nationalism is a part of historical and individual experience, and it provided a metaphor, a discourse, for redefining group relations. Throughout human history, people construct others whom they define in opposition to culturally constructed selves. These boundaries are never firmly fixed but are subject to negotiation and redefinition. This is also true in the Balkans. In the recent past, other dimensions of personal and group identities took precedence over ethnic nationality, at least in some of the south Slav regions. Ethnic nationality, as one dimension of identity, did not disappear, but for some, perhaps many, former Yugoslav citizens, giving primacy to ethnic-nationality identity ceased to make rational sense in the socialist years. In the recent war, political leaders and elites used ethnic nationality to gain backing for political agendas that may not have been motivated by nationalism itself. This tactic, however, could not have worked if nationality had been entirely a nonissue.

Political and economic variables contributed to the resurgence of nationalism and the start of war. But they alone didn't *cause* either the war or the brutalities against women, children, and the elderly. Another contributing factor was discourse about the past.

Experience, Recollection, and Reinvention

Wariness of others grows out of the experience of deprivation, violence, and loss. Because life was difficult, and because others protected their own interests, not yours, families and small groups tended to look inward for mutual support and protection against the insecurity of the world outside. Boundaries were closely drawn to insulate and protect. But they could also be opened to admit someone who proved trustworthy or useful. This attitude of wariness tended to be fostered in families where grandparents took an important role in child care and in passing on cultural values (Gilliland 1986; Olsen 1989, 1990; Olsen, Spoljar-Vrzina, Rudan and Barbaric-Kersic 1991). But younger people also had a direct experience of shortages and inflation in the period following Tito's death, which perpetuated expectations that others were not to be trusted and that your family and your network of connections were needed to get ahead or sometimes even to survive. This perception of others, as looking for opportunities to take advantage and promote their own interests, was fairly easily translated to ethnic-national levels.

My research in the early 1980s focused on questions of social change and cultural reproduction in families and small communities. I was concerned not only with the behavior of household groups (Olsen, Spoljar-Vrzina, Rudan, and Barbaric-Kersic 1991) but with the symbolic construction of concepts of family and household and the notions of belonging to family, neighborhood, or community groups (Gilliland 1986; see also Baric 1967; Denich 1977; Erlich 1966; Halpern 1963, 1965, 1967, 1969; Halpern and Kerewsky-Halpern 1986; Hammel 1972; Hammel and Yarbrough 1973; Simic 1972, 1982, 1983). In Slavonski Brod before 1990, the interests of families, households, and personal networks (*drustvo* and *veze*, literally "company" and "connections") took precedence over those of ethnic-national affiliations, particularly among people who were of mixed nationality. I describe elsewhere concerns that focus on family, household, and network boundaries (Olsen 1989, 1990). To be socially viable, these groups had to allow the entry of new members. This raised questions, even in the early 1980s and before, of the degree to which outsiders (however defined) could be trusted. This included women marrying into families, people from different neighborhoods, and new colleagues, neighbors, and friends. I argued that the drawing of very close boundaries, the emphasis on the family, household, and kin group and on the local community or immediate personal networks, were survival strategies known to the oldest members of families from earlier remembered days of hardship and war (Gilliland 1986; Olsen 1990). People depended on family and friends to see themselves through periods of difficulty that sometimes threatened basic physical survival.

The new construction (or reconstruction) of nationalities was accomplished through a language of belonging, familiar from the recent and the more distant past. The right or the necessity to protect the interests of oneself and other members of a salient social group was expressed in part through metaphors of suffering, deprivation, and self-sacrifice (Olsen and Rudan 1992). Others have hurt oneself or members of one's group in some way. Those who made these kinds of claims also claim that they have, in fact, helped those who now later turned against them. They are therefore entitled to protect themselves and to exclude or turn against those who have done them wrong. This language was evident in public discourse and was seemingly used to justify behavior on all sides of the political crisis. It is the same language of protest, justification, and claim to privileged status commonly used in families (before *and* since the wars). Women particularly made claims to moral superiority based on self-sacrifice (Breuner 1992; Gilliland 1986; Olsen 1989; Olsen and Rudan 1992).

The notion of a unified Yugoslavia, a nation of southern Slavs who shared a common past and future, was predicated largely on the events of the Second World War, the success of Tito and his partisans, a nationally mixed group. The media, political leaders, and individuals began to talk again (during the build-up to the recent wars) of a history prior to the Second World War. The times and the events they invoked depended on the claims they wished to further. Croats claimed that Mostar, for example, which had belonged to Croatia in the eleventh century, should really be a part of Croatia in present times. For Serbs, Greater Serbia included the Dalmatian coast, and Bosnia. Who did what during the Second World War, the ratio of Croats to Serbs in the Partisan Army, traditions of "democracy and hard work" as opposed to "authoritarianism and patronage" were invoked in heated discussions, television interviews, and films. Religious holidays became once again important, primarily as markers of ethnic-national identity.[8] Weddings, baptisms, and funerals began more often to be associated with church services (Gilliland 1986). Selective histories, religion, ethnic-national (rather than the federal Yugoslav) flags, the changes of public place names—these and other very powerful symbols were selectively promoted.

The first instances of nationalist violence in the early winter of 1991 were also aired on television. Each side was eager to show mutilated bodies. This was very effective in rousing anti-Serb feelings among Croats and was undoubtedly used in a similar way in other republics. Living in Zagreb, I had access primarily to Croatian news. I had occasion, however, to travel to Beograd and received information about the media secondhand from individuals living in Serbia, both Serbs and Americans. The media continued to play a central role in the ongoing war as evidenced by a letter I received in December 1992 from my former landlady's niece, Draga. She is a young wife and mother living near Deronje in the Backa region of Serbia. In 1982 and 1983, Draga lived with her aunt, my landlady in Slavonia. She seemed at that time unconcerned about nationality or religion. Many of her friends were Croats, and her family is mixed. In 1992, Draga's husband was in the Serbian volunteer reserve. "You cannot believe," she wrote, "what our lives are like. The news you hear is nothing compared to the reality of the situation. *Ustashas* and Muslims are raping four- and five-year-old girls. [This she heard on Serbian news.] They are not normal humans." She didn't believe that Serbs committed atrocities. She considered that Serbs had been betrayed by the West and were the victims in the war.

Draga's new or heightened sense of *Srpstvo* (Serbian identity) and her redefinition of other ethnic nationals as enemies appear to have come about since the war began (sadly, I have had no contact with her since 1995). She did not, however, say anything against her cousin who married a Croat and who left the country rather than be caught in the war. How she resolved this in her own mind, I do not know. On all sides, however, people redefined themselves and others. "Slavonians" became Croats, Serbs, or Muslims. In 1980, I knew many "Bosnians." These people all became Bosnian Croats or Catholics, Bosnian Serbs, and Bosniacs. The associations with place became secondary to nationality (and religion as its marker).

Conclusion

I asserted earlier that in 1982 and 1983, nationality was relatively unimportant. At that time, people talked about economic difficulties. They were preoccupied with the cost and availability of certain items and with the cultivation of networks that would provide access to goods, services, or jobs. Celebrations traditionally specific to one ethnic nationality or another often included guests who were ethnically different. This was another indication that ethnicity did not much matter. I was many months into my research before I began to learn about my neighbors' ethnic histories.

There were some incidents in which ethnicity or religious affiliation came up. My landlady's great-aunt insisted she spoke Croatian, not Serbo-Croatian or the Yugoslav language (as it was commonly then called). The celebration of a wedding between a Bosnian Serb and a Croat was nearly ruined by hostility between the families, expressed initially as crude jokes and later as open ethnic prejudice. These incidents and the general unwillingness of people to speak of nationality, and even the sense I had on some occasions that this was a forbidden topic, should have indicated to me that there were more tensions over ethnic nationality than I realized at the time. But these were isolated incidents, and it is indeed the case that there are still more people surprised that war broke out than expected it.

When I look through my notes and recall conversations, there are clear indications of a lingering ethnic-nationalist prejudice under the surface of good relations. There was an implicit hierarchy in which Gypsies hardly counted and Albanians were only a little better. Muslims were regarded by some as inferior to Croats or Serbs, though Bosnian Muslims were generally more acceptable to Croats and Serbs than were Albanians (most of whom are also Muslim). My landlady's sister-in-law had married a Muslim whom the family never entirely accepted. While this man was active in the community and was treated to his face as an equal by his neighbors and near associates, comments behind his back about his lack of initiative (a trait commonly attributed to ethnic minorities) were not infrequent. A young man who brought back a bride from Kosovo (where he served in the army) was cut off by his parents (she was Albanian Muslim). Jokes were made at the expense of Bosnian Muslims, a good indication that Serbs and Croats regarded them with ambivalence at best. Anti-Muslim sentiments may have been a source of solidarity between Serbs and Croats. Grandma Ana said that Muslims in a village near her own had provided her with food and shelter when she had to flee her own home during the Second World War. Because she was a Catholic, it surprised her they had done so. A neighbor explained to me early in my stay that Muslims "married four wives." This erroneous belief was enough for her to describe them as "animals," not even human, and justified her disdain, at least in her own eyes. No one contradicted her, though four other people were in the room at the time. Whether they agreed or not, I do not know.

At the other end of the scale, Croats did not denigrate Slovenians or Hungarians. Sometimes Slovenians were said to be "colder" than other Slavs, "more like Germans." This explanation was given often to account for the unwillingness of one of my neighbors to participate in gossip. Jokes were made about the way Hungarians spoke Serbo-Croatian (their confusion about gender was exaggerated). Slovenes and Hungarians did, however, more often differentiate themselves from others as being superior.

While good relations generally held between Serbs and Croats, people still sometimes made comments in private about the events of the Second World War. In 1982, the names *Ustasha* or *Chetnik* were not spoken publicly, as a rule, but the stories of personal losses were recounted in private, as I described earlier. By 1991, however, references to these groups were being made in public and were used by Croats and Serbs to dehumanize each other and to justify separateness and then violence.

The experience of nationality in Slavonski Brod seems to be a special case, as it may be in other border regions or even urban areas where there is an ethnic mix. Over a period of more than forty years, for many people, not only the children of mixed marriages but also believing Communists, ethnic nationality ceased to be a primary marker of social advantage and social distance. Yet a folklore of ethnic nationality remained. There was continued discrimination in public against the groups who remained marginal—Muslims, Albanians, Roma, and Jews. More important, perhaps, the private family histories kept ethnic-nationalist sentiments and fear alive. These memories were there waiting to be called into action if the times were right, if someone wanted to make use of them, and if the means of communication were available.

In the recent southern Slav wars, all three conditions were met. The economy was falling apart, and people were impatient for change. The current leaders of the Croats and the Serbs emerged in this climate. They had something to gain—power—and needed legitimacy. The Marxist idiom of deprivation by a ruling class was bankrupt, since people realized that socialist economic policies had failed. Moreover, all the would-be leaders had themselves been associated with socialism in the past.

Serbs who lived in minority enclaves within Croatia began to blame Croats for keeping them in a disadvantaged situation. Croats blamed Serbs in Beograd, and less developed regions of Yugoslavia in general, for the Yugoslav and Croatian economic decline. Serbs countered with further concerns for the welfare and safety of Serbs in Croatia. Stories of past oppression began to move from private discourse into the public realm. And so the situation escalated in spite of an initial levelheadedness, in spite of the mixture of ethnic nationality, and in spite of the many people on all sides who resisted secession or war. The media played a central role. Censorship and sensationalism added to the growing climate of fear.

The experience of ethnic nationality in a border region such as Brod is, in some ways, unique. But it does highlight the inadequacy of explanations for the war that claim nationalism to have been "always" a part of life in the Balkans.*At the same time, however, without a history of nationalism, divisions along these particular lines would have been less likely to have occurred. Economic and political variables alone will not explain why people move from disagreements about the distribution of resources to unmitigated hatred.

Notes

I would like to acknowledge grants from IREX and CIES-Fulbright, which made research in Yugoslavia and Croatia possible. I would also like to acknowledge the Institute for Anthropological Research in Zagreb, Croatia, for its kind and generous sponsorship and collegiality in 1991, 1993, 1995, and 1996–1997.

1. It bears noting that many of those countries regarded as part of the Balkan region claim themselves not to be (Bakic-Hayden and Hayden 1992; Pavlovic 2003, 10; Hayden 2002; Bradatan 2003, 43).

2. Fox, in discussing the rise of a Hindu national identity in India, emphasizes the roles of changing material conditions and class relations in India since independence. "Without this class analysis, I could say only that nationalist ideologies are cultural constructions—which is not very illuminating by itself" (1990, 65).

3. In 1991, sentiments had also changed among people in Brod. Even strong supporters of the state in 1982, such as my landlady's son, regarded the federal government differently in 1991. The failure of economic reform contributed largely to this change, as did perceived discrimination on the basis of nationality and associated emotions such as resentment, anger, and fear.

4. The new Croatian flag replaced the Communist red star with a "chessboard" of red and white squares at the center. This chessboard had also been used at the center of the wartime flag of the *Ustasha* state. While Croats deny that it has anything to do with fascism, Serbs see this as a symbol of exclusion of all non-Croats in the territory and associate the symbolism with Serbian genocide (see Denich 1994, 378).

5. Names with socialist associations were replaced by names associated with Croatian heroes and history. Some of the "new" Croatian names were actually old pre-1945 names that had been resurrected. Square of the Republic in Zagreb, for example (*Trg Republika*), had previously been Square of Ban Jelacic and has now been named once again Square of Ban Jelacic (*Trg Ban Jelacica*).

6. In fact, in the past, religion did matter to people who wanted to practice their religion openly. Old people went to church anyway, but many young people felt they were not really free to make that choice. One young man who openly attended church and professed his religious feelings claimed that this was the reason

for his lack of success in advancing at his job. This issue became more complicated during and just after the war for people who were, in fact, reconstructing their own histories. Some who have chosen not to publicly deny that they were once supporters of socialism criticize those who pretended to be socialists for personal gain and now pretend to have been devout Catholics all along.

7. *Yug*, or *Jug*, means south in the Croatian, Serbian, Slovenian, and Macedonian languages; thus Yugoslavia was a nation of southern Slavs, compared to the northern Slavs, who are Russians, Poles, Czechs, Slovaks, and others.

8. My husband and I spent Christmas 1996 on the Adriatic coast. We watched a broadcast of Christmas Mass from the St. Stephen's Cathedral in Zagreb. One of our friends commented wryly that the church was filled because Croats now felt they had to be publicly seen as Catholic. The same policemen who used to wait outside church to take down names were still there. Under socialism, the people attending Mass would be fired the next week; just after the war, the people who *failed* to attend Mass would be fired the next.

References

Anderson, Benedict. 1991. *Imagined communities*. London: Verso. (Orig. pub. 1983.)

Andric, Ivo. 1977. *The bridge on the Drina*. Chicago: University of Chicago Press. (Orig. pub. 1945.)

Bailey, F. G. 1988. *Humbuggery and manipulation: The art of leadership*. Ithaca: Cornell University Press.

———. 1996. *The civility of indifference: On domesticating ethnicity*. Ithaca: Cornell University Press.

———, ed. 1971. *Gifts and poison: The politics of reputation*. New York: Schocken Books.

Bakic-Hayden, Milica, and Robert M. Hayden. 1992. Orientalist variations on the theme "Balkans": Symbolic geography in recent Yugoslav cultural politics since 1987. *Slavic Review* 51:1–15.

Baric, Lorraine. 1967. Traditional groups and new economic opportunities in rural Yugoslavia. In *Themes in economic anthropology*, ed. Raymond Firth, 253–81. London: Tavistock Publications.

Botev, Nikolai, and Richard Wagner. 1993. Seeing past the barricades: Ethnic intermarriage in Yugoslavia during the last three decades. *Anthropology of East Europe Review Special Issue: War among the Yugoslavs* 11 (1–2): 27–34.

Bradatan, Cristina. 2003. Cuisine and cultural identity in the Balkans. *Anthropology of East Europe Review Special Issue: Food and Foodways in Post-Socialist Eurasia* 21:43–47.

Breuner, Nancy F. 1992. The cult of the Virgin Mary in Southern Italy and Spain. *Ethos* 1 (20): 66–95.

Bringa, Tone. 1993. Nationality categories, national identification and identity formation in "multinational" Bosnia. *The Anthropology of East Europe Review Special Issue: War among the Yugoslavs* 11 (1–2): 69–76.

———. 1995. *Being Muslim the Bosnian way: Identity and community in a central Bosnian village.* Princeton, NJ: Princeton University Press.

Denich, Bette S. 1977. Women, work and power in modern Yugoslavia. In *Sexual Stratification,* ed. Alice Schlegel, 215–44. New York: Colombia University Press.

———. 1993. Unmaking multi-ethnicity in Yugoslavia: Metamorphosis *observed.* *The Anthropology of East Europe Review Special Issue: War among the Yugoslavs* 11 (1–2): 43–53.

———. 1994. Dismembering Yugoslavia: Nationalist ideologies and the symbolic revival of genocide. *American Ethnologist* 21 (2): 367–90.

Devereaux, George. 1975. Ethnic identity: Its logical foundations and its dysfunctions. In *Ethnic identity: Cultural continuities and change,* ed. George De Vos and Lola Romanucci-Ross, 42–70. Chicago: University of Chicago Press.

De Vos, George. 1975. Ethnic pluralism: Conflict and accommodation. In *Ethnic identity: Cultural continuities and change,* ed. George De Vos and Lola Romanucci-Ross, 5–41. Chicago: University of Chicago Press.

———. 1983. Achievement motivation and intra-family attitudes in immigrant Koreans. In *The Journal of Psychoanalytic Anthropology* 6 (1): 25–71.

Erlich, Vera St. 1966. *Family in transition: A study of 300 Yugoslav villages.* Princeton, NJ: Princeton University Press.

Filipovic, Zlata. 1994. *Zlata's diary: A child's life in Sarajevo.* New York: Viking Press.

Foster, Charles, ed. 1980. *Nations without states.* New York: Praeger.

Fox, Richard G. 1990. Hindu nationalism in the making, or the rise of the Hindian. In *Nationalist ideologies and the production of national cultures,* ed. Richard G. Fox, 2:63–80. Washington, DC: American Anthropological Association.

Gilliland, M. K. (see also M. K. G. Olsen). 1986. *The maintenance of family values in a Yugoslav town.* PhD diss. in anthropology, University of California, San Diego.

———. 1995. Nationalism and ethnogenesis in the former Yugoslavia. In *Ethnic identity: Creation, conflict and accommodation,* ed. Lola Romanucci-Ross and George A. De Vos, 3rd ed., 197–221. Walnut Creek, CA: AltaMira Press.

Gilliland, M. K., S. Spoljar-Vrzina, and V. Rudan. 1995. Reclaiming lives: Variable effects of war on gender and ethnic identities in the narratives of Bosnian and Croatian refugees. *Anthropology of East Europe Review* 13 (1): 30–39.

Gladney, Dru. 1991. *Muslim Chinese: Ethnic nationalism in the people's republic.* Harvard East Asian Monographs. Cambridge: Harvard University Press.

Glenny, Misha. 1996. *The fall of Yugoslavia.* 3rd ed. London: Penguin Books. (Orig. pub. 1992.)

Green, Linda. 1994. Fear as a way of life. *Cultural Anthropology* 9 (2): 227–56.

Halpern, Joel M. 1963. Yugoslav peasant society in transition—stability in change. *Anthropological Quarterly* 36:156–82.

———. 1965. Peasant culture and urbanization in Yugoslavia. *Human Organization* 24:162–74.

———. 1967. Farming as a way of life: Yugoslav peasant attitudes. In *Proceedings of the Conference on Soviet and East European Agriculture,* ed. Jerzy Karcz, 356–84. Berkeley, CA: University of California Press.

————. 1969. *A Serbian village*. New York: Harper. (Orig. pub. 1958.)

Halpern, Joel M., and Barbara Kerewsky-Halpern. 1986. *A Serbian village in historical perspective*. Prospect Heights, IL: Waveland Press. (Orig. pub. 1972.)

Hammel, E. A. 1972. The Zadruga as process. In *Household and family in past times*, ed. Peter Laslett and Richard Wall, 335–74. Cambridge: Cambridge University Press.

————. 1993. The Yugoslav labyrinth. *The Anthropology of East Europe Review Special Issue: War among the Yugoslavs* 11 (1–2): 35–42.

Hammel, E. A., and C. Yarbrough. 1973. Social mobility and the durability of family ties. *Journal of Anthropological Research* 29:145–63.

Hayden, Robert M. 2002. Imagined communities and real victims: Self-determination and ethnic cleansing in Yugoslavia. In *Genocide: An anthropological reader*, ed. Alexander Hinton, 231–53. Malden, MA: Blackwell Publishers.

Helms, Elissa. 2003. The "nation-ing" of gender? Donor policies, Islam and women's NGOs in post-war Bosnia-Herzegovina. *Anthropology of East Europe Review Special Issue: Ethnographies of Postsocialism* 21 (2): 85–93.

Hobsbawm, Eric, and Terence Ranger, eds. 1989. *The invention of tradition*. New York: Cambridge University Press. (Orig. pub. 1983.)

Huseby-Darvas, Eva V. 1993. But where can WE go? Refugee women in Hungary from the former Yugoslavia. In *Selected papers on refugee issues: III*, ed. Jeffrey L. MacDonald and Amy Zaharlick, 63–77. Arlington, VA: American Anthropological Association (a publication of the Committee on Refugee Issues, a committee of the General Anthropology Division of the American Anthropological Association).

Jambresic-Kirin, Renata. 1996. Narrating war and exile experiences. In *War, exile and everyday life: Cultural perspectives*, ed. Renata Jambresic-Kirin and Maja Povrzanovic. Zagreb, Croatia: Institute of Ethnology and Folklore Research.

Jelavich, Charles. 1990. *South Slav nationalisms: Textbooks and Yugoslav Union before 1914*. Columbus: Ohio State University Press.

Lewin, Carroll McC. 1993. Negotiated selves in the Holocaust. *Ethos* 21 (3): 295–318.

McKay, James, and Frank Lewins. 1978. Ethnicity and the ethnic group: A conceptual analysis and reformulation. In *Ethnic and Racial Studies* 1:412–27.

Milicevic, Aleksandra Sasha. 2003. Joining the war: Draft-dodgers and volunteers from Serbia, 1991–1995. Paper presented at annual meeting of the American Anthropological Association, Chicago, Illinois, November.

New Yorker. 1993. Comment: Quiet voices from the Balkans. *New Yorker*, March 15, 4–6.

Olsen, M. K. G. 1989. Authority and conflict in Slavonian households: The effects of social environment on intra-household processes. In *The household economy: Reconsidering the domestic mode of production*, ed. R. Wilk, 149–70. Boulder, CO: Westview Press.

————. 1990. Redefining gender in rural Yugoslavia: Masculine and feminine ideals in ritual context. *East European Quarterly* 23 (4): 431–44.

———. 1993. Bridge on the Sava: Ethnicity in Eastern Croatia 1981–1991. *The Anthropology of East Europe Review Special Issue: War among the Yugoslavs* 11 (1–2): 54–62.

Olsen, M. K. G., and Vlasta Rudan. 1992. Childlessness and gender: Example from the island of Hvar. *Collegium Antropologicum* 16 (1): 115–24.

Olsen, M. K. G., S. M. Spoljar-Vrzina, V. Rudan, and A. M. Barbaric-Kersic. 1991. Normal families? Problems in cultural anthropological research methods and methodology. *Collegium Antropologicum* 15 (2): 299–308.

Patrias, Carmela. 1993. Tales of Teleki Square. *Oral History: Ethnicity and National Identity* 21 (1): 22–34.

Pavlovic, Zoran. 2003. *Croatia*. Philadelphia: Chelsea House Publishers.

Peoples, James, and Garrick Bailey. 1991. *Humanity*. 2nd ed. St. Paul, MN: West Publishing Company.

Perks, Robert. 1993. Ukraine's forbidden history: Memory and nationalism. *Oral history: Ethnicity and national identity* 21 (1): 43–53.

Petrovic, K., and B. Belic. 1970. Prehistoric cultures in the area of Brodsko Posavlje. Materijali VII: Simpozijum praistorijske sekcije arheoloskog drustva Jugoslavije [Materials VII: Symposium of the prehistoric group of the Archaeological Society of Yugoslavia]. Beograd: Slavonski Brod.

Plejic, Irena. 1992. All that we had, all that we were, reduced to memories: Personal accounts and letters of displaced persons from Eastern Slavonia. In *Fear, death and resistance: An ethnography of war, Croatia 1991–1992*, ed. Lada Feldman, Ines Prica, and Reana Senjkovic, 229–39. Zagreb, Croatia: Institute of Ethnology and Folklore Research.

Popis stanovnistva i stanova [Census records]. 1981. Republicki zavod za statistiku SR Hrvatska [Census of population and dwellings (or residences)]. Zagreb, 1983.

Povrzanovic, Maja. 1992. Culture and fear: Everyday life in wartime. In *Fear, death and resistance: An ethnography of war, Croatia 1991–1992*, ed. Lada Feldman, Ines Prica, and Reana Senjkovic, 119–50. Zagreb, Croatia: Institute of Ethnology and Folklore Research, Matrix Croatica X-Press.

———. 1993. Ethnography of war: Croatia 1991–1992. *The Anthropology of East Europe Review Special Issue: War among the Yugoslavs* 11 (1–2): 117–25.

Reineck, Janet. 1993. Seizing the past, forging the present: Changing visions of self and nation among the Kosovo Albanians. *Anthropology of East Europe Review Special Issue: War among the Yugoslavs* 11 (1–2): 85–92.

Rodman, Margaret C. 1992. Empowering place: Multilocality and multivocality. *American Anthropologist* 94 (3): 640–56.

Romanucci-Ross, Lola. 1995. Matrices of an Italian identity. In *Ethnic identity: Creation, conflict and accommodation*, ed. Lola Romanucci-Ross and George A. De Vos, 3rd ed., 73–96. Walnut Creek, CA: AltaMira Press.

Rubic, Ivo. 1953. *Slavonski i Bosanski Brod: Zbornik za narodni zivot i obicaje juznih slavena* [Slavonski and Bosanski Brod: Journal for folk life and customs of the Southern Slavs]. Jugoslavenska akademija znanosti i umjetnosti [Yugoslav

Academy of Science and Arts]. Vol. 36. Zagreb, Croatia. (This particular "article" consumes an entire volume. Usually these volumes contain articles about several different regions. Slavonski Brod and Bosanski Brod are both names of towns, one in Croatia [a region known as Slavonia] and one in Bosnia.)

Rudan, Pavao, Guy Heyden, Damir Caric, Snjezana Colic, Sanja Martic-Biocina, Vlasta Rudan, Anita Sjuoldzic, Josip Santic, Sanja Spoljar-Vrzina, and Mary Kay Gilliland. 1997. *The study and care of displaced persons and refugee families.* Zagreb, Croatia: Croatian Anthropological Society.

Silber, Laura, and Allan Little. 1996. *Yugoslavia: Death of a nation.* New York: TVBooks/Penguin U.S.A.

Simic, Andrei. 1972. *The peasant urbanites: A study of rural-urban mobility in Serbia.* New York: Seminar Press.

———. 1982. Urbanization and modernization in Yugoslavia: Adaptive and maladaptive aspects of traditional culture. In *Urban Life in Mediterranean Europe*, ed. M. Kenny and D. Kertzer, 203–24. Urbana: University of Illinois Press.

———. 1983. Machismo and Cryptomatriarchy: Power, affect and authority in the contemporary Yugoslav family. *Ethos* 11 (1–2): 66–86.

———. 1991. Obstacles to the development of a Yugoslav national consciousness: Ethnic identity and folk culture in the Balkans. *Journal of Mediterranean Studies* 1 (1): 18–36.

Suarez-Orozco, Marcelo M. 1990. Speaking of the unspeakable: Toward a psychosocial understanding of responses to terror.

———. 1994. Doing anthropology at the *Fin de Siecle.* In *The making of psychological anthropology II*, ed. Marcelo Suarez-Orozco, George Spindler, and Louise Spindler, 158-94. Fort Worth, TX: Harcourt Brace College Publishers.

Verdery, Katherine. 1991. *National ideology under socialism: Identity and cultural politics in Ceausescu's Romania.* Berkeley, CA: University of California Press.

West, Richard. 1999. *Tito and the rise and fall of Yugoslavia.* New York: Carroll and Graf Publishers. (Orig. pub. 1994.)

Zebec, Tvrtko. 2004. The challenges of applied ethnology in Croatia. *Anthropology of East Europe Review Special Issue: Dance and Music in Eastern Europe* 22 (1): 85-92.

Cultural Identity and Minority Status in Japan

4

GEORGE A. DE VOS AND HIROSHI WAGATSUMA

APAN WAS THE FIRST NON-WESTERN, non-Caucasoid country to become an industrialized nation. This occurred in a surprisingly short period of time, after 1868, following three hundred years of feudalism and isolation. Since the end of World War II in 1945, Japan has accomplished a miraculous industrial recovery, again within a brief time. Today, Japan is the third largest industrial complex in the world. As a major industrial state, it has lost any isolation that once insulated it from other areas of Asia, and it is reluctantly interchanging residential population with other areas of the globe. In this process, at least, Japan is the polar opposite of the United States, though it is still problematic as to who is to be included or excluded in an American identity.

Definitions of American citizenship begin with awareness of diverse origins constituting its citizenry. Determination of who is a Japanese citizen starts from completely different traditional premises—that Japanese are of a totally homogeneous origin. Given the effects of its recent colonial past, contemporary worldwide labor mobility, and international industrial interpenetration, three important questions arise about present-day Japanese ethnic identity.

First, there is the question of a shared continuing national purpose in the homeland as related to its past historical cultural identity, individual and collective. Is Japanese ethnic identity to remain coterminous with the nation-state and its traditional population? Does being Japanese remain a racial question? The second unresolved issue is how Japanese at home view themselves physically, intellectually, and culturally vis-à-vis their Asian neighbors and the European American Caucasoid Westerners who opened up Japan to foreign commerce and industry in the nineteenth century. Third is the modern dilemma of all modern nation-states, namely the relationship of citizenship to an exclusively defined ethnic identity. How does the state recognize, socially and legally, and without discrimination, the increasingly diverse origins of many newer, permanent residents in Japan within a nonethnic definition of full citizenship? The latter is particularly difficult for Japanese, given their still-abiding belief in a mythological assertion that Japanese are of a unique, homogeneous racial and cultural origin. For most Japanese, citizenship or social acceptance cannot as yet be well distinguished from a racially defined ethnicity.

What Is It to Be Japanese?[1]

Commodore Perry first came to Japan with his black warships in 1853. His visit helped instigate the overthrow of the Tokugawa Shogunate. In the years after the symbolic restoration of the emperor in 1868, Japan transformed itself from a feudal country into an industrialized nation by learning from the West. A second vigorous wave of Westernization occurred from the mid-1920s to the mid-1930s. During that time, not only Western technology but also liberal democratic ideas and even American music, movies, and fashions had an impact on urban Japanese. Then came the war in 1941. Following defeat in 1945, Japan found itself once again learning "lessons of democracy" from its American teachers during the occupation.

As a result of mass media, the impact of American culture was unprecedented. Things American flooded Japanese society. When the occupation ended, the flood began to subside. Recent political, diplomatic, and economic developments indicate a new increase of exclusionary nationalistic feelings. Intellectual and political leaders seem to be grappling continuously with the problem of relating a uniquely conceived national purpose and cultural pride to present economic affluence.

Identity problems were first recognized by Japanese intellectuals soon after Japan had begun its vigorous efforts to "Westernize itself in order to resist the West" (Passin 1962). Japanese intellectuals struggled to escape from their "historical predicament" (Pyle 1969); the conflict involved national pride and the desire for cultural borrowing—in short, the need to be both modern and Japanese. The "cultural colonization" (Passin 1962) during the postwar occupation shattered once and for all not only militarism and ultranationalism but everything that appeared to be associated with it, namely Japanese tradition itself. Amid economic affluence, the hundred-year-old question seems to remain largely unanswered, the dilemma unresolved. How can Japanese become modernized yet remain Japanese? What makes the Japanese uniquely Japanese and something they can be proud of? Japanese intellectuals are still trying to find some meaningful way of relating their isolate past to an interactive present and future, but apparently without much success.

Influences on the Purity of Language

Certain sectors of contemporary Japanese life, and the language describing them, are Westernized. Although not limited to Japan, fads and fashions in dress, music, and the arts come directly from U.S. and European cities, arriving in Japanese cities perhaps more quickly than they reach corners of rural America and Europe. Well-known books by Western intellectuals, particularly Americans such as Herbert Marcuse or Peter Drucker, are quickly translated (or mistranslated) into Japanese and avidly read by white-collar workers in overcrowded commuter trains. In television commercials, two-thirds or more of the words used for brand names and descriptions of products are English or French, although such words are systematically mispronounced so that they fit into the Japanese phonological system, a process that renders them quite incomprehensible to actual speakers of English or French. Some linguists estimate that a Japanese needs to know about 2,200 foreign words for ordinary daily conversation and about 3,000 additional words to engage in sophisticated discourse. The number of words of foreign origin (*gairai-go*) included in Japanese dictionaries published at different times in Japan's modern history indicates a definite increase in words that first came into Japanese as foreign words (*gaikoku-go*) and were eventually adopted (Yazaki 1964).

One can also point out the "conceptual Westernization" of Japanese academic theory. For example, Japanese social psychologists omit the variable "Japan" in most of their recent writings. They do not pay enough attention to the social psychological reality that is uniquely Japanese but tend to be satisfied with Western theories that are based upon a Western psychological reality and are not necessarily directly applicable to Japan (Wagatsuma 1969).

Racial Aesthetics

Westernization is also found in what one might call the "racial" sexual aesthetics of the Japanese. As analyzed elsewhere in detail (Wagatsuma 1967, 1969, 1972), prior to any sustained contact with the Caucasoid Europeans, the Japanese valued white skin as beautiful and depreciated "black" (that is, suntanned) skin as ugly. With the introduction of Western technology and values in 1868, the Japanese perception of feminine beauty also began to change. Although they admired the white skin of the Westerners, they considered Caucasian hair color and hairiness as distasteful. Wavy hair was not attractive to the Japanese until the mid-1920s, for curly hair was considered characteristic of animals.

During the second peak of Westernization in the 1920s and 1930s, the Japanese, especially those in cities, adopted Western customs and fashions, including singing American popular songs and dancing in dance halls. They watched motion pictures with delight and made great favorites of Clara Bow, Gloria Swanson, and Greta Garbo. Motion pictures seem to have had a strong effect in finally changing hairstyles and notions of beauty. During this period, many Japanese women had their hair cut and, in spite of the exhortations of proud samurai, had it waved and curled. They took to wearing long skirts with large hats and emulated the clothes worn by Greta Garbo. Anything Western was considered modern and therefore superior.

This trend lasted until the mid-1950s, when, under the pressure of the ultranationalist militarist regime, ties with Western fads and fashions were systematically broken. On the other hand, the subtle, almost unconscious trend toward an idealization of Western physical features apparently became of increasing importance in the 1920s. It remained, it seems, a hidden undercurrent even throughout the last war, when Japan, as the "champion" of the Asian nations, fought against the whites.

Plastic surgery, especially to alter eye folds and to build up the bridge of the nose, has become standard practice among Japanese movie actors and actresses and among many ordinary people. Japanese women also attempt to increase the actual or apparent size of their breasts by surgery or by wearing padded brassieres. These various attempts by younger Japanese, women in particular, to alter their physical appearance suggest that the Caucasian standards of beauty and sexual attractiveness became the standards for the Japanese.

Attitudes toward the skin of Caucasians fall into opposites of likes and dislikes, which may coexist within an individual, either appearing alternately or being expressed simultaneously. White skin may be considered inferior to that of the Japanese because it is rough in texture, with many wrinkles, blemishes, and furrows, whereas Japanese skin is smooth, tight, and resilient, with far fewer spots and speckles. Most Japanese, however, admit that Caucasian facial and body structures are more attractive than the "flat face" and "less shapely body" of the Japanese.

Japanese men, especially those over forty years of age, tend to be concerned more with the skin texture of a Japanese woman than with the measurement of her bust and hips, whereas Western men will first think of the shape of a woman rather than her skin texture. One might say that the Japanese man's taste with respect to sexual aesthetics has traditionally been "surface oriented," whereas the Western man's is "structure oriented." Among younger Japanese, however, structure orientation is quickly replacing surface orientation, as the popularity of plastic surgery shows. Japanese in the United States admire the beauty of white skin in Caucasian women but also point out their inaccessibility.

Finally, Westerners smell different. They have stronger body odors than do Japanese. The ambivalence about Western physical attributes leads to mixed feelings of admiration, envy, fear, and disgust, along with the sense of being overwhelmed or threatened that is evoked in the Japanese mind by the image of a hairy giant whose great vigor and strong sexuality can easily satisfy an equally energetic and glamorous Caucasian female.

Spiritual-Racial Values versus Material Intrusion

Such trends have certainly invited criticism from intellectuals. Particularly among the older generation, one observes dissatisfaction and irritation with "too much Westernization." For example, Takeo Kuwabara, a professor of French literature at the University of Kyoto and a prolific writer, used bitter words in criticizing the Japanese preoccupation with things Western: "I want the Japanese to be more proud of themselves as modern people (*kindai-jiri*) with human dignity and individual rights. The Japanese should have 'guts' (*konjo*) as a nation. They should stop worshipping foreign countries and stop regretting that Japan never had the same history as the West" (1963).

But in spite of plastic surgery, Japanese know very well, perhaps too well, who they are, and especially who they are not. For the Japanese, group identity is an assured given. They tend to believe that there is a greater degree of physical homogeneity among themselves than actually exists. And they tend to believe that they look uniquely alike and always different from other Asians. In the Japanese mind, only those born of Japanese parents are genetically Japanese—nobody can *become* Japanese.

By 1867, toward the end of the Tokugawa feudal era, the sense of crisis was expressed in two contrasting ways. The first was based on recognition of the material superiority of Western civilization and of the necessity to learn from it in order to maintain Japan's political independence. The second was based on the recognition of fundamental differences between Japanese and Western civilizations and of the necessity to reject Western influences so as to maintain Japan's cultural autonomy. The followers of the first line of thought emphasized that Japan should open itself up to the West; they were called *kaikoku-ha* (the open-country wing). Those who followed the second line of thought insisted that Japan drive the Westerners away; they were called *joi-ha* (the expulsionist wing). Both groups, despite fierce and often bloody battling between them, shared the same goal: Japan's survival in the face of the Western threat.

Following the visit of Perry's ships to Uraga in 1853, the Tokugawa government changed its policy from "expulsion of the barbarians" to "opening up the country." After complicated changes of alliances among the lords and among the antigovernment forces, and after battles and bloodshed, the Tokugawa regime was overthrown in 1867. The Meiji emperor was restored to the throne, and the building of a new modern nation was begun under those who were anti-Tokugawa, some of whom had favored expulsion of the outsiders and others of whom had advocated opening up the country. All these young leaders agreed on the goal of making their country as rich and powerful as Western ones so that Japan would not become a foreign colony of the West. Most were former samurai, and they were sensitive to the grave threats that the Western powers posed to Japan's independence and autonomy. They focused their efforts on building a rich nation and a strong army (*fukoku kyohei*).

Some intellectual leaders even advocated the "physical" Westernization of the nation. Twenty-four-year-old Arinori Mori, later the first minister of education, was in the United States in 1871 as Japan's first ambassador. He declared that Japanese students in the United States should marry American women and bring them home so as to produce physically and mentally stronger children (Nagai 1965). In 1883, a book proposed that the Japanese import women from the West and marry them, in order to produce "racially superior offsprings" (Takahashi 1883). Incredible as it may sound today, the prime minister, Prince Hirobumi Ito, took this proposition seriously enough to write to Herbert Spencer,[2] asking for his opinion. At about the same time, a newspaper article advised the Japanese to eat more meat and drink more milk. "Japanese are intellectually smart by nature, but, unlike the Westerners, they lack persistence and tenacity," said an article. "Japanese lack persistence and tenacity because they do not eat beef and drink milk. . . . Cows are stupid animals but they are persistent and tenacious. Those who eat their meat and drink their milk become persistent and tenacious like cows" (Kosaka et al. 1938). As a matter of fact, Emperor Meiji, setting up a model for the nation, had begun drinking milk twice a day in 1871, and in 1872, the imperial family had started eating meat regularly (Sabata 1971).

In 1885, *Youth of the New Japan* was published. Urging youth to seek total Westernization of Japan, the book soon became very popular among young people (Tokutomi 1885/1931). Its author, Soho Tokutomi, organized young intellectuals into a group called the *Min'yusha* (Friends of Nation). Writing for the group's periodical, *Kokumin no Tomo* (subtitled in English "The Nation's Friends"), he became the leading spokesman of the new generation. Following Herbert Spencer, Tokutomi believed that a universal process of social evolution, impelled by historical forces, was molding all nations, including Japan, along similar lines. When the government made it an official policy (particularly with the promulgation of the Imperial Rescript on Education in 1890) to adopt the past-oriented Confucian ethics as the moral backbone of national education, Tokutomi severely attacked the policy as proceeding with industrialization while maintaining identification with the East.

An alternative to the *Min'yusha's* Westernism was proposed by a second group of intellectuals, the *Seikyosha* (Society for Political Education), founded in 1888. Their emphasis on the preservation of Japan's cultural autonomy gained increasing popularity. Although its members had been strongly influenced by Western values and were committed to the adoption of many Western institutions, they believed that only by maintaining a distinct identity could the Japanese feel equal to the Westerners and recover their own national pride.

In 1894 and 1904, Japan won its wars with Qing Dynasty China and czarist Russia. Japan was able to make the Western nations agree to relinquish their extraterritorial privileges only after winning these two wars, not after the *Rokumeikan* masquerade of 1887, when high Meiji government officials and their families dressed in Western clothes and invited foreign diplomats to balls to persuade the foreigners that the Japanese were civilized enough to deserve equal treatment. The improvement in their international status made the third answer to the problem of cultural identity increasingly convincing.

The Meiji government formulated and propagated a national ideology that justified its power and called for great loyalty on the part of the people to achieve the nation's industrial and military goals. In the newly established universal education and military training, the government reasserted the old values of loyalty, filial piety, solidarity, and duty to superiors, and it promoted ethnic-racial myths about the sacredness of the emperor. The pressure to conform to this national orthodoxy came not so much from the government as from "forces within Japanese society" (Jansen 1965). The receptivity to a national ideology was a natural revivalist reaction to the sense of uprootedness and the emotional stress and dislocation produced by the rapid changes during the first two decades of the Meiji period. This national ideology of the past helped the Japanese compensate for their new lost sense of security.

During the 1920s, following its industrial expansion and economic depression, Marxism also became popular among urban intellectuals, as did certain political and labor movements. As mentioned before, things Western (this time, mainly American)—jazz, dress, dance, and movies—also attracted the urban Japanese. The countries of the West continued to be regarded as advanced nations (*senshin koku*), and Japan as backward (*koshin koku*). Ishida describes the period after World War I as "an extension of the previous age of inferiority feelings among the Japanese toward the West."[3]

Then came the war, first in Manchuria in 1931, then spreading to north China, then to the whole of China, and finally to the Pacific and Pearl Harbor. Ultranationalism, with its mythical glorification of the "descendants of the Sun Goddess," drowned all liberal thought. The problems of cultural-racial identity were answered by a clear definition of the national goal of the "sacred war," in which Japan's role was to become the leader and protector of the Asian nations and to drive out the Western imperialists. During this disastrous war, the importance of "Japanese soul and spirit" was greatly stressed. The chauvinistic emphasis on the superiority of the traditional warrior-Confucian-Shinto value system over the "corrupt Western civilization" became almost hysterical, for the "corrupt" West proved to be much more powerful, and there was no sign of the "divine wind" (*kamikaze*) blowing to protect the "land of gods."

When the war ended, the Japanese began to receive a "democratic education" from their American teachers, toward whom they felt rivalry mixed with admiration. Japanese society and traditions were all put on trial, not by Americans, but by Japanese intellectuals. Historians separated Japanese history from the myth of the origins of the imperial line. The mechanisms of Japanese fascism were analyzed for the first time in scientific terms (Maruyama 1963). Sociologists pointed out the predominance of small communities in Japan, and particularly the institution of the patriarchal family (Kawashima 1948). Psychologists analyzed the "irrational," "premodern," or "feudal" characteristics of the Japanese (Minami 1949; Miyagi 1950, 1956; Takagi 1955) and emphasized the necessity of overcoming such characteristics so as to accomplish the democratization of the Japanese people.

All this demonstrated a "wide-spread realization of Japan's backward-ness" (Kato 1965). Anything associated with defeated Japan—whether the emperor cult, calligraphy, judo, "a father who tells his daughter to come home before supper," or "a mother who wants her son to marry her best friend's daughter"—was condemned as feudal (*hoken-teki*) and was there-fore to be rejected. Intellectuals, through lectures and writings, urged the Japanese to become modern *(kindai-teki)*; rational *(gori-teki)*; democratic *(minshu-teki)*; and, the implication not infrequently was, "like the Ameri-cans." To those intellectuals, as to Min'yusha members of the 1880s, there seemed once again to be an assumption that Japan should move along the ladder of unilineal social evolution, from the feudal or premodern stage to the modern and democratic stage. Moreover, many of them, pointing out what the Japanese should no longer be, seemed too busy to think what the Japanese would eventually become when they were fully democratized and modernized.

The occupation ended, and the flood of things American subsided. In terms of economy and in the sphere of material life, the Japanese rebuilt everything they had lost and more, "except for a sense of values and na-tional purpose to replace those shattered by the war" (Rosenthal 1963). Bad as the old system might have been, "it had given meaning and purpose to life, a way of viewing the world, and an opportunity for service and sac-rifice to a larger cause" (Passin 1962). "The thought that the Japanese were not passively accepting Western civilization, but were holding themselves as the last fortress in Asia against the Western powers, gave the nation pride and a sense of mission" (Kosaka 1968). This was all lost, and the rapid changes, the confusion, the "transvaluation of values," and the discrediting of the old authority without replacement by a new one created what the Japanese themselves refer to as "a spiritual void."

The drive toward Westernization has slowed down somewhat since the middle of the 1950s, especially with the recent economic prosperity of the country. Japanese intellectuals now seem again increasingly concerned with the century-old question of cultural identity. An anthropologist, Mitsusada Fukasaku (1972), contends that with these basic "unchanging" characteris-tics, the Japanese have adopted various foreign cultural elements "without ever really understanding their essential nature." He asserts that the Japan-ese adoption of foreign cultures has been no more than "monkey's imita-tion" (*saru-mane*, a "superficial imitation"), and that the Japanese have remained essentially the same in the relative isolation afforded by a self-sufficient rice agriculture. But Japan is no longer geographically isolated from the international community; agriculture is no longer the basis for the

Japanese economy; and Japan's once-beautiful natural, traditional settings have been destroyed by pollution, urbanization, and commercialization.[4]

The issues raised above by Wagatsuma in his original chapter, written in 1970 and summarized here, remain. Intellectuals of the 1990s do not insist on Japanese uniqueness, but they recognize a continuing Japanese isolation within the international community. A Japanese brand of exclusory racism persists in the general public. There is aversion to extending citizenship toward those of non-Japanese origin and toward a segment of its population that bears the stigma of past premodern outcaste status, still attributed by many to some supposed non-Japanese ancestors. In international business ventures, the Japanese have difficulties in creating organizations at home or abroad that include foreign personnel on an equal basis. These are issues to which we now turn in the context of ethnic identity and minority status in Japan.

Minorities within the Japanese State

By most serious estimates, Japan has various minorities that probably total about 4.5 percent of its population (De Vos and Wetherall 1983). Some are technically citizens; some are not. The issues of social self-identity in some instances, strictly speaking, are not of an "ethnic" nature. Nevertheless, from the standpoint of the majority of Japanese, all of these individuals, regardless of the category into which they are placed, are not "true" Japanese. They therefore, at least occasionally, face some form of social discrimination.

The largest minority group consists of the former outcastes of Japan, Burakumin, comprising close to three million individuals, including many who are secretly "passing."[5] They are the premodern descendants of hereditary pariahs who were a debased caste beneath the four classes of ordinary Japanese.

The three next largest groups result from Japanese expansion into Okinawa and Taiwan as a result of its war with China in 1894 and its official takeover of Korea in 1910. There are over a million Okinawans, whose languages were similar to but distinct from that of the majority Japanese. These languages are rapidly disappearing, but Okinawans, seen as smaller and hairier, still face various degrees of nonacceptance when they move to the four main islands of Japan. There are close to a million people of Korean descent, most of whom remain technically noncitizens and live in large ghettos in many urban areas. Some have taken citizenship, many with fabricated Japanese names and practicing various degrees of hiding ancestry. Those of Taiwanese background are fewer in number and less conspicuous, but they occasionally suffer slights when they venture into ordinary business relationships. Children of Japanese and Korean or Taiwanese parents are considered *konketsuji*, or racially of "mixed blood."

There remain relatively small remnants of Ainu, indigenous people who were driven to their remaining villages in the northern island of Hokkaido over a period of eight hundred years in the Japanese early occupation of the northeastern territories. They are treated in much the same way as is the native population of North America. That is, they are often considered quaint or primitive. Now much intermixed with ordinary Japanese, they nevertheless maintain, in many instances, a sense of separate identity.

Of more immediate moment are residential minorities created by more recent events. There are the *hibakusha*, survivors of the atomic bombs dropped on Japan at the close of World War II. Considered irrevocably contaminated, they have been shunned by other Japanese.

There have been a number of intermarriages and other liaisons during and after the postwar American occupation of Japan. Children resulting from these relationships have been subjected to various forms of continuing discrimination by members of their extended family as well as by unrelated neighbors and others who come in contact with them in various circumstances. More than any other minority group in Japan, offspring of Japanese and non-Asian foreigners are maliciously stereotyped in mass media, including popular literature, films, and comic books. Unlike white Japanese *konketsuji*, who may have physical features that many Japanese find exotically attractive, black Japanese tend to have the kinds of features that some Japanese openly despise (Wagatsuma 1967).

Increasingly, Japan hosts many foreign residents of long-term duration, both as skilled professionals and, now more recently, unskilled labor. Given the complex legal difficulties, only a very few are able to obtain Japanese citizenship. A recent notable group are South Americans of Japanese ancestry, mainly from Brazil, who come to Japan to do unskilled work, receiving a much higher rate of payment than it is possible to gain for professional, let alone skilled, work in their homeland. Despite their Japanese ancestry, they do not gain social acceptance among ordinary Japanese, given their problems with language and, more offending, their "un-Japanese" bodily comportment and their more openly expressive social habits.

We shall examine in some detail identity issues raised by two of these groups that we have researched in some detail, namely the Burakumin and the Koreans. The first group is fully Japanese and are legally so. However, the majority population questions their origins since they are considered innately inferior people. The second group, the Koreans, have for the most part maintained a separate identity as Koreans and wish to have this ethnicity respected without losing the opportunity of being able to receive Japanese citizenship and equal treatment in professional and commercial careers. They, too, are considered unrefined and inferior. Polls rating relative acceptability place them just above Africans or African Americans on so-called social distance scales.

Citizenship Is Not Enough:
The Outcaste Tradition in Modern Japan[6]

Discussed only briefly, if mentioned at all in general histories, are two subgroups of the traditional, premodern society. They are the *hinin* (nonpeople)—a heterogeneous mélange of beggars, prostitutes, itinerant entertainers, mediums, and religious wanderers—and felons or former felons who had fallen out of the four-tier class system. These are not inherently polluted and can be rehabilitated by proper purification ceremonies.

Beneath these outcasts are the true hereditary outcastes, officially called Eta, a defiling word written with characters meaning "full of filth." They traditionally performed tasks considered ritually polluting, including animal slaughter and disposal of the dead. By extension, they worked on armor and musical instruments (which contained animal products such as leather). Some other professions, such as basket weaving, for now unknown reasons, were also consigned to Eta. During the modernization period, the Eta were declared "new citizens," but their status did not change much, and they were still people of special villages, *Tokushu Buraku*. Burakumin, village people, became a generally used neutral, nonpejorative term of reference. This word is beginning to be rejected by some in favor of more euphemistic terms such as "yet unliberated people."

There are striking functional parallels between the social problems and sense of social alienation resulting from the discrimination encountered by the Japanese Burakumin and the problems faced by African Americans in the United States. However, these striking parallels may be obscured by a number of seeming dissimilarities. First, the Burakumin are not physically distinct or visibly discernible in any way. Second, a major, collectively exercised "coping" technique of contemporary Japanese society with respect to members of this group is avoidance or direct denial that any such group continues to exist, or indeed that there is any problem. Consciously or not, a Burakumin must choose between four limited alternatives in social self-identity and group belonging, available also in other cultural settings to many disparaged minorities who are not visibly distinct.

1. Maintain an overt and *direct identity* with one's past and with a present minority status, whatever that implies with respect to social degradation. By so doing, one may be *passively receptive and resigned* to the stigmata of past definitions of the society.
2. Gain increased social advantages or changes in status through *concerted cooperative action* with others sharing a demeaned status.
3. Go into a *selective disguise*, in which one maintains expressive family affiliations and group membership within the Buraku community, but for occupational and other instrumental purposes, one may lead a life of semidisguise among members of the majority population.
4. Attempt to *pass* completely; move from the home community and cut off overt contacts with family, forging an entirely new identity, and in some cases fabricating a new past.

Many complex societies have parallel situations in which the difficult process of social assimilation to full status within a majority culture is likely to face similar problems. Utilizing a psychocultural framework,[7] let us illustratively explore some Burakumin minority status problems and their psychological consequences. Erik Erikson (1959), discussing the nature of identity formation, provides excellent theoretical background for this discussion.

Relative Social Status and Occupation

In Buraku communities, caste separation from the majority Japanese does not preclude the appearance of internal class distinctions in social participation. This is also true of American colored communities, though these have the further complication of complex attitudes about shades of skin color and kinds of hair. Such distinctions do not function among the Burakumin, but differences in occupation do (Cayton and Drake 1962).

In our work in Japan starting in the early 1950s, we did not find it difficult to apply an index of class-status characteristics to the 2,400 majority Japanese interviewed in both city and village, which distinguished them into upper-, middle-, and lower-class patterns. Our indexes[8] were slightly modified from those developed by Lloyd Warner and his colleagues in his intensive urban anthropological study of Newburyport, Massachusetts, in the 1930s (Warner et al. 1963). Occupation, education, internal conditions of the home, area lived in, and source of income generally held up as significant variables.

Specifically within an outcaste community, area lived in, in most instances, was a known ghetto, but we also interviewed some who were passing by living in majority areas. With regard to other class-variant characteristics, Burakumin differed among themselves in line with internally considered class distinctions that regulated their relationships.[9] Also, a number of high-status families lived outside these enclaves in good housing. They passed in public situations but maintained socially stratified class contacts within close-by Buraku communities. The Buraku community had a great deal of social stability. A few families within each community owned land and rented out houses; their status was that of families whose wealth continued through several generations.

Most inhabitants were unskilled day laborers in construction or similar work—"lower-lower" in the system of Warner et al. (1963). A number worked for the city, often on a daily or temporary basis, doing street cleaning, garbage collecting, or (at the time we studied them) night-soil collecting. Some members of the community achieved Warner's "upper-lower class"—blue-collar status—within the community. Workers under the direction of a local *oyabun*, or boss, worked with leather for the shoemaking industry, a stigmatic sign that marked a traditionally degraded occupation in the community. This *oyabun* occupied a status somewhat below that of others generally acting as supervisors of ordinary daily laborers.

General stores within these communities sold fried tripe, a favorite Buraku snack, the taste of which is considered repugnant by other Japanese. Butcher shops within a Buraku community also sold raw tripe, hence their slang name, *iremon-ya* (literally, a "container"—i.e., "stomach"—shop). The owners of these shops were also upper-lower class, perhaps because the scorn of lowly merchants typical of Tokugawa Japan had persisted longer in Buraku society. The proprietors of other establishments—a barber shop, a public bathhouse, or a dry-cleaning store—were accorded somewhat higher prestige. There were a good number of women among those employed in small stores, and in some cases as factory workers. If the husband worked in a store or factory, generally the social status of the family seemed to be classifiable as upper-lower class. If, however, the father worked as a day laborer or casual construction worker and his wife or daughter worked as a factory hand, the family was considered by our informants to be in the lowest class position. This also was the case if the father or the household head was dead or an invalid.

Almost every member of some communities, including those who had moved out and were then more or less successfully passing, maintained strong religious affiliation with one or another Buddhist temple. Middle- and upper-status families sent their children to kindergartens outside the community.

Markers of Identity:
Distinct Customs within the Urban Buraku

FOOD. Eating meat was once exclusively a Buraku habit, disapproved of by other Japanese in accordance with Buddhism. Only since the end of the nineteenth century has it become general. Most butchers are still thought outcastes, and, except for increased consumption of liver and kidney among the young postwar generations, eating internal animal organs continues to be an abhorred Buraku characteristic.

DRESS. Within the Buraku community itself, dress is extremely informal and can be described as careless, however well-off the family. At the time of our study, one specific article of dress in one Kyoto Buraku was a special sandal, *setta zori*. This was a somewhat self-conscious tradition, and there are indications that the continued use of this form of *zori* evokes some feeling of belonging and self-enhancement.

SPEECH AND COMPORTMENT. Those familiar with the intricacies of local dialects agree that the Buraku have speech patterns of a more "informal" and "less refined" nature than the general society. There are distinctive definable characteristics in vocabulary and pronunciation. Patterns of speech, dress, and comportment shared by all individuals help maintain a strong sense of in-group social solidarity, though individuals of the wealthier families may also learn to behave in a style acceptable to the outer society.

Within the Buraku, given its small perimeter, it is very difficult for individuals with higher incomes to isolate their children from the rest of the community. Although children are sometimes sent to schools outside their community, the speech patterns and modes of behavior are generally shared, whatever the economic means of the family. Emotional alienation occurs in individuals deciding to pass. But if they desire, they can easily reassume language patterns and other gestures of communication spontaneously, since they have had ample firsthand experience growing up with peers in the community. They can "code switch" when necessary.

In-Group Solidarity

In order to live in the face of strong social discrimination and prejudice, the ordinary Burakumin has to rely heavily on the group. With the exception of government service, a man cannot easily take a job in the majority society unless he has the capacity to successfully pass, and few succeed in getting into the big firms. A considerable number of individuals living in Buraku communities are on some form of public relief, having little opportunity for self-support.

Those who work within the community depend upon their employer. Usually the relationship with the employer is a very paternalistic one, the traditional pattern of mutual obligation involving financial protection and income security. Occupations within the communities studied in Kobe and Kyoto were mainly in the leather industry, shoemaking, animal slaughtering, metal or rag picking, and the handling of corpses and burial of the dead. As long as an employee remains passively loyal and hardworking, he can enjoy a modicum of emotional and financial security. If, for instance, he or his family members get ill, the boss will protect him and help defray medical expenses.

Endogamy is still the rule. Only occasionally will an individual make a "love" marriage with a person of nonoutcaste background in the face of the difficulties engendered. As with relations between blacks and whites in the United States, differences in caste position prevent marriage, but not love affairs. A sense of family solidarity is coupled with a high rate of endogamy; everyone knows everyone else. Parents do not worry when a child does not show up at home for two or three days, as long as they are sure the child is within their community. There is usually a very well-built, large Buddhist temple in the middle of many Buraku communities, in impressive contrast to the shabby-looking houses in the vicinity. There is some indication that Burakumin, as a mark of solidarity, tend to maintain adherence to their Buddhist religion with a greater tenacity than is now noted generally in Japan.

Problems of Passing

Not physically different, only one's place of residence might identify outcastes with any degree of certainty. Many outcaste individuals succeed in passing, as far as external conditions are concerned. Nevertheless, the intrapsychic tensions and difficulties over self-identity make it impossible for most to continue their passing role.

Successful passing, therefore, requires moving and changing both one's place of registry and one's family register. Although now an illegal requirement, a copy of one's registry is still expected to be provided when applying for a job. The procedure to change is very complicated. Even when a change of residence is recorded, the previous address is recorded. Therefore, to be secure in not revealing Buraku residence, the family must make at least two changes of residence. But, by and large, they remain bound to bosses within the community by both psychological and economic ties, and since they have little direct social contact with outsiders, they are not continuously exposed to the feelings of rejection they are likely to face if they move in among majority Japanese. For some upper-class Buraku families, motivation for passing has not been compelling for other reasons. First, their sources of income and prestige lie within the community itself. Second, if they are particularly wealthy, they can afford to visit hot-spring resorts and be treated as ordinary guests in good hotels. In effect, they can pass when they wish in recreational activities. The pressure to pass is felt most strongly among the middle-class families who are sufficiently well-off to provide the education and financial support for their children necessary for them to become established as white-collar workers. The Japanese emphasize family interdependence. They are not socialized for independent individualism. Passers are therefore particularly prone to alienation and marginality.

It is especially on the issue of intermarriage that caste feelings toward the Burakumin remain strong. Neighbors may be friendly and sociable although suspicious of the Buraku origin of a family until the family seeks to establish marital liaisons in their new neighborhood. Then latent suspicions will come to the fore, and deliberate investigations might be made. A frequent solution is for a boy of a passing family to marry an eligible girl of another passing family. In the period before World War II, a good number of matches between American-born nisei were broken off when one family's register was found to record an old Buraku address in Japan. Even in the 1950s, a Japanese woman student at the University of Chicago was astonished to find that several nisei who took her out volunteered at the start of their acquaintance that they were not of Eta origin. I met a group of Japanese artists in Paris in the 1970s. One revealed to me that many of the older members were minority outcastes and that some others were Korean with Japanese names.

Socialization, Social Identity, and Burakumin Status

DIFFERENTIAL SOCIALIZATION WITHIN THE COMMUNITY. Interviews both within and outside the communities revealed that Burakumin are considered somewhat more impulsive and volatile than other Japanese and, related to that, hostile and aggressive to individuals from the outside society.[10] There is some evidence that in socialization practices, the Burakumin tend to be less restrained than other Japanese in expressing aggression toward their children. According to some informants, parents, especially fathers, do not hesitate to resort to physical punishment in handling children. Not only shouting loudly and wildly but also slapping and hitting on the head or cheeks are common expressions of disfavor when provoked. There is less hiding of sexual relationships in Burakumin households. Many Burakumin children have a shorter latency period than those in more restrained Japanese households; some do not have any latency period. In general, there seems to be less stringent impulse control demanded of either sexuality or aggression of the Buraku child. The adult relationships witnessed in childhood also illustrate that role-modeling adults do act impulsively and can give vent to their feelings when they are under the influence of strong emotions.

DIFFERENTIAL ROLE EXPECTATIONS IN SEX, PROPERTY, AND AGGRESSION. In certain Buraku communities, at least among their lower strata, there is considerable casualness about marriage ties and sexual fidelity. A husband who goes to a distant place to work for a year or two is likely to find another partner where he lives and works, and his wife may take another man if the opportunity occurs. In the majority society, such a situation would provide a good subject for gossip and criticism. The Burakumin consider it necessary for a Burakumin woman to have someone to rely on for income and training of children, as well as for her own pleasure, which is an acknowledged part of the relationship of the sexes. According to the opinion survey by a Japanese sociologist quoted by Cornell (1956), Burakumin think they have "inferior" sexual morals compared with people of the majority society. The stringent double standard of majority society does not apply in the Buraku. However, relative sexual freedom does not seem to imply general equality of status between man and wife. Women among the Burakumin, as in the traditional society, are required to be subservient and docile and to appear nonaggressive, at least toward their husbands. Husbands beat their wives, but wives are not supposed to hit back. Mothers are also less violent with their children than fathers are, but they are probably more violent than mothers of the majority society. Physical attacks between women are known to occur.

Self-Image as Part of Social Identity[11]

Informants shared memories of shame about self-discovery. One boy, as an art assignment at school, was asked to draw his father at work. He drew a picture of his father as a shoe cobbler. When he brought the picture home, his parents were very upset. They forbade him from ever again revealing his father's occupation to outsiders, but the boy was not told why. Living away from the Buraku, his parents had hoped the child would pass at school. From the serious reaction and the tone of his parent's voice, he could sense that he had done something seriously wrong, that there was something secret about his family that should be hidden from the eyes of others. This was his painful initiation into understanding that he was marked as a Burakumin. Once, when this same informant delivered shoes to a customer, the money was given to him tied to the end of a bamboo pole—an ancient way of avoiding the "unclean" by those needing the services of outcastes in Kyoto. This cruel reminder of his unclean status made him feel somehow very lonely and helpless.

Another painful memory included discovering his mother's deep capacity for violence. On a fearful occasion, she, normally a calm, gentle woman, wildly hit out at the wife of another shoemaker family that was also partially passing. Angered by something the boy had done, this woman had shouted "Eta!" and "Yotsu!" (four-legged beast) at him. The incident reminded the boy of fights he had seen between other women in the Buraku who pulled each other down into the street, rolling in the dirt. It forever destroyed his idealized picture of his mother and simultaneously undermined the self-identity he had tried to create of himself as a non–Buraku person. He then felt consciously that he could never escape his debased group.

CONSERVATIVE, PASSIVE, AND INTRAPUNITIVE ELEMENTS OF SELF-IMAGES. A very difficult aspect of minority status is a continual need to cope with a negative self-image, automatically internalized as a child becomes socialized within an enclave surrounded by a disparaging outer society. In *Japan's Invisible Race* (De Vos and Wagatsuma 1966), our most poignant case material was about the conscious as well as unconscious negative self-images that various informants showed to us. There are severe inner problems with developing a conscious negative self-image, but a developing negative self-image is not always conscious.

Some revealing materials have been gathered by a few Japanese social scientists concerning the Burakumin's group identity. For example, Koyama (1953) illustrated the mixture of active resentment against the majority society and a passive sense of personal inferiority in Burakumin attitudes. These attitudes reflect, though not completely passive helplessness, a great deal of intrapunitive thinking, such as "we should behave better; we should give up our slovenly behavior and keep our houses and domes clean; we should seek more education; we should cooperate with one another; we should move out of this dirty area; we should change our occupations to more decent and respectable ones," and the like.

Deviant Attitudes toward Authority in Educational, Legal, Medical, and Welfare Matters

The social role expectations of adult Burakumin do not induce as strong a conformist identification with prevailing authority as is found in middle-class Japanese. They are loathe to internalize the forms of responsibility more readily assumed by the majority. A basic means of expressing discontent with discrimination is through cooperative political action. Some of this behavior is expressively quite hostile; some is persistently instrumental. The more educated Burakumin find outlets for discontent through leftist political organizations that seek to change social attitudes through changing their society's pattern of political-legal sanctions. A basic defensive maneuver is to find methods of trickery to outwit authorities. By so doing, the minority-group member salvages some self-esteem and "gets back" at an authority structure that is perceived as operating to maintain degradation or to hinder freedom rather than to benefit the individual in any way. One may refuse to conform to expected patterns. Deviant attitudes become emblematic of a minority identity.

Selective Permeability and the Educational Experiences of the Burakumin

One striking parallel between the value systems of American and Japanese culture is the emphasis of both on occupational and educational achievement. Although minority members, whether African American or Burakumin, are well aware that they should seek personal training and education, they also know they will be faced with a highly problematical situation when applying for a job in the profession or skill for which they have received training (Ogbu 1974, 1978). Our study in Kobe reported the truancy rate among Buraku children to be as high as that reported for African American and Mexican American children in California.[12]

Dependency, Deviousness, and Apathy in Relation to Health and Welfare Authorities

Members of a minority group who have experienced a long tradition of discrimination commonly exhibit a combination of defensive hostility toward the dominant group and attitudes of economic dependency. This is evident in response to U.S. welfare policies to "help" Native Americans, or in the welfare policies set up to aid single-parent families, a large proportion of which are black.

Deviousness is a balm to the ego and allows the individual to maintain a shred of self-respect by not having one's dependent needs make one feel completely helpless. Individuals in the majority culture sometimes are angered when they discover some form of "relief cheating." It confirms their prejudice concerning the worthless nature of the individuals who are being helped by the efforts of the more humane elements within their community.

Burakumin have developed certain expectations that they are "due" economic assistance from the majority society. They deem it a right that goes with their minority status. We have cited graphic evidence of the prevalence of such attitudes among Burakumin as compared to their relative absence among ordinary Japanese (De Vos and Wagatsuma 1966; Wagatsuma and De Vos 1984).

Relative Indexes of Delinquency and Crime

Members of the Kobe family court, when interviewed, indicated that although the Burakumin are a small minority in Kobe City, they comprise a disproportionate number of cases of both family problems and delinquency coming before the court. There is also court evidence from Kobe, as well as in Kyoto, that Burakumin inspire fear in the rest of the population. A criminal career is one available for passing. *Yakuza*, the generic name now used for the organized underworld, draw into their ranks youth who can contribute talent to their organizations.[13] If a Buraku youth is successful in becoming a member of a criminal gang or *Yakuza* group, his outcaste background is discreetly forgotten.[14] Therefore, the Buraku youth may feel more readily accepted in this career activity than in attempting to face the more overt discrimination that occurs in other occupational pursuits. In the same manner, Buraku women who become entertainers, bar girls, or prostitutes find it an easy way to pass and remove themselves from the Buraku community.

Overt Recognition of Psychocultural Problems and Their Possible Amelioration

Personal individuation and maturation among the Burakumin is a more difficult challenge than among ordinary Japanese, for to become a mature adult, one must overcome any need to obtain ready acceptance from members of the majority culture. One must avoid a regressive acquiescence to a debased self-image while noting that others of one's group have incorporated such images of themselves, and yet they, too, must be accepted and loved with a shared feeling of belonging.

Today, the Japanese government, in its official policies at least, is eager not to discriminate among its citizens; it seeks to be more "universalistic" rather than "particularistic" in the field of human rights. It is now seeking to alleviate the position of the Burakumin by general welfare programs, providing relief for the unemployed and the destitute in the manner of other modern states.

The situations described in our 1966 volume (De Vos and Wagatsuma 1966) have not been much altered by educational programs and the improvements in public housing now put into the areas with the worst slums. Like numerous African Americans, many former Burakumin outcastes have been able, with great difficulties, to make noted contributions to their society and live felicitous lives. Nevertheless, a disproportionately large number of the Buraku minority do suffer psychologically, as do members of discriminated minority groups in other cultures.

Law enforcement officers seem to be, generally speaking, attempting to be more nondiscriminatory than in the past, but tensions and animosities persist. In the United States, African Americans today are still trying to overcome a general fear inspired by a continuing potential for violence on the part of the police toward them. The majority American public, aware of the greater amount of violence in the black community, fear that the internally inflicted black violence will spread beyond city ghettos into the more protected urban suburbs. To some degree, the situation in Japan is similar, in that now the general public is more in fear of the Burakumin than the Burakumin are in fear of the majority. Generally, the contemporary Burakumin themselves fear being demeaned rather than being physically attacked.

Modern Japanese society no longer supports either the economic base or the rationale underlying the caste system that prevailed during Tokugawa times. The rigid hereditary hierarchy has given place to a fluid industrial class and underclass structure in which occupational adaptation is subject to the marketplace, and social standing depends largely on occupational function. Lineage is less emphasized. There are no hereditary prescribed behavior patterns, deviation from which can make one an outcaste, and there are, in principle, no unclean occupations.

Yet, as with African Americans, where caste status developed out of the feudal plantation system of the South, remnants of former attitudes continue into the present. The question arises, therefore, as to what the functions are of a continuing caste attitude in Japan. The persistence of these attitudes could be ascribed to conservative beliefs concerning hierarchy and biological continuity in talent. But there are other functions of the outcastes that, once established, become a continuing part of the society, and one has to explore these as well. Elsewhere, I have discussed at length the expressive forms of social exploitation that are still in evidence.[15]

Implications for a Theory of Social Exploitation[16]

There are functional similarities in the treatment of Japanese outcastes and of African Americans, despite the fact that in Japan it is not phenotypic visibility that leads to racism. There is no physiological difference that singles out the Burakumin, or the Koreans, to be discussed below. For me, the bases for cross-cultural generalization about caste or racism are the psychocultural mechanisms involved.

Various visibly different physical characteristics may be suggested as necessary criteria for differentiation, but nonvisible features can be used with the same force to segregate a portion of the population of a society as essentially inferior, or, in religious terms, "impure." Particular language forms and modes of physical comportment or eating practices, just as much as physical differences, can come to be interpreted as genetically transmitted forms of "ugliness" if they differ from the standards aimed at by the majority. Equally among American minorities or Japanese Burakumin and Koreans, prejudice categorizes. Such attitudes overlook individual differences within any outcaste group and categorize the group as genetically inferior.

Most Japanese still believe that Burakumin are of an alien origin. In this sense, they remain an ethnic minority, despite their official citizenship. The caste concept is not consciously used in either the United States or Japan. We use race; Japanese use ethnicity in a pejorative sense. For me, it is generically an example of caste endogamy based on a concept of special hereditary inferiority.

It is obvious that purely economic explanations of caste are comparable to those of class in the Marxist system of thought. Such lack of distinction among the structural forms of minority status is inadequate. Human behavior has expressive as well as instrumental aspects, and every culture defines certain forms of expressive behavior as highly valued, whereas others are reprehensible and disavowed.

For caste differences, the disavowal is accompanied by abhorrence—the abhorrent activities having to do with oral, anal, and genital functions, all initiated as well as responded to with the human autonomic nervous system. It is these aspects, examined anthropologically and psychologically, that ensure the endogamy of caste groups and their hereditary perpetuation. These considerations find no explanation in Marxist theory. Just as the economic exploitation of blacks within a plantation economy is no full explanation of the attitudes toward them in modern America, so, too, we must look for deeper psychological feelings that maintain the untouchable status of the Burakumin. The outcaste, whether black, Burakumin, or witch, is in one sense a scapegoat. The kind of scapegoat he or she is depends on the particular kind of behavior the culture is most concerned with disavowing and attributing to others who are less virtuous, in short, what is "projected" out. Thus, as Dollard (1957) has shown in his now classic work, a predominant element in the southern white's stereotype of the "Negro" was his potent and primitive sexuality. Dirtiness and aggressiveness were also components.

Japanese stereotypes directed toward both Burakumin and Koreans contain the same basic components. In the case of the Burakumin, the relative emphasis on unacceptable sexuality and aggression found directed toward African Americans is reversed. Concern with the aggressiveness and crudeness of the Burakumin or Korean is more intense than worry about their sexuality. Although there is ample evidence that the sexual behavior of the Burakumin is "looser" than allowed in the majority society, it is their "unclean" habits with reference to language and manners, as well as their supposed tendencies to be inordinately violent and aggressive, that are emphasized. Within Japanese society, sexual experience is more tolerated if exercised at the right time and place, but there is a great need to disavow the appearance of direct aggression in everyday relations and to emphasize specific rules of propriety. In both cases, however, "purity" remains the prime cultural concern.[17]

There is no doubt that caste prejudice may involve feelings of economic competition. Nevertheless, the main psychological factors maintaining prejudice with any force in society are these deeply expressive intrapsychic conflicts over internalized social values[18] and expectations that are also projected outward. A thorough understanding of these psychological forces, as well as the society's cultural history and the economic functions of discrimination, is necessary if we are ever to understand the nature of continuing prejudice in modern society. What has been considered about the Burakumin situation also applies directly to the Koreans, a more recently acquired, overtly ethnic minority.

Japan's Colonial Heritage: The Case of the Koreans

The central political and social issues facing minority Koreans in Japan today are strongly influenced by the deeply subjective ethnic feelings developed between Japanese and Koreans long before the defeat of Japan in 1945. The political and legal difficulties resulting from the subsequent reestablishment of an independent Korean state cannot be settled without some necessary modernization of the concept of citizenship, as distinct from that of ethnic identity.

Both Japanese and Koreans have great difficulty arriving at such a distinction due to certain cultural-historical continuities in both countries. Ethnicity is a complex combination of both expressive and instrumental motivations that operate within any conflict-ridden, changing social structure. Former colonial people who live in the territory of the former colonizer face similar difficulties that are often compounded by persistent racist attitudes. They are prevented from merging into the general population. But many, as in the case of the Koreans, have strong motives for maintaining their ethnicity, even when they are tempted to pass.

Space will only allow a partial illustration of the categories I have used in my research to describe the interpersonal interactions involved in maintaining a defensively protective separate ethnic identity. Following are some attitudes about affiliation and belonging—and the personal sensitivities to social degradation that can occur in many of these situations—as they relate to Koreans in Japan. These issues are discussed more fully in Lee and De Vos (1981).

Affiliation versus Isolation

A sense of belonging can be expressed through one's identity with a group. It is a means of finding one's harmonious place in a spiritual entity larger than oneself. The need for affiliation, however, can also be directed more toward the satisfaction to be gained from intimacy and close contact between specific individuals, either in bonds of friendship or in heterosexual attachments. Being alone, isolated, or alienated is intolerable for most human beings. Marginality and apartness are sources of inner agony and tension. General ethnic-group membership may supply the forms of contact and affiliation necessary for day-to-day living. But some individuals may feel such a strong need for personal autonomy and independence that they find themselves capable of doing without sustained social contact.

For Koreans in Japan, as for Burakumin, resolving the need for affiliation is related to whether or not an individual chooses to pass, leaving one's own family and childhood friendships behind in seeking an individual route of social mobility in Japanese society. Individuals who seek to leave a group are subject to various forms of sanctioning. The principal threat, of course, is that of ostracism and rejection. A group that, in turn, feels rejected by a former member can even become physically destructive toward a perceived deserter or traitor. For some, the threat of isolation or of aggressive rejection can be a very heavy sanction that keeps them within the group.

For Koreans, a sense of intimacy is first fostered within a primary family strongly influenced by a Confucian tradition. I have noted elsewhere (De Vos 1992, 1993a) that Korean and Japanese families may provide a deep sense of psychological security without necessarily supplying intimate companionship to any of its members. Regardless of the priority given to direct companionate types of intimacy and contact, the majority Japanese family continues to afford other forms of warmth and a sense of dependent belonging for the individual.

With Koreans in Japan, however, the psychological-test material we have collected thus far emphasizes a very strong sense of alienation in many youth (De Vos and Kim 1993). In contrast with the more positive family concerns found in majority Japanese records, one may infer that many Korean families in Japan have suffered internal breakdown generationally, due to the chronic unemployment and degradation of family heads. In many instances, mothers have been forced to become the economic support of the family. This has undermined the dignity of the traditional male family role. Working mothers do not devote as much time at home as do traditional ones. As a consequence, children experience less expressive gratification, not only in intimacy but in harmony, self-respect, and affection.

Many Korean children seem to do relatively poorly in school for reasons similar to those found to operate in some American minorities, such as among African Americans or Mexican Americans (De Vos 1992). Individuals do not identify or internalize standards and expectations set for them by members of the external majority (De Vos 1993a). Instead, for some, a deviant peer group becomes the main source of affiliative gratification, discouraging acquiescence and conformity to the school as an institution. Such a peer group can also become the arena for demonstration of prowess and competence, the source of appreciative judgment from other youth (De Vos 1993a, chap. 7). Attitudes of protective association and antagonism toward the outside are sometimes perpetuated into adulthood.

Korean Japanese seem to seek out individual affiliations in marriage. Although their Confucian tradition emphasizes family role patterns rather than intimate companionship, today they seem less prone to concern themselves with family considerations. Among younger Koreans, just as among younger Japanese, there is a greater desire for closeness and intimacy in the marital bond. Indeed, romantic love today in some few instances transcends the social barriers set up between Koreans and Japanese. In some, but not all, instances, such marriages can compound problems of identity on the part of the Korean partner. He or she is faced with the necessity of affirming or denying Korean affiliations outside the marriage and at the same time of maintaining solidarity with his or her mate. There are numerous instances of difficulties arising in mixed marriages owing to external pressures of family or internal problems of divided loyalty. In turn, mixed marriages produce children with their own identity problems as *konketsuji* (mixed-blood children); they, too, must make decisions as to their principal allegiances and the principal groups from which they will seek out companions.

Appreciation versus Disparagement

Ultimately, perhaps, the issue of social acceptance and dignity is the main concern of any ethnic minority. The Japanese, themselves sensitive to appreciation or depreciation from outsiders, generally have been deprecatory and derogatory toward Koreans. They cannot accept different Korean customs; they cannot even accept Korean eating habits. The poverty to which Koreans have been historically subjected is used to classify them as inherently uncouth and uncivilized.

The Japanese cannot accept some aspects of the freer interpersonal expressions, both positive and aggressive, that Koreans manifest. Freer, less restrained behavior goes against the greater degree of self-constraint exercised by Japanese generally.[19] More rigid forms of self-constraint have been particularly apparent in Japanese society from the time of the annexation of Korea through the prewar militaristic period, and they have been maintained by many into the postwar era. It is difficult for any majority group to accord equal value to the behavioral patterns of others who may stimulate tension in themselves. Only a very open, self-possessed individual who arrives at his or her own behavior out of choice rather than out of severely internalized constraints can accept others who behave differently than they do.

As we shall presently discuss, the Japanese have great difficulty feeling comfortable in cultural settings other than their own. This discomfort is not limited to situations with Koreans alone but includes contacts with other peoples throughout eastern and southeastern Asia. The Japanese have been quick to disparage and derogate what is different from their own expectations. Their sense of uniqueness, their susceptibility to criticism, and their need for approval are the opposite sides of their readiness to disparage and disapprove of others. In short, Koreans have been vulnerable to scapegoating because their behavior is not thoroughly Japanese.

Their anomalous status within Japanese society continues. The deviant behavior of some is used by many Japanese as supportive evidence to maintain a massive deprecatory attitude toward all. One need not belabor the point that Koreans are deprecated not because they eat garlic or have a higher delinquency and crime rate, but because they are vulnerable objects for psychological projection and displacement. This brings up again the crucial problem that some members of a disparaged ethnic minority may be subject to self-hatred and self-disparagement (De Vos and Wagatsuma 1966). Lee and I garnered poignant evidence, similar to that given us by the Burakumin, from Koreans in several urban settlements (1981). No theoretical statements can better express these processes at work than the actual writings and comments Wagatsuma and I gathered from those who must deal with their own damaged self-esteem (1966).

Because of their Confucian traditions, Koreans and Japanese continue to revere their family lineages. A particular point at issue is that Japanese expect equally Confucian Koreans to give up their family names in order to gain better social acceptance in Japan. This expectation implies that being of Korean ancestry has less value than being of a Japanese family lineage. To change one's name is, to some degree, to accept this implication.

There is, at present, no consensus among Korean parents in Japan as to whether a child should use his or her Korean name in public.

Intermarriage occurs in any multiethnic state, raising questions of identity for the children of parents of different ethnic backgrounds. In a racist society where certain ethnic groups are considered inferior, marriages between members of the dominant and inferior groups are deemed contaminated, and the children of such liaisons are identified with their less acceptable minority heritage (De Vos 1967).

In situations of conflict, children faced with the need to choose between parental heritages will sometimes opt for the minority identity, seeking to protect the heritage of the demeaned parent out of a sense of honor and personal integrity. But in situations imputing nothing pejorative to either ancestry, a child will happily identify with a more complex heritage. When the school teaches the cultural history and language of both, the child acknowledges both ancestral backgrounds without conflict over the expediency of the integrity of being one or the other.

A relatively democratic Japanese state cannot long sustain the illusion of separate origin. Scientific archaeological inquiry in Japan is presently not being repressed. New findings increasingly reveal how their cultural heritage has been interwoven with that of Korea. Prehistorically, there is good evidence to suggest that the mythological imperial lineage might have been from the Korean peninsula. Later in the sixth century, it was Sinicized refugees from elite Paekche families, with their artisans and priests, not Chinese, who brought literacy, medicine, and architecture, as well as the Buddhist and Confucian religious heritages, to Japan. This elite intermarried with the local Japanese rulers. The later invasion of Korea by Japan in the sixteenth century brought in new neo-Confucian learning and ceramic traditions. The latter are still the pride of Japan, but current historians in Japan recognize their Korean origins.

Education, Legislation, and Ethnic Maintenance

By and large, Korean children growing up in Japan, even those sent to special Korean schools, are becoming culturally, if not socially, Japanese.[20] Korean language schools in Japan are steadily declining, despite the interest in ethnic education on the part of some Japanese as well as many ethnically Korean educators who want to bring about a more open cultural pluralism in Japanese society. Koreans in Japan are culturally Japanese.

However, *social* assimilation, without a denial or a problematic sense about one's ethnic background, can only take place when there is genuine respect accorded by the majority toward those of a different background. The present legally anomalous status of remaining "Korean" in Japan makes any assuagement of social disparagement a particularly difficult task (De Vos and Kim 1993). Some ameliorative measures are being attempted. In Osaka, for example, which contains a large Korean population, there is a public school program of after-school classes in Korean cultural traditions. A program of this sort stimulates some self-consciousness about being *ethnically* Korean, but it does not keep the children *culturally* Korean.

As is apparent in Japan as well as in the United States, it is often the peer group rather than the family that carries on a contrastive, defensive ethnic identity (De Vos 1992). Especially for the socially disparaged minority child, if home influence is relatively tenuous due to a lack of intrafamilial closeness, it is the peer group rather than a formal school program that has the strongest influence on how ethnic separateness is maintained. Some form of contrastive peer group ethnic maintenance occurs regardless of any complete loss of separate language or other cultural content supposedly integral to that identity. In fact, a separate idiom or intonation pattern may develop instead of a genuine language difference.

Thus, to the degree the peer group becomes the predominant reference group (De Vos 1978; De Vos and Wagatsuma 1966, 25ff), a social identity is produced more through peer group interaction both in and out of school than through effects of programs instituted by officials or families. Given these limitations of school influence on the social attitudes of students, I contend that it is the more important role of the school to see to the education of the majority in regard to ethnic diversity. There is a yet-to-be-completed task of demythologizing Japanese youth about their own supposed racial uniqueness.

If the past American experience of Japanese Americans teaches us anything, it is that family patterns and food habits may persist, but language and other specific features of a separate culture cannot be maintained in an enveloping dynamic society. The immigrant Japanese made notable efforts to preserve their separate cultural heritage in the United States. Some children, the so-called Kibei, were sent back to Japan. Special language and culture schools were set up. The nisei children who were sent to these schools by and large refused to learn Japanese. They identified themselves as Americans culturally but continued to associate with one another socially as Japanese Americans. The peer group had decided. For most, there remains some prideful identity with the Japanese past, but most live in the American present. The Japanese family survived despite prejudice and rejection by a racist majority.

Although the Japanese schools have instituted instructional programs to gain social acceptance for Korean students within their public schools, the problems inherent in defensively maintaining a minority identity cannot be so easily resolved by well-intentioned efforts on the part of some Japanese educators. For some Korean students, emphasis on immediate, practical, instrumental adaptation may sacrifice pride, the validity of being Korean, and one's sense of self-worth. Conversely, a too rigid insistence that being Korean resides in objective criteria, such as language proficiency or dress, may be impractical for Koreans who plan to continue to live in Japan. Furthermore, it represents acceptance of the adversary view of those Japanese who equate Japanese ethnicity with Japanese citizenship.

If Korean identity in Japan can be maintained only through attending a Korean language school, which handicaps the individual in the formal Japanese school system, then the individual becomes subject to continuous conflict, both external and internal. Conversely, if the Japanese school system derogates the assumption that it is legitimate and dignified to be Korean in ancestry, then the child perhaps has no alternative but to resist education at a cost to his or her sense of personal worth. The fact is that most children of Korean ancestry growing up in Japan will not speak Korean as their native tongue. They will speak Japanese.

Both Japan and the United States have a dynamic nature that absorbs youth, sometimes in ways not appreciated by older generations. To me, one fact is obvious; both Japanese and Koreans have to come to terms with the fact that most Korean residents will remain in Japan. They cannot remain as a marginal group without proper citizenship in a Japanese state that both legally and socially continues to confuse nationalism with ethnicity. Although most Koreans are physically indistinguishable from Japanese, they nevertheless continue to be considered racially distinct by Japanese. Whether they avow it openly, many Japanese still consider Koreans their biological inferiors.

Ethnic Identity and Continuing
Difficulties in External Relationships

As a final consideration of Japanese ethnicity, I wish to point out that there are features of Japan's cultural heritage that cause them continuing difficulty in establishing emotional bonding with outside others in reaching common goals. Japanese internally can develop their unique forms of economic and social organizational abilities. At the same time, a sense of belonging as Japanese inhibits or prevents any greater contribution to international social, economic, and political organizations.

But the future is always partially present in the past. Cultural beliefs in their own uniqueness persist despite conscious attempts of a people to alter their own institutions. This is true for all societies; Japan is no exception. There are features of Japanese cultural psychology and social organization that are maintained despite the modernized institutions that give them new content and new challenges for adaptation. Japanese continue to be socialized toward behavioral conformity, both in the intimate confines of the family and in the no-less-intimate groups that characterize schools and business concerns. Many of these learned patterns of group thought, emotional expression, and social perception are highly adaptive to situations of change in Japan. At the same time, in many, these patterns are sources of personal tension and difficulty in external relations. The Japanese sense of social belonging, especially in an international context, remains exclusionary.

Japan's industrial community is based on forms of hierarchy. Age-progressive social organizations demand a great deal of personal closeness in mentorship. These patterns have been well described elsewhere by James Abegglen (1958), Ronald Dore (1967), Masao Maruyama (1963), Chie Nakane (1970), Ezra Vogel (1975), and others. There are obvious competitive advantages to the resultant high per capita productivity and relatively high morale of Japanese commercial and industrial workers. The cultural heritage of a strong work ethic is far removed from the problems of animosity and low morale found in Great Britain, for example.

Japanese social organizations are often very close and intimate, depending heavily on informal implicit patterns. Contractual, impersonal understandings do not carry the same set of expectancies. In dealing with one another, Japanese organizations also depend heavily on personal obligations. In dealing with outsiders, Japanese feel less at ease with the formal contractual structures and impersonal attitudes developed in Western settings, both internally in dealings between labor and management and externally in dealing with one another. Individual outsiders coming into a Japanese setting, whatever their special talents may be or however much they are needed for the benefit of the organization, find it difficult to overcome this sense of remaining alien beings.[21]

As discussed above, there is still the social dilemma of Japan-born Koreans who technically remain foreigners although for four generations they have been born in Japan, have gone to Japanese schools, and know no language other than Japanese. They cannot easily belong to a society that discriminates against them legally and in the more subtle forms of discrimination they face day by day. In common with many discriminated groups in other countries, many become bitter and antisocial in conduct, a social liability not only because they lack productive potential, but because social inequality experienced from early youth breeds bitterness and malaise.

In a curious way, one might say Japan needs more expatriates—independent intellectuals and scholars who can make it more necessary for the European intellectual community to study contemporary Japanese art, technology, and social thought and to take into account the considerable Japanese contribution to the arts and sciences of the twentieth century. Realistically, the Japanese have to take on the task of conversing in other languages in international communication, but if the Japanese government were so inclined, it could provide the monetary means of enticing more Europeans to Japan to take on the task of learning Japanese and learning about Japanese culture and society firsthand. Japanese living abroad permanently can form social liaisons. They can be a means of opening up and broadening channels of communication. Here, one sees the dilemma of Japanese ethnicity.

Few Japanese feel they can remain comfortably Japanese when they are not surrounded and immersed within their own society. Cultural marginality is discomforting. Japanese, by cultural tradition, find a cosmopolitan career difficult and uncomfortable. There is often a vague sense of disloyalty and loss of responsibility if one lives abroad for too long.

One does note in the younger generation under thirty in Europe, the United States, and Japan a communality of outlook and experience that brings them more easily together. For Japanese students, though, internationalism may come at the expense of a loss of interest in the contribution of Japanese cultural traditions, which take considerable discipline to continue with any sense of high standards. Be that as it may, the price of communication, ironically, may be at times at the expense of having something unique to communicate. It is not at the student level that difficulties in communication are most noticeable, but on the part of those already established. Today's students, however, are tomorrow's leaders.

It is difficult for any successful assertive nation to develop a cultural perspective that accepts and embraces its own heritage without depreciating others in so doing. It is the first lesson, nevertheless, for those making international contacts—a lesson, alas, no better learned by many Americans than by many Japanese.

Notes

1. Space limitations do not allow more than a summary of the late Hiroshi Wagatsuma's original contentions from the previous edition about the cultural and physical identity of Japanese vis-à-vis Caucasoid Westerners. Here we are focusing on the continuing reluctance of the Japanese to deal with minority status problems. The unresolved issue to be examined is a continuing Japanese confusion of citizenship and ethnicity (De Vos and Mizushima 1967). This is unresolved to some degree in most modern states. When the word *I* is used in this chapter, it refers to De Vos.

2. At the turn of the century, Spencer was perhaps the sociologist best known internationally. Strongly influenced by Darwin, he advocated an evolutionary approach to human society.

3. In 1918, Japan sent its army to Siberia; in 1921, the liberal premier Hara was attacked by an assassin; in 1923, members of the Japanese Communist party were arrested in great numbers; in 1925, the notorious Law for Maintenance of the Public Peace (*chian iji ho*) was enacted; in 1928, the Special Secret Police (*tokubetsu koto keisatsu*) was instituted; in 1931, Japan sent its army to Manchuria; and in 1933, it seceded from the League of Nations.

4. Such characteristics as cited by Fukasaku have become anachronistic. By the 1990s, less than 7 percent of Japanese were engaged in agriculture, and, despite bitter opposition and desperate subsidies, a good percentage of rice is now imported, as are other agricultural products.

5. See the discussion of passing in chapter 1.

6. Excerpts were taken principally from De Vos and Wagatsuma (1966), chapter 9, 373–405. Other materials were taken from chapters 11, 13, 16, and 17.

7. I shall draw on the concept of ethnic identity and other related concepts defined in some detail in De Vos and Suarez-Orozco (1990), chapter 1.

8. These indexes are discussed in detail in Wagatsuma and De Vos (1984), chapter 10.

9. In this respect, the class distinctions operative in urban African American communities have parallels in the urban Buraku.

10. People too readily assume that the problems caused by social discrimination can be soon resolved if the majority society changes its attitudes and becomes more accepting of the discriminated individual. This overlooks the fact that there are often strong inducements in the socialization pattern of discriminated individuals that make the maintenance of their minority status important to them in their psychological integration, regardless of amelioration of outside attitudes toward them. Some of the reputation of the Burakumin for being aggressive seems to have a basis in fact. There is a relationship between aggressive behavior, out-group enmity, and patterns of socialization in the Buraku. Hatred of the outer society and hostility toward the majority society become part of the individual's total personality structure; they are not simply immediate angry reactions to prejudice and discrimination.

11. See a much fuller discussion of this material in De Vos and Wagatsuma (1966), passim.

12. The subsequent work of Ogbu (1974, 1978, especially 1978) has reaffirmed these contentions. See also De Vos (1992, chapter 7).

13. See an extensive discussion of the history of Japanese organized crime in De Vos and Mizushima (1967), 289–325.

14. Some police we interviewed claimed that close to 70 percent of the underworld is of Buraku or Korean origin.

15. See especially chapter 17 in De Vos and Wagatsuma (1966) and chapter 5 in De Vos and Suarez-Orozco (1990).

16. These issues are discussed at length in chapters 4 and 5 of De Vos and Suarez-Orozco (1990).

17. See the detailed discussion of this in De Vos and Suarez-Orozco (1990), chapter 5.

18. I discuss the particular culturally prevalent concerns of Japanese with purity and pollution in De Vos and Wagatsuma (1966), chapter 17. See also my more general discussion of pollution in respect to caste and race (De Vos 1967).

19. In an analogous manner, as indicated above, Japanese Brazilians are considered too loose in their comportment to be socially acceptable. They make ordinary Japanese uncomfortable (Takeyuki Tsuda, personal communication).

20. Specialists in ethnic relations (e.g., Gordon 1978) recognize this difference between cultural and social assimilation of ethnic minorities.

21. Japanese academic organizations find it difficult to meet the challenges of intellectual leadership. They remain internally oriented toward group inclusion rather than being competitively oriented as are American universities. Europe as a whole is slowly struggling toward greater exchange and mobility in its universities. There is, in effect, however, more worker mobility and business mobility than movement of intellectuals between nations. European universities are only beginning to realize the potential development of a true exchange of intellectuals by faculty appointments across national boundaries.

References

Abegglen, J. G. 1958. *The Japanese factory: Aspects of its social organization*. Glencoe, IL: Free Press.

Cayton, Horace, and Sinclaire Drake. 1962. *Black metropolis*. New York: Harper & Row.

Cornell, John. 1956. Matsunagi—a Japanese mountain community. *Occasional Papers*, no. 5. University of Michigan: Center for Japanese Studies.

De Vos, George A. 1967. Psychology of purity and pollution as related to social self-identity and caste. In *Caste and race: Comparative approaches*, ed. A. V. S. de Reuck and Julie Knight, 292–315. Ciba Foundation Symposium. London: J. and A. Churchhill.

————. 1978. Selective permeability and reference groups sanctioning: Psychocultural continuities in role degradation. In *Major social issues—a multi-community view*, ed. Milton Yinger, 9–24. New York: Free Press.

————. 1986. Japanese citizenship and Korean ethnic identity: Can they be reconciled? A psychocultural dilemma. *Seoul Law Journal* 27 (1): 75–100.

————. 1992. *Social cohesion and alienation: Minorities in the United States and Japan.* Boulder, CO: Westview Press.

————. 1993a. A cross cultural perspective: The Japanese family as a unit in moral socialization. In *Family, self, and society: Towards a new agenda for family research*, ed. P. Cowan, J. Field, D. Hansen, M. Scolnick, and G. Swanson, 115–42. Hillsdale, NJ: Erlbaum Associates.

————. 1993b. Problems with achievement, alienation, and authority in Korean minorities in the United States and Japan. In *Studies of Koreans Abroad*, ed. K. K. Lee, 137–94. Seoul: Society for the Study of Overseas Koreans.

De Vos, George A., and Eun-Young Kim. 1993. Koreans in Japan: Problems with achievement, alienation, and authority. In *California immigrants in world perspective*, ed. Ivan Light and Parminder Bhachu, 145–80. New Brunswick, NJ: Transaction Books.

De Vos, George A., and Keiichi Mizushima. 1967. Organization and social function of Japanese gangs. In *Aspects of social change in modern Japan*, ed. R. P. Dore, 289–325. Princeton, NJ: Princeton University Press.

De Vos, George A., and Marcelo Suarez-Orozco. 1990. *Status inequality: The self in culture.* Newberry Park, CA: Sage Publications.

De Vos, George A., and Hiroshi Wagatsuma. 1966. *Japan's invisible race.* Berkeley: University of California Press.

De Vos, George A., and William O. Wetherall. 1983. Japan's minorities: Burakumin, Koreans, Ainus and Okinawans. Updated by Kate Stearman. *Minority Rights Group*, report no. 3. London: Minority Rights Group.

Dollard, John. 1957. *Caste and class in a southern town.* New York: Doubleday.

Dore, R. P., ed. 1967. *Aspects of social change in modern Japan.* Princeton, NJ: Princeton University Press.

Erikson, Erik. 1959. Identity and the life cycle: Selected papers. *Psychological Issues* 1:1–171.

Fukasaku, Mitsusada. 1972. *Nippon Bunka oyobi Nipponjin Ron* [A study in Japanese culture and people]. Tokyo and Kyoto: San'itsu Shobo.

Gordon, M. 1978. *Human nature, class and ethnicity.* New York: Oxford University Press.

Jansen, Marius. 1965. Changing Japanese attitudes toward modernization. In *Changing Japanese attitudes toward modernization*, ed. Marius Jansen, 43–89. Princeton, NJ: Princeton University Press.

Kato, Shuichi. 1965. Japanese writers and modernization. In *Changing Japanese Attitudes toward Modernization*, ed. Marius Jansen, 245–445. Princeton, NJ: Princeton University Press.

Kawashima, Takeyoshi. 1948. *Nihon Shakai no hazoku-teki Kosei* [The familial structure of Japanese society]. Tokyo: Yuhikaku.

Kosaka, Masaaki, et al. 1938. Meiji Bunka Shi [Meiji cultural history]. In *Shiso Genron Hen* [A volume on thoughts and speech]. Tokyo: Yuzankaku.

Kosaka, Masataka. 1968. *Sekai Chizu no Naka de Kangaeru* [Thinking in the world map]. Tokyo: Shincho Sha.

Koyama, Takashi. 1953. Buraku ni okeru shakai kincho no seikaku [The nature of social tension in outcaste communities]. *Shakaiteki Kincho no Kenkyu* [Studies on social tensions], 395–410. Nihon Jinbun Kagakkai, Tokyo: Yuhikaku.

Kuwabara, Takeo. 1963. *Nippon Bunka no Kangae Kata* (The way to think about the Japanese culture]. Tokyo: Hakusui Sha.

Lee, Changsoo, and George A. De Vos. 1981. *Koreans in Japan: Ethnic conflict and accommodation*. Berkeley: University of California Press.

Maruyama, Masao. 1963. *Gendai Seiji no Shiso to Kodo* [Thoughts and behavior in contemporary politics]. Tokyo: Hakusuisha.

Minami, Hiroshi. 1949. *Nippon no Shinri* [Psychology of the Japanese]. Tokyo: Iwanami Shoten.

Miyagi, Otoya. 1950. *Kindaiteki Ningen* [Man of the modern age]. Tokyo: Kaneko Shobo.

———. 1956. *Atarashii Kankaku* [New tastes]. Tokyo: Kawade Shobo.

Nagai, Michio. 1965. *Nihon no Daigaku Sangyo Shakai ni Hatasu Yakuwari* [Japanese universities—their roles in an industrial society]. Tokyo: Chuo Koron Sha.

Nakane, Chie. 1970. *Japanese society*. London: Weidenfeld and Nicolson.

Ogbu, John. 1974. *The next generation*. New York: Academic Press.

———. 1978. *Minority education and caste: The American system in cross-cultural perspective*. New York: Academic Press.

Passin, Herbert. 1962. The source of protest in Japan. *The American Political Science Review* 54 (2): 91–403.

Pyle, Kenneth. 1969. *The new generation in Meiji Japan—problems of cultural identity 1885–1889*. Stanford: Stanford University Press.

Rosenthal, A. M. 1963. New Japan—future beckons to timorous giant in search of an identity. *New York Times*, June.

Ryoichi, Ishii. 1937. *Population pressure and economic life in Japan*. Chicago: University of Chicago Press.

Sabata, Toyoyuki. 1971. *Sekai no Naka no Nippon—Kokusaika Jidai no Kadai* [Japan in the world—her task in the era of internationalization]. Tokyo: Kenkyusha.

Takagi, Masataka. 1955. *Nihonjin—Sono Seikatsu to Bunka no Shinri* [The Japanese psychology of their life and culture]. Tokyo: Kawade Shobo.

Takahashi, Yoshio. 1883. *Nippon Jinshu Kaizyo Ron* [Proposal for physical improvement of the Japanese race]. Quoted in Ryoichi 1937, 38–39.

Tokutomi, Soho. 1885/1931. Shin Ninon no Seinen [Youth of new Japan]. Vol. 5 of *Gendai Nippon Bungaku Zenshu* [Contemporary Japanese literature]. Tokyo: Kaizosha.

Umezao, Tadao. 1959. Bunmei no Seitai Shi Kan Josetsu [An introduction to the ecological history of civilizations]. *Chuo Koran* [Tokyo, Monthly Journal], February.

Vogel, Ezra, ed. 1975. *Modern Japanese organization and decision making*. Berkeley: University of California Press.

Wagatsuma, Hiroshi. 1967. The social perception of skin color in Japan. *Daedalus*, Spring, 407–43.

———. 1969. Recent trends in social psychology in Japan. *American Behavioral Scientists* 12 (3): 36–45.

———. 1972. Mixed-blood children in Japan: An exploratory study. Paper prepared for the Conference on Ethnic Relations in Asian Countries, State University of New York, Buffalo, NY, October 20–21.

Wagatsuma, Hiroshi, and George A. De Vos. 1967. The outcaste tradition in modern Japan: A problem in social self-identity. In *Aspects of social change in modern Japan*, ed. R. P. Dore, 373–407. Princeton, NJ: Princeton University Press.

———. 1984. *Heritage of endurance: Family patterns and delinquency formation in urban Japan*. Berkeley: University of California Press.

Warner, W. Lloyd, et al. 1963. *Yankee city*. Chicago: University of Chicago Press.

Yazaki, Genkuro. 1964. *Nihon no Gairai Go* (Words of foreign origin in the Japanese language). Tokyo: Iwanami Shoten.

MIGRATION AND ETHNIC MINORITIES

II

INTERNATIONAL MIGRATION HAS BEEN RESPONSIBLE for the creation of many of the world's ethnic minority groups. Many advanced industrialized (as well as developing) countries have experienced significant influxes of foreign immigrants who have become targets of discrimination and socioeconomic marginalization because of their ethnic differences. Although many of these migrants were part of the majority society back home, when they cross national borders and settle in foreign countries, they become immigrant ethnic minorities that are racially and culturally different from the dominant populace. For instance, this is the case with the Arab Moroccans discussed in Philip Hermans's chapter, "Ethnic Identities of Moroccans in Belgium and the Netherlands," who are the dominant group in Morocco but become a Muslim immigrant minority in Europe. Likewise, Fabienne Doucet and Carola Suárez-Orozco's chapter, "Ethnic Identity and Schooling: The Experiences of Haitian Immigrant Youth in the United States," examines how Haitians (a vast majority of whom are of African descent) are treated as a black ethnic minority when they immigrate to the United States. Other immigrants were already ethnic minorities in their countries of origin and have simply become a different type of ethnic minority in the receiving country. For instance, Takeyuki Tsuda's chapter, "When Minorities Migrate: The Racialization of Japanese Brazilians in Brazil and Japan," deals with Japanese Brazilians, who are treated as a racially and culturally distinct "Japanese" minority in Brazil but become a culturally Brazilian ethnic minority when they "return" migrate to their ethnic homeland of Japan. Since migration to a foreign country entails such radical ethnic changes, immigrants are often forced to reconsider their ethnic identities when confronted by a completely different sociocultural and racial environment.

The manner in which immigrant minorities are received in the host society greatly affects their ethnic experiences and identity outcomes. In the United States, Haitian immigrants face an exclusionary environment in which they are not only socioeconomically marginalized but face considerable racism and discrimination as poor black immigrants who are stigmatized because of negative images of Haiti. In general, the greater the ethnic and socioeconomic marginalization that immigrants experience, the more likely they will adopt oppositional minority identities. However, even when the context of immigrant reception is more inclusionary (and even assimilationist), immigrants do not always develop a more accommodating identification with the majority host society. For instance, although Belgium and the Netherlands have attempted to incorporate ethnic minorities through multicultural policies that have granted them generous public services, political rights, and naturalization, Moroccan immigrants are still subject to strong ethnic prejudice as well as social and occupational marginalization and do not identify with majority Belgians and Dutch. In Japan, the context of reception for the Japanese Brazilians is assimilationist, based on essentialized ethnic assumptions that those of Japanese descent should be culturally Japanese. Nonetheless, the Japanese Brazilians are still ethnically and socioeconomically excluded as culturally Brazilian, unskilled immigrant workers, causing many to assert an oppositional Brazilian counteridentity in Japan (see Tsuda 2003, chap. 3).

As Doucet and Suárez-Orozco and other contributors to this book note, ethnic identities are defined in relation to significant others in contexts of power. Therefore, the identity experiences of immigrant minorities are also influenced by the racial categories and identities that are imposed on them by the dominant host society. Frequently, these externally ascribed ethnic identities are different from and conflict with their own ethnic understandings that they bring from their home country. For instance, although Haitians did not use race as a means of social differentiation back home (social-class differences were much more prominent), they are homogeneously racialized as "blacks" in the United States and even grouped together with African Americans. Internal social-class divisions between earlier elite, French-speaking Haitian immigrants and more-recent lower-class Haitian immigrants are not recognized by mainstream Americans. In other cases, the ethnoracial categories that the dominant host society ascribes to immigrants are the same as those used in their home countries, but the cultural meanings attached to these categories in the host society are very different. As Hermans notes, an Arab Moroccan identity that may have been a source of prestige and pride in Morocco is associated in Europe with Islamic fundamentalism, terrorism, illegal immigration, drug trafficking, and female oppression (again, Europeans do not differentiate between Arab and Berber Moroccan immigrants). In the case of the Japanese Brazilians, they are racialized as "Japanese" in both Brazil and Japan, but the cultural standards for being Japanese in Japan are much higher than in Brazil.

The impact of such dominant ethnic perceptions on immigrant identities can be quite negative when they are derogatory and racist, as is the case with the Haitians and Moroccans, making it difficult for immigrants to maintain ethnic self-esteem. In general, first-generation immigrants are more resilient to such majority ethnic prejudice and discrimination, since their point of reference continues to remain their country of origin and their compatriots. For instance, when racialized and denigrated as "blacks" in the United States, many of the earlier elite Haitian immigrants distanced themselves from African Americans by taking pride in their Haitian national identities and their backgrounds as French speakers. Even after living in Europe for decades, most of the Moroccan immigrants in Hermans's chapter retain a strong national loyalty to Morocco, value their Muslim heritage, and are quite critical of Belgium or Dutch society, therefore preferring to remain culturally unassimilated and socially segregated.

In contrast, a discriminatory racial context has a much more powerful effect on second-generation immigrant descendants, who are no longer oriented toward their parents' homeland and are more likely to internalize the negative ethnic identities imposed upon them because of their greater interaction with majority society (and peer groups). A number of the Haitian youth studied by Doucet and Suárez-Orozco have come to view dominant society and its institutions as racist and oppressive and have developed defensive, adversarial minority identities in opposition to majority society. Others have attempted to avoid the shame and derogation associated with being Haitians by hiding their ethnic background and assimilating to majority white society or even identifying with African Americans ("ethnic flight"). Only a relative few seem to adopt a "transcultural" identity based on a balanced dual affiliation with both minority and majority cultures. Although racism and prejudice toward Moroccans in Europe may not be as intense (Hermans reports that most lead satisfying lives), some members of the second generation that Hermans profiles continue to identify as Moroccans or Arabs and have a negative opinion of aspects of Belgium or Dutch society (including its racism), although not necessarily in a defensive or adversarial manner. However, a notable number of second-generation individuals seem to be developing a more accommodative bicultural identification in which their identities as Moroccans and Muslims are accompanied by an acknowledgement of their majority identities and a willingness to assimilate to mainstream society. There seems to be less evidence of ethnic flight where cultural assimilation is based on a wish to distance themselves from a negatively perceived Moroccan culture and immigrant community.

Even when the ethnoracial categories and identities through which immigrants are understood are not derogatory, they may still reject such majority ethnic perceptions and respond in an oppositional manner. Because of their presumed ethnic affinity with the Japanese, Japanese Brazilian immigrants in Japan do not confront overt discrimination. However, because they are racialized as "Japanese" because of their descent, they come under considerable assimilationist cultural pressure. Although some Japanese Brazilians with bicultural abilities adopt a "Japanese" (or transcultural) identity and conform to Japanese cultural standards (see Tsuda 2003, chap. 6), a majority of them resist such ethnic demands by asserting a Brazilian nationalist identity in order to ethnically differentiate themselves from the Japanese.

The ethnic identity of second-generation immigrant minorities is not merely a matter of inner self-consciousness but also has significant implications for their future socioeconomic success and integration in majority society. As Doucet and Suárez-Orozco make clear in the case of the Haitians, the adoption of adversarial minority identities among immigrant youth in response to majority discrimination can be quite detrimental to school performance. Since such ethnic identities involve a rejection of dominant institutions, academic achievement in accordance with majority cultural standards is often equated with ethnic betrayal and "acting white," which becomes a powerful sanction among youth peer groups against school success. Although some youth constructively harness their adversarial resistance against majority society into achievement-oriented behavior in order to defy and overcome its discriminatory barriers, many fall into despair and self-doubt or channel their sense of injustice and anger into criminal and gang activity. In contrast, those youth who wish to avoid majority discrimination by distancing themselves from their disparaged minority peers and identifying with majority cultural norms may enjoy school success and self-advancement, but at the expense of ostracism and alienation from their own ethnic group. This is one reason why few second-generation Moroccans attempt to pass as Belgians or Dutch; the instrumental benefits of such an identification (better majority acceptance and socioeconomic mobility) are clearly outweighed by the expressive need to maintain family and ethnic attachments and a sense of belonging.

A similar pattern can already be observed among first-generation Japanese Brazilians in Japan (see Tsuda 2003, chaps. 5–6). Those that resist Japanese cultural pressures in Japan by asserting their Brazilian counteridentities face greater ethnic prejudice and stigma from the Japanese, reinforcing their ethnic and socioeconomic marginalization in Japan. In contrast, the more assimilation-oriented Japanese Brazilians are more socially accepted by the Japanese and have access to higher-level jobs, but at the expense of having their ethnic loyalty questioned by their immigrant peers. According to Doucet and Suárez-Orozco, second-generation youth who develop a transcultural identification with both the immigrant minority and the majority cultures are the most socially adaptable, enabling them to assimilate to the dominant culture while maintaining their attachment to the culture of their immigrant parents. Such bicultural competence enables them to become academically and socioeconomically successful in mainstream society without threatening their sense of ethnic self or denying their immigrant heritage. Many times, such individuals are able to conform to mainstream cultural norms and language in public while maintaining their immigrant language and customs in the privacy of their homes or ethnic communities.

It is quite evident that many factors influence the eventual academic and socioeconomic success of immigrant minority youth, including their migration histories (voluntary or involuntary), their parents' legal status and educational levels, the amount of poverty and discrimination they confront, and the level of community and family support they enjoy. However, there is no doubt that the different types of ethnic identities immigrants adopt in response to varying contexts of immigrant reception have a significant impact on whether they will remain a socioeconomically excluded and ethnically disparaged minority or will eventually be incorporated as members of mainstream society.

Takeyuki Tsuda

Reference

Tsuda, Takeyuki. 2003. *Strangers in the ethnic homeland: Japanese Brazilian return migration in transnational perspective.* New York: Columbia University Press.

Ethnic Identity and Schooling: The Experiences of Haitian Immigrant Youth

5

FABIENNE DOUCET AND CAROLA SUÁREZ-OROZCO

L ARGE-SCALE IMMIGRATION, A PHENOMENON THAT is actively blurring and challenging our constructions of nation, state, and identity, is a global event. Estimates suggest that around the world today there are more than 130 million immigrants and refugees. Societies worldwide are being transformed in remarkable ways as a result of these unprecedented changes in the world population, and even the United States, with its long-running history of immigration, is being stretched in new ways (M. M. Suárez-Orozco 2001). In contrast to the first large wave of immigration (roughly between 1880 and 1930), during which 80 to 90 percent of immigrants to the United States were Western European, post-1965 immigration has been marked by an increase in immigration from Latin America, Asia, the Caribbean, and Africa, with a decrease in Western European immigration. Thus, although in the middle of the twentieth century less than 15 percent of our population was considered to be "ethnically marked minorities," currently more than 25 percent of the population is so classified. Demographers have projected that by the middle of this century, approximately half of our population will be "minority"—a term that obviously will need rethinking (C. Suárez-Orozco 2000).

Immigrant children are the fastest-growing sector of the child population (Schmidley 2001) and thus represent a vitally important subpopulation of immigrants. Today, one in five children in the United States is the child of immigrants, and by 2040, one in three children will fit this description (Rong and Preissle 1998). These dramatic shifts are having a profound impact on U.S. schools faced with the opportunity and the challenge of bringing these children to their full potential (C. Suárez-Orozco 2000).

Typically schools are the first setting of sustained contact with a new culture for immigrant children, and academic outcomes are a powerful barometer of current as well as future psychosocial functioning. How immigrant children fare in our schools will, in many cases, forecast their contributions as citizens to our society. While this has long been true, schooling is a particularly high-stakes process in the new economy (M. M. Suárez-Orozco and Gardner 2003).

In this chapter, we examine ethnic identity within the context of schooling, focusing specifically on the experiences of Haitian youth. The Haitian immigrant population in the United States has been estimated conservatively at 500,000 and growing (Frérère 1999), and others suggest that the combined population of documented and undocumented Haitian immigrants in the United States is closer to 1 million (Zéphir 2004). Yet there is a dearth of empirical knowledge regarding this group.

Haitians represent an interesting case on multiple levels. Flore Zéphir (2001) aptly demonstrates how race, ethnicity, class, and immigration together have created a daunting set of obstacles for Haitian youth as they try to assimilate into American society. From a conceptual standpoint, black immigrant groups in general have added important complications to our existing understanding of "assimilation" (Glick-Schiller and Fouron 1990; Laguerre 1984, 1998; Portes and Rumbaut 2001; Portes and Stepick 1993; Portes and Zhou 1993; Rumbaut and Portes 2001; Waters 1990, 1996a, 1996b, 1999). In the United States, where skin color is the most powerful characteristic for social stratification and discrimination (Appiah and Gutman 1998; Glick-Schiller and Fouron 1990; Omni and Winant 1986), black immigrants face particular obstacles as they attempt to become integrated into U.S. society, most notably racism. But there is important diversity within this immigrant category. Among black immigrants, Haitians in particular consistently have been stigmatized and discriminated against by the U.S. government (Glick-Schiller and Fouron 1990). Haitians also are represented disproportionately among the working-class and the poor in the United States, and Zéphir (2001) clearly articulates the impact of socioeconomic status on the development of ethnic identity.

The history of the migration of Haitians to the United States serves as an important backdrop to the story of how Haitians craft identities around class and skin color, though the concept of "race" as it is understood in the United States is foreign to the way they construct the social structure. Haitians have emigrated from Haiti since the colonial era, when the children of enslaved African women and male French colonists were sent to France to be educated (Zéphir 1995). In the twentieth century, Haitian migration has been generally characterized as marked by two major waves. The first wave, triggered by the dictatorial presidency of François Duvalier, began in the 1950s and represented the mass exodus of upper-class, professional, and educated individuals and families to the United States, Europe, Canada, and Africa (Glick-Schiller and Fouron 1990; Mintz 1974; Stepick and Portes 1986). These families established themselves in their new countries of origin, and many were able to find employment in the occupational sectors for which they were educated or trained (Buchanan 1983; Woldemikael 1989). In the United Sates, these families settled primarily in New York and Boston, with a smaller group opting for the Chicago area.

The late 1970s and early 1980s marked the beginning of the second wave. The more recent émigrés were more impoverished than their counterparts who migrated during the first wave (Stepick and Portes 1986). Political upheavals in Haiti in the mid-1980s engendered conditions of traumatic experiences and interrupted schooling for children (Desir 2004), and conditions for living in Haiti became unbearable for many impoverished families who saw the United States as a land of opportunity. The arrival of these new Haitians of lower social status was disturbing to many of the "old" immigrant families who perceived this new group as more vulgar and less educated, and as painting a negative image of Haitians in the eyes of Americans (Buchanan 1983).

In the following examination of ethnic identity in the context of schooling, we will first discuss conceptual and theoretical constructs that help us to understand the complex set of factors implicated in the development of ethnic identity. We then focus on how these constructs have informed our research examining the academic trajectories and outcomes of immigrant youth. Finally, we detail a typology of ethnic-identity styles (C. Suárez-Orozco and M. M. Suárez-Orozco 2001) that helps provide insight into the choices that immigrant youth make regarding academic engagement.

Throughout the chapter, we draw from research we conducted under the umbrella of the Harvard Immigration Projects. The primary study of the projects was the Longitudinal Immigrant Student Adaptation (LISA) study, a five-year investigation of the experiences of newly arrived (1.5 generation) immigrant Central American, Chinese, Dominican, Haitian, and Mexican youth, directed by Carola and Marcelo Suárez-Orozco. Data were collected with a sample of approximately 400 youth in Boston and in the San Francisco Bay Area from 1997 to 2002 (C. Suárez-Orozco and M. M. Suárez-Orozco 2001). From 2000 to 2002, Doucet conducted a parallel study of U.S.-born (second generation) Haitian immigrant youth called Communicating Values across Generations of Haitian Immigrants. Mirroring the methods of the LISA study, Doucet collected interview data with youth, their parents, and their teachers and conducted participant observations in several Boston middle and high schools.

Contributors to Identity Formation

Generational Status

Country of birth, length of residence in the host country, and age at migration are additional dimensions to be considered in examining the adaptation of immigrant groups to a new context. As Carola Suárez-Orozco (2004) has argued, the challenges faced by the first generation—that is, immigrants who come as adults—are considerably different from those of the second generation. The first generation is concerned primarily with surviving and adjusting to the new context. They may go through a variety of normative adverse reactions following the multiple losses of migration, including anxiety and depression. However, the first generation is protected by several factors. The dual frame of reference by which immigrants can compare their current situation with that left behind allows them to often feel relatively advantaged in the new context (C. Suárez-Orozco and M. M. Suárez-Orozco 1995). Optimism is at the very heart of the immigrant experience; the possibility of a better tomorrow acts as both a tremendous motivator as well as a form of inoculation against encountered frustrations and barriers. Further, first-generation immigrants often are energized by the desire to support loved ones—by sending remittances home to those left behind—as well as by the desire to build the best possible life for their children. While it is not an easy road, it is one with a clear path of identity. Immigrants who come in adulthood maintain a sense of identity rooted deeply in the birthplace. Many expatriates are, of course, quite comfortable in their new homeland. However, they may retain outsider status as the cultural and linguistic hurdles are simply too high to be surmounted within one generation (C. Suárez-Orozco and M. M. Suárez-Orozco 2001). The path for their children—the second generation—is less singular, offering a variety of forks to be taken. For these youth, forging a sense of identity may be their single greatest challenge (Erikson 1968; C. Suárez-Orozco 2004). For Haitian youth, this identity often is crafted under tenuous circumstances. Not only must they contend with ethnic discrimination, but they must also learn the meaning of race in this country.

There is no curriculum for this learning; these youth must glean their information from interactions with members of the majority group, from the ways in which their status as "bilingual" students is framed, from their parents (who may themselves struggle to understand it), and of course from their peers.

The Ethos of Reception

The general social climate, or ethos, of reception plays a critical role in the adaptation of immigrants and their children (C. Suárez-Orozco and M. M. Suárez-Orozco 2001). Unfortunately, intolerance for newcomers is an all-too-common response all over the world. Discrimination against immigrants of color is particularly widespread and intense in many settings receiving large numbers of new immigrants; this is true in Europe (M. M. Suárez-Orozco 1996), the United States (Espenshade and Belanger 1998), and Japan (Tsuda 2003). As today's immigrants are more diverse than ever in terms of ethnicity, skin color, and religion, they are particularly subject to the pervasive social trauma of prejudice and social exclusion (Rubin 1994; Tatum 1997).

The exclusion can take a structural form (when individuals are excluded from the opportunity structure) as well as an "attitudinal" form (in the form of disparagement and public hostility). These structural barriers and the social ethos of intolerance and racism encountered by many immigrants of color intensify the stresses of immigration. Although the structural exclusion suffered by immigrants and their children is tangibly detrimental to their ability to participate in the opportunity structure, prejudicial attitudes and psychological violence also play a toxic role. Philosopher Charles Taylor argues that "our identity is partly shaped by recognition or its absence, often by the misrecognition of others, and so a person or group of people can suffer real damage, real distortion, if the people or society around them mirror back to them a confining or demeaning or contemptible picture of themselves" (Taylor 1994, 25).

Waters asserts that in this "race conscious society a person becomes defined racially and identity is imposed upon them by outsiders" (Waters 1999, 6). She reports that her black West Indian immigrant informants are shocked by the level of racism against blacks in the United States. Though they arrive expecting structural obstacles (such as discrimination in housing and promotions), what they find most distressing is the level of both overt and covert prejudice and discrimination they experience in everyday interpersonal interactions. Although black immigrants tend to bring with them a number of characteristics that contribute to their relative success in the new setting, for their children, "over the course of one generation the structural realities of American race relations and the American economy undermine the cultures of the West Indian immigrants and create responses among the immigrants, and especially their children, that resemble the cultural responses of African Americans to long histories of exclusion and discrimination" (Waters 1999, 6).

While cross-sectional data have been used to identify this transgenerational pattern, preliminary data from our longitudinal study suggest that among many immigrant youth of color, this process is unfolding at a rapid pace within a few years of migration. In contrast to the white immigrants from Europe in the early 1920s who struggled to transcend social-class boundaries, new immigrants often have to contend with prejudice due to both color and class (Rumbaut 1994). This is a relatively new experience for Haitians, whose social structure is built primarily around class, with skin color playing only a secondary (though arguably important) role in relation to position in the social hierarchy (Zéphir 1996; Doucet, forthcoming).

The Social Mirror

Child psychoanalyst D. W. Winicott suggests that the child's sense of self is profoundly shaped by the reflections mirrored back to her by significant others (Winicott 1971). Indeed, for identity development, all human beings are dependent upon the reflection of themselves mirrored by others. "Others" include not just the mother (which was Winicott's principal concern), but also relatives, adult caretakers, siblings, teachers, peers, employers, people on the street, and even the media (C. Suárez-Orozco 2000). When the reflected image is generally positive, the individual (adult or child) will be able to feel that she is worthwhile and competent. When the reflection is generally negative, it is extremely difficult to maintain a coherent sense of self-worth.

These reflections can be accurate or inaccurate. In some cases, the reflection can be a positive distortion. In such a situation, the response to the individual may be out of proportion to his actual contribution or achievements. In the most benign case, positive expectations can be an asset. In the classic "Pygmalion in the Classroom" study, when teachers believed that certain children were brighter than others (based on the experimenter randomly assigning some children that designation, unsubstantiated in fact) they treated the children more positively and assigned them higher grades (Rosenthal and Feldman 1991). It is possible that some immigrant students,

such as Asians, benefit somewhat from positive expectations of their competence as a result of being members of a "model minority"—though no
doubt at a cost (Lee 1994; Louie 2004; Takaki 1993).

It is the negative distortions, however, that are most concerning. While
all groups face structural obstacles, not all groups elicit and experience the
same attitudes from a dominant culture. Some immigrant groups elicit more
negative attitudes—thus encountering a more negative social mirror—than
others do. Such is the case with many immigrant and minority children
(Maira 2004). Iraqi American Nuar Alsadir, for example, shortly after September 11, eloquently stated, "The world shouldn't be a funhouse in which
we're forced to stand before the distorting mirror, begging for our lives"
(Alsadir 2002). The legacy of racism in the United States is such that the
immigrant children most likely to encounter these vitriolic messages are
black and brown children, whether from the Caribbean and Latin America,
the Middle East, or Africa. For Haitian children, the issue of race is compounded with ethnic discrimination; Haitians are known as AIDS carriers,
boat people, and the poorest people of the Western Hemisphere (Zéphir
2001). In *Haiti's Bad Press* (1992), Robert Lawless argues that since the
eighteenth century, the characteristics of Haitian people, culture, and religion have been painted as dangerous and frightening, creating a historical
record in the public imagination of Haiti and Haitians as problematic and
undesirable.

Facing such charged attitudes that assault and undermine their sense of
self, minority children may come to experience the institutions of the
dominant society—and most specifically its schools—as alien terrain reproducing an order of inequality (De Vos and M. M. Suárez-Orozco 1990).
W. E. B. DuBois famously articulated the challenge of what he termed
"double-consciousness"—a "sense of always looking at one's self through
the eyes of others, of measuring one's soul by the tape of a world that looks
on in amused contempt and pity" (DuBois 1903/1989, 3). When the expectations are of sloth, irresponsibility, low intelligence, and even danger,
the outcome can be toxic. When these reflections are received in a number of mirrors, including the media, the classroom, and the street, the outcome is devastating (Adams 1990).

Our research suggests that immigrant children are keenly aware of the
prevailing ethos of hostility in the dominant culture (C. Suárez-Orozco
2000). We asked our sample of 400 children to complete the sentence "Most
Americans think that [Chinese, Dominicans, Central Americans, Haitians,
Mexicans—depending on the child's country of origin] are . . . ." Dis-
turbingly, fully 65 percent of the respondents provided a negative response

to the sentence-completion task. The modal response was the word "bad"; others, even more disconcerting, included "stupid," "useless," "garbage," "gang members," "lazy," and "we don't exist."

Social Disparagement and Academic Outcomes

Schools represent one site where all children receive messages from the broader society about who they are. Children of color in particular are subject to negative expectations that have profound implications for their academic performance (Weinstein 2002). Cross-cultural data focused on a variety of disparaged minorities in a number of contexts all over the world suggest that exposure to a negative social mirror adversely affects academic engagement. Furthermore, anthropological cross-cultural evidence from a variety of different regions suggests that the social context and ethos of reception play an important role in immigrant adaptation. Ogbu (1978) has argued that minorities who were originally incorporated against their will through slavery and conquest are more likely to give up on educational avenues as a route to social mobility than are those of immigrant origin who enter a new society voluntarily. De Vos and Suárez-Orozco (1990) have demonstrated that the cultural and symbolic ethos of reception saturated with psychological disparagement and racist stereotypes has profound implications for identity formation of minority and immigrant children as well as for their schooling experiences.

For groups in places where racial and ethnic inequalities are highly structured, such as for Algerians in France, Koreans in Japan, or Haitians in Miami, "psychological disparagement" and "symbolic violence" may permeate the experience of many minority youth. Members of these groups are not only effectively locked out of the opportunity structure (through segregated and inferior schools and by work opportunities in the least desirable sectors of the economy), but they also commonly become the objects of cultural violence. Stereotypes about immigrants—they are inferior, they steal work from natives, and they pose a threat to public safety—justify the sense that they are less deserving of partaking in the dominant society's opportunity structure.

In past generations, assimilationist trajectories demonstrated a correlation between length of residence in the United States and better schooling, health, and income outcomes (Gordon 1964; M. M. Suárez-Orozco and Paez 2002). While assimilation was a goal and a possibility for immigrants of European origin, resulting in a generally upwardly mobile journey (Child 1943; Higham 1975), this alternative is more challenging for the new immigrants of color. Further, increasing "segmentation" in the American economy and society is shaping new patterns of immigrant adaptation (Gans 1992; Portes and Rumbaut 2001; Rumbaut 1997; Waters 1999; Zhou 1997).

Certainly, a preponderance of evidence suggests that structural factors such as neighborhood segregation and poverty (Massey and Denton 1993; Orfield and Yun 1999), as well as family-level factors (including parental education and general socioeconomic status), are significant predictors of long-term educational outcomes for children (Coleman et al. 1966). In a society powerfully structured by "the color line" (DuBois 1903/1989), however, race and color are significant vectors for understanding the adaptations of immigrant youth of color.

Stanford University social psychologist Claude Steele has been at the forefront of new theoretical and empirical work on how "identity threats," based on group membership, can profoundly shape academic achievement. In a series of ingenious experimental studies, Steele and his colleagues have demonstrated that under the stress of a stereotype threat, performance goes down on a variety of academic tasks. For example, when high-achieving African American university students were told before taking an exam that the test had proven to differentiate between blacks and whites (in favor of whites), their performance was significantly worse than when they were not told that the test they were about to take differentiated between groups (Steele 1997). Steele maintains that when negative stereotypes about one's group prevail, "members of these groups can fear being reduced to the stereotype" (Steele 1997, 614). He notes that in these situations, self-handicapping goes up. This "threat in the air" has both an immediate effect on the specific situation that evokes the stereotype threat and a cumulative erosive effect when continual events that evoke the threat occur. He argues that stereotype threat shapes both intellectual performance and intellectual identity.

How are identity and agency implicated in educational processes and outcomes? John Ogbu and his colleagues have done seminal work in the area of immigration, minority status, and schooling in plural societies (Matute-Bianchi 1991; Ogbu 1978, 1987a, 1987b). Inspired by the work of George De Vos's comparative studies of social stratification and status inequality (De Vos 1973; De Vos and M. M. Suárez-Orozco 1990), Ogbu argued that parental and other socioeconomic factors explain only part of the variance; when these factors are controlled for, differences become evident. Immigrants tend to develop cultural models and social practices that seem to serve them well in terms of educational adaptations and outcomes. Ogbu distinguished between the experiences of immigrant (voluntary) versus nonimmigrant (involuntary) minorities. He posited that involuntary minorities are in a castelike position and have been "incorporated into a society more or less involuntarily and permanently through slavery, conquest, and colonization" (1987a, 258–59). This description can be applied to African Americans.

According to Ogbu, dominant-group members place castelike minorities in positions of denigration and rationalize themselves into thinking that these minorities are biologically and/or socially inferior. The response of castelike minorities to such classification is to reject this denigrated status and to develop their own explanations for caste status. One manifestation of such responses is the development of collective identities and cultural systems that are oppositional to the dominant group's cultural system. In the school setting, black Americans may adopt a stance of cultural inversion whereby being a good student and a high achiever is defined as inappropriate for them because it is characteristic of white Americans (Ogbu 1987a, 1987b).

In contrast, among immigrant (or voluntary) minorities, academic achievement and adoption of the cultural values for success typical of the dominant group are not perceived as giving up any part of one's identity (Ogbu 1987a, 1987b). Immigrants may even be more willing to suffer discrimination and prejudice because they perceive these as a natural reaction to outsiders (Gibson 1988). Unlike involuntary minorities, immigrants perceive school success as necessary to obtain good jobs and wages (Gibson 1988). Rather than adopting a cultural frame of reference that is *oppositional* to the dominant group, immigrants' frame of reference is simply *different* from that of the dominant group. School and school success are not perceived as the property of whites, and conforming to requirements for success in this setting is not seen as equivalent to assimilation into white culture. Instead, immigrant groups often retain their own cultural values and practices but develop an "alternation model of schooling" (Ogbu 1987a, 275), the essence of which proposes that it is possible to simultaneously participate in two different but not oppositional cultures. This framework assumes a certain degree of uniformity within voluntary immigrant groups, such that considerations of immigrant generation and social-class status are missing. We found in our research that members of the dominant culture are not the only gatekeepers to access to educational opportunities in the United States.

Haitian Bilingual Classrooms:
"Haitian on Haitian" Discrimination

Among the demands created by the influx of new immigrants and refugees from Haiti in the 1980s was a dire need for teachers who could provide these children with language instruction. In Massachusetts, native speakers of Haitian Creole (Kreyol) were in high demand. This led to heavy recruiting of members of the Haitian community to be teachers in the school, even though some of these people had no formal training as teachers. Aside from the logical consequences we might anticipate from allowing minimally trained adults to teach in classrooms, one unintended consequence has been the negative treatment some students have received at the hands of their teachers. During the course of our research, several school personnel, from guidance counselors to bilingual program directors to a school psychologist, shared with us their concerns that Haitian students in the Boston and Cambridge public schools were being verbally abused by their teachers with epithets berating their social status (e.g., *abitan, sòt, gwo soulye, moun mòn, restavèk*)[1] and suggesting that they did not belong in the United States, or that being here still should not be taken as an indication that they had transcended their origins. By invoking status distinctions that hold meaning in the Haitian context, these teachers actively engaged in redrawing the boundaries around social class and status. The meaning of such practices can be understood as "putting people in their place" so that they would not become overly confident or overstep their bounds (Buchanan 1983). Language also holds significance with regards to social status in Haiti. All Haitians speak Haitian Creole, but because of Haiti's legacy as a French colony, French has remained an important marker of educational status among Haitians (Zéphir 2004). The essential presence of language in bilingual classrooms thus created another source of opportunity for the re-creation of class-based hierarchies.

In her exploration of the differentiated meanings of French and Kreyol for monolingual and bilingual speakers, Flore Zéphir (1995) argued that, contrary to expectation, it is not only the bilingual bourgeoisie who have resisted attempts to reform Haitian education by using Kreyol as the primary language for instruction. Indeed, the monolingual lower class has a vested interest in acquiring French "because of its symbolic power for social mobility" (190).

One way to understand these practices is to recall the history of Haitian migration to the United States, in that for the first wave of educated, elite, or middle-class migrants, being Haitian was a source of pride that distinguished them from black Americans, whose marginalized and oppressed status in the United States made them an undesirable reference group (Woldemikael 1989). These Haitians enjoyed the prestige associated with being speakers of French, a language that invokes images of sophistication and refinement, and they relished being nicknamed "Frenchies" (Woldemikael 1989; Zéphir 1995). By contrast, representations in the media of the second wave of Haitian migrants as deprived, godless boat people—concurrent with the steady barrage of images of Haiti as "the poorest country in the Western Hemisphere" and of Haitians as the harbingers of AIDS—shifted Haitian identity from being a source of pride to being a source of shame (Buchanan 1983; Stepick and Portes 1986). It became a matter of self-preservation for members of Haiti's bourgeoisie living in the United States to maintain their distance, both physical and psychological, from the "masses" now arriving on U.S. shores. While in Haiti material wealth was one way for the Haitian upper class to create distance between themselves and the "masses," the U.S. economic structure is such that a larger percentage of the population can amass the "material symbols of high status, such as cars, televisions, stereo sets, expensive furniture, etc." (Buchanan 1983, 14). In response, social markers such as the knowledge of French, a well-known family name, proper upbringing, and good manners take on the functional purpose of determining status among Haitians, even if this differentiation cannot be detected by mainstream U.S. Americans, for whom only one social marker separates "the elite" from "the masses," and that is race.

Youth Responses

What meanings do youth construct, and how do they respond to this negative social mirror? One possible pathway is for youth to become resigned to the negative reflections, leading to hopelessness and self-depreciation that may in turn result in low aspirations and self-defeating behaviors. The general affect associated with this pathway is one of depression and passivity. In this scenario, the child is likely to respond with self-doubt and shame, setting low aspirations in a kind of self-fulfilling prophecy: "They are probably right. I'll never be able to do it." Other youth mobilize to resist the mirrors and injustices they encounter. Carola Suárez-Orozco (2004) draws a distinction between two types of resistance. The first is a project infused with hope, a sense of justice, and a faith in a better tomorrow. The other form of resistance is eventually overcome by alienation, leading to anomie, hopelessness, and a nihilistic view of the future. In this latter case, youth may actively resist the reflections they encounter but are unable to maintain hope for change or a better future. Without hope, the resulting anger and compensatory self-aggrandizement may lead to acting-out behaviors including the kinds of dystopic cultural practices typically associated with gang membership. For these youth, the response is one of, "If you think I'm bad, let me show you just how bad I can be" (C. Suárez-Orozco and M. M. Suárez-Orozco 2001).

The social trajectories of youth are more promising for those who are actively able to maintain and cultivate a sense of hope for the future. Whether they are resigned, oblivious, or resistant to the reflections in the social mirror, those who are able to maintain hope are in fundamental ways partially inoculated to the toxicity they may encounter. These youth are better able to maintain a sense of pride and preserve self-esteem. In these circumstances, their energies are freed-up and mobilized in the service of day-to-day coping. Some may not only become focused on their own advancement but may also harness their energies in the service of their communities by volunteering to help others, by acting as role models, or by actively advocating and mobilizing for social change. In this scenario, youth respond to the negative social mirror by being goaded into "I'll show you I can make it in spite of what you think of me" (C. Suárez-Orozco and M. M. Suárez-Orozco 2001).

Among our Haitian participants, we found evidence of these two types of resistance. Doucet and Desir (2003) have proposed that the sense of hope detected among Haitian youth was constructed from the development of a critical consciousness about education as the vehicle for success, or, more specifically for the Haitian children who were the focus of our research, education *in the United States* as the vehicle for success. Over and over again, we heard from our interviewees that "the most important thing in life is school." One of our students, Rodny,[2] stated, "If you stay in school and get good grades, you'll go to college and you'll be able to get a good job." Parents also strongly pushed this belief in the primary role of education as the key to helping their children build a successful life in this country. In some families, the push for education was understood in the context of the adversities children would face because of their race or ethnicity. As another young man, Johnny, told us, "They (Americans) don't really respect people especially if you are black. I don't think the white people like blacks too much." Nonetheless, this same young man believes Americans and Haitians have the same chance of getting ahead, "but Haitians have to work very hard." His mother also displayed an awareness of the negative light through which blacks and Haitians are viewed, stating, "Discrimination exists in school. White kids have priority," further nothing that, "as blacks, we work hard, so I trust and respect my children and am their friend."

While this kind of lucid understanding of the obstacles to education that racism presents was a motivating factor for some, for others it brought on feelings of anger and/or helplessness. Joseph, another of our participants, was sure about the importance of school to one's future. When asked what advice he would give to a cousin who just arrived to the United States on how to be successful, he answered, "Go to school and learn." But he also felt the brunt of discrimination at school: "Most of the time when black students go to the office for issues with white students, the black students are always at fault." In Joseph's case, however, there was not as strong a sense that his family was fully aware of the issues he was dealing with in school, and so they were not able to provide the same kind of support that Johnny's family was. As the eighth child in a family of nine, Joseph faced a particular set of challenges due to his parents' age and failing health, and the seeming absence of support from his older sisters. Yet these two cases illustrate an important discovery in our exploration of the issues surrounding the hopes and dreams of Haitian immigrant youth. That is, children who seem most able to hang on to the hope that an American education will be their ticket to success have an important combination of awareness of the racism and discrimination they will face, learned both in the social curriculum of the "peer classroom" and sometimes in the home, *and* adequate support mechanisms, whether in the home or from outside sources, such as mentors or strong after-school programs. Those youths who are never able to shatter the image reflected to them by society's mirror, whether because they internalize it or feel overpowered by it, are those whose dreams "shrivel like raisins in the sun" due to a lack of strong personal determination and/or social support.

Identity Styles: Pathways and Adaptation

Carola Suárez-Orozco and Marcelo Suárez-Orozco (2001) define a typology of identity styles that recognizes the incredibly fluid nature of ethnic identification among youth. Identities and styles of adaptation are powerfully linked to context and social mirroring. The identity style chosen by a young person has implications for adaptation to the new society, including schooling experiences. In some cases, the identity that is forged is highly focused on the culture of origin, with coethnics as the primary point of reference. In some of these cases, an identity that is adversarial to the dominant culture may emerge. Alternatively, youth of immigrant origin may embrace total assimilation and complete identification with mainstream American culture. And for some other youth, a new ethnic identity that incorporates selected aspects of *both* the culture of origin and mainstream American culture is forged. Within the same family, each child may adopt his or her own way, resulting in various siblings occupying very different sectors of the spectrum.

Coethnic Identities

Some immigrant-origin youth maintain a largely coethnic focus. Some may do so because they have limited opportunity to make meaningful contact with other groups in the host culture. Others may be responding to an understanding that a group with which they may have extensive contact is even more disparaged than they are as immigrants. Hence, Caribbean-origin individuals may distinguish themselves from African Americans in an attempt to ward off further disparagement (Waters 1999; Zéphir 1996). In conducting her research with second-generation Haitian youth, Zéphir (2001) found that those youth who had migrated at high school age and who thus retained their French accents bore these as a point of pride because they felt it distinguished them from African Americans. Compared to her participants who were born in the United States or who had migrated at younger ages, those who migrated as young adults were far more critical of African American culture and made conscious efforts not to associate with African Americans.

Other youth of immigrant origin may develop an adversarial stance constructing identities around rejecting—after having been rejected by—the institutions of the dominant culture. Princeton sociologist Alejandro Portes observes, "As second generation youth find their aspirations for wealth and social status blocked, they may join native minorities in the inner-city, adopting an adversarial stance toward middle-class white society, and adding to the present urban pathologies" (Portes 1993). Immigrant children who find themselves structurally marginalized and culturally disparaged are more likely to respond to the challenges to their identities by developing an adversarial style of adaptation (Vigil 1988). These children of immigrants are responding in similar ways to that of other marginalized youth in the United States, such as many inner-city, poor African Americans or Puerto Ricans. Likewise, gazing back to previous waves of immigration, many of the disparaged and disenfranchised second-generation Italian American, Irish American, and Polish American adolescents demonstrated a similar profile.

Among children of immigrants who gravitate toward adversarial styles, embracing aspects of the culture of the dominant group is equated with giving up one's own ethnic identity (Fordham and Ogbu 1986). Like other disenfranchised youth, children of immigrants who develop adversarial identities tend to encounter problems in school and drop out, and they consequently face unemployment in the formal economy. Among youth engaged in adversarial styles, speaking the standard language of the host culture and doing well in school may be interpreted as a show of hauteur and as a wish to "act white" (Fordham and Ogbu 1986). Navarrette recalls the taunts from his less successful peers: "They will call me 'Brain' as I walk through hallways in the junior high school. . . . They will accuse me, by virtue of my academic success, of 'trying to be white'" (Navarrette 1993, 260). When adolescents acquire cultural models that doing well in school is symbolically viewed as an act of ethnic betrayal, it becomes problematic for them to develop the behavioral and attitudinal repertoire necessary to succeed in school.

One of our Haitian participants, Anne-Marie, articulated the difficulty of being in a college preparatory track while the majority of her Haitian friends were not. When asked if her friends helped her in school, she responded, "No. They're not doing anything I'm doing. Where I am is too different from where they are. We have different classes, different work, different interests." And though she tried both to pursue her academic interests and remain connected to her Haitian peers, there were tensions: "I sometimes feel like I have to sit with Haitians, even if I don't want to, because otherwise they would talk and say that I am ignoring them."

The children of immigrants who are not able to embrace their own cultures and who have formulated their identities around rejecting aspects of the mainstream society may be drawn to gangs. For such youth, in the absence of meaningful opportunities, gang membership becomes incorporated into their sense of identity. Gangs offer their members a sense of belonging, solidarity, protection, support, discipline, and warmth. Gangs also structure the anger many feel toward the society that violently rejected their parents and them. Although many second-generation youth may look toward gangs for cues about dress, language, and attitude, most remain on the periphery and eventually outgrow the gang mystique after working through the identity issues of adolescence. Others drawn to the periphery—and even to the epicenter of gangs—are disproportionately represented in the penal system. The gang ethos provides a sense of identity and cohesion for marginal youth during a turbulent stage of development while facing urban poverty and limited economic opportunity, ethnic-minority status and discrimination, lack of training and education, and a breakdown in the social institutions of school and family (Vigil 1988).

While many adversarial youth may locally enact delinquent behaviors within their immediate neighborhood, an adversarial stance may lead to extreme nationalism or radicalism. Algerian-born Kamel Daoudi was raised in France and arrested on suspicion of being part of an al-Qaeda plot to blow up the American embassy in Paris. In an essay sent to TV network France 2, Daoudi said, "I became aware of the abominable social treatment given all those potential 'myselves' who have been conditioned to become subcitizens just good for paying pension for the real French. . . . There are only two choices left for me, either to sink into a deep depression, and I did for about six months . . . or to react by taking part in the universal struggle against the overwhelming unjust cynicism" (Sciolino 2002).

Clearly, adversarial styles quite severely compromise the future opportunities of immigrant-origin youth who already are at risk of school failure because of poverty, inequality, and discrimination.

Ethnic Flight

At the other end of the spectrum, some children of immigrant origin shed their cultures, identifying most strongly with the dominant mainstream culture (Berry 1997). Taking ethnic flight, these youth may feel most comfortable spending time with peers from the mainstream culture rather than with their less-acculturated peers. For these youth, learning to speak standard English serves not only an instrumental function of communicating, but it also becomes an important symbolic act of identifying with the dominant culture. Among these youth, success in school may be seen both as a route for individualistic self-advancement and as a way to symbolically and psychologically move away from the world of the family and the ethnic group.

Often this identification with the mainstream culture results in the weakening of ties to members of their own ethnic group. These young people all too frequently are alienated from their less-acculturated peers; they may have little in common or may even feel they are somewhat superior to them. While they may gain entry into privileged positions within mainstream culture, they still have to deal with issues of marginalization and exclusion.

Even when they do not feel a sense of hauteur toward their ethnic peers, they may find their peer group unforgiving of any behaviors that could be interpreted as "ethnic betrayal." It is not necessary for the child of an immigrant to consciously decide to distance himself from his culture. Among some ethnic groups, merely being a good student will result in sanctioning by peers. Accusations of "acting white" or of being a "coconut," a "banana," or an "Oreo" (brown, yellow, or black on the outside and white on the inside) are not infrequent (Fordham and Ogbu 1986).

In an earlier era of scholarship, this style of adaptation was termed "passing" (De Vos 1992). While there were gains for the children of immigrants who "disappeared" into the mainstream culture, there were also hidden costs—primarily in terms of unresolved shame, doubt, and self-hatred. While passing may have been a common style of adaptation among those who phenotypically "looked" like the mainstream, it is not easily available to today's immigrants of color who visibly look like the "Other." Further, while ethnic flight is a form of adaptation that can be adaptive in terms of "making it" by the mainstream society's standards, it frequently comes at a significant social and emotional cost.

Among Haitians, the term for youth who adopt this identity style is "undercover Haitians." Zéphir (2001) describes them in this way:

> Undercover second-generation Haitian immigrants go to great length [sic] to conceal any trace of their Haitian identity directly associated with Haiti. They endeavor to camouflage as much evidence of their origin as they can. For them, Haiti and Haitians are symbols of shame and embarrassment and are constant reminders of a difficult past that must be discarded. Undercover Haitian youth believe that there is absolutely nothing to be gained from claiming any sort of Haitianness. On the contrary, they are convinced that it is an invitation to be ridiculed, to be labeled, to be marginalized, and to be excluded altogether from meaningful participation in American life. (99)

Haitian youth born in the United States who choose to go undercover often identify as African Americans, while those who migrated later in life and thus still carry an accent claim to be from Canada, France, or some other French-Caribbean country. In our studies, we did not have occasion to interact with young people who were in denial of being Haitian altogether, though Doucet had difficulty recruiting U.S.-born participants in certain schools, partly because some students chose not to identify as Haitian or Haitian American.

Transcultural Identities

In between the coethnic and ethnic-flight gravitational fields, we find the large majority of children of immigrants. The task of immigration for these children is crafting a transcultural identity. These youth must creatively fuse aspects of two or more cultures—the parental tradition and the new culture or cultures. In so doing, they synthesize an identity that does not require them to chose between cultures; rather, they are able to develop an identity that incorporates traits of both cultures, all the while fusing additive elements (Falicov 2002).

For those of Latino origin, this state is what Ed Morales refers to as "living in Spanglish." He defines "the root of Spanglish [as] a very universal state of being. It is displacement from one place, home, to another place, home, in which one feels at home in both places, yet at home in neither place. . . . Spanglish is the state of belonging to at least two identities at the same time, and not being confused or hurt by it" (Morales 2002, 7–8). Such is the identity challenge of youth of immigrant origin—their developmental task requires crafting new cultural formations out of two systems that are at once their own and foreign. These children achieve bicultural and bilingual competencies that become an integral part of their sense of self.

Among youth engaged in bicultural styles, the culturally constructed social strictures and patterns of social control of their immigrant parents and elders maintain a degree of legitimacy. Learning standard English and doing well in school are viewed as competencies that do not compromise their sense of who they are. These youth network, with similar ease, among members of their own ethnic group as well as with students, teachers, employers, colleagues, and friends of other backgrounds. A number of studies in recent years have demonstrated a link between racial- and ethnic-identity pathways and academic outcomes (Gibson 1988; Ogbu and Herbert 1998). These studies suggest a pattern that implies that those who forge transcultural identities are the most successful academically.

Many who successfully "make it" clearly perceive and appreciate the sacrifices that loved ones have made to enable them to thrive in a new country. Rather than wishing to distance themselves from parents, these youth come to experience success as a way to "pay back" their parents for their sacrifices. At times, they experience a form of "survivor guilt" as a result of the deprivation their parents and other family members have suffered in order to move to the new land. Among many such adolescents, success in school serves not only the instrumental function of achieving self-advancement and independence, but also, perhaps even more importantly, the expressive function of making the parental sacrifices worthwhile by "becoming a somebody." To "make it" for such youth may involve restitution by "giving back" to parents, siblings, peers, and other less-fortunate members of the community.

We view the transcultural identities as the most adaptive of the three styles in this era of globalism and multiculturalism. They blend the preservation of affective ties to the home culture with the acquisition of instrumental competencies required to cope successfully in the mainstream culture. This identity style not only serves the individual well, but it also benefits the society at large. It is precisely such transcultural individuals who Stonequist argued would be best suited to become the "creative agents" who might "contribute to the solution of the conflict of races and cultures" (Stonequist 1937, 15).

By acquiring competencies that enable them to operate within more than one cultural code, immigrant youth are at an advantage. These styles of adaptation are highly context dependent and fluid. An immigrant youth might first gravitate toward one style of adaptation. Over time, as she matures and as her context changes, she may be drawn into new attitudes and social behaviors. The unilinear assimilationist model that results in styles of adaptation we term ethnic flight is no longer feasible. Today's immigrants are not unambivalently invited to join the mainstream society. The rapid abandonment of the home culture implied in ethnic flight almost always results in the collapse of the parental voice of authority. Furthermore, lack of group connectedness results in anomie and alienation. The key to a successful adaptation involves the acquisition of competencies that are relevant to the global economy while maintaining the social networks and connectedness essential to the human condition. Those who are at ease in multiple social and cultural contexts will be most successful and will be able to achieve higher levels of maturity and happiness.

Conclusion

Given that today nearly 80 percent of the new immigrants are of color emigrating from the "developing world"—Latin America, the Caribbean, and Asia (Edmonston and Passel 1994; Fix and Passel 1994)—a pattern of racialization and adversarial identity formation within the school context is deeply concerning. In our increasingly globalized world, education becomes ever more crucial for functioning (M. M. Suárez-Orozco and Qin-Hilliard 2004; Bloom 2004). Formulating identities that allow the individuals involved to move fluidly from context to context becomes critical to future functioning as a global citizen.

As educators, we have a responsibility to place the tolerance—and even celebration—of cultural differences at the very core of our educational agenda. Such an "end" could serve to provide a core meaningful educational narrative that "envisions a future . . . constructs ideals . . . prescribes rules of conduct, provides a source of authority, and above all gives a sense of continuity of purpose" (Postman 1995, 5–6). Tolerance must be fostered not only in those who already reside in the receiving context but also among the widely diverse newcomers who are sharing the new social space. We must allow newcomers to retain a sense of pride in their cultures of origin while facilitating their entrance into the new milieu. Preparing youth to successfully navigate in our multicultural world is essential to preparing them to be global citizens.

Notes

1. Peasant, uneducated, unrefined, hillbilly, servant.
2. Participant names are fictitious.

References

Adams, Paul L. 1990. Prejudice and exclusion as social trauma. In *Stressors and adjustment disorders*, ed. J. D. Noshpitz and R. D. Coddington. New York: John Wiley & Sons.

Alsadir, Nuar. 2002. Invisible Woman. *New York Times Magazine*, November 17, 98.

Appiah, Kwame Anthony, and Amy Gutmann. 1998. *Color conscious: The political morality of race*. Princeton, NJ: Princeton University Press.

Berry, John W. 1997. Immigration, acculturation, and adaptation. *International Journal of Applied Psychology* 46:5–34.

Bloom, David E. 2004. Globalization and education: An economic perspective. In *Globalization: Culture and education in the new millennium*, ed. M. M. Suárez-Orozco and D. B. Qin-Hilliard. Berkeley, CA: University of California Press.

Buchanan, Susan Huelsebusch. 1983. The cultural meaning of social class for Haitians in New York City. *Ethnic Groups* 5:7–29.

Child, Irving L. 1943. *Italian or American? The second generation in conflict*. New Haven, CT: Yale University Press.

Coleman, James S, Ernest Q. Campbell, Carol J. Hobson, James McPartland, Alexander M. Mood, Frederic D. Weinfield, and Robert L. York. 1966. *Equality and educational opportunity*. Washington, DC: U.S. Government Printing Office.

Desir, Charlene. 2004. Lòt bò dlo/Across waters: Haitian students search for identity in U.S. schools. Unpublished thesis proposal, Harvard University, Cambridge, MA.

De Vos, George. 1973. *Socialization for achievement: Essays on the cultural psychology of the Japanese*. Berkeley: University of California Press.

———. 1992. The passing of passing. In *Social cohesion and alienation: Minorities in the United States and Japan,* ed. G. De Vos. Boulder, CO: Westview Press.

De Vos, George, and Marcelo M. Suárez-Orozco. 1990. *Status inequality: The self in culture.* Newbury Park, CA: Sage Press.

Doucet, Fabienne. Forthcoming. The reproduction of color and class in Haitian bilingual classrooms. In *Out of one, many: The communities of the Haitian diaspora,* ed. R. O. Jackson.

Doucet, Fabienne, and Charlene Desir. 2003. What happens to a dream deferred? Framing the educational experiences of Haitian children within the context of migration. Paper read at biennial meetings of the Society for Research in Child Development, Tampa, Florida.

DuBois, W. E. B. 1903/1989. *The souls of black folks.* New York: Bantam.

Edmonston, Barry, and Jeffrey Passel, eds. 1994. *Immigration and ethnicity: The integration of America's newest arrivals.* Washington, DC: Urban Institute.

Erikson, Erik. 1968. *Identity: Youth and crisis.* New York: Norton.

Espenshade, Thomas, and Maryann Belanger. 1998. Immigration and public opinion. In *Crossings: Mexican immigration in interdisciplinary perspective,* ed. M. M. Suárez-Orozco. Cambridge, MA: David Rockefeller Center for Latin American Studies.

Falicov, Celia Jaes. 2002. The family migration experience: Loss and resilience. In *Latinos: Remaking America,* ed. M. M. Suarez-Orozco and M. Paez. Berkeley: University of California Press.

Fix, Michael, and Jeffrey Passel. 1994. *Immigration and immigrants: Setting the record straight.* Washington, DC: Urban Institute.

Fordham, Signithia, and John U. Ogbu. 1986. Black students' school success: Coping with the burden of "acting white." *Urban Review* 18 (3): 176–206.

Frérère, Gérard Alphonse. 1999. *Haiti and its diaspora: New historical, cultural, and economic frontiers.* www.webster.edu/~corbetre/haiti-archive/msg00868.html (accessed January 12, 2006).

Gans, Herbert. 1992. Second-generation decline: Scenarios for the economic and ethnic futures of the post-1965 American immigrants. *Ethnic and Racial Studies* 15 (April): 173–92.

Gibson, Margaret A. 1988. *Accommodation without assimilation: Sikh immigrants in an American high school.* Ithaca, NY: Cornell University Press.

Glick-Schiller, Nina, and Georges Fouron. 1990. "Everywhere we go, we are in danger": Ti Manno and the emergence of a Haitian transnational identity. *American Ethnologist* 17 (2): 329–47.

Gordon, M. M. 1964. *Assimilation in American life: The role of race, religion, and national origins.* Oxford: Oxford University Press.

Higham, John. 1975. *Send these to me: Jews and other immigrants in urban America.* New York: Atheneum.

Laguerre, Michel S. 1984. *American odyssey: Haitians in New York City.* Ithaca, NY: Cornell University Press.

———. 1998. *Diasporic citizenship: Haitian Americans in a transnational America.* New York: St. Martin's Press.

Lawless, Robert. 1992. *Haiti's bad press*. Rochester, VT: Schenkman Books.

Lee, Stacy J. 1994. Behind the model-minority stereotype: Voices of high- and low-achieving Asian American students. *Anthropology & Education Quarterly* 25 (4): 413–29.

Louie, Vivian. 2004. *Compelled to excel: Immigration, education, and opportunity among Chinese Americans*. Palo Alto, CA: Stanford University Press.

Maira, Sunaina. 2004. Imperial feelings: Youth culture, citizenship, and globalization. In *Globalization: Culture and education in the new millennium*, ed. M. M. Suárez-Orozco and D. B. Qin-Hilliard. Berkeley, CA: University of California Press.

Massey, D., and Nancy Denton. 1993. *American apartheid*. Cambridge, MA: Harvard University Press.

Matute-Bianchi, Maria E. 1991. Situational ethnicity and patterns of school performance among immigrant and non-immigrant Mexican descent students. In *Minority status and schooling: A comparative study of immigrant and involuntary minorities*, ed. M. A. Gibson and J. U. Ogbu. New York: Garland Publishing.

Mintz, Sidney W. 1974. *Caribbean transformations*. Baltimore: Johns Hopkins University Press.

Morales, Ed. 2002. *Living in Spanglish: The Search for Latino Identity in America*. New York: St. Martin's Press.

Navarrette, Ruben, Jr. 1993. *A darker shade of crimson: Odyssey of a Harvard Chicano*. New York: Bantam.

Ogbu, John U. 1978. *Minority education and caste: The American system in cross-cultural perspective*. New York: Academic Press.

———. 1987a. Variability in minority responses to schooling: Nonimmigrants vs. immigrants. In *Interpretive ethnography of education: At home and abroad*, ed. G. Spindler and L. Spindler. Hillsdale, NJ: Lawrence Erlbaum Associates.

———. 1987b. Variability in minority school performance: A problem in search of an explanation. *Anthropology and Education Quarterly* 18 (4): 312–34.

Ogbu, John U., and Simmons Herbert. 1998. Voluntary & involuntary minorities: A cultural-ecological theory of school performance with some implications for education. *Anthropology & Education Quarterly* 29: 155–88.

Omni, Michael, and Howard Winant. 1986. *Racial formation in the United States from the 1960s to the 1980s*. New York: Routledge and Kegan Paul.

Orfield, Gary, and John T. Yun. 1999. *Resegregation in American schools*. Cambridge, MA: The Civil Rights Project, Harvard University.

Portes, Alejandro. 1993. "The New Second Generation." Press release, School of International Relations. Baltimore, MD: Johns Hopkins University Press, June 3.

Portes, Alejandro, and Rubén G. Rumbaut. 2001. *Legacies: The story of the second generation*. Berkeley, CA: University of California Press.

Portes, Alejandro, and Alex Stepick. 1993. *City on the edge: The transformation of Miami*. Berkeley, CA: University of California Press.

Portes, Alejandro, and Min Zhou. 1993. The new second generation: Segmented assimilation and its variants. *The Annals of the American Academy of Political & Social Science* 530:74–96.

Postman, Neil. 1995. *The end of education: Redefining the value of school.* New York: Knopf.

Rong, Xue Lang, and Judith Preissle. 1998. *Educating immigrant students: What we need to know to meet the challenges.* Thousand Oaks, CA: Corwin Press.

Rosenthal, Doreen A., and S. Shirley Feldman. 1991. The influence of perceived family and personal factors on self reported school performance of Chinese and Western high school students. *Journal of Research on Adolescents* 1:135–54.

Rubin, Lilian B. 1994. Is this a white country, or what? In *Families on the fault line: America's working class speaks about the family, the economy, race, and ethnicity.* New York: HarperCollins.

Rumbaut, Rubén G. 1994. The crucible within: Ethnic identity, self-esteem, and segmented assimilation among children of immigrants. *International Migration Review* 28: 748–94.

———. 1997. Passages to adulthood: The adaptation of children of immigrants in Southern California. Report to the Russell Sage Foundation.

Rumbaut, Rubén G., and Alejandro Portes. 2001. Introduction-ethnogenesis: Coming of age in immigrant America. In *Ethnicities: Children of immigrants in America,* ed. R. Rumbaut and A. Portes. Berkeley, CA: University of California Press.

Schmidley, Dianne. 2001. *Profile of the foreign-born population in the United States: 2000.* Washington, DC: U.S. Census Bureau.

Sciolino, Elaine. 2002. Portrait of the Arab as a young radical. *New York Times,* September 22, A14.

Steele, Claude. 1997. A threat in the air: How stereotypes shape intellectual identity and performance. *American Psychologist* 52 (6): 613–29.

Stepick, Alex, and Alejandro Portes. 1986. Flight into despair: A profile of recent Haitian refugees in South Florida. *International Migration Review* 20 (2): 329–50.

Stonequist, Everett V. 1937. *The marginal man.* New York: Scribner & Son.

Suárez-Orozco, Carola. 2000. Identities under siege: Immigration stress and social mirroring among the children of immigrants. In *Cultures under siege: Social violence & trauma,* ed. A. Robben and M. Suárez-Orozco. Cambridge: Cambridge University Press.

———. 2000. Meeting the challenge: Schooling immigrant youth. *NABE News,* November/December, 6–9, 35.

———. 2004. Formulating identity in a globalized world. In *Globalization: Culture and education in the new millennium,* ed. M. M. Suárez-Orozco and D. B. Qin-Hilliard. Berkeley, CA: University of California Press in association with the Ross Institute.

Suárez-Orozco, Carola, and Marcelo M. Suárez-Orozco. 1995. *Transformations: Immigration, family life, and achievement motivation among Latino adolescents.* Stanford, CA: Stanford University Press.

———. 2001. *Children of immigration.* Ed. J. Bruner, M. Cole, and A. Karmiloff-Smith. The Developing Child Series. Cambridge, MA: Harvard University Press.

Suárez-Orozco, Marcelo M. 1996. Unwelcome mats. *Harvard Magazine*, July–August, 32–35.

———. 2001. Psychosocial themes in changing cultures. Paper read at the Culture and Human Development Conference, Harvard University Graduate School of Education.

Suárez-Orozco, Marcelo M., and Howard Gardner. 2003. Educating Billy Wang for the world of tomorrow. *Education Week* 23 (8): 34, 44.

Suárez-Orozco, Marcelo M., and Mariela Paez. 2002. *Latinos: Remaking America.* Berkeley, CA: University of California Press.

Suárez-Orozco, Marcelo M., and Desirée Baolian Qin-Hilliard. 2004. Globalization: Culture and education in the new millennium. In *Globalization: Culture and education in the new millennium*, ed. M. M. Suárez-Orozco and D. B. Qin-Hilliard. Berkeley, CA: University of California Press in association with the Ross Institute.

Takaki, Ronald. 1993. *A different mirror: A history of multi-cultural America.* New York: Little, Brown.

Tatum, Beverly. 1997. *"Why are all the black kids sitting together in the cafeteria?" and other conversations about race.* New York: Basic Books.

Taylor, Charles. 1994. *Multiculturalism: Examining the politics of recognition.* Princeton, NJ: Princeton University Press.

Tsuda, Takeyuki. 2003. *Strangers in the ethnic homeland: Japanese Brazilian return migration in transnational perspective.* New York: Columbia University Press.

Vigil, James D. 1988. *Barrio gangs: Street life and identity in Southern California.* Austin, TX: University of Texas Press.

Waters, Mary C. 1990. *Ethnic options: Choosing identities in America.* Berkeley, CA: University of California Press.

———. 1996a. Ethnic and racial identities of second-generation black immigrants in New York City. In *The new second generation*, ed. A. Portes. New York: Russell Sage Foundation.

———. 1996b. The intersection of gender, race, and ethnicity development of Caribbean American teens. In *Urban girls: Resisting stereotypes, creating identities*, ed. B. J. Leadbeater and N. Way. New York: New York University Press.

———. 1999. *Black identities: West Indian dreams and American realities.* Cambridge, MA: Harvard University Press.

Weinstein, Rhona. 2002. *Reaching higher: The power of expectations in schooling.* Cambridge, MA: Harvard University Press.

Winicott, D. W. 1971. *Playing and reality.* Middlesex, UK: Penguin.

Woldemikael, Tekle. 1989. A case study of race consciousness among Haitian immigrants. *Journal of Black Studies* 20 (2): 224–39.

Zéphir, Flore. 1995. Role of the Haitian middle class and the social institutions in forging the linguistic future of Haiti. *Research in Race and Ethnic Relations* 8:185–200.

———. 1996. *Haitian immigrants in black America: A sociological and sociolinguistic portrait.* Westport, CT: Bergin & Garvey.

———. 2001. *Trends in ethnic identification among second-generation Haitian immigrants in New York City.* Westport, CT: Bergin & Garvey.

———. 2004. *The Haitian Americans.* Ed. R. H. Bayor. The New Americans Series. Westport, CT: Greenwood Press.

Zhou, Min. 1997. Growing up American: The challenge confronting immigrant children and children of immigrants. *Annual Review* 23:63–95.

Ethnic Identities of Moroccans in Belgium and the Netherlands

6

PHILIP HERMANS

Moroccans in Belgium and the Netherlands

IN BELGIUM AND THE NETHERLANDS,[1] two small countries in the coastal region of northwestern Europe, Moroccans have become among the largest immigrant groups. In 2004, the number of people of Moroccan origin living officially in Belgium was estimated at more than 215,000, where they form the second-largest group after Italians; in the Netherlands, there live more than 306,000 people of Moroccan origin (Statistics Netherlands 2004). Here they form the third-largest group after Turks and Surinamese. In both countries, most Moroccans are concentrated in the bigger cities; both capitals (Brussels and Amsterdam); and other cities such as Antwerp, Rotterdam, and Utrecht. Immigration from Morocco[2] in northwest Africa started in the 1960s, when many West European countries opened up their borders because of their need for a cheap labor force. The first generation of Moroccans was mainly of rural origin; many were Berbers from the north of Morocco, and only a few had received some formal education. They were employed as unskilled workers. For a long time, Moroccan guest workers, as they were called, were seen as a temporary phenomenon. Only gradually did the authorities, as well as the immigrants themselves, realize that their immigration would be permanent. This meant that it took a long time before governments started to develop immigration and integration[3] policies and programs. Large-scale immigration from Morocco was halted in the 1970s. The enforcement of stricter immigration laws was introduced progressively. Even now, a few thousand Moroccans still immigrate every year by marrying a person already residing here. In this way, a first generation is created again and again. In the meantime, second- and third-generation immigrants[4] have reached adult-hood (Obdeijn, De Mas, and Hermans 2002, 213–15, 229).

After the economic recession of the 1970s, guest workers were no longer in demand. Many people lost their jobs, and the uneducated immigrants were among the first to be laid off. Youngsters from the second generation often had unsuccessful school careers and had difficulty gaining access to the already saturated labor market. Guest workers were soon perceived as stealing the jobs of the original inhabitants or as taking advantage of the social security system. In both countries, Moroccans came to symbolize the foreigner who embodies all sorts of threats and dangers for society. Soon they were blamed for everything that was going wrong in society. This has dominated many political and societal debates during the last two decades and has given rise to right-wing and populist political parties that owe their huge successes—winning over a quarter of the vote in some regions—to their anti-immigrant stands. The dominant discourse lumps Moroccans together with Islamic fundamentalism, illegal immigration, and drug trafficking. They are often presented as rejecting the basic principles of democracy and the constitutional state, such as freedom of speech, separation of church and state, and equality of the sexes. After the attack on the World Trade Center Towers in New York on September 11, 2001, the climate changed for the worse. More than before, it was stated that something was wrong with Islam and Arab cultures. More than ever, Moroccans were expected to declare themselves as pro-Western and to distance themselves from Islam.[5]

Of course, not everybody in the low countries dislikes immigrants. Society seems to be divided over the "immigrant issue." One side, leftist, progressive, and humanist, is positive toward immigrants and believes they can be integrated into society and given equal rights while at the same time allowing them to maintain their own culture. The other side, rightist, wants to see all immigration from non-European countries halted and would like to send many immigrants back to their countries of origin, or at least demand that they assimilate into the dominant culture, all while continuing to consider them as second-class citizens. These attitudes are translated in daily life into behavior ranging from "cuddling to death" and paternalism to indifference toward complaints of discrimination and overt racism.

However, over the last two decades, the authorities have invested a lot in the integration and emancipation of ethnic minorities and the organization of a multicultural society. Among other things, advisory centers for immigrants were founded and subsidized; all kinds of measures that promoted the interests of ethnic minorities in education, employment, and housing were stimulated and subsidized; language courses were organized; immigrants were more involved in decision processes that concerned them; public services were stimulated to reach out and enlist immigrants in their programs and aims; and the right to vote in municipal elections was accorded to certain categories of immigrants (Clyck, Timmerman, and Martens 2004; Smeets 2003).

Moroccans find themselves in the lower socioeconomic strata of society. There are improvements in the level of education and income of Moroccans, but the gap between their situation and that of native Belgians and Dutch still remains wide (Clyck, Timmerman, and Martens 2004; Groeneveld and Veenman 2004). However, some people of Moroccan origin have managed to attain important positions in Belgian and Dutch society, for instance in politics, business, popular music, and literature. The majority of Moroccans probably lead satisfying lives in Belgium and the Netherlands. Remigration hardly ever occurs, and many inhabitants of Morocco still hope and try to immigrate to the West. Most Moroccans live their private lives among their own Moroccan relatives and acquaintances. In day-to-day relations between Moroccans and the native born, both in the public arena and on the work floor, things run, on the whole, more smoothly than the discourses mentioned above would have us believe.

Moroccan Identity and Culture

Moroccan identity, just as other ethnic identities, is neither a monolithic nor a clear-cut phenomenon. Historically the idea of a Moroccan (national or ethnic) identity is recent and relative. In the past, many of the peoples living within the borders of the current kingdom of Morocco identified themselves in terms of the tribes they belonged to or the towns they resided in. Only parts of the country stood under the direct control of the sultanate. Sultans were always competing and waging war to control dissenting tribes, religious brotherhoods, and important families who controlled large parts of the country and maintained their independence (Hart 1976; Obdeijn, De Mas, and Hermans 2002). Only in the face of the Christian enemy did the sultan and tribes reunite temporarily. It was the French (and Spanish) colonizers (1912–1956) who succeeded in consolidating the sultanate in the 1930s. At the same time, they unwillingly provoked a strong independence movement in which virtually the whole population, Arabs as well as Berbers, united to throw out the colonizers. Modern Moroccan identity was thus born. During the process of nation building that followed independence, Islam; the Arabic language; and loyalty to the sultan (modernized into king), who had become a symbol of resistance and Moroccan unity, were promoted as essential components of a Moroccan identity. Only the first principle was not disputed. Virtually all Moroccans embrace Islam, but not all Moroccans are Arabs. Especially Berbers in the Rif continued their tradition of mistrusting and opposing the central government. Berber languages never received any official status, and pleading the cause of Berber was interpreted as an act of insubordination by the regime. This has changed. Berber is more and more conceived of as being part of Moroccan culture instead of detracting from it. The regime has had to fear leftist, nationalist, and separatist threats, but since the 1980s, these have been superseded by political fundamentalist Islam. In any case, the ethnic label *Moroccan* probably took on more meaning and made more sense for people after they had migrated to Europe.

It is even more difficult to define Moroccan culture.[6] Moroccan culture(s) and peoples can be, and have been, described for instance by Westermarck (1926); Eickleman (1976); Hart (1976); Geertz, Geertz, and Rosen (1979); Combs-Schilling (1989); and Mernissi (1994), to name but a few excellent examples. Describing a culture is one thing; defining it is another. Important elements, traits, and aspects of Moroccan culture include the importance of Islam ("lived" in a Moroccan way); the importance of the family beyond the nuclear unit and governed by a patriarchal and patrilineal ideology; the use of Moroccan Arabic or Moroccan Berber; and a varied combination of traits concerning, among other things, arts, dress, cuisine, customs, and beliefs seen as typical Moroccan. Just like all cultures, Moroccan culture is diverse, dynamic, open, and permeable. Morocco was colonized by the French and the Spanish in the beginning of the last century and has remained under neocolonial influence ever since. As much as any developing country, it has modernized and has been affected by processes of globalization. Material culture, infrastructure and technology, consumer culture, political structures and ideologies, education and health care, legal systems, media and popular culture, and labor systems, to name but a few, are heavily influenced by Western culture. Moroccans who live in the Netherlands and Belgium are, of course, even more affected by Western culture. Seen from an individual's perspective, it would be very difficult to decide where a person's Moroccan culture ends and his Western culture begins. On the other hand, as time and distance have become less important obstacles in our globalizing world—a flight from Brussels to Tangier in north Morocco takes about three hours and costs less than $400—it is fairly easy for Moroccans to visit their country of origin and stay in contact with their relatives in Morocco and with the Moroccan way of life. Satellite television is another means by which Moroccans in Europe have access to Moroccan and Middle Eastern culture.

The aim of this article is to get an understanding of the way Moroccans in Belgium and the Netherlands define themselves and their culture in relation to the dominant cultures they live in. How do they understand their ethnic identity? How do they cope with living in these other cultures? My insights are based on long-term commitment and contacts with Moroccans in Belgium, the Netherlands, and Morocco (Hermans 1985, 1995), and more specifically on four research projects that took place between 1996 and 2004 (Hermans 2002). In these projects, ethnographic interviewing (Heyl 2001; Spradley 1979) was used to focus on Moroccan parents' concerns over the upbringing and education of their children in the Western society they were living in. The related topics of identity, culture, and "integration" into Western society were also brought up for discussion. However, concerns about education and upbringing were relevant, as they are related to preserving one's culture and identity. In total, sixty-five men and fifty-five women were interviewed in several Belgian and Dutch cities. In order to best represent the Moroccan population, I tried to obtain varied and differentiated groups of fathers and mothers from various backgrounds and origins, as well as from different generations, but who all had children they were bringing up in Belgium or the Netherlands.[7] More than half of the interviews took place in the homes of the interviewees.

I chose to start with the presentation of six cases to illustrate some typical opinions and positions that Moroccans living in Belgium and the Netherlands hold about their ethnic and cultural identities. For the analysis and discussion that follow, I relied, of course, on the complete set of data. I made use of the computer program ATLAS.ti (Scientific Software Development 2000) to further manage and investigate them.

Six Case Studies

1. Mr. Tanjaoui is in his fifties and migrated in 1973 from Tangier (Morocco) at the age of twenty-two. His education consisted of a few years of Koranic school and some years of primary school. His parents were of Riffian origin. He lives in Antwerp (Belgium). He worked in a metal factory for more than ten years but has been on welfare since he was laid off. He married a second cousin and brought her to Belgium in the late 1970s. She never worked outside the home. They have five children now, of which the older ones are adult and married. Moroccan Arabic is the family language,

but his children often speak Dutch among themselves. He does not really like this and even considers it impolite when he hears Moroccan children speaking Dutch with their parents. His own Dutch is poor; his French is better. Mr. Tanjaoui considers himself a 100 percent Moroccan and feels proud because of this. He finds that he differs fundamentally from Belgians. According to him, the Belgian way of life has no religious or moral rules or principles anymore. People just do what they want. He is naturalized and now possesses Belgian and Moroccan nationality.[8] But he says this does not mean anything: "My Belgian nationality is only a piece of paper that gives me certain rights and that makes life in Belgium easier and more secure. It does not change my ideas, values, or customs." He does not want to assimilate into Belgian culture, and he does not believe in the idea of integration: "I obey the law, what more do they want me to do? I just want the right to do things in my own way." He practices his religion strictly and spends much time in his local mosque and the adjacent Moroccan club. Here he plays cards and drinks tea with his friends. Together they watch Moroccan and other Middle Eastern television programs via satellite dish. All Moroccan holidays and religious feasts are celebrated here. However, his family life is also important: "Moroccans value their families; a Moroccan family is a warm and lively place, and we enjoy visiting and receiving our relatives and spending time together." He did his best to give his children an Islamic upbringing. He wants his wife and daughters to wear head scarves when they go out. It is important for him that his children remain Muslim and Moroccan. He finds this difficult to achieve because Western society does not endorse those values that are important for Moroccans, such as respect, discipline, morality, and chastity. He believes that girls need a different education from boys and that the roles of women and men are fundamentally different. According to him, a lot of Moroccan boys get into trouble not because their parents are unable to give them a correct upbringing, but because Belgian society is too free and does not allow Moroccan parents to hit their children to prevent them from going astray. He would like to see Arabic, Islam, and Moroccan geography and history included in the curriculum, certainly in schools that have a majority of Moroccan pupils. But instead, schools do not give any attention to Moroccan culture and even influence children to give up their Moroccan culture and become Belgians. For this reason, he experiences extracurricular activities as threatening. Furthermore, in his eyes, many teachers are racist. They do not like their Moroccan pupils; they see them as troublesome and their culture as backward. Because of the existing racism in society at large, it will be difficult for his children to find good jobs later. There is also the racism of the street and of political parties. He would have liked to send his children to an Islamic school, but there is none in Antwerp. He sent them to a Koranic Sunday school. He also tries to take them to Morocco every year to keep the link with their country of origin. He would be terribly disappointed if his children ceased to be Moroccans or left the Islamic faith. For this reason, he would also find it dreadful if one of his children married a European, certainly a non-Muslim.

2. Mrs. Berjaoui is twenty-nine. She was born in Brussels, where she still lives. She followed general secondary education but never completed her studies. She does not have a job. Her parents come from Oujda in north Morocco. Her husband grew up in Morocco and was able to come to Belgium after marrying her. He works as a cleaner. They have two daughters that are going to primary school now. She calls herself Moroccan and Arab. She made a telling lapse when talking about her Riffian neighbor: "I am Moroccan, but she is Rif." But she calls herself a modern Moroccan. This means, among other things, that she sees herself on equal terms with her husband, that she tries to get hold of religious information herself, and that she does not just accept what the imam in the mosque or her husband tells her. On the other hand, she believes that it is her task to bring up their children and her husband's task to have a job and earn a living. But this does not mean she would never consider taking up a job. Islam has not always been important for her, but this has changed. Her parents gave her a free education in which Islam did not figure much, and she did not learn much about her religion. Only later, when her brother was killed in a car accident, did she start to reflect upon her life and situation. Her family became more important to her, and she got more and more interested in Islam. Islam was the only thing that gave sense to her life, and she started to educate herself about it. Now Islam is the basis of her life. She finds herself more religious than her relatives in Morocco. She does her daily prayers, though not always at the exact times; she never drinks alcohol; and she even refuses to put her savings in an account that gives interest, as this is considered usury in Islam. She wears a head scarf, but not because her husband or her family tell her to do so: "I understand that this is an important tenet in my religion, but it should be worn out of your own free will. Wearing a head scarf brings me more respect in some circles, but in others I feel I am frowned upon and seen as old-fashioned, even by other Moroccans." She also wants her daughters to wear head scarves when they grow up, but she will not force them to do so. The home language is Moroccan Arabic, the only language her husband speaks well. She herself speaks fluent French and catches herself more and more

speaking French with her daughters. With her parents and siblings, she usually speaks French. She does not have any of the complaints Mr. Tanjaoui made about Belgian schools, and she appreciates the two-hour Islamic instruction her children receive at school. She voices the opinion that many Moroccan parents do not pay attention to the education of their children, especially the Berbers. She prefers for her daughters to marry Moroccans, but adds that it is better for them to marry a Belgian Muslim than a Moroccan drug addict. She also has Belgian nationality but says it does not mean anything really. About Belgian culture, she says, "Europeans have no family life; they amuse themselves individually and do as they please and are not hindered by religion or customs. But I have to admit that I do not really know how Belgians live because I do not have much contact with them. I have never visited the home of a Belgian family."

3. Mrs. Hosima is forty-two years old. She joined her father in Brussels with the rest of the family when she was five. They migrated from the Rif. She followed some vocational training and left school at sixteen, which was still possible at that time. Her marriage was arranged by her parents and enabled her husband to come to Belgium. They have six children. She considers herself a housewife but has worked as a cleaning woman for some years to earn some additional income for the family. Her husband worked as a janitor in a school but is now unemployed. She says she is Moroccan, but she also sees herself as Belgian. All of the family are of Belgian nationality. For her, it is no problem that her children will become "real" Belgians. She and her husband speak Berber or some Arabic, but the home language has become French. She laughs and says, "None of my children speak fluent Arabic or Berber, they do not like to spend their holidays in Morocco, and we hardly eat Moroccan dishes at home." She thinks that the values she finds important are also those that are important in school. She has no problem with schools not organizing Arabic or Islamic lessons, but she sends her children to a private school on the weekend to learn at least some Standard Arabic. "We live in a foreign country, so we cannot demand a Moroccan education here. But even more, I want my children to be integrated; it is necessary for them to learn the languages of this country and to understand other religions as well." For her and her husband, it is important that their children do well in school so that they can have proper jobs later in life. For this reason, she spent weeks going from one place to another finding a Flemish school in Brussels for one of her younger sons. She sees this as instrumental in making her son bilingual (in Dutch and French), which is important for him in finding a job later. However, because Dutch was not spoken at home, many schools turned down her re-

quest to enroll her son. This was experienced as racism by the family, but she finally found the school she wanted. In her eyes, a good school is a school that does not have too many foreign pupils. One of her older sons studied engineering, but he has not yet managed to find a decent job. She is convinced that this is because of his Moroccan origin. "But these people are wrong," she exclaims, "my son is Belgian!" She considers herself a Muslim but not as fanatical: "We are not against other religions. But we do want to practice our religion, and this is not always made possible. On several occasions and despite our insistence, my children were served pork during school outings!" Boys and girls get the same education in her family. She is not very strict and finds it important that children are content and happy. It would be no problem if her children did not consider themselves Moroccans anymore, but she wants them to stay Muslim.

4. Mr. Ouahhabi lives in Helmond. He is thirty-five and grew up in the Netherlands. His parents originated in the Rif. He completed higher education and works as a social worker. He has Dutch nationality. He married a Moroccan woman who grew up in the Netherlands, had a secondary education, and now works as a secretary. They have two children, a boy in secondary school and a daughter in primary school. About Moroccan culture, Mr. Ouahhabi says on the one hand that it is not fundamentally different from traditional Dutch culture, though he adds that in Europe the extended family with all its implications has given way to extreme individualism. On the other hand, he finds that the culture of Moroccans is not respected in school, nor in society at large. From the beginning, children are raised according to Western principles, and all their own values and customs such as the wearing of head scarves, the use of henna, and the protection of girls and women are demeaned. They also undergo a lot of racism and paternalism. Moroccan boys are taken for delinquents or terrorists in the making; Moroccan girls are portrayed as the helpless victims of a harsh patriarchal culture. Society decides how their children will develop, not the parents. Because of this, many Moroccan children start to hate themselves and their background and start to turn away from their culture of origin. "I have seen some of my friends starting to act like Dutchmen. They felt superior, and they were praised by the Dutch as models of integration. But soon they realized that they were not really accepted, they did not get jobs, and finally they understood they had been denying their real natures." He raises his children in a strict way, just as he was educated by his own father. He will send his children to an Islamic school, if possible, or at least to a Koranic Sunday school and to Arabic classes, just as his father sent him. He loathed it as a child, but now he understands the importance of it.

It has been important for his personal development. He is a Moroccan, and he is a Muslim, but he has grown up in and lives in the Netherlands. He has to accept both components. The deeper root of all problems is Western capitalism that spares nobody. Moroccans are exploited by Western states and businesses. The Moroccan state is only too glad to cooperate in this process. Western laborers are only a bit better off than Moroccans. By providing native laborers with a competitor and a scapegoat in the immigrant, capitalism divides and rules. His language toward the Dutch society is harsh, but at the same time he likes his job, which involves collaborating with Dutch colleagues and mediating between Moroccan youth, their parents, and Dutch institutions.

5. Mrs. Ouazzani, now a psychologist in her late thirties, grew up near Antwerp. Her parents are of Berber origin. She calls herself Belgian, or rather European, and to the dismay of her parents has renounced Islam completely. She acknowledges her Moroccan roots though and is especially interested in her Berber origins. She says she is happy to have had the opportunity to grow up and study in Belgium. She admits that her parents have given her the opportunity to study, but she also says that it has been a constant process of struggle and manipulation. "My studies became my own private thing, which my parents did not understand much about, and which I did not share much with my family. I had to fib a lot even to be able to go to the library. As soon as I was about seventeen, I had to ward off the suitors that were proposed by my parents. Fortunately, they did not put too much pressure on me, and I always used the argument that I wanted to complete my studies first. Because of my good grades, they could not do anything but let me continue. Afterward, I immediately found a job, and then I could go and live on my own. This was a big drama for my parents, who still lament to this day the fact that they gave me too much freedom." She finds the traditional Moroccan culture of her parents very backward. She lives with a Belgian partner, and they have a daughter. Marriage with a Moroccan was out of the question because she would never have found anyone who would have accepted her as she was. She considers herself completely integrated into society, but this does not mean she feels completely accepted. To start with, she looks Moroccan, and she has a Moroccan name. Her experience is that people see her as different and behave accordingly. "For instance, Belgian boys never flirted with me because they saw me as an unapproachable, chaste Moroccan girl." She is aware of the general racism that exists in society; in some cases she understands it, and in other cases she is dumbfounded by the irrational fear or hate that seems to underlie it. She considers herself "integrated" but asks

herself at what cost: she is not really accepted and has lost the love of her family.

6. Mrs. Belhaj was born in Amsterdam and still lives there. She is thirty-two. Her parents came from Tetouan and were Arabic speakers. She completed higher education and, after having held several short jobs, now runs her own business. In the course of her studies, she was often confronted with the fact that her teachers underestimated her capacity, but thanks to a few exceptions who believed in her potential and stimulated her, she succeeded. She is married to a Moroccan and has a son of six. She defines herself in the first place as Moroccan: "I am Moroccan, but yes, I am also an 'Amsterdammer.' It also depends on where I am and what I am doing; when I am visiting my parents, I am a Moroccan, but at university and at work, I consider myself Dutch." About her religion, she says, "I do not fast during Ramadan, I was not a virgin when I married, I never wear a head scarf, and sometimes I eat pork sausages. Still I consider myself a Muslim. It is in me. Nevertheless, I am a Muslim in my own way, and I do not accept being talked to by anyone about my religious conduct. Religion and the Koran are often used by Moroccans to maintain obsolete customs and to subdue women, and that of course I will not put up with." About Dutch culture, she says that everything is overregulated and that everything has to be discussed: "Dutch life misses a kind of warmth and spontaneity. You cannot just drop round at people's homes without making an appointment. You will only get a meal if you were invited officially." On the other hand, she admires their punctuality, openness, and righteousness, qualities she often finds lacking in Moroccans. In her job, she has never felt any overt racism or discrimination: "People are on the whole usually very friendly toward me, but you are never sure what they have in the back of their minds. Sometimes people tell me that my Dutch is excellent. They mean it as a compliment. But I grew up here, I had all my education here, and I even went to university here! Do they still expect me to talk gibberish? It shows they still perceive us as dumb immigrants and are amazed when we turn out to be smart."

Further Results and Discussion

One of the first conclusions that can be drawn from these cases and the other data is that there is a lot of variety in the way these Moroccans experience and discuss their ethnic identity, their culture, and their relation with the larger society and culture they live in.

Most of the people interviewed continue to consider themselves Moroccans. Instances of individuals denying, refusing, or rejecting their Moroccan identity, or of "passing" as Dutch or Belgian, were rarely if ever reported. Seeing themselves as Moroccan is something that goes without saying. There is also an important psychological and emotional component; there is a sense of belonging and attachment. Just as a person belongs to her family, giving up her Moroccan identity would be felt as betrayal, by herself as well as by her acquaintances. Generally, they conceive their ethnic identity in primordialist terms. They conceive of their Moroccan identity as something that is given and permanent. It is "in the blood or in the genes," or "God created them Moroccans." It has to do with belonging to a family, which in turn implies being part of a people and a nation. People's phenotypes also play an important part in this. After all, Moroccans look like Moroccans. People living and mixing in multiethnic cities such as Brussels or Amsterdam usually have no difficulties in distinguishing Moroccans from Turks, Spaniards, or Surinamese. It is not only a question of self-identification. There is also always the other who will label you Moroccan by your looks, your accent, or your name.

This given or natural aspect of their identity is formed and developed further through upbringing, socialization, living together, and other life experiences. For first-generation Moroccans, Moroccan identity is even more natural; they experience an enormous cultural and social gulf between themselves and the native-born of their host country, while their frame of reference remains that of their culture and country of origin. Many of the second and third generations living in Belgium and the Netherlands continue to call themselves Moroccan, but, having been educated and much more exposed to the culture of the country they live in, they acknowledge Dutch or Belgian aspects or layers in their identity. On the whole, the more people have studied and the higher the educational level they have attained, the more they recognize Dutch or Belgian aspects of their identity.

Religion is a very important aspect in the ethnic identity. There is a great deal of overlap between the two aspects. For many Moroccans, being Muslim is an important, if not the most important, aspect of their Moroccan identity. For others, and this is more typical for people of the second and third generations, their Muslim identity is more important than their Moroccan identity. Nobody considered him- or herself a Moroccan but not a Muslim. However, several younger people of the second generation said that they considered themselves Muslim in the first place and were not so sure about their Moroccan identity.

The ease with which Moroccans naturalize seems to contradict some of the above conclusions. As part of the integration policy in Belgium and the Netherlands, it has been made easier for immigrants to obtain Belgian or

Dutch nationality, and for people of the third generation, it is even conferred automatically. More than half of the people interviewed had applied for and received their new nationality. A few decades ago, this was still unthinkable. Then, applying for Belgian nationality was tantamount to converting to Roman Catholicism. Now people see it as obtaining a document that grants certain rights but that does not change their identity.

Though Moroccan identity is usually understood in a general way, internal differentiation also occurs. Moroccans make "ethnic" distinctions between themselves. The difference between Arabs and Berbers is mentioned most often. Arabs typecast Berbers as uncivilized and unsophisticated. Berbers think Arabs pretentious, chauvinistic, and condescending. It is also revealing that Arabs and Berbers often have separate mosques not only in the bigger cities, as those of my interviewees, but also in smaller municipalities. This is also indicative of the fact that there is no real evolution toward a European Islam in which Moroccan, Turkish, and other immigrants, as well as European converts, could overcome their ethnic loyalties and idiosyncrasies.

Tracing ethnic boundaries is one thing; understanding what the boundaries contain—the "cultural content"—is another. While anthropologists have become skeptical of the concept of cultural difference and are wary of specifying cultural differences (Bashkow 2004, 454), most of my interviewees had no problems in stating what was typical for Moroccan culture and how it differed from Belgian or Dutch culture. When talking about their own culture, Moroccans usually stressed the importance of Islam and the way their interpersonal relationships were characterized by family honor, clearly defined sex roles, warmth, solidarity, hospitality, propriety, and respect. Other traits were seen as less essential and concerned aspects such as their cuisine, dress, and courtesy. Belgian and Dutch culture were characterized as unreligious, immoral, and too free, while interpersonal relationships were seen as cool and overregulated. On the other hand, the affluence, high technology, organization, democracy, and welfare of the Belgian and Dutch societies were recognized and valued. The attitudes toward these aspects also varied; some people valued the democracy, freedom, and tolerance they see as typical for the West, and others found they go too far.

Appraising their position in Belgian and Dutch society, their opinions varied considerably, but they also expressed ambivalence. This was also the case with the way the interviewees evaluated the education their children received in Belgian and Dutch society, a topic that received my special attention. On the one hand, parents believed that their children received a decent education in Belgian or Dutch schools and that they acquired the necessary knowledge and skills to enable them to function and participate in society later in life. They were convinced that their children would get better jobs than they themselves ever had. Some parents praised Western education as a means to emancipation and empowerment. On the other hand, most interviewees, even those that otherwise spoke out positively, voiced a lot of discontent. I will focus on this dissatisfaction because it probably represents that part of the thoughts and feelings that affect interethnic attitudes and relations in particular.

First, many of the interviewed parents considered their way of raising children to be much better than the Dutch or Belgian way. Respect and morality were crucial aspects of the Moroccan way of upbringing for which Islam provided guidelines. Therefore Islam could not be absent from any education. In Western education, at least in the eyes of many parents, these qualities were deemed lacking. Further, many Moroccan parents asserted they had the right and the duty to be severe with their children if necessary. All sorts of rumors circulated about parents who had been reported to the police by overzealous teachers or social workers because a child had complained he or she got a clip around the ear. According to some of my interviewees, problems with Moroccan youngsters were due to the fact their parents were not allowed to act with severity when necessary. Therefore, if children did not do their best at school or if they got into trouble, it should not be the parents who deserved the blame but schools and society. Parents had the feeling that their authority over their children was being denied. In addition, Moroccan parents had the impression that schools and society thwarted their specific educational aspirations. Schools gave children too much freedom and encouraged them to have their own opinions and to question everything too much, even the certainties they were taught at home. This again undermined the authority of the parents. Certain extracurricular activities organized by the school, such as swimming lessons for girls and school trips, were felt to be especially threatening. In many other respects, parents said that their religious values and traditions were not respected. Schools forbade girls from wearing head scarves, did not have holidays on Islamic feast days, did not always respect religious dietary laws, and provided sexual education that was contrary to Islamic principles. Parents felt that their culture was denigrated at school. Their children received the message that their culture was backward, primitive, and problematic. Morocco was always portrayed as an underdeveloped country, Moroccan traditions and customs were presented as old-fashioned. Moroccan youngsters were portrayed as academically hopeless and in danger of becoming drug addicts or criminals. Women and children were represented as the victims of a harsh patriarchal and traditional culture. It was high time that Moroccans gave up their quaint customs and started to integrate into modern Western society. Because of such experiences, some Moroccan parents became convinced that the schools had a hidden agenda. They said that in the name of integration, children of immigrants had to distance themselves from their original culture and loosen the links with their parents. In fact, parents feared that their children would lose their Moroccan identity, values, and customs.

When children presented problems at school, their parents were met with prejudices and paternalism. Parents got the feeling they were being held accountable for the problems their children caused. They got the message that they were not concerned enough with the education of their children or that they were too authoritarian. Already in advance, parents were viewed as not sufficiently integrated in society. Parents also found that teachers were not really interested in their Moroccan pupils and did not have enough insight into Moroccan culture to intervene adequately when problems occurred. Parents felt that they did not have enough power to influence things at school and that their voices were not heard. For some parents, it was only a small step from these negative experiences to arrive at the conclusion that schools and the educational system discriminated against them. In their eyes, many of the above problems amounted to the fact that teachers and other pupils were prejudiced and racist. Racism at school was nothing more than a manifestation of the racism that existed in society at large. They pointed to racism in the street and in politics. They also pointed to discrimination in the housing and job markets. Even when Moroccans studied hard and adapted, they did not get many opportunities. This, in particular, rendered the situation of young Moroccans desperate and undermined their academic motivation.

These utterances show that the ethnic identity of many of my interviewees had an important defensive component that can be seen as a reaction to cultural differences but also to the ongoing discourses on Moroccans in the dominant society (Hermans 2006). They are also influenced by developments on the international scene, where Islam and the West seem to be waging wars.

This opposition and polarization between Moroccans and the native-born belongs to reality and may not be underestimated. In extreme cases, it translates into serious incidents like those referred to in endnote 5. Incidents like these receive much attention from the media. What receives much less attention is the fact that in their daily life, Moroccans are probably more acculturated to Western culture than they themselves or Westerners realize or even want to admit. This is certainly the case for people from the second and third generation. For instance, many never learn Standard Arabic, while Dutch (in Belgium, Dutch or French) has become their most important language. Even if second- and third-generation Moroccans define themselves as Muslims, some are very free in the way they experience and practice their religion. Many also have progressive opinions about sex roles and the relations between spouses. In all this, women measure up to men. Moroccan girls are very ambitious and are amongst the most diligent students at school. Moroccans know they live in Europe, and they know they will have to deal with and mix with Europeans, and they actually do so. The life they lead in Belgium and the Netherlands is very different from that which their relatives are living in Morocco. Only in the privacy of their homes, and for some, in their mosques, do they succeed in preserving important aspects of their Moroccan culture. Moroccans seem to be adapting to many aspects of the dominant culture while maintaining aspects of their original culture, especially those that have to do with religion and basic familial and interpersonal relationships. This process has been described as accommodation by Gibson (1988). In a way, accommodation is not really different from what people in Belgium and the Netherlands usually call integration. In this sense, Moroccans are undeniably integrating in Belgian and Dutch societies.

Notes

1. Dutch is the official language of the Netherlands. Belgium has become a federal state with a Dutch-speaking region in the north (Flanders), a French-speaking region in the south, a very small German-speaking region in the southeast, and the officially bilingual (French and Dutch) region of Brussels, the capital, in the center.

2. Morocco's official language is Standard Arabic. Notwithstanding a policy of Arabization, French has the status of a semiofficial second language remaining important in education and commerce. However, the mother tongue of Moroccans is Moroccan Arabic, a colloquial form of Arabic, or one of the varieties of Berber. Neither Moroccan Arabic nor Berber is written. Most Berbers are familiar with Moroccan Arabic, the lingua franca of Morocco. Because of its relation with Islam—the Koran is written in Classical Arabic, the language of Allah—Arabic holds a lot of prestige for everybody. About three-quarters of the Moroccans living in Belgium and the Netherlands are of Berber origin, and of these, most originate from the Rif in North Morocco.

3. The notion of integration in this context refers to the idea that immigrants should become part of mainstream society by participating in and accepting its

laws and core values while at the same time being allowed to preserve their own culture and religion. Integration is seen as a "duty" for immigrants, who should be willing to adapt; the authorities and public services should facilitate and encourage this process; and the general public should be hospitable. Integration has become a key notion in Belgian and Dutch policy documents, as well as in the social debate about immigration. Some criticize the notion of integration for its vagueness and arbitrariness. After all, who decides what the core values of a culture are? What are the values of the host country that have to be accepted, and what are the original ones that can be preserved?

4. The term immigrant is of course not very correct when it is applied to persons who were born or even whose parents were born in Europe. For want of a better term and to avoid wordiness, I keep using the word.

5. How strained the ethnic relationships are came to light recently when a young Islamic fundamentalist of Moroccan origin, but having dual nationality (Moroccan-Dutch), shot and stabbed a Dutch columnist and filmmaker in Amsterdam. The filmmaker was known for his outspoken anti-Islamic opinions and crude and insulting remarks about Muslims and Moroccans. He had just released a movie criticizing the brutal treatment of women in Islam. He did not survive the attack; his murderer was arrested. In reaction, Islamic schools have been bombed and set on fire. Mosques have been smudged with paint and graffiti. Elsewhere, a Catholic school was set on fire. Meanwhile, the authorities have asked the population to remain calm and renounce all violence, but they have proclaimed at the same time that the country is in a state of war and that they will push for stricter laws to combat Islamic terrorists more efficiently. In another city, combined police and military forces besieged a house that was taken over by terrorists. After a day, they managed to overpower them and make some arrests. Other terrorists have also been arrested. They were planning to kill members of parliament that voiced negative opinions about Islam. Moroccan and Muslim spokespersons condemned the murder. Many Moroccans expressed their horror at what happened, but others said that the filmmaker got what he asked for. In neighboring Belgium, the incidents have received a lot of attention. Politicians and press have wondered aloud if Muslim fundamentalism is out of control. A few days later, some politicians received death threats by telephone. One of them was a senator of Moroccan origin who had condemned the murder and challenged the Islamic authorities to do the same, which they soon did. She was threatened by a Belgian Muslim convert!

6. When qualifying culture and identity as Moroccan, Dutch, or Belgian, or even European, I am using these adjectives as gross generic terms, and I am aware of their problematic status. They are not only too broad, but they also essentialize and exaggerate the boundaries and differences between cultures while minimizing intercultural diversity as well as similarities between cultures. My interviewees, however, often spoke in these terms. To avoid wordiness, I keep using phrases such as "Dutch culture."

7. Because of this focus on parenting in Belgium and the Netherlands, issues relating to the identities and cultures of Moroccan youngsters as well as of recent immigrants fall outside the scope of this article.

8. As it is not possible for Moroccan nationals to lose or forfeit their Moroccan nationality, they possess dual nationality after naturalizing in Belgium or the Netherlands. In Morocco, they will always be considered as Moroccans.

9. This was also the conclusion of a report by the Dutch Scientific Council for Government Policy of 2001 (as cited in Obdeijn, De Mas, and Hermans 2002, 228). Other findings were that the integration of Moroccan youngsters was higher than that of their Turkish age mates and the difference between the first and the second generation was more outspoken among Moroccans than among other immigrants.

References

Bashkow, I. 2004. A neo-Boasian conception of cultural boundaries. *American Anthropologist* 106:443–58.

Clyck, N., C. Timmerman, and A. Martens. 2004. Immigratie en het integratiebeleid: Een schets van (on)gelijke kansen? In *Wachten op gelijke kansen*, ed. S. Pee, I. Lodewyckx, A. Motmans and M. Van Haegendooren, 51–63. Antwerpen: Garant.

Combs-Schilling, M. 1989. *Sacred performances: Islam, sexuality and sacrifice.* New York: Columbia University Press.

Eickelman, D. 1976. *Moroccan Islam: Tradition and society in a pilgrimage center.* Austin: University of Texas Press.

Geertz, C., H. Geertz, and L. Rosen. 1979. *Meaning and order in Moroccan society: Three essays in cultural analysis.* Cambridge: Cambridge University Press.

Gibson, M. 1988. *Accommodation without assimilation. Sikh immigrants in an American high school.* Ithaca, NY: Cornell University Press.

Groeneveld, S., and J. Veenman. 2004. De sociaal-economische positie van etnische minderheden. In *Jaarboek Minderheden 2004*, ed. H. Smeets, S. Groeneveld, and J. Veenman, 37–198. Houten: Bohn Stafleu Van Loghum.

Hart, D. 1976. *The Aith Waryaghar of the Moroccan Rif.* Tucson: University of Arizona Press.

Hermans, P. 1985. *Maatschappij en individu in Marokko: Een antropologische benadering.* Brussels: Cultuur & Migratie.

———. 1995. *Opgroeien als Marokkaan in Brussel: Een antropologisch onderzoek over de educatie, de leefwereld en de "inpassing" van Marokkaanse jongens.* Brussels: Cultuur & Migratie.

———. 2002. Opvoeden in een "multiculturele" samenleving: Opvattingen, idealen, praktijken en problemen van Marokkaanse ouders. In *Allochtone jongeren in het onderwijs. Een multidisciplinair perspectief*, ed. C. Timmerman, P. Hermans, and J. Hoornaert, 95–148. Leuven: Garant.

———. 2006. Counternarratives of Moroccan parents in Belgium and the Netherlands: Answering back to discrimination in education and society. *Ethnography
and Education* 1, 87–101

Heyl, B. 2001. Ethnographic interviewing. In *Handbook of Ethnography*, ed.
P. Atkinson, A. Coffey, S. Delamont, J. Lofland, and L. Lofland, 369–94. London: Sage.

Mernissi, F. 1994. *Dreams of trespass: Tales of a harem girlhood*. Reading, MA: Addi-
son-Wesley.

Obdeijn, H., P. De Mas, and P. Hermans. 2002. *Geschiedenis van Marokko*. Amsterdam: Bulaaq.

Scientific Software Development. 2000. *ATLAS.ti 4.2 (build 58)—the knowledge
workbench: Visual qualitative data analysis, management and theory building*. Berlin:
Scientific Software Development.

Smeets, H. 2003. Beleidsontwikkelingen. In *Jaarboek minderheden 2003*, ed.
H. Smeets, S. Dominguez Martinez, S. Groenveld, and J. Veenman, 11–77.
Houten: Bohn Stafleu Van Loghum.

Spradley, J. 1979. *The ethnographic interview*. New York: Holt, Rinehart & Winston.

Statistics Netherlands. 2004. *Population statistics 2004*. http://statline.cbs.nl.

Westermarck, E. 1926. *Ritual and belief in Morocco*. Macmillan: London.

When Minorities Migrate: 7
The Racialization of Japanese
Brazilians in Brazil and Japan

TAKEYUKI (GAKU) TSUDA

Various immigration scholars have documented how the same ethnic group can be racialized quite differently when they migrate to other societies. For instance, peoples of African descent from the Caribbean and Latin America who were considered Creole, mulatto, or *mestiço* back home are quite surprised when they migrate to the United States and are racialized as "black" and grouped together with African Americans (Basch et al. 1994; Charles 1992; Freeman 2000) (the category of "black" was used to refer only to people of very dark complexion in their homelands). In this manner, the experience of race is de-essentialized through the migratory process as immigrants realize that their racial identities, which seemed to be based on primordial physical characteristics, are contextually relative and subject to redefinition in a different society abroad.

This chapter examines the impact of different racial ideologies on the ethnic identities of transmigrants by examining the ethnic "return" migration of second- and third-generation Japanese Brazilians to Japan as unskilled foreign workers. The Japanese Brazilians began migrating to Japan in the late 1980s because of a severe economic crisis in Brazil coupled with a severe shortage of unskilled labor in the Japanese economy. Even though they are relatively well educated and mostly of middle-class background in Brazil, they still earn five to ten times their Brazilian salaries in Japan as factory workers. The return migration flow was enabled by an open Japanese immigration policy toward the *nikkeijin* (Japanese descendants born and raised abroad), which was based upon an assumption among Japanese government officials that the Brazilian *nikkeijin* would assimilate smoothly into Japanese society, providing much-needed immigrant labor without disrupting Japan's cherished ethnic homogeneity. Although most Japanese Brazilians migrate to Japan with intentions of working only for a couple of years and then quickly returning home with their savings, many have already called over their families, and the process of long-term immigrant settlement has begun. Because a vast majority of them are of the second and third generations who were born and raised in Brazil, do not speak Japanese very well, and have become culturally Brazilianized to various degrees, they are ethnically marginalized in Japan despite their Japanese descent, and they have become the country's newest ethnic minority.

In contrast to other migrants, who are racialized quite differently in the home and host societies, the Japanese Brazilians are racialized as "Japanese" in both Brazil and Japan. However, although the same racial category is used to classify them in both countries, the cultural meanings attached to this category are quite different, causing them to assert very different ethnic identities in the two social contexts. In Brazil, the Japanese Brazilians are always called "japonês" by majority Brazilians because of their distinctive Asian racial appearance. Because there are a number of positive ethnic stereotypes about Japan and Japaneseness associated with this racial category, the Brazilian *nikkeijin* have capitalized on these positive images by embracing their Japanese identities instead of emphasizing their status as Brazilian nationals. When the Japanese Brazilians return migrate to Japan, they are again racialized as Japanese by their appearance, but as a means of assimilationist homogenization instead of differentiation. In addition, this racial category in Japan is associated with complete Japanese cultural and linguistic proficiency, because the Japanese naturally expect those who look Japanese to be culturally Japanese as well. As a result, the Japanese Brazilians, as culturally Brazilianized Japanese descendants, do not meet these racialized Japanese expectations and are seen as ethnic anomalies. In order to avoid ethnic confusion and embarrassment, the Japanese Brazilians assert their Brazilianness in Japan in order to ethnically differentiate themselves from the Japanese and resist assimilationist cultural expectations. In this manner, the different meanings attached to the same racial category can produce different processes of racialization among transmigrants and result in divergent ethnic outcomes.

This chapter is based on over twenty months of intensive fieldwork and participant-observation in the mid-1990s in both Japan and Brazil. Nine months were first spent in Brazil among two separate Japanese Brazilian communities in the cities of Porto Alegre (Rio Grande do Sul) and Ribeirão Preto (São Paulo). During my one-year stay in Japan, I conducted fieldwork in Kawasaki (Kanagawa prefecture) and Oizumi-Ota cities (in Gunma prefecture), where I worked for four intensive months as a participant-observer in a large electrical appliance factory with Japanese Brazilian and Japanese workers. Close to one hundred in-depth interviews (in Portuguese and Japanese) were conducted with Japanese Brazilians and Japanese workers, residents, and employers, as well as with local and national government officials.[1]

The Racial Essentialization of Japanese Ethnicity in Brazil

Racial Markers of Difference

As Brazil's oldest and by far largest Asian minority (with a population over 1.2 million), the Japanese Brazilians are now relatively well-integrated in Brazilian society, both socioeconomically and culturally. Most of them live in large cities in the most economically developed states of São Paulo and Paraná and have become part of Brazil's middle class as professionals and business owners, with educational levels and incomes that are considerably higher than the Brazilian average. Considerable cultural assimilation has also occurred among the second and third generations, and most of them do not speak Japanese very well or maintain Japanese customs at home.

Despite their high level of sociocultural integration, however, the Japanese Brazilians continue to be racialized as a Japanese ethnic minority because of their distinctive physical appearance. In Brazilian society, the *nikkeijin* are immediately recognizable because of their *traços orientais* ("oriental features"), which are seen as markedly different from those of whites, blacks, and mixed-descent *mestiços* of all types (cf. Maeyama 1984, 455). Much attention is given by Brazilians to these phenotypic differences because of the high Brazilian sensitivity to racial characteristics, including slight differences in skin color.[2] Therefore, the Japanese Brazilians are always referred to as "japonês" by other Brazilians simply because of their facial features, not only in unfamiliar contexts when names are not known (such as in the streets, stores, and public areas) (cf. Maeyama 1984, 448), but also when they are talked about among familiar acquaintances. Their distinctive racial appearance is much more prominent as an ethnic marker of Japaneseness in Brazil than for the Japanese Americans in the United States, where there are many Asian Americans of non-Japanese descent. As a result, an Asian phenotype does not denote Japanese ancestry as it usually does in Brazil, where most Asians are of Japanese descent.[3]

The experience of being racially identified as *japonês* is undoubtedly familiar to anyone of Japanese descent who has lived in Brazil. It happened to me for the first time a few days after I arrived in Brazil. I was walking innocently down the street in downtown Porto Alegre (state of Rio Grande do Sul), when suddenly,

"*Oi, japonês!* (Hey, Japanese!)"

Startled, I turned around to find a Brazilian street vendor beckoning to me, trying to interest me in his goods.

"*Só três mil cruzeiros, japonês*," he was holding up a bag of apples. "*Mais barato do que nas lojas.*" Realizing that he had caught my attention, he continued his upbeat sales pitch, telling me how fresh and delicious his apples were. I hesitated before the proper words in Portuguese came out.

"*Não obrigado* (No thank you)."

My hesitation was less the result of my still inadequate Portuguese than the way I had been addressed directly by my race. It was the first time in my life that I had been greeted by a stranger in such a manner.

I reached the downtown bus station where a row of buses waited, the open doors beckoning passengers inside. I checked the signs designating the various routes. My bus had not yet arrived. However, because I was still unfamiliar with the bus system, I approached the attendant to confirm that I was waiting at the right spot (and also to practice my Portuguese). After indicating that I had the correct bus stop, he gestured toward the bench.

"*Espera aqui, japonês* (Wait here, Japanese)."

There it was again. I was beginning to realize that this would be a common occurrence in Brazil. In the following days, I would experience it numerous times—strangers calling me *japonês* in public (sometimes for no apparent reason), store clerks referring to me as *japonês*, a pedestrian muttering "*japonês*" as I walked past, questions ending with the ethnic designation *japonês*.

"You might as well get used to it," one of my Japanese Brazilian friends told me. "There are so few Japanese living in Porto Alegre that you have Brazilians here who have hardly ever seen a Japanese person."

Of course, children are merciless in this regard since they react with an unrefined spontaneity that adults have politely learned to suppress. I will never forget the little Brazilian boy who grabbed his mother's skirt and pointed to me as I walked past, saying, "Mommy, Mommy. Look! A *japonês!*" Nor will I ever forget the group of smiling Brazilian children who surrounded me on the street and greeted me with every Japanese word they knew. "*Sayonara, arigato . . . .*"

The other experience that remains vividly in my mind was a particular bus ride I took from downtown Porto Alegre. A little girl who sat next to her mother across from me spent most of the bus ride staring at me, her large and cute eyes studying my features intently. I shifted uncomfortably in my seat, averted my eyes for a while, and then glanced back at her. The stare continued. After a few minutes, I realized that it was hopeless; there was no way I could shake her probing eyes off me. My Japanese ethnicity was being located and essentialized by the silent gaze of a mere child! Yet the gaze was more powerful and meaningful for me than any utterance. I could easily fill the absence of words with my own imagination: "So, this is what a Japanese looks like. The slanted eyes, the flat face, the small nose. How intriguing." Even after I got off the bus, the gaze seemed to follow me relentlessly. In contrast to children, the ethnic curiosity is expressed in a more muted form among adults, as concerns for decorum intervene and the novelty wears off after numerous ethnic encounters. Yet the gaze was always there, making me acutely aware of my peculiar Japanese racial appearance that clearly differentiated me from the surrounding blend of Brazilian faces.

In fact, this racial designation as japonês is not simply confined to places like Porto Alegre where the sight of a Japanese descendant is quite rare. It prevails throughout Brazil, including the city of São Paulo, which has the highest concentration of Japanese Brazilians in the country. Of course, in such areas, it is less frequent and more of a confirmation of ethnic difference than a reaction to ethnic novelty. Nonetheless, when ethnic appellations are based on physiognomy, it inscribes a racially constituted ethnic awareness (cf. Fanon 1967, 109–12). Although my distinctive Asian appearance had never been a real focus of attention in the United States, my race was suddenly thrust into my self-consciousness in Brazil, becoming a prominent component of my "Japanese" ethnic identity.

Was it ethnic prejudice? For a moment, I was reminded of Frantz Fanon's experience in France as a black man from Martinique:

"Look, a Negro!" It was an external stimulus that flicked over me as I passed by. I made a tight smile.

"Look, a Negro!" It was true. It amused me.

"Look, a Negro!" The circle was drawing a bit tighter. I made no secret of my amusement.

"Mama, see the Negro! I'm frightened!" . . . Now they were beginning to be afraid of me. I made up my mind to laugh myself to tears, but laughter had become impossible.

... I subjected myself to an objective examination, I discovered my blackness, my ethnic characteristics; and I was battered down by tom-toms, cannibalism, intellectual deficiency, fetishism, racial defects, slave-ships. ...
... What was it? Color prejudice. (1967, 111–12, 118)

Of course, the issue is one of subjective interpretation. The external ethnic stimulus I received in Brazil was somewhat similar, but, unlike Fanon, I was not ethnically burdened by a historical legacy of colonialism, exploitation, and slavery at the hands of the Brazilians. Even during my first week in Brazil, I had fully realized that Japaneseness did not have the negative connotations that blackness had in France for Fanon. For me, the Brazilian insistence on racially inscribing me as japonês was simply a recognition of *diferença* and not a prejudicial reaction in which difference is negatively perceived (cf. Park 1999, 682). At worst, there may have been a tint of ridicule or banter at times, but never overt denigration or dislike. In general, I was much more amused than offended. After a while, it became routine, expected.

Yet the emphasis placed on racial difference in Brazil is not always this subtle. I soon realized that certain Brazilians pull their eyes upward with their fingers to indicate the *olhos puxados* (slanted eyes, or literally "pulled eyes") of the Japanese Brazilians. However, this ethnic gesture is not necessarily intended as an affront directed at the *nikkeijin*, but simply as an amusing commentary on their different physiognomy. In contrast to the United States, where the gesture is considered to be an ethnic insult, when it was used in Brazil to refer to people or things Japanese, the context was basically neutral or playful. One of the most typical examples I observed was when my landlady in Riberão Preto (state of São Paulo) described the children of her Japanese Brazilian friend to an acquaintance. "Their father is Brazilian, but they still look very Japanese," she remarked, pulling her eyes up with her fingers for emphasis. I have also seen the gesture used when referring to products made by the Japanese. The "worst case" that I encountered was actually personally solicited—one of my many attempts to gather derogatory ethnic humor about the Japanese Brazilians. "Why do the japonês have eyes like this?" my Brazilian friend asked, repeating the now familiar gesture. "Because they spend all their time frying pot stickers."

The peculiar Japanese physiognomy has even been conveniently appropriated by Brazilian commercials. A television ad for Toshiba products ends with a magnifying glass passing over the eyes of a Japanese face. "*Abre os olhos*" (Open the eyes), the ad exhorts. The commercial undoubtedly pokes fun at the Japanese, but it seemingly has a double connotation that asks consumers to open their eyes to the quality of Japanese products. Again, local context is everything, making an unmitigated ethnic insult in one society a good-humored advertising gimmick in another.

My Japanese Brazilian informants seemed to generally share my interpretation of such ethnic experiences in Brazil. In fact, most were very accustomed to their constant racial designation as *japonês* in Brazil, whether by appellation or gesture, and very few were bothered by it.[4] "It's simply how people behave here in Brazil," one *nikkeijin* man explained. "And it happens to other ethnic groups as well. Brazilians frequently say, 'Hey, black!' 'Hey, German!' or 'Hey, Jew!'" A few mentioned that they would be offended if they were called "Jap," but most claimed it did not happen.

Others even read positive meanings into the experience. "My kids came home from school one day somewhat bothered that they are always called *japonês* by the other kids," one Japanese Brazilian mother remarked. "I told them that the Brazilians are not making fun of them. I told them that being Japanese is a source of pride. The Japanese are respected and admired in Brazil."

Even the slanted-eyes gesture was taken in stride as simply ethnic humor. "It's just a joke. No one takes it seriously," one man expressed as a common opinion. It was quite remarkable that only one informant was personally offended by the gesture, claiming that behind the jovial exterior was a serious attempt to ridicule the funny appearance of the Japanese. Yet even she admitted that the Brazilian tendency to express ethnic prejudice in a jocular manner takes much of the bite out of ethnic discrimination in Brazil.

Despite the apparent lack of pejorative connotations, the tendency among mainstream Brazilians to single out the Brazilian *nikkeijin* by their race essentializes them as an ethnically different, Japanese minority. As some Japanese Brazilians mention, regardless of how culturally Brazilian they may become, they will be forever marked as *japonês* because of their distinctive physical appearance (see also Reichl 1995, 47). "Even if we become completely Brazilian and act as Brazilian as possible, we will always be seen by Brazilians as Japanese because of our faces. There's no way to avoid this," a young Japanese Brazilian student said, a hint of resignation in his voice. "We can go to a soccer game and cheer on our favorite São Paulo team, or even dance samba in the streets, and in the midst of it, someone will say, 'Oi, japonês.'"

Since minority identities always imply a certain amount of ethnic marginalization, by racially essentializing the Japanese Brazilians as "Japanese," many Brazilians partake in a discourse of ethnic exclusion (whether inadvertently or not). Despite the cultural assimilation of Japanese Brazilians in

Brazil, mainstream Brazilians continue to find it difficult to conceptualize them as part of majority society because they do not belong to one of the three "founding" races of the Brazilian nation (white, black, and Indian), a notion popularized by the famous Brazilian scholar Gilberto Freyre (Capuano de Oliveira, n.d., 18). As a result, those Brazilian *nikkeijin* who wish to be fully accepted as majority Brazilians and do not want to be treated as an ethnic minority sometimes say, "*a cara não ajuda*" (the face does not help) (cf. Smith 1979, 59).

However, most of them have no problem with being racially differentiated as japonês, since they do not wish to discard their minority Japanese ethnicity in favor of a Brazilian national identity in the first place. In fact, their Japaneseness is less of an ethnic stigma to be avoided than a positive asset to be maintained.

The Positive Cultural Meanings of Japonês

The racial category of "japonês" in Brazil is associated with various positive cultural meanings about Japan and Japaneseness. Because their racialization involves such favorable images, the Japanese Brazilians have become a "positive minority" in Brazil who are respected, if not admired, for their "Japanese" cultural attributes, in contrast to most minority groups, which usually suffer from low socioeconomic status, prejudice, and discrimination (e.g., see Giddens 1989, 245; Ogbu 1978, 21–25). As a result, many of them take pride in their ethnic heritage and have developed a rather strong Japanese ethnic identity while generally distancing themselves from what they perceive negatively as "Brazilian."

These favorable cultural perceptions of Japaneseness in Brazilian society are undoubtedly a product of Japan's prominent and respected position in the global order as an economic superpower. Plenty of positive images about Japan's industrial development, prosperity, and advanced technology have been transmitted to Brazil through global mass media and telecommunications networks (see Tajima 1998, 191). Reports and stories about Japan in Brazilian newspapers, magazines, and television programs have saturated Brazilian society with favorable impressions and information.[5] In addition to current news, there are plenty of stories featuring Japan's economic accomplishments and prosperity[6] as well as new Japanese products and technological innovations. The effectiveness of these images is further enhanced by the limited but increasing availability of high-quality Japanese products in Brazil (video and electronic equipment as well as automobiles), which are admired for their reliability and technological superiority.

This favorable Brazilian perception of Japan is based not only on specific knowledge and commodified images about the country but also on general impressions of the First World (*primeiro mundo*) that come mainly from the United States, which dominates the global flow of mass media and popular culture. In fact, when specific knowledge about Japan is lacking, generalized and rather idealistic images about the First World are quickly substituted as if they were synonymous with Japan. Although very few of the Brazilians I spoke with had a clear idea of the actual living conditions in Japan, because images of relatively privileged and luxurious Euro-American standards of living are readily available through American movies and TV shows, they were automatically applied to Japan by virtue of the country's First World status.

This global dissemination of positive impressions about Japan as a techno-economic power and First World nation has greatly enhanced the amount of ethnic respect Japanese Brazilians receive in Brazil. Virtually all of my older informants agreed that their ethnic status in Brazil has increased considerably with Japan's postwar rise in the world order. The observations of a *nikkeijin* woman were representative of her contemporaries:

> Although we were not involved in Japan's postwar growth, we have certainly benefited from it. Japan's great success has always reflected well on us, and as a result, our standing in Brazil has improved dramatically. Indeed, some act as if we actually participated in Japan's economic miracle.

The influence of Japan's global stature on the Japanese Brazilians is especially strong because of the Brazilian tendency to closely associate them with Japan by virtue of their racial appearance. "Some Brazilians don't clearly differentiate the Japanese in Brazil from the Japanese in Japan," one informant observed. "For them, a Japanese is a Japanese, regardless of whether he lives in Brazil or Japan. Therefore, what the Japanese [in Japan] do instantly becomes a reflection of who we [Japanese Brazilians] are."

Indeed, the Japanese Brazilians have capitalized on the currently pro-Japanese climate by asserting and embracing their racialized "Japanese" distinctiveness. In fact, because Japan is now part of the First World, there is a certain prestige in being associated with the country, in contrast to Third World Brazil. In this manner, by developing a strong transnational ethnic identification with Japan, the Japanese Brazilians are able to distance themselves from negative images of Brazil (cf. Linger 2001, 25; Reichl 1995; Saito 1986, 246). Undoubtedly, with the development of modern communications and mass media, which reach out to people across national borders, it has become easier for second- and third-generation immigrant minorities to identify transnationally with distant ethnic homelands by appropriating positive images that circulate in the global ecumene (cf. Gupta and Ferguson 1992, 10–11; Harvey 1989, 289).[7]

In addition, being racially Japanese in Brazil also has various positive *cultural* connotations associated with Japanese culture and Japaneseness. The dissemination of positive images about Japan in Brazil has been accompanied by favorable portrayals of Japanese culture. In fact, there is considerable interest among some non-*nikkeijin* Brazilians in Japanese culture, which has lately come to be seen as refined, fashionable, chic, and exotic (Maeyama 1996, 491; Moreira da Rocha 1999, 289, 295; Reichl 1995, 45). As Moreira da Rocha remarks, "Lately, it has become fashionable in Brazil to know about Japanese things, to learn cookery, to be able to read some *kanji* [Japanese characters], and to sit *zazen* [and to] learn . . . *chanoyu* [Japanese tea ceremony]" (1999, 295). Although many of these Brazilians are introduced to Japanese culture by their Japanese Brazilian friends, much of their interest is also generated by their exposure to Japanese cultural images through television, films, and print media. When I lived in Porto Alegre (which has only a small Japanese Brazilian population), the local Catholic university held a series of demonstration classes on Japanese culture, including tea ceremonies and flower arrangement. I was surprised to find not only that these classes were well attended but consisted overwhelmingly of non-*nikkeijin* Brazilians (cf. Moreira da Rocha 1999, 290–91). Indeed, Japanese language classes offered both at the university and in more informal contexts consist not only of *nikkeijin*, but a good contingent of Brazilian students as well. "It's amazing how many Brazilians want to learn Japanese," one Japanese Brazilian university student remarked. "It has no practical value for them—they just do it out of personal interest in Japanese culture. I am frequently asked by my [Brazilian] friends how long it will take them to learn the language."

Although most Japanese Brazilians are culturally assimilated and have not retained Japanese cultural practices, they have attempted to preserve their cherished "Japanese" cultural traditions through the symbolic recreation of Japanese festivals, rituals, food, music, and dress within their ethnic communities, which run a multitude of ethnic activities and events ranging from festivals, large dinners, and performances featuring Japanese karaoke, theater, traditional music, and dance to various sporting events and Miss Nikkei beauty pageants (see also Cardoso 1973). In fact, the Japanese Brazilians show much more interest in Japanese music and other aspects of Japanese culture than do Japanese Americans (Centro de Estudos 1992).

In addition, the Japanese Brazilians are regarded by majority Brazilians as having inherited various positive Japanese cultural qualities by virtue of their racial descent and ancestry. There is notable consensus among Brazilians that the japonês are hardworking, honest, intelligent, trustworthy, and responsible (cf. Saito 1986; Smith 1979, 58–59), which is partly the result of their notable success as a socially mobile and highly educated immigrant minority. The Japanese Brazilians are also sometimes seen as more timid, reserved, and calm than Brazilians, characteristics that can have positive connotations. Such positive stereotypes and attitudes were quite evident in my interactions with mainstream Brazilians, which resulted in numerous unsolicited ethnic comments about the Japanese Brazilians such as the following:

"The japonês are very respected. They do the work of ten Brazilians," a Brazilian waiter told me, when he found out that I had interviewed a Japanese Brazilian woman in his restaurant.

"Japonês, eh?" an agent at a Brazilian bus terminal confirmed when I gave him my name, mistaking me for a Japanese Brazilian. "They are good people. Very intelligent, hardworking."

"We trust the japonês very much, much more than Brazilians," an old Brazilian lady told me. "I have many japonês friends and they are always honest, responsible."

"You see, he is japonês," my professor in Porto Alegre observed when one of his students showed up unexpectedly to fulfill an obligation he did not need to honor. "He has a sense of responsibility lacking among Brazilian students."[8]

In addition to such stereotypic ethnic images of the *nikkeijin*, many Brazilians directly racialize the perceived cultural differences of the Japanese Brazilians in positive terms (cf. Maeyama 1984, 448; 1996, 312). There is a strong tendency among a good number of Brazilians to favorably interpret many of the distinctive aspects and behaviors of the Japanese Brazilians (such as their high academic achievement, politeness, greater social reserve, cleanliness, etc.) as positive "Japanese" cultural qualities that are a product of their different racial descent and ethnic heritage. A Japanese Brazilian mother gave a typical example of this type of Brazilian ethnic reasoning in regards to her son:

> When my son gets good grades in school, they say, "Of course, it's because he's Japanese." When he does a really careful and neat job on a class assignment, they say, "Of course, it's because he's Japanese." When he keeps his desk clean in the classroom, they say, "Of course, he is Japanese."

WHEN MINORITIES MIGRATE   219

In fact, as a Japanese descendant in Brazil, my behavior was also sometimes attributed to essentialized Japanese cultural traits. My "Japanese" intelligence was credited for my relatively quick mastery of Portuguese more than a few times. On the day I left Porto Alegre, I told my Brazilian friends who drove me to the bus terminal that I had spent much of the previous night cleaning my apartment before I moved out. Again, the inevitable ethnic conclusion: "*Ele é japonês*" (He is Japanese).

These racialized cultural definitions of Japaneseness are not only hegemonic constructs that are simply imposed on the self-consciousness of the Japanese Brazilians. Because of their positive connotations, they are actively asserted by the Japanese Brazilians themselves. When talking about their cultural differences, my *nikkeijin* informants agreed with the way they were ethnically characterized in Brazilian society and claimed that they *are* indeed more hardworking, diligent, honest, educated, intelligent, and responsible than most Brazilians, whom they stereotypically portrayed as lazy, easygoing, irresponsible, immature, and dishonest (see also Flores 1975, 95; Reichl 1995, 49, 51, 55; Saito 1986; Smith 1979, 58).[9] In fact, it was remarkable how the comments that they made about their positive cultural qualities were frequently accompanied by negative images of majority Brazilians. For example, consider the reflections of one young Japanese Brazilian man:

> We feel lots of cultural differences in relation to other Brazilians. Lots. Our cultural level is higher. We work harder, are more diligent, and intelligent. Brazilians like the beach too much and spend too much time partying and enjoying themselves. If you ask a Japanese [Brazilian] to do something, you can be assured it will be done. If you ask a Brazilian, who knows what will happen? They aren't serious about work and are unreliable.

In this manner, although the racial differentiation of the *nikkeijin* as "Japanese" in Brazil prevents them from being considered as part of majority Brazilian society, it apparently has its advantages because it invokes a positive contrast between First World Japan and Third World Brazil and between Japanese and Brazilian culture. In fact, the Japanese Brazilians have themselves become all-too-willing participants in their positive racialization by asserting a culturally distinct "Japanese" ethnic identity while distancing themselves from the negative aspects of Brazilianness. For many of them, their ethnic-minority status is a source of much pride and self-esteem, and for some it even leads to a sense of superiority over what is considered Brazilian.[10] The result is a relatively strong self-identification as ethnic "Japanese," which continues to take precedence over their identities as Brazilian nationals.

Racial Homogenization and Ethnic Differentiation in Japan

Essentialized Racial Perceptions of Japanese Brazilians

When the Japanese Brazilians return migrate to Japan, race obviously loses its power of ethnic differentiation. However, the lack of phenotypic difference between the migrants and their hosts[11] does not mean that the Japanese Brazilians are no longer subject to racial ideologies in Japan. Although they are no longer racialized as culturally different, they are still racialized in Japan, but this time as culturally *similar* "Japanese." Needless to say, however, what it means to be culturally Japanese in Japan is very different from what it means to be culturally "Japanese" in Brazil. These different cultural meanings attached to the racial category of Japanese in Japan lead to a very different ethnic response among Japanese Brazilian immigrants in Japan.

When the Brazilian *nikkeijin* are racialized as culturally "Japanese" in Japan, they are obviously held to much higher standards than those in Brazil. According to one of my Japanese Brazilian friends in Japan,

> We think we are Japanese in Brazil, but in Japan, we find out that we were wrong. If you act differently and don't speak Japanese fluently, the Japanese say you are a Brazilian. To be considered Japanese, it is not sufficient to simply have a Japanese face and eat sushi with chopsticks. You must think, act, and speak just like the Japanese.

Another informant had similar feelings:

> In Brazil, we are considered Japanese because we speak some Japanese, eat Japanese food, and maintain some Japanese customs from our parents. This is Japanese enough for Brazilians, but for the Japanese, it means nothing. We appear quite Brazilian to them and are seen as foreigners.

Japanese ethnic perceptions of Japanese Brazilians are based on a presumed correspondence between race and culture that seems to develop in nations such as Japan in which an ideology of ethnic homogeneity is maintained. In other words, since all Japanese are seen as the same race and are perceived as culturally similar in thinking and behavior, those who are "racially" Japanese (i.e., who have a "Japanese face") are assumed to be culturally Japanese as well (see also Kondo 1986). The comments of a local neighborhood doctor who treats foreign workers was quite representative of this type of essentialized ethnic perception:

"When you live in Japan, you come to take this for granted. Everyone looks Japanese, and we all think and act in more or less the same way. So when we see someone who has a Japanese face, we end up thinking that they are like the Japanese, that they will speak and behave like the Japanese."

This perceived correlation between racial descent and culture applies not only to the Japanese in Japan but also to a lesser extent to those of Japanese descent born abroad, because it is assumed that Japanese culture will be transmitted through family socialization to those of Japanese descent regardless of national boundaries. Therefore, there was a strong expectation among most of my Japanese informants that the Brazilian *nikkeijin* should be culturally similar since they are expected to have literally inherited Japanese customs from their parents, even if they were born in a foreign country. The Japanese undoubtedly realize that the Japanese Brazilians have become culturally foreign to a certain extent, and some are not sure how much of the Japanese language and behavioral patterns they have retained abroad. Despite this, however, the anticipation is that there will be strong cultural similarities. Such ethnic attitudes toward the *nikkeijin* are clearly expressed in the following statement by a local storeowner, which echoes the feelings of many of my Japanese informants:

> We think the Brazilian *nikkeijin*, as descendants of Japanese, must have retained good Japanese traditions because even if born abroad, they grew up in Japanese families. So they must be like the Japanese, at least a little. If their face is pure Japanese, we have the idea that their customs and attitudes will be at an above-average Japanese level.

Because of such essentialized Japanese ethnic understandings in which those of Japanese descent are assumed to be culturally similar, Japanese Brazilians come under considerable assimilative ethnic pressure in Japan. However, most cannot meet such Japanese cultural demands because they lack sufficient Japanese linguistic and cultural competence. Jefferson, a young second-generation *nikkeijin* man, spoke about such frustrations:

> The Japanese make many more demands on us than on whites or other foreigners in Japan because of our Japanese faces. They think we should speak the language and understand Japanese ways because we are Japanese descendants. They must realize that we can't understand and act like them because we are from a foreign country. But the Japanese always demand this. They say, "You are *nikkei*. Why don't you speak Japanese?" Our adaptation is harder because of this pressure.

The greater cultural demands on Japanese Brazilians affect even their children in Japanese schools. One Japanese teacher noted how *nikkeijin* students, because of their Japanese faces, suffer more than those of mixed descent (cf. Hirota 1993) because they experience greater pressure to culturally conform at school. However, Japanese cultural standards are sometimes imposed even on the mixed-descent *mestiços*. Maria, a second-generation *mestiça* woman, spoke about how the Japanese women at her factory during one social outing told her not to sit Indian style on the tatami floor but in *seiza* style,[12] as is expected of Japanese women. "I just can't sit on my legs," she complained. "I'm simply not used to it. I always get leg pains after a few minutes." Maria was also reminded by her female Japanese coworkers not to use the rough Japanese to which she was accustomed, which is unbecoming of a Japanese woman.

Acting Brazilian in Japan

A number of Japanese Brazilian immigrants therefore decide to resist such assimilative Japanese cultural pressures by acting in conspicuously Brazilian ways in Japan in order to demonstrate to the Japanese that they are *not* Japanese despite their Japanese racial appearance and therefore cannot be held to Japanese cultural expectations. By asserting their Brazilian identities, they are able to ethnically differentiate themselves from the Japanese, therefore challenging their racialization as Japanese and the essentialized cultural demands that are placed on them.[13]

A common way in which the *nikkeijin* display their Brazilianness to the Japanese is through dress, which is among the most frequent emblems used to symbolize ethnic difference. Although their manner of dress is normally different from the Japanese, some Japanese Brazilians deliberately wear distinctive Brazilian clothes to catch the attention of the Japanese. Jefferson was quite explicit about his intentions:

> At first, I tried to dress like the Japanese. I knew that the Japanese manner of dressing was different from ours, so I went out and bought new clothes at the department store. But now, whenever I go to the bank or to stores, I wear Bermudas or Brazilian T-shirts. The Japanese never dress like this, so they can always tell I am Brazilian. I feel better this way because I don't want to be seen or mistaken as Japanese.

The ethnic effectiveness of clothes as an identifying marker of Brazilianness has actually increased the demand for Brazilian clothes in Japan. As a result, Brazilian clothing stores have opened in areas of Japan with high concentrations of *nikkeijin*. Of course, some Japanese Brazilians wear Brazilian clothes in Japan purely out of physical comfort or habit, but for others it is a prominent ethnic display of cultural difference. The manager of a Brazilian clothing store explained that the clothes she sells have distinctive designs, fashions, and colors that cannot be found in Japanese department stores. Jeans have colorful ornamental features, and those for women tend to be tighter around the hips (as the buttocks, not the breasts, are the primary locus of female sexual attention in Brazil). Shirts have strong (even loud) colors and may have mosaic patterns, while T-shirts with the Brazilian flag, national colors, or the country's name prominently displayed are also popular. Many of these Brazilian styles are undoubtedly exaggerated constructions that have appropriated stylistic images of Brazil without necessarily representing any particular cultural style in Brazil. When national symbols are appropriated by migrants abroad, they are frequently culturally decontextualized and reconstructed. Such clothes are meaningful as symbolic makers of ethnicity only in Japan, where the Japanese Brazilians suddenly feel a desire to express their cultural identities as Brazilians.

The Japanese Brazilians also culturally differentiate themselves as Brazilians through the use of language and greetings. Although some *nikkeijin* are sensitive to Japanese opinions and social pressures and lower their voices when speaking Portuguese in public areas, others take the opposite approach. For instance, Martina mentioned that although she speaks Japanese well, whenever she walks into a store, she makes a point of speaking Portuguese loud enough so that the Japanese will notice. "I don't want to be confused as Japanese," she said. "So I always show them I am Brazilian." Likewise, the tendency of some *nikkeijin* to greet each other loudly and affectionately in public by embracing or kissing is similarly a display of Brazilian behavior that is completely incongruous with Japanese culture and thus serves as another means of ethnic differentiation.

Some individuals take their cultural resistance further by exaggerating their Brazilian behavior in Japan in a rebellious, exhibitionist manner by purposefully acting more Brazilian in Japan than they ever did in Brazil. As one informant observed a bit cynically, "Some of these Brazilian youth have this attitude toward the Japanese: 'Hey, I'm Brazilian, and I am going to act Brazilian in Japan. And if you don't like it, screw you.' As a result, they are seen less favorably by the Japanese. However, in Brazil, they would never have acted like this and do it only in Japan." Even among those who do not take such a rebellious approach, the public assertion of their Brazilian identities is frequently a way to tell the Japanese that despite their racialization as

"Japanese," they are Brazilians who cannot be expected to behave like Japanese and speak the language fluently.

Others engage in much more subdued performances of their Brazilian identity. This is especially true among the more acculturated *nikkeijin*, who are more accommodating toward Japanese cultural expectations and feel more pressure to act in accordance with Japanese norms. For such individuals, the assertion of their Brazilianness is much less ostentatious than their peers and is usually limited to introducing themselves as Brazilians or foreigners. Of course, the need to make self-introductions is not as relevant to those Japanese Brazilians who do not speak much Japanese, since it is apparent to the Japanese that they are foreigners when they open their mouths. However, for *nikkeijin* who can speak Japanese well enough to communicate, the issue becomes critical when they meet Japanese who are unfamiliar with them and therefore assume that they are native Japanese because of their racial appearance. In such cases, their imperfect Japanese leads to some confusion and disorientation among the Japanese. Therefore, by introducing themselves as Brazilians when meeting Japanese for the first time, such individuals are able to avoid being mistaken as Japanese and therefore relieve themselves of the resulting Japanese cultural expectations that would otherwise be imposed. Geraldo spoke about how he finds it beneficial in this regard to introduce himself as a Brazilian in order to avoid cultural embarrassment or ill-treatment:

> If I just ask simple questions at a store, there is no problem, but if they start using technical terms or the conversation continues, they are surprised at my lack of comprehension and find my accent really strange because they think I'm Japanese. So it's better to say from the beginning that I am Brazilian, so that the Japanese will understand and explain things to you more carefully without looking down on you. When I first got to Japan, I would try to act like a Japanese, but now I always say I'm Brazilian. It's a way to apologize beforehand for my inability to understand Japanese perfectly.

Such concerns are most salient among those *nikkeijin* who speak fluent Japanese and are students or office workers in Japan. These individuals are the most likely to be mistaken as Japanese because of their cultural and linguistic abilities and their unwillingness to overtly display Brazilian behavior. Therefore, they sometimes find subtle ways to culturally differentiate themselves as Brazilians and avoid being held to the same social standards as the Japanese. This includes not only introducing themselves as *nikkeijin*, but writing out their Japanese last names in *katakana* (a phonetic alphabet used for foreign names) instead of using Japanese characters. Those who have both Brazilian and Japanese first names sometimes intentionally use their Brazilian name in Japan, although they may have been called by their Japanese name in Brazil. "It is my way of identifying myself as someone who is not Japanese," a Japanese Brazilian graduate student remarked. "It is my way to ask permission from the Japanese to forgive me because I behave differently from them."

Other individuals use not only public symbols such as names and self-introductions, but also personal symbols in order to ethnically mark themselves as Brazilians in Japan. For instance, Marcos, a Japanese Brazilian journalist, wears a goatee as his "little rebellion against the Japanese," an idiosyncratic emblem of his ethnic differences with Japanese men, whom he believes do not like facial hair. He also told me that he was clean shaven in Brazil, again showing how his goatee is a symbol of his Brazilian identity that has significance only in Japan. In order to resist the cultural pressures of Japanese society, Marcos, like many others, finds a need to assert his Brazilianness—a desire he had not had in Brazil. In this manner, there is considerable variation in the conscious expression of Brazilian cultural difference, ranging from aggressive displays of cultural difference in public to the subtle use of introductions, names, and other personal symbols for proper identification in order to avoid Japanese cultural pressures and ethnic embarrassment.

The enactment of Brazilian identities in Japan occurs not only in individual behavior but in collective ritual performances as well. The most important example is the samba parades that the Japanese Brazilians organize in local communities with high *nikkeijin* concentrations. Although most Japanese Brazilians never participated in samba in Brazil and even scorned it as a lowly Brazilian activity, they find themselves dancing samba for the first time in their lives in Japan and actually finding it a lot of fun. However, as was the case with the emblematic use of Brazilian clothes, considerable decontextualization and modification again occur when nationalist symbols from back home are conveniently appropriated for ethnically demonstrative purposes by Japanese Brazilian migrants in Japan.

Since the *nikkeijin* never really danced samba in Brazil, they have insufficient cultural knowledge of this national Brazilian ritual. As a result, their ethnic performance in Japan is not structured or regulated by preordained cultural models of samba but is a spontaneous cultural form generated by them in the context of enactment. For example, the samba parade I observed (in Oizumi town, Gunma prefecture) was a somewhat random cultural performance that was improvised, haphazard, and casual. The "samba costumes" the Japanese Brazilians wore were randomly chosen and ranged from simple bathing suits, clown outfits, and festival clothes with Brazilian national colors (yellow and green), to T-shirts and shorts. Apparently, few of the *nikkeijin* knew how to design or construct any real Brazilian samba costumes or had the resources to do so. In addition, most of them did not seem to know how to properly dance samba, and even if some of them were familiar with the dance form, almost no one had the experience or will to execute it properly. Therefore, instead of properly schematized body movements, most of the participants seemed to be moving and shaking their bodies randomly, some in a lackadaisical manner. The general result was simply a potpourri of costumes and individuals moving their bodies randomly without any pattern, definition, or precise rhythm that resembles actual Brazilian samba. The only part of the parade that required any explicit cultural knowledge was the singer of the samba theme and the *bateria* (the drum section that beats out the samba rhythm), both of which were composed almost exclusively of non-Japanese descent Brazilians.

Therefore, the final cultural product that emerged had little in common with samba as it is practiced in Brazil and would have been barely recognizable back home. Nonetheless, given the Japanese context in which this "samba" was being enacted, it was seen as very "Brazilian" because of its cultural distinctiveness in Japan. In other words, as long as the *nikkeijin* could find some costume that looked vaguely Brazilian and could shake their body in one way or another, the performance remained effective as a collective assertion of their Brazilian ethnic identity. This process of cultural authentication is also unintentionally supported by the presence of attentive Japanese spectators, who showed active interest in the unusual and different festivities of another nation. Since the Japanese have even less knowledge about samba than the Japanese Brazilians, they are unable to provide any cultural critique of the performance as "inauthentic," like a Brazilian audience. For them, anything that seems culturally different and novel is accepted and appreciated as bona fide Brazilian samba. Therefore, the implicit collusion between participant and observer in a foreign context validates and authenticates the spontaneously generated and random performance as a true display and assertion of a distinctive Brazilian culture.

Conclusion: Racialization and the De-essentialization of Ethnic Difference

As the case of Japanese Brazilian return migration demonstrates, what is important about racialization processes is not the racial category per se that is used to classify immigrant groups ("black," "Asian," "Mexican," "Japanese," etc.) but the cultural understandings that are attached to them in different local contexts. Although the Brazilian *nikkeijin* are racialized as "Japanese" in both Brazil and Japan, what it means to actually be Japanese is quite different in the two societies. In Brazil, Japanese racial appearance was automatically associated with positive images and cultural stereotypes, which enabled the Japanese Brazilians to claim a respected Japanese minority identity almost by fiat. As a result, their Japanese ethnic distinctiveness could easily be validated by their perceived behavioral characteristics and their symbolic deployment of Japanese tradition and ethnic festivities. When they migrate to Japan however, the *nikkeijin* find that having a "Japanese face" is an ethnic burden because of the Japanese insistence that they be culturally Japanese by virtue of their shared descent. This causes the Japanese Brazilians to assert their Brazilianness in order to defy such unreasonable cultural demands. Therefore, although the *nikkeijin* touted their distinctive Japanese cultural qualities when racialized as "Japanese" in Brazil, they ironically find themselves asserting their Brazilian cultural differences when racialized as Japanese in Japan, in order to resist assimilative cultural pressures. In this manner, the different cultural meanings of the same racial category can produce different processes of racialization among transmigrants in the sending and receiving countries, leading to divergent ethnic responses and outcomes.

Not only does race take on different meanings in different societies, it can also be used for very different ethnic purposes. The same racial category of "Japanese" that is used to inscribe cultural differences onto the Japanese Brazilians and forever confine them to minority status in Brazil is used in Japan to forcibly incorporate them under an assimilation-oriented and homogeneously constituted Japanese majority ethnicity. It is important to remember that domination and control does not always involve portraying others as *different* and inferior as the critics of Orientalism have emphasized (Said 1979; Gupta 1994). Perceptions of the other as *similar* also facilitate hegemonic projects of incorporation and assimilation based on efforts to remake the other in one's own image (cf. Todorov 1982/1984).

Regardless of its varying uses, when race becomes a fundamental component of ethnic identification, it produces an essentialized understanding of ethnicity. In Brazil, the "Japanese" ethnic identities of the *nikkeijin* were essentialized by their racial appearance, and therefore their supposedly distinctive cultural behavior was seen as a natural product of their Japanese descent. In turn, the Japanese Brazilians also understood their "Japanese" ethnicity through racialized notions of culture, laying personal claim to the positive images of Japanese culture in Brazilian society by virtue of their Japanese ancestry. When the perception of cultural difference is racially essentialized in this manner, it is removed from the contingencies of context and practice, rendering ethnic identities relatively immobile. The Brazilian preoccupation with racial appearance forever defines the *nikkeijin* as a culturally Japanese minority regardless of their level of cultural assimilation. On their side, many Japanese Brazilians continue to insist that the positive "Japanese" cultural qualities they have inherited from their parents and grandparents have persisted despite generations in Brazil, a claim made partly credible by symbolic re-creations of "Japanese" tradition in their communities. As a result, both majority Brazilians and minority *nikkeijin* were somewhat blinded to their substantial cultural similarities, which greatly outweigh any lingering differences.

Although race in Japan no longer inscribes cultural difference, the Japanese Brazilians are still confronted by essentialized notions of ethnicity in which Japanese culture is closely related to notions of racial essence. However, Japanese attempts to culturally assimilate the *nikkeijin* on the basis of their racialization as "Japanese" eventually fail as the Japanese Brazilians prove unable and unwilling to meet Japanese ethnic expectations. Many Japanese Brazilian immigrants eventually escape the racial essentialization of their ethnicity through assertive demonstrations of their Brazilian cultural differences. By disassociating culture from race in this manner, they effectively de-essentialize racialist conceptions of Japanese ethnicity among both the Japanese and themselves, causing them to mutually question their previous assumptions of cultural similarity based on common descent (see Tsuda 2003, chap. 5). If anthropology has attempted to de-essentialize the self by disengaging it from notions of biological or universal essence (Kondo 1990, 34),[14] my *nikkeijin* and Japanese informants seemingly came to the same conclusion in their ethnic encounter, although few of them attain this level of theoretical reflexivity.

In this manner, ethnic identity for Japanese Brazilian immigrants changes from something that is racially inscribed (essentialized) to something that is culturally contingent and actively negotiated in various social contexts (de-essentialized). Racially essentialized ethnic identities become harder to sustain under transnational migration because it disengages relatively static ethnic meanings from a certain locale and reengages them in a new social context, causing them to be challenged and redefined. As a result, the contextually relative and contingent nature of ethnic identity becomes more apparent, making it more dynamic and subject to contestation.

Notes

1. See Tsuda (2003, introduction) for a detailed analysis of my fieldwork experiences.

2. Because of the considerable racial intermixture in Brazil, Brazilians (unlike Americans) have a wide array of racial categories. Harris and Kottak (1963), in their study of racial categories among Brazilians in a fishing village in coastal Bahia, uncovered forty categories used to describe phenotypic differences.

3. It is interesting to note that those of Korean and Chinese decent in Brazil are also called japonês and frequently have to correct this misnomer (cf. Maeyama 1984, 455).

4. Maeyama claims that many Japanese Brazilians become angry when they are called japonês and say "I am not japonês. I am Brasileiro" (1996, 322). However, his impressions seem to be based on earlier postwar experiences and are no longer true today.

5. Some have even claimed that favorable images of Japan, fostered by the mass media, prevail throughout Latin America (e.g., see Nakagawa 1983, 63).

6. When the author was in Brazil, Japan's serious and prolonged recession did not receive prominent media coverage.

7. Some researchers have noted a desire among second- and third-generation immigrant minorities to explore and assert their past ethnic heritage (e.g., Hansen 1952). This type of "ethnic revival" occurs not only because they feel that they are losing their ethnic distinctiveness due to assimilation. Since they are now well established and secure in majority society, they are able to assert a minority ethnic identity without compromising or threatening their social position.

8. In fact, the only notable negative image of the Japanese Brazilians that I encountered in Brazil was a sense that the japonês are somewhat unreceptive toward ethnic outsiders. I have also heard Brazilians mention how the "japonês" are too timid and restrained and that women are too submissive to men, although the reference was more to Japanese in Japan. Although much of Brazilian ethnic prejudice is expressed through joking behavior, the jokes about the "japonês" that I actively collected from Brazilians tended to emphasize the positive aspects of the Japanese Brazilians such as their high academic achievements (although my own "Japanese" ethnic status undoubtedly made complete access to any nasty jokes difficult). The most popular ethnic joke in Brazil about the Japanese Brazilians is undoubtedly the following: "If you want to enter the University of São Paulo [the Harvard of Brazil], kill a Japanese" (like Asians in the United States, the Japanese Brazilians are overrepresented at top Brazilian universities). The other joke of this type that I heard involves plugging a Japanese into an intelligence-measuring machine. The reading goes off the scale, causing the machine (made in Brazil) to break and the Japanese to come out stupid like a Portuguese (in contrast to American attitudes toward the British, the Portuguese are frequently portrayed in Brazilian jokes as bumbling idiots). Other jokes poked fun at either the facial features or strange and complicated last names of the Japanese Brazilians. Also, the stereotype

of Asians in the United States as "geeks" or "nerds" seems to be much less prominent in Brazil.

9. Many Japanese Brazilian respondents in Saito's survey (1986) characterized Brazilians in this unfavorable manner. Few saw Brazilians as educated, hardworking, intelligent, or responsible. In fact, according to a 1995 *Datafolha* poll of Japanese Brazilians living in São Paulo, 59 percent admitted that they are prejudiced against Brazilians, whereas only 35 percent felt that Brazilians were prejudiced against them (cited in Linger 2001, 25).

10. Studies have shown very high levels of self-confidence and esteem among the Japanese Brazilians (Saito 1986, 249–50). In fact, Kitagawa's study of two Japanese Brazilian communities found that 86 percent of those surveyed have lots of pride in their Japanese descent, and 11 percent have some pride, rates higher than for Japanese *in Japan* (Kitagawa 1996, 188; 1997, 133).

11. There are relatively few Japanese Brazilians of mixed descent in Japan.

12. *Seiza* is when one sits on folded legs with the knees together. The sitting position is very uncomfortable for those who are not accustomed to it, and the author himself cannot endure *seiza* for more than several minutes, although men are allowed to sit Indian style on the tatami floor.

13. It is very important to note that the desire to resist Japanese cultural pressures is not the only reason the *nikkeijin* express their Brazilian identities in Japan. See Tsuda (2003) for an extensive analysis of the development of Brazilian migrant nationalism among the Japanese Brazilians in Japan.

14. This has also been emphasized by those studying the cultural construction of emotion as part of the self (e.g., see Lutz 1988; Rosaldo 1980, 1984).

References

Basch, Linda, Nina Glick Schiller, and Cristina Szanton Blanc. 1994. *Nations unbound: Transnational projects, postcolonial predicaments, and deterritorialized nation-states.* Amsterdam: Gordon and Breach Publishers.

Capuano de Oliveira, Adriana. n.d. Migration and identity: Brazilian Dekasegi in Japan. Unpublished manuscript.

Cardoso, Ruth Corrêa Leite. 1973. O Papel das Associações Juvenis na Aculturação dos Japoneses [The role of youth associations in the acculturation of the Japanese]. In *Assimilação e Integração dos Japoneses no Brasil* [The Assimilation and Integration of the Japanese in Brazil], ed. Hiroshi Saito and Takashi Maeyama, 317–45. Petrópolis, Rio de Janeiro: Editora Vozes.

Centro de Estudos Nipo-Brasileiros [Center for Japanese-Brazilian Studies]. 1992. *Pesquisa de Comportamento e Atitude de Japoneses e seus Descendentes Residentes no Brasil.* São Paulo: Centro de Estudos Nipo-Brasileiros.

Charles, Carolle. 1992. Transnationalism in the construct of Haitian migrants' racial categories of identity in New York City. In *Towards a transnational perspective on migration: Race, class, ethnicity, and nationalism reconsidered,* ed. Nina Glick

Schiller, Linda Basch, and Cristina Blanc-Szanton, 101–23. New York: New York Academy of Sciences.

Fanon, Frantz. 1967. *Black skin, white masks*. Trans. Charles Lam Markmann. New York: Grove Press.

Flores, Moacyr. 1975. Japoneses no Rio Grande do Sul [The Japanese in Rio Grande do Sul]. *Veritas* 77:65–98.

Freeman, Carla. 2000. *High tech and high heels in the global economy: Women, work, and pink-collar identities in the Caribbean*. Durham, NC: Duke University Press.

Giddens, Anthony. 1989. *Sociology*. Cambridge: Polity Press.

Gupta, Akhil. 1994. The reincarnation of souls and the rebirth of commodities: Representations of time in "East" and "West." In *Remapping memory: The politics of TimeSpace*, ed. Jonathan Boyarin, 161–83. Minneapolis: University of Minnesota Press.

Gupta, Akhil, and James Ferguson. 1992. Beyond "culture": Space, identity, and the politics of difference. *Cultural Anthropology* 7 (1): 6–23.

Hansen, Marcus. 1952. The third generation in America. *Commentary* 14:492–500.

Harris, Marvin, and Conrad Kottak. 1963. The structural significance of Brazilian racial categories. *Sociologia* 25:203–9.

Harvey, David. 1989. *The condition of postmodernity*. Cambridge, MA: Blackwell.

Hirota, Yasuo. 1993. Toshi Esunikku Comyunitei no Keisei to "Tekiyo" no Iso ni Tsuite: Tokuni Yokohama-shi Tsurumi no Nikkeijin Comyunitei o Taisho to Shite [About the construction of urban ethnic communities and the phase of adaptation: Especially within the Nikkeijin communities in Tsurumi, Kanagawa-ken]. *Shakai Kagaku Nenpo* 27:289–325.

Kitagawa, Toyoie. 1996. Hamamatsushi ni Okeru Nikkei Burajirujin no Seikatsu Kozo to Ishiki: Nippaku Ryokoku Chosa o Fumaete [The lives and consciousness of the Brazilian Nikkeijin in Hamamatsu City: Based on surveys in both Japan and Brazil]. *Toyo Daigaku Shakai Gakubu Kiyo* [Bulletin of the Department of Sociology at Toyo University] 34 (1): 109–96.

———. 1997. Burajiru-taun no Keisei to Deasupora: Nikkei Burajirujin no Tei-jyuka ni Kansuru Nananen Keizoku Oizumi-machi Chosa [Diaspora and the formation of Brazil-town: A continuing seven-year Oizumi-town survey about the settlement of Brazilian Nikkeijin]. *Toyo Daigaku Shakai Gakubu Kiyo* [Bulletin of the Department of Sociology at Toyo University] 34 (3): 66–173.

Kondo, Dorinne K. 1986. Dissolution and reconstitution of self: Implications for anthropological epistemology. *Cultural Anthropology* 1 (1): 74–88.

———. 1990. *Crafting selves: Power, gender, and discourses of identity in a Japanese workplace*. Chicago: University of Chicago Press.

Linger, Daniel T. 2001. *No one home: Brazilian selves remade in Japan*. Stanford, CA: Stanford University Press.

Lutz, Catherine. 1988. *Unnatural emotions: Everyday sentiments on a Micronesian atoll and their challenge to Western theory*. Chicago: University of Chicago Press.

Maeyama, Takashi. 1984. Burajiru Nikkeijin ni Okeru Esunishitei to Aidenteitei: Ishikiteki Seijiteki Genjyo to Shite [The ethnicity and identity of the Nikkeijin in Brazil: Politico-cognitive phenomena]. *Minzokugaku Kenkyu* [Ethnicity Research] 48 (4): 444–58.

———. 1996. *Esunishitei to Burajiru Nikkeijin* [Ethnicity and Brazilian Nikkeijin]. Tokyo: Ochanomizu Shobo.

Moreira da Rocha, Cristina. 1999. Identity and tea ceremony in Brazil. *Japanese Studies* 19 (3): 287–95.

Nakagawa, Fumio. 1983. Japanese–Latin American relations since the 1960s: An overview. *Latin American Studies* 6: 63–71.

Ogbu, John U. 1978. *Minority education and caste: The American system in cross-cultural perspective.* New York: Academic Press.

Park, Kyeyoung. 1999. "I am floating in the air": Creation of a Korean transnational space among Korean-Latino American remigrants. *Positions* 7 (3): 667–95.

Reichl, Christopher A. 1995. Stages in the historical process of ethnicity: The Japanese in Brazil, 1908–1988. *Ethnohistory* 42 (1): 31–62.

Rosaldo, Michelle, Z. 1980. *Knowledge and passion: Ilongot notions of self and social life.* Cambridge: Cambridge University Press.

Rosaldo, Michelle. 1984. Toward an anthropology of self and feeling. In *Culture theory: Essays on mind, self, and emotion,* ed. Richard A. Shweder and Robert A. LeVine, 137–58. Cambridge: Cambridge University Press.

Said, Edward W. 1979. *Orientalism.* New York: Vintage Books.

Saito, Júlia Kubo. 1986. Auto-Estima e Auto-Conceito entre os Jovens Descendentes de Japoneses [Self-esteem and self-concepts among Japanese-descent youths]. In *O Nikkei e Sua Americanidade* [The Nikkei and their Americanness], ed. Massao Ohno, 241–55. São Paulo: COPANI.

Smith, Robert J. 1979. The ethnic Japanese in Brazil. *The Journal of Japanese Studies* 5 (1): 53–70.

Tajima, Hisatoshi. 1995. Laten Amerika *Nikkeijin* no Teijyuka [The settlement of Latin American *Nikkeijin*]. In *Teijyuka suru Gaikokujin* [Foreigners who settle], ed. Hiroshi Komai, 165–98. Tokyo: Akaishi Shoten.

———. 1998. Socio-cultural differentiation in the formation of ethnic identity and integration into Japanese Society: The case of Okinawan and Nikkei Brazilian immigrants. *JCAS Symposium Series* 8:187–97.

Todorov, Tzvetan. 1982/1984. *The conquest of America.* New York: Harper & Row.

Tsuda, Takeyuki. 2003. *Strangers in the ethnic homeland: Japanese Brazilian return migration in transnational perspective.* New York: Columbia University Press.

ETHNIC ASCRIPTION VERSUS SELF-DEFINITIONS III

A S THE CHAPTERS IN THE PREVIOUS SECTION HAVE ILLUSTRATED, ethnic identity is not only internally developed through the individual's self-consciousness of racial and cultural differences, but it is also externally imposed by the dominant society onto the ethnic group. Since there is often a conflict between internally experienced and externally defined identities, the development of ethnic identity is inherently a process of competing ethnic constructs and contestation over cultural meanings. In most cases, either the external or internal aspects of identity become dominant, or some type of compromise or synthesis is achieved between these two components. Otherwise, the ethnic self may become conflicted and fragmented.

Because the individual's experience of self is always partly constituted by external ethnic ascription in this manner, the development of identity is always embedded within dominant contexts of power and inequality, especially for ethnic minority groups. Some minority individuals resist these hegemonic ethnic categories and understandings that are imposed on them, while others may conveniently appropriate or promote them for their own uses. In cases where the externally ascribed ethnic identity is derogatory, individuals may simply attempt to escape such definitions by deploying other identities or forgoing minority ethnicity altogether by passing as part of the majority group. The construction of ethnic identities is therefore an ongoing struggle and negotiation between the inner self and society that is never fully resolved as individuals continue to engage in relationships with different people and institutions and contend with the shifting nature of state power.

As the chapters in this section illustrate, such identity struggles are not merely over ethnic and cultural definitions. Often, what is at stake is none other than the socioeconomic well-being and livelihood (if not survival) of an ethnic minority group. In such cases, the struggle over ethnic identity can involve political resistance against oppressive state power or mobilization for minority rights and socioeconomic justice. The most apparent example is Yos Santasombat's chapter, "Peasants, Ethnicity, and the Politics of Location in Thailand," which describes an ongoing conflict between the Thai government and the Lua, an indigenous minority group of highland peasants. In response to environmental problems created by decades of commercial logging and deforestation, the Thai government has enforced a forest conservation policy that has established national parks on territory inhabited by the Lua. As a result, the Lua have been threatened with relocation and the loss of their land as well as the disruption and prohibition of their traditional rotational swidden agricultural practices, which are critical for their subsistence and economic survival.

According to Santasombat, this is not simply a conflict over land ownership and use but a struggle over ethnic symbols in which the Lua are deploying their own ethnic self-definitions to actively contest how they are being externally represented by the Thai state. The ethnic identity of the Lua is intimately tied to their territory, since their agricultural as well as religious practices and historical memories that define them as a people are based on their attachment to their land and the cultural meanings of specific locations and places. Therefore, the spatial domination of the state is also a form of ethnic domination, in which the Thai government is attempting to justify its appropriation and confiscation of Lua land by externally defining the Lua in a denigrating manner as illiterate savages who are destroying the forest with their primitive agricultural practices. This conflicts with the Lua's own ethnic self-understandings as traditional guardians and managers of the forest who have developed a sophisticated system of controlled land use and conservation through institutionalized cultural, religious, and kinship processes. As a result, the Lua have begun to challenge and resist the state's hegemonic ethnic representations and the suppression of their cultural identity through positive ethnic self-assertion in a cultural politics of location and protest against the state. The Lua are also engaged in a cultural struggle for property rights by ethnically representing themselves through their religious rituals and sacred practices as first inhabitants who have a natural and spiritual claim to the land. Therefore, by challenging the territorial encroachment of the state, the Lua are defending a threatened cultural system that is the basis for their ethnic identity and agricultural livelihood.

However, ethnic minorities do not always contest hegemonic ethnic representations of themselves but may actually appropriate and perpetuate such stereotypes for their own purposes, even when they are derogatory. An example are the Maasai, a former "tribal" people in Kenya discussed by Lotte Hughes in her chapter, "'Beautiful Beasts' and Brave Warriors: The Longevity of a Maasai Stereotype." Hughes notes the remarkable longevity of the stereotype of the Maasai as brave and ferocious warriors and free-roaming pastoralists (as well as dignified noble savages) who have been impervious to administrative control and modernity. This dominant image continues to persist in current accounts, advertisements, films, and the tourist industry, despite its inaccuracy, especially in terms of the contemporary lives of the Maasai, who have now urbanized and are ordinary wage laborers.

Hughes historically examines how this erroneous stereotype was developed and perpetuated during British colonialism for various purposes. Early travelers portrayed the Maasai as "beautiful beasts" in their accounts in order to sell books and deal with their own sense of personal and sexual inadequacy. Such portrayals were then readily appropriated by British authorities to justify their colonial policies and attempts to civilize what were perceived to be primitive and wild savages. Maasai territory was confiscated on the grounds that they were aimless pastoralists who did not fully appreciate and utilize their land. Pacification and relocation of the Maasai was justified by their supposed aggression and danger to nearby Europeans. Their refusal to submit to capitalist wage labor produced images of the Maasai as stubborn, uncontrollable primitives who refused to modernize, which further justified coercive and repressive measures against them. Although there were dissenting accounts and administrators who questioned, and even refuted, this dominant ethnic stereotype, their voices eventually were not heard.

In contrast to the Lua, however, the Maasai have not contested this externally imposed ethnic stereotype. Instead, they have bought into these derogatory images and have appropriated (and even enacted) them for their own purposes, contributing to their contemporary persistence. Undoubtedly, this is partly an attempt by the Maasai to increase tourism revenue from foreign visitors seeking authentic encounters with exotic and wild tribal peoples. Maasai activists who are demanding land restitution are also invoking this dominant ethnic stereotype by erroneously representing themselves as a former warrior people who fought and died in order to defend their lands against colonial intrusion in the past. It also seems that the Maasai are attempting to nostalgically recover a sense of self-respect and past glory in response to apparent concerns that they are "losing their identity" in the face of urbanization, land deprivation, and the demeaning, urban jobs that they currently perform. Unlike the Lua, for whom the construction and assertion of an alternative ethnic self-consciousness against the state was critical for their cultural identity and economic survival, the Maasai have become all-too-willing promoters of their externally ascribed ethnic identities for exactly the same purposes. Nonetheless, considerable internal disagreement within the Maasai community remains over such strategies of ethnic advancement.

In other cases, it is not the specific details of an ethnic identity that are the source of contention, but the ethnic category itself. In other words, the ethnic identification that is imposed by dominant society on the minority group may not be recognized by its members, who view themselves in terms of other identities. This is the case with the Roma (gypsies) of Eastern Europe, analyzed by Andrea Boscoboinik in her chapter, "Becoming Rom: Ethnic Development among Roma Communities in Bulgaria and Macedonia." Although the category of "Roma" is commonly used by outsiders to refer to Gypsy peoples, they themselves do not use this ethnic label, nor do they identify as Roma. There are a number of reasons for this. First, Roma peoples are very heterogeneous and divided according to differences in culture, language, religion, socioeconomic level, and national affiliation, and they therefore have little in common. As a result, they do not share a coherent and collective ethnic identity and instead identify according to much more specific ethno-linguistic and regional groups. In addition, since they were nomadic and have been scattered over a broad geographical area for many generations, they are not unified by a shared affiliation with a land of ethnic origin (unlike other diasporic groups like the Jews and Armenians, where the ethnic homeland provides a common identity). Finally, as is the case with many ethnic groups, they reject the externally imposed "Roma" label because of its pejorative connotations.

However, according to Boscoboinik, there is currently a process of "ethnicization"—the emergence of a collective ethnic identity—among the disparate Roma groups. This is partly the result of the constant imposition of a homogeneous Roma identity on them by dominant society as well as common experiences of discrimination, scapegoating, and cultural difference from surrounding communities. However, this movement is mainly being led by elite, educated Roma who are attempting to develop a shared ethnic consciousness across national borders in order to politically unify and mobilize the Roma in the struggle for human rights and socioeconomic justice. However, such calls for unity and collective ethnic identification have not affected ordinary Roma, who remain divided and do not show interest in ethnic mobilization or trust the various Roma organizations that have proliferated in recent years. Therefore, there is yet little evidence that this process of ethnicization will become a viable means to improve the socioeconomic situation of Roma groups, and it may even exacerbate the division between elite and ordinary Roma. Like with the Maasai, efforts to appropriate externally ascribed ethnic categories for instrumental political purposes by ethnic minorities are fraught with ambiguity and internal dissension.

Instead of manipulating or contesting dominant ethnic representations and identities, minority individuals may sometimes attempt to escape them altogether (especially when they are derogatory) by not only rejecting the external category imposed upon them, but by also attempting to become ethnically invisible. Such a case is briefly discussed in Eugeen Roosens's chapter, "Subtle 'Primitives': Ethnic Formation among the Central Yaka of Zaire." Similar to the Roma Gypsies, the ethnic group known as the Yaka (or Bayaka) in Southwestern Zaire actually consist of disparate peoples who have been grouped together by outsiders under one ethnic category in a process of "ethnogenesis" (ethnic formation). The ethnic labels that these peoples actually use to refer to themselves range from the general category of Yaka to more particular ethnic affiliations (such as Baluunda and Suku), depending on the social situation. The internal ethnic diversity of the group is further reinforced by those who consider themselves Luunda (the political and social elite who are descendants of people who once conquered and dominated the region) and non-Luunda (known as landowners and descendants of the original indigenous people living in the region). These are mutually exclusive ethnic identifications, although in reality, there has been considerable intermixing between the two groups.

However, when these peoples internally migrate to the city of Kinshasa, they are collectively referred to as Yaka by urban residents, who do not recognize the ethnic diversity inherent in the group. A small number of individuals vehemently reject the Yaka category because of its pejorative connotations as rural primitives untouched by modernity who are currently performing dirty, unskilled jobs at low wages. However, unlike the Maasai and Roma, who either reject homogenizing external classifications or have selectively adopted them to further their own ethnic causes, most Yaka in Kinshasa have attempted to hide their ethnic background in public by speaking vernacular Lingala and not teaching the Yaka language to their children in an attempt to pass as part of the majority urban population. In other words, for disparaged ethnic minorities, there seem to be two opposed types of ethnic advancement: (1) the assertion of ethnic identities through political mobilization in an effort to improve their minority status by fighting discrimination and socioeconomic marginalization, and (2) the concealment of ethnic identity through cultural assimilation in an attempt to avoid and escape a disadvantaged minority status. It is still an open issue whether ethnic visibility or invisibility is a more effective strategy among minority individuals for social integration and mobility in mainstream society.

Takeyuki Tsuda

Peasants, Ethnicity, and the Politics of Location in Thailand

8

YOS SANTASOMBAT

Introduction

SOUTHEAST ASIA HAS LONG BEEN A CROSSROADS where the most diverse ethnic and indigenous groups have come into contact and mixed with each other. Sociocultural and ethnic diversity have served as modes of adaptation for peoples that live on the margins and in the interstices of the major civilizations of the region and that have patterned power relations with representatives of these civilizations. Although most of the ethnic groups of the region were found in the highland areas, sharp boundaries did not develop between the hill and lowland peoples. Rather, throughout most of Southeast Asia, hill peoples were incorporated into social systems dominated by the lowland peoples. The hill peoples provided the lowlanders with forest products while obtaining metal, salt and, other needed trading items from the lowlanders.

The ethnic groups of Southeast Asia found themselves caught up in the formation of the nation-states during the colonial period and the nationalist struggles that swept the region after World War II. Many Southeast Asian governments pushed a policy of assimilation of ethnic minorities. Access to and the use of forestland for swidden cultivation became more restricted. The lives of various ethnic groups have been transformed by the expansion of state control first unleashed during the colonial period and by subsequent development programs designed to ensure the domestication of these ethnic minorities.

Today, however, the struggle between the state and ethnic groups in Southeast Asia is not merely a struggle over forestland, property rights, and territorial integrity. It is also a struggle over the appropriation of symbols, a struggle over how the past and present shall be understood and represented, and a contentious effort to give meaning to local history and ethnic identity. This chapter is an attempt to present a case study of how a sense of ethnic identity of a highland minority group is situationally reconstructed in northern Thailand. It explores the relationship between the concept of place and the production of ethnic identity. The ethnic highlanders on the one hand, and the Thai state on the other, have different conceptions of rights over forestland based on different conceptions of the meaning and usage of forest. The Royal Forestry Department deploys technologies of territorialization to assert its rights of control over the forest. This in turn gives rise to struggles in which ethnic identity is produced and reproduced. The ethnic identity of a minority group is thus constructed in a continuous process, not only by external forces and labeling by the state and other outsiders with whom they interact, but also through their own sociocultural process of creating a self-definition. The perplexing notion of the ethnic group is largely attributable to this imagined construction. An ethnic category can be examined only when we can account for the continual processes of imagined construction, both subjective and externally enforced, viewing them both together in their historical context. Ethnic identity is thus a "complex and dynamic construct which takes place within the context of changing power relations and socio-economic conditions where the past is reconstructed to give meaning to the present and hope for the future" (Yos 2001, 166).

The Lua Highlanders of Northern Thailand

In the afternoon of January 10, 1999, a family of Lua swidden cultivators of Baan Toey, Phu Kha mountain of Nan province, northern Thailand, were confronted by Royal Forestry Department (RFD) officials on a paved road near the entrance to their village. Two men were picked up and taken to the nearby police station. They were subsequently charged with trespassing, occupying, and illegally practicing slash-and-burn cultivation within the national park. They were detained at the police station for eight days and later released on bail after a large group of Lua peasants threatened to stage a massive rally in front of the district office.

This incidence is by no means isolated. As powerful demands for resources, land, and military control have guided state expansion to the farthest corners of the kingdom, the autonomy and mobility of the marginal cultural groups of once inaccessible places—tropical forests, rugged mountains—have increasingly been threatened. In fact, during the past decade, many ethnic minority groups of the northern highlands have been victimized by a militant conservation policy to protect watershed areas. In August 1990, twenty-four Karen of two villages in Doi Suthep National Park were arrested for practicing swidden agriculture in an area where they had lived for centuries. In 1991, the Hmong of Khun Klang village in Inthanon National Park were forced to abandon their agricultural practice and were threatened with relocation. Since 1992, the RFD has strengthened its forest conservation policy by establishing more national parks and reforestation programs and has stepped up its threat of relocation. From then on, the forest conservation policy became highly politicized and contested because the RFD strictly enforced the policy on certain marginal groups, especially the ethnic highlanders and poor lowlanders, while favoring the richest and their investment in terms of eucalyptus plantations and resort construction on forestland. In 1994, the RFD started to relocate the Mien villages of Mae San and Pha Daeng in Doi Luang National Park, and they stepped up relocation programs in various parts of the upper north.

In addition to the relocation schemes, the rapid expansion of conservation forests by establishing more national parks and reforestation programs has threatened the security of tenure of local villagers who usually have only customary access to land in the forests. Several Karen villages in Mae Wang district of Chiang Mai, for instance, had their rotational swidden lands taken away for reforestation. Without legal recognition of community rights and communal property regimes, the RFD began to establish new national parks and expand the old ones in both highland and lowland areas, often encroaching upon and enclosing community forests that many villages had been preserving as their graveyard, watershed areas, or multipurpose communal woodland. Changes in forest conservation policy and its harsh implementation provoked so many disputes and conflicts that local villages have begun to form a network to protest against enclosure by the state (Anan 1998, 72–73).

Indeed, the relocation and reforestation programs are part of the RFD's use of the spatial technologies of domination. The RFD produces space through cutting up and differentiating between parcels of space; through the use and abuse of maps, borders, and markers; and through the control of movement within and across different kinds of boundaries, assigned forest types, zones, and so on. These boundaries, forest types, and zones are authorized spaces of domination. They are what Pile (1997, 3) called the "spatial practices of oppression."

In addition to the spatial technologies of domination, the RFD also uses brutal tactics to suppress the expression of cultural identity or opposition by indigenous groups. These tactics include the machinery of fear: surveillance, border guarding, controlling movement, dividing and ruling, pitching the lowlanders against the ethnic-minority highlanders, and so on. The state power is also mobilized through the imposition of a system of values—forest conservation for the entire nation, watershed area protection for the common good—that the indigenous peoples must recognize, even while they might despise it.

The forestry officials and the Lua look at each other suspiciously, each needing to know where the other is. Nevertheless, neither sees the other accurately; every contact between the officials and the indigenous is a falsehood. The officials have to figure out who it is they are oppressing. In one sense, their power is the power to have control over space, to occupy it, and to guarantee that hegemonic ideas about that space coincide with those of the nation and national identity. In order to impose and maintain control over people, they have to work out what exactly has to be suppressed and what does not, while not really understanding what is going on. The RFD officials seek to construct a nominal image to describe what the indigenous people are like, and then they denigrate them on the basis of those descriptions. The forms of knowledge through which the officials came to know the indigenous, and significantly through which they became the power wielder, are fantasies. They are built out of stories, anecdotes, misconceptions, lies, and so on—fantasies about the untamed hill peoples, shifting cultivation, the use of fire, opium production, and so on and so forth. These fantasies, however, serve to legitimize their power of exclusion (Yos 2003, iii).

The Lua, on the other hand, are in a different position. They have to recognize that the officials are more powerful, and this puts them in the position of having to *misrecognize* themselves (Bourdieu, 1990, 16; 1991, 164) and their culture as having less value, because it is the RFD's values that have authority and give meaning, however fantastic. In a way, the indigenous are battered into place by phantasm—savagery, untamed hillbillies, illiteracy, animism, and so on—within powerful discourses on development and progress. Their images are formed in the imagination of the Thai state and the civilized majority (Yos 2003, 209–10).

Yet these powerful, dominant discourses do not have an unquestioned hegemony: Lua respond, reinterpret, and challenge even as they accept and are shaped by these forms of discourse. It may, at first glance, appear that the powerful control space and that the Lua are weak, passive, and controlled. But as the arrested were charged, Lua began to fight back. The spatial practices of resistance, or what Mohanty (1987) calls a "politics of location," has begun.

In Mohanty's understanding, the politics of location involves not only a sense of belonging, of where one is in the world, but also the political definitions of the "grounds" on which struggles are to be fought. In this sense, location has more to do with the active constitution of the grounds on which political struggles are to be fought and the identities through which people come to adopt political stances, than with the latitude and longitude of experiences of circumscription, marginalization, and exclusion (Pile 1997, 28). Moreover, location conveys a sense of having to take up positions in activism and struggle in order to change the plot of power. These locations cannot, however, be presumed in advance of activism and struggle. If politics is about making history, then it is also about changing space: political locations are constituted through the struggles that are supposedly fixed in them. Location is both the ground that defines struggle and a highly contested terrain, which cannot provide any secure grounding for struggle (28). Thus, in the case of the Lua, ethnicity is produced as well as uncovered in their definitions of experience, with attendant notions of unity and difference forming the basis of this production. Location is simultaneously about history, community, ethnicity, and unity, about definitions of boundaries, of who occupies the same place and who does not. It is strategic, tactical, and mobile.

In this sense, politics of location involves boundaries, movement, and territorialization. They are the spatialities of struggle within which ethnic identities are formed, boundaries are drawn and redrawn, and history is constructed and reconstructed, and resistance can be analyzed as a reaction to the injurious effects of power relations.

The Territorialization of Ethnicity

The case of the Lua makes it necessary for us to rethink the question of roots in relation to ethnic identity and the forms of its territorialization. Examining the question of roots in relation to ethnic identity illuminates the complexity of the ways in which people reconstruct, remember, and lay claim to particular places as homelands and nations.

For instance, the Lua still *remember* a kingdom that could have been formed in the north of Thailand by Khun Luang Wilangka, the great Lua leader. The existence of this kingdom shows through in the different chronicles written several centuries after the Tai Yuan had assured their domination over the region. In them, we see the Lua recognized as the first inhabitants and founders of most of the towns and settlements of the north. The ancient Tai Yuan chronicles give Doi Ngen (Suthep) as the site of the former capital of the Lua, which was founded prior to the creation of the Mon kingdom of Haripunjaya in the eight century AD (Condominas 1990, 10–19).

Similarly, the Lua of Doi Phu Kha in Nan province still remember themselves to be the first inhabitants of the lowland areas in Woranakorn or Pua. It was a group of Tai Lue who were forced to migrate en masse from Sipsong Panna more than two centuries ago who attained domination over the Lua country. The Lua subsequently fled to seek refuge in the hills of Doi Phu Kha and began the practice of rotational swidden agriculture, as flat land suitable for wet rice cultivation was nowhere to be found.

Territorial displacement is not, of course, new to northern Thailand. Peoples have always moved through violence or through personal desire. Cultural groups were swept away as prisoners of war when their kings were defeated, the same way marginal groups are now evicted from their home to pave way for dam construction, forest conservation, and other large-scale government projects. In recent years, however, place is becoming more important, to the degree that the authenticity of dwelling is being undermined and encroached upon by politico-economic processes of spatial transformation and forest conservation. In other words, it is under conditions of challenge and threat that identities are most vehemently and at times violently spatialized.

The following sections of this chapter explore the relationship between place and the reproduction of a flexible peasant ethnic identity. It will argue that the Lua ethnic identity is a *continuing production* based on sets of opposition between the self and multiple others. The perspective taken here is that ethnic identity is the unstable, contingent reflection of a dialogic process in which a number of voices are raised. The information exchanged in this dialogue is constituted in, on the one hand, positive assertions of group self-identity and, on the other hand, labels affixed to the identities of others. Some of the voices in the dialogue may be more powerful than others, conjuring up more domineering symbols of inclusion and exclusion. Some may be, moreover, more authoritative than others, possessing the power to enforce their interpretation of identities through the attachment of either benefits or liabilities to them. Yet the dialogue is ongoing; none really has the last word. This perspective insists on joining the cultural politics of location to those of identity in a manner that connects them in terms of "contextualized political strategies." Location, or

"ground for struggle," then becomes a chosen spatial metaphor for emphasizing the situated practices that shape, but do not necessarily determine,
the formation of identities and places.

The Lua Swidden Fields and "Ground for Struggle" in Doi Phu Kha

The hills of Doi Phu Kha are the result of the state-making project. Although its geographical location prevented extensive settlement, the area
has, since the mid-eighteenth century, formed part of an internally complicated hierarchical network of power relations among various ethnic
groups including the Lua, the Tai Lue, and the Tai Yuan lowlanders
(Cholthira 1987, 24–28). "The valleys made the hills," in the words of Scott
(1999), and the Lua "not only live in marginal territory but they also occupy marginal land" (Hirsch 1990, 56).

Doi Phu Kha in Pua district of Nan province is now home to approximately 1,152 small-holder families of Lua peasants (some thirteen official
villages with 4,407 residents) spread across a vast area of rugged mountains,
prime forest, and steep river valleys, including more than 22,386 hectares
of rotational swidden fields.

In multifarious ways, the forests and fallow fields are central to the successful practice of swidden agriculture. They are the prime sources of food,
medicinal herbs, fodder, and grazing ground. The Lua are also blessed by
the abundance of *miang* (forest tea), *makwaen*, and other nontimber forest
products, which are the major sources of cash income for the hill peasants.
The dependence of the Lua on forest resources has been institutionalized
through a variety of social and cultural mechanisms. Through religious beliefs, folklore, and traditional practices, the village communities have drawn
a protective ring around the forests and fallow fields. Across the hills and
steep valleys of Doi Phu Kha, there exists a highly sophisticated system of
conservancy that takes various forms. Hilltops are dedicated to local deities,
and the surrounding trees and small patches of forests are regarded as sacred ground. Many wooded areas are not of spontaneous growth and bear
marks of the local practice of forest preservation; indeed, the lushness of
what is now Doi Phu Kha National Park, extending over mountain ranges
and hillsides, bears testimony to the care bestowed upon them by the successive generations of the Lua and other indigenous groups.

While sacred forests testify to the role played by traditional beliefs in the
preservation of nature, in other instances, it is informal management practices that regulate the utilization of forest. While no formal management

system exists, practical protection is secured by customary limitations on users. In many patches of forest, there are rules that prohibit the felling of trees in gullies and water courses. These rules have an obvious role in stabilizing water flows and preventing landslides. Furthermore, with the planting of *miang, makwaen,* and other tree species, a fairly common phenomenon, the forests preserved within the local boundaries are zealously guarded by the villagers.

As this description of traditional conservation systems suggests, these hill peasants are primed for collective action. The absence of economic differences among local villagers greatly facilitates social solidarity, as do the ties of kinship shared by them. In their egalitarian characteristics and almost total reliance on natural resources, the Lua are representative of highland societies in which ecological constraints to the intensification and expansion of agriculture have resulted in an emphasis on the close regulation of the common-property resources so crucial for the survival of the households. The detailed rules and regulations for the management and utilization of forests and fallow fields account in large measure for the stability and persistence of many mountain communities.

All Lua hill villages in Doi Phu Kha are swidden landholding units. The village social structure is organized around the control and utilization of swidden lands. Swidden fields are held in common, but household use-rights, established by previous use, are recognized and inheritable by descendants of the households. In practice, most if not all households return to the spot they cultivated during the previous rounds of swidden cultivation. Household use-rights to swiddens are often shared between siblings, even after they are married. The individual household, composed of husband, wife, and children, is the primary labor group. Most agricultural work, however, is organized around the exchange of labor between relatives and friends. Labor exchange groups are organized at planting and harvesting times when a great deal of work must be handled swiftly. There is very little wage labor, either in cash or in kind. All Lua families in Doi Phu Kha are strictly monogamous. The usual pattern of postmarital residence is matrilocal. The children adopt their father's family names according to Thai law but worship their maternal ancestral spirits.

The annual cycle of cultivation in Baan Toey begins in January, when the choice of cultivation site is chosen by the village elders. Even though the elders know the next field to be cultivated should be in the orderly round of cultivation and fallow, they must verify that the fallow field has reached the proper stage of forest regrowth, that the soil is not "*jeud*" (tasteless) or infertile, and that there is no evidence that a recent fire has burned through the chosen site. If these conditions are not met, they go on to the next field in the rotational cycle. Each household traditionally had eight to ten swidden plots, but in recent years, increasing pressures from the RFD have forced many swiddeners to relinquish parts of their swidden lands, and the rotational cycle is reduced to three to five years. This means, in effect, that the choice of fields is becoming more limited, that the chosen field may not be fully fertile, and that the yield may not meet the household's subsistence needs.

The clearing of swidden fields starts in January and usually lasts ten to fifteen days. Family members work together in the harsh labor of slashing the fallow fields. Small trees and brush are slashed as close to the ground as possible; larger trees are cut, leaving about one- or one-half-meter-high stumps, but their branches are trimmed close to the main trunk so that any immediate regrowth will not shade the rice stalks. The Lua strictly forbid cutting trees on the ridge tops and along gullies and water courses in a conscious effort to preserve the watersheds and prevent soil erosion. The cleared fields are allowed to dry for about six to eight weeks to ensure a complete burn. The burn is preceded by a communal ceremony to propitiate the field spirits and to insure that the fields will burn completely and not out of control. The Lua are extremely careful to construct firebreaks around the sides and tops of the cleared fields before they burn them by clearing an eight-to-ten-meter-wide firebreak and sweeping it clear of underbrush to protect other fallow fields. Field burning involves community coordination and cooperation because of the perceived dangers to the village and communal land resources.

After the fields have been cleared and reburned, each household prepares a shelter in their swidden. The small, low-roofed shelter is erected on short poles, flooring is made of split bamboo, and the roof is covered with leaves. The swiddeners retreat to shelter during heavy rains or extreme heat of the day, and their older children may stay in the fields overnight to guard them before and during harvest.

The full mobilization of friends and relatives in labor-exchange groups is seen in planting and harvesting the fields. Planting begins early in April before the rains have begun and the loose ash and topsoil have been swept down the slopes. Before or on the first day of planting their fields, each household must slaughter a chicken and make sacrifice to the spirits of the locality. Each household must also make sacrifice to the ancestor spirits. On April 12, just before the northern Thai New Year celebration, all Lua villages join together to make sacrifice to Phii Khun Nam Pua (Chao Luang Pua, or Spirit of the Watershed). The households of all villages are obliged to donate money for sacrificial offering of chicken, pig, or buffalo on this occasion, which symbolizes the common interests of the villagers in the agricultural process and reaffirms the connection between the Lua villagers and their claims to their swidden fields through their relationships with the spirits.

In planting the fields, men thrust the iron tips of their planting sticks eight to ten centimeters into the soil while women and small children follow behind and throw a few seeds in each hole. A wide variety of crops is planted in the *Lua* swidden fields. Rice is certainly the primary crop. Each field contains a number of different varieties of rice classified as glutinous or nonglutinous; as heavy, medium, or light ripening; by color and shape of grain (short, long, golden, red, yellow, etc.); and by sources of germplasm (for instance, rice varieties obtained from other places or ethnic groups are named after them). In Baan Toey, the most commonly planted varieties are glutinous, heavy- and slow-maturing rice, with a fairly short, rounded grain. Over forty varieties are planted each year because of their taste and other specific qualities. Each household normally plants eight to ten different rice varieties in the swidden, keeps its own seeds separate from all other rice, and prefers its own to that of other households. Poorer families, who cannot afford to wait the extra month for heavy rice to mature, plant large amounts of light- and early-ripening rice varieties. The planting of different varieties of rice over a period that stretches out three to four weeks is highly beneficial when it comes to harvest time because different ripening dates reduce the amount of labor needed to harvest. Different varieties and ripening dates also reduce the risk of total production loss due to pest or unseasonable storm near harvest time. Several varieties of flowers, maize, beans, mustard, taro, sweet potatoes, yams and other tuber crops, and many varieties of melons, cucumbers, gourds, and squashes are also grown in the swidden. Each variety of plant is placed according to its growth habits and its soil and water requirements.

The most labor-consuming, tedious, and disliked aspect of swidden agriculture is weeding. The weeding season starts shortly after the first rains have come and ends only when the rice is about to ripen. All Lua swiddeners assert that rice production increases according to the number of times a field is weeded during the growing season. All farmers confirm that the reason they do not clear larger plots is that they recognize the limitations of their household's labor supply, and larger plots, though they could be cleared and planted, could not be weeded. Weed growth is also a primary reason why swidden fields in the area are not farmed for more than one year. Lua swiddeners recognize the need for a long fallow period in order to restore fertility to the fields and reduce weed growth. Fallow fields are also vital sources of food and medicinal plants. The number of non-cultivated plants in the fallow fields totals about two hundred varieties (Kunstadter 1978, 91). Thus the eight-to-ten-year rotational cycle appears to be a stable pattern. A decrease in the length of fallow would undoubtedly lead to a decline in soil fertility and crop yield. A shortening of the rotational cycle might also lead to a change in forest regrowth from predominantly leafy species to grassy species, making further use of land for cultivation increasingly difficult.

In recent years, increasing pressure from the RFD is forcing the Lua in Doi Phu Kha to shorten their cultivation-fallow cycle from eight to ten years to three to five years. Consequently, the average landholding in Baan Toey has declined markedly. Whereas each household traditionally had eight to ten swidden plots (each plot containing 1.6 to 2 hectares of farmland), today there has been a remarkable drop in the numbers down to three to five plots for each household. This change has had the predictable result of destabilizing subsistence security and may be leading to changes in the pattern of swidden practices. For instance, repeated use of swidden fields without a long fallow period has led to increasing problems of weed growth. Baan Toey's swiddeners have resorted to the practice of spraying salted water for limiting weed growth. Increasing saline content and soil contamination may be one of the most important side effects of the use of salt in swidden agriculture in the coming years.

The swiddens, however, continue to be productively used by the villagers after the harvest and during the fallow period as important sources of food, animal fodder, and medicinal plants. After the harvest, the major economic activity and primary source of income for the Lua is the gathering of *makwaen*, *kong*, and *miang* (forest tea) from the uncultivated portions of the environment and the surrounding forest area. The fact that the Lua derive most of their livelihood from their own environment, that swidden agriculture is the most important base of their subsistence, and that fallow swiddens and other uncultivated portions of their environment make important contributions to the economy of the indigenous group reinforces their strong ties to the land. The "field" (*rai*) thus continues to be a spatial metaphor for emphasizing the situated practices that shape the formation of Lua identities in Doi Phu Kha.

A Peasant Economy and Indicators of Social Differentiation

In contrast with many lowland villages in northern Thailand, internal differentiation among various social classes in Baan Toey is minimal. There is

Table 8.1.   Percentage of Village
Household and Social Differentiation

Social Class Status	Percentage
Poor	49
Middle	26
Well-to-do	21
Rich	4

no landless household in the village, and all households derive most of their subsistence needs from swidden agriculture. However, a deeper under-standing of the dynamics of village formation and household economy is facilitated by a survey of 198 households taken as representatives of poor, middle, well-to-do, and rich households in Baan Toey.[1]

From table 8.1, it can be clearly seen that there are only a handful of rich villagers in Baan Toey, and class differentiation is minimized by very little disparity in terms of swidden landholdings or the size of farmland among different classes.

As shown in tables 8.2 and 8.3, even though the sizes of swidden farms seem to reflect structural differences in the economic situations of the households, poorer households can still manage to reproduce themselves in terms of subsistence farming without any real necessity to supplement their income by engaging in wage labor. As shown in table 8.5, 98 per-cent of all poor households in Baan Toey depend for their survival on sub-sistence production, while 78 percent of all middle households depend on swidden farming for their survival. In contrast with lowland peasant vil-lages, where wage labor far exceeds farm income, in Baan Toey, on the average, more than 75 percent of the households are completely devoted to swidden production, and wage labor plays only a minor role in the to-tal income of these households (see tables 8.4 and 8.5). More importantly, inequality in access to resources as well as differences in the pattern of uti-lization of land and natural resources does not exist in the village, render-

Table 8.2.   Distribution of Households and Farmland in Baan Toey

Type of Household (rai)	No. of Households	Percent	Size of Swidden Farm
Poor (6,000 Baht/year)	91	49.5	7.1020
Middle (6,001–12,000/year)	51	25.8	9.0392
Well-to-do (12,001–60,000/year)	51	20.7	13.2927
Rich (60,000+/year)	8	4.0	14.2500
Total	198	100	Mean = 9.1717

Table 8.3.   Average Land Holdings and
Social Class

Social Class Status	Landholding (rai)
Poor	7.10
Middle	9.04
Well-to-do	13.29
Rich	14.25

ing notions of "egalitarian rice-producing" society or "homogenous peas-ant units" definitely applicable. More importantly, the traditional practice of a land-sharing, close-knitted network among kin, and flexibility and openness in terms of land-use management leave large numbers of peas-ant households in possession and access of swiddens capable of providing a livelihood.

If differentiation involves accumulation and a permanent process of change in the ways in which different groups in Baan Toey gain access to the products of their own or others' labor based on their differential control over production resources and on increasing inequalities in access to land, then differentiation in Baan Toey is minimal. Even though income inequal-ities are increasing and some peasant households become richer than others, social relations between them remain practically unchanged. There is no transfer or extraction of surplus generated in the village economy.

Moreover, factors that contribute to the dispossession and increasing marginalization of lowland peasants, especially indebtedness and inability to repay at high interest rates, are totally nonexistent in Baan Toey. The Lua villagers lead a modest, traditional way of life, with very little conspicuous consumption. As shown in table 8.6, average household expenditures, in-cluding food for daily consumption, clothing, transportation, and educa-tional fees among other things, are very low.

Table 8.4.   Percentage of Household
Occupation

Household Occupation	Percentage
Agriculture	75
Agricultural wage labor	1
General wage labor	17
Factory wage labor	4
Trade	1
Civil service	2

Table 8.5.   Occupation and Major Sources of Income in Baan Toey (baht)

Social Class	Agriculture	Wage Labor in Agriculture	Wage Labor Outside Village	Factory Worker	Trade	Civil Service	Total
Poor	96	1	1	—	—	—	98
Middle	38	1	8	4	—	—	51
Well-to-do	15	—	19	3	1	3	41
Rich	2	—	5	—	—	1	8
Total	151	2	33	7	1	4	198

Similarly, as tables 8.7 and 8.8 clearly show, the average annual income of Lua villagers far exceeds their expenditures. In contrast with lowland villagers, the Lua swiddeners of Doi Phu Kha are not increasingly drawn into commodity circuits in the sphere of exchange. On the contrary, it seems highly likely that most if not all village households are able to maintain and reproduce themselves independently of these circuits, and they are still in control of strategic means of production and labor processes.

Nevertheless, during the past decade, their subsistence security and control over means of production and local forest resources are increasingly undermined by the state. Another system of forest management, propelled by powerful economic and political forces and rested on a radically different set of priorities, is threatening the stability and persistence of the mountain communities. It is to the conflict between the imperatives of scientific forestry and the socioeconomic and cultural values of the highland peasantry that we shall now turn.

The Science of Domination and the Art of Resistance

The landmark in the history of Thai forestry is undoubtedly the political reform program of King Rama V during the time of colonial conquest in Southeast Asia. An attempt to maximize the commercial exploitation of the forest in northern Siam, as the country was then called, and to minimize the power and control of local lords over the forest concessions led to the creation of a forest department, set up with the help of British experts in 1892.[2] The first task before the new department was to oversee all teak logging concessions in the north, and for this the assertion of state monopoly right was considered essential. Initial attempts at asserting state monopoly through the Teak Conservation Act of 1898 and the Forest Reservation Act of 1913 having been found wanting, a comprehensive forest act was promulgated in 1941. This act provided for the constitution of national reserves or protected forests. Since then, the national forestry policy has been guided

Table 8.6. Average Household Expenditures in Baan Toey (baht)

Social Class	Food	Clothes	Medicine	Construction	Transport	Education	Household Appliances	Debt Payment	Other
Poor	5393	535	132	51	256	212	892	—	50
Middle	5015	422	61	925	336	412	899	101	37
Well-to-do	6624	670	152	2056	959	482	1155	—	103
Rich	13000	1487	156	27500	1875	875	1626	75	—
Total	5858	572	119	1800	487	346	966	29	55

Table 8.7. Household Annual Income, Expenditure, and Debt (baht)

Social Class Status	Income	Expenditure	Debt
Poor	6,000	7,102	0
Middle	12,000	8,613	101
Well-to-do	60,000	14,200	0
Rich	80,000	33,772	75

by two popular misconceptions, namely the overemphasis on short-term economic benefits and the separation of people and forest.

Predicated on the ideological setting in which they operated, the techniques of scientific forestry were designed to reorder both nature and customary use in its own images. Reserved forests were cut up into pieces, and areas of forest deemed commercially profitable were granted logging concessions. At a deeper epistemic level, the language of scientific forestry worked to justify the shift toward commercial working. The terms *mai me kha* ("valuable woods") or *mai huang harm* ("restricted woods"), used mainly to refer to teaks and few other species, bear no relation to the ecological and other functions the species may perform for the surrounding communities. By a similar act of redefinition, one that rested on a prior usurpation of legal ownership by the state, local forest users were designated its enemies. Thus the national forest policies indicated that possible sources of injury to the forest include *chao baan* (villagers, local people) and particularly *chao kao* (highlanders) in the same category as natural hazards and forest fires.[3]

The strategies forged by forestry science and legislation manipulated agrarian practices by carefully regulating the intrusion and exclusion of *chao baan*, classified in the terminology of forestry science as one of the enemies of the forest. Consequently, forestry policy has been based on the assumption that local communities are not part of the ecological system and that local people are the main cause of deforestation. This particular misconception has greatly undermined the traditional role and customary rights of the local communities as guardians, custodians, and managers of the forest.

Table 8.8. Household Annual Expenses and Debt (baht)

Social Class Status	Expenditure	Debt
Poor	7,102.14	317.35
Middle	8,613.53	1,117.65
Well-to-do	14,200.00	1,219.51
Rich	33,772.50	875.00

Even though the local people were classified in the terminology of forestry science as one of the enemies, intrusion into the reserved forests was seldom strictly enforced at the local level. However, in 1989, after many decades of extensive commercial logging and exploitation, including the massive expansion of agricultural land, the forest destruction and the resulting environmental problems led to a public outcry and a demand for a total logging ban. Even though factors contributing to the rapid destruction of the forest have included unbalanced growth between urban and rural sectors, skewed land distribution and insecure land tenure, unsustainable exploitation of forests for industrial timber production and export, and inappropriate policies of centralization and mismanagement of natural resources, none of these problems have been seriously tackled (Yos 1992, 107). On the contrary, conservation became top priority and led to a radical shift in the management practices of the forestry department.

At the instrumental level, new national parks, conservation forests, watershed areas, and reforestation programs were set up and expanded, and the RFD carefully regulated peasant access into these conservation zones. The radical shift in the management priorities, from commercialism to conservation, has threatened the security of local villagers who usually have only customary access to land in the forests. Moreover, the establishment and expansion of conservation forests often encroached on community forests and swidden fields. The radical shift to a conservation policy has also led to a redefinition of customary practices of forest use. Rotational swidden agriculture and the use of fire, for instance, were outlawed and strictly enforced. In the application of these techniques, consideration of control was paramount. Not surprisingly, the dislocation of agrarian practices that followed was to have far-reaching consequences.

It is important to reiterate the impact of the imposition of national parks and conservation forest management on the dislocation of agrarian practices. The working of a forest for conservation necessitates its closure to local communities that have traditionally protected and utilized the surrounding forest areas. Closure to local people is regarded as integral to successful reforestation and conservation of watershed and biodiversity-rich areas. Furthermore, protection from fire is necessary to ensure the regeneration and growth to maturity of young saplings. Thus the practice of swidden agriculture—of firing the forests—had to be regulated or stopped in the interest of scientific forestry.

The loss of control over forests and swidden fields has been acutely felt by the hill peasants of Doi Phu Kha, leading to a deep sense of discontent. Lung In, one of the Lua peasants who were arrested on January 10, 1999, gave the following comment: "The RFD is taking away our forests and our rice fields. They are robbing us of our own property. We have been living here for hundreds of years."

The belief obstinately persists in the minds of all Lua cultivators that the RFD is taking away their property. The notion seems to have grown up from the complete lack of restriction or control over the use of forest by the local people during the past decades. The oldest inhabitants are therefore most assured of their rights to the use of the forest. Subsequent regulations—all very recent—only appear to them as an abrupt encroachment upon their rights, culminating in the final acts of confiscation and arrest.

The RFD officials, on the other hand, claim that the Lua peasants were stubborn and disobedient. A local RFD official contends thus: "We have repeatedly warned them that burning the forest areas in the national park is no longer acceptable. It is against the law, and we had to arrest them in order to teach them a lesson."

The root cause of the conflict between the RFD and the highland peasants over forest rights thus lay in differing conceptions of property rights and ownership. According to the swidden cultivators, all forestland and swidden fields are communally owned and managed, and rights of individual household users are established by previous claim and utilization. With the forestland and swidden fields never having attracted the attention of the RFD, there exists strong historical justification for the popular notion that all forestland within the village boundaries is the property of the Lua.

In more ways than one, the recurrent conflicts are a consequence of the struggle for existence between the peasants and the RFD—the former to live, the latter to conquer. In its most elementary form, local discontent is a result of the restrictions on customary patterns of use entailed by scientific forestry. The takeover of the forests and their subsequent management are at once a denial of the state's traditional obligations and a threat to the "subsistence ethic" (Scott 1976, 2) and security of the hill peasantry.

Initially, defiance of the hegemony of the forestry officials and state control on forests took direct forms. In 1997, the Lua of Doi Phu Kha staged a massive rally against the declaration of Doi Phu Kha National Park. They managed to unite as a militant movement and even threatened to burn down the local national park office. This rebellious act is very similar to the cases in Andra Pradesh and Udaipur, where forest dwellers attacked forestry officials (Haimendorf 1982, 90–92); the case of armed men disguised as women (Demoiselles) who attacked the forest guard and the police in the mountain region of Ariege in nineteenth-century France (Sahlins 1994); the forest rebellion in Uttarakhand (Guha 2000, 187–89);

and the Jharkhand and Chipko movements (Sengupta 1988, 111–12). Lately, however, the relationship between forest dwellers and the state has come to be mediated through NGOs and people's groups, and through these organizations, the Lua articulate with great tenacity their need to subsist by being peasants in the forest and demand access to forests and swidden fields. While the dialogue between them and the RFD is ongoing, the Lua continue to practice rotational swidden cultivation and use the forests in their everyday life.

In addition to noncompliance, the hegemony of the forest officials is eroded by other forms of resistance. In day-to-day functioning, the Lua accept the domination of forest officials, who are feared and respected. At the same time, the Lua may refuse to have anything to do with local forestry officials. Many Lua villagers, for instance, have been reluctant participants in the wage labor with the national park office. In fact, wage employment of a few Lua teenagers in a local reforestation program alienates the elders, many of whom forbid their children to work for the RFD. In the mind of the forest dwellers, forest areas that they have not been able to use, especially those fenced off for regeneration or that are under reforestation, bring out a deep sense of hostility, and communal struggles are organized through their experience of injustice, injury, and inequality.

In recent years, forests and swidden fields have become a spatiality of resistance in the sense that they have to be struggled for and toward. The unity of communities of resistance is formed through the production of location, the redefinition of boundaries, and identity formation. A politics of place is thus undeniably also a politics of identity in which group boundaries are constantly being emplaced, repositioned, opened up, and closed down. Resistance thus involves the spatiality of location and boundary formation, and in the case of Doi Phu Kha, it is also constituted through religious ritual.

Every year, on the second week of April, the Lua reproduce and redefine a sense of place in their experiment in forging locally internalized ethnic identity as a form of solidarity. Right before the annual planting of the rice fields, the Lua propitiate the spirit of Chao Luang Pua, the most powerful local deity. Chao Luang Pua has a definite foundation myth that, as it happens, is connected with the displacement of the Lua from lowland areas to the mountains of Doi Phu Kha. Lung Moon, a respected religious leader of Baan Toey, gave the following version of it, corroborated by other adepts:

A long time ago, Chao Luang Pua was a lowlander who lived in Baan Gam on the foothill of Doi Phu Kha. On the bank of the nearby river Pua that runs down from the mountain, there existed a "Satoke" stone, a sacred stone that is shaped like a small table. Local people shared a popular belief that the sacred stone had the power to protect its believers from wounds or accidents. As increasing numbers of lowlanders moved in and settled down, more forestland were cleared, and competition and conflict over land between the newcomers and the Lua who were the first inhabitants became more rampant. Then one year came a flash flood resulting from forest depletion. The whole lowland area was under water. When the water receded, the villagers found that the sacred stone was missing. Many of them went downstream in search of the stone, but Chao Luang Pua, for some unknown reason, led a number of his men upstream in search of the sacred stone. He propitiated the spirits of the forest who are supposed to watch over the fortunes of the people to help him, and after weeks of searching, he found the sacred stone where it now lies, on a bank of a small tributary in Doi Phu Kha. Years later, the Lua fled to seek refuge on the hills of Doi Phu Kha, and every year a sacrifice of a buffalo is offered to Chao Luang Pua who now watches over the fortunes of the Lua people.

In the preparation of the sacred feast, the Lua spend a week performing the "*yum kwaen*" ceremonies. These festivities are partially to effect a reconciliation between friends and relatives and to reconstruct a sense of solidarity. All members of Baan Kok village parade to the home of Kao Jum (a religious practitioner) where they spend an entire day eating, drinking, singing, and dancing with fellow villagers. The following day, a group of Lua people from Baan Kok travels to Baan June, another Lua village, where the *yum kwaen* feast is held, and the next day, the celebrations move to Baan Toey and so on and so forth until the processional pattern has come to a full circle.

The *yum kwaen* ceremony is held in each and every Lua village in Doi Phu Kha, with a belief that Chao Luang Pua will accompany them to give blessing to "his children." The ceremonies take place when the cycle of the year has come round and a new agricultural calendar is about to begin. They provide, in effect, a discharge of all the ill feelings during the previous year and reanimate the spirit of "*communitas*" (Turner 1969, 180). The ceremonies also serve to reestablish their sense of place as the first inhabitants and rightful owners of the forests and swidden fields in Doi Phu Kha. When the *yum kwaen* ceremonies have been completed, the entire "Lua" community works together to prepare for the propitiation of Chao Luang Pua. The day before the propitiation, a spirit house is erected near the sacred Satoke stone, and the whole area is cleared and cleaned in order to symbolize the clearing of all hostilities among the Lua people. The en-

tourage of religious practitioners and representatives of all the Lua villages
are present at the sacred site where they spend the night with Chao Luang
Pua. On the next day, the boundaries of the Lua people are redrawn in the
prayer of Kao Jum as he makes the offering of the buffalo to Chao Luang
Pua, the greatest of the local spirits:

> We invite the Mother Earth, Chao Luang Pua, and the guardians of the
> hills, forests, and waters to come and join us at this sacred site. We, your
> humble children, are here to sacrifice an animal on your behalf. We have
> not forgotten you, so we beg you to come and accept our sacrifice. We
> have now cleared our forests and our fields, and we beg you for protection
> and blessing.

In the reproduction of this ritual, the Lua unequivocally assert continuing rights of control and use of forestland in Doi Phu Kha. Through a
mix of religious beliefs and ritual, the peasants have redrawn a protective
ring around the forest and the boundary of their ethnic group. The continuity of their world rests on continuity in their relationship with the forest. Scientific forestry threatens to disrupt this continuity, most obviously
by denying access and by imposing an alien system of management on the
forest. In this manner, peasant resistance has brought to the fore, on the one
hand, conflicting conceptions of property and ownership and, on the
other, conflicting conceptions of forest management and use. The conflicting perspectives rest on fundamentally different conceptions of the forest, on radically different systems of meaning. Scientific forestry represents
a threat to the subsistence and the cultural survival of the hill peasants; opposition to its working has necessarily to invoke an alternative system of
use and of meanings.

In their search for alternative meanings, Doi Phu Kha is conceptualized
as a site of struggle, a fiercely contested terrain of symbolic and material
practices. It is not just a mountain but a *place*; it invokes a sense of belonging and of where the Lua people are in the world, and it is the ground on
which struggles against the RFD are to be fought. Doi Phu Kha is simultaneously about history, community, ethnicity, and unity. It involves
boundaries, movement, and territorialization. It is a spatiality of struggle
within which ethnic boundaries are drawn and redrawn and history is constructed and reconstructed.

The Lua's assertions of their exclusive rights to territory are multivo-
cally expressed through everyday forms of resistance, including their
agricultural production and ritual performance. Their legitimate claims
are based on their status as the first inhabitants of Doi Phu Kha, on their

continuing residence, and on the linkage between ethnic identity and local landscape. Their sense of place and ethnic identity, however, are not fixed and immobile. On the contrary, their space-identity formations are tactical and strategic. They are continuing productions based on sets of opposition between the Lua and multiple others, especially the RFD and the lowlanders.

Doi Phu Kha has a politics and is produced through material and symbolic struggles. It is a ground for struggle and a spatial metaphor that has history woven into its very fabric. Resistance to scientific forestry and the RFD's use of spatial technologies of domination hinges critically on the social memory of past displacements, their evictions from lowland areas. Their refusal to comply with the spatial practices of oppression is shaped by attachments to the specific site, hence their struggle for place and identity.

Conclusion

Ethnic identity, for many peasants on the margins, stands for a community, a safe place, where there is no need to explain oneself to outsiders; it stands for home; more problematically, it can elicit a nostalgia for the good old days that never were, a nostalgia that elides exclusion, power relations, and difference. Motifs of home, community, and identity animate works by peoples on the margins (Kondo 1996, 97). Identity, then, is the product of work, of struggle; it is inherently unstable and contextual, and it has to be constantly reevaluated in relation to critical political priorities; and it is the product of interpretation—interpretation based on constant attention to history (Martin and Mohanty 1986, 210).

Ethnic identity is not a commodity that is formed naturally as a by-product of descent, culture, and genetic transmission (Miron 1999, 80–81). Rather, identity is relationally and situationally constructed and reconstructed across a shifting network of social relations through time. The central point about understanding ethnic identity as relationally and situationally constructed (Yos 2001, 165–66) is that there is no personal ethnic identity apart from a relationship to other identities. Furthermore, the processes of identity formation within the social context of ethnicity are inseparable from the broader social relations of power and material and ideological structures. A postmodern concept of ethnic identity embraces consciousness of other groups. It also calls for social action through a constant reflexive monitoring of the intentions, motivations, and reasons that propel groups into action. The process of collective ethnic-identity formation moves substantially beyond the notion of the autonomous modern self to embrace the recognition of ethnicity as a contested cultural terrain whose borders are constantly drawn and redrawn. This redrawing of boundaries assumes a considerable degree of conflict over values and a shared sense of common purpose. Within this framework, conflict is elevated to a normative status.

The increasing recognition of the issue of ethnicity on a global scale creates an alternative identity politics that challenges the conventional notions of the political subject of late modernity. It also provides a social space within which the marginal peasants can effectively challenge and destabilize the state.

Notes

1. Field research was carried out in Baan Toey from March 1999 to February 2000. Of all the 305 households in the villages of Baan Toey Klang, Toey Kew Hen, and Toey Huan Ngon, an overview of 198 households was obtained in order to derive baseline indicators like landownership, size of farm operation, migration, and indicators of social differentiation.

2. For detailed accounts of the history of the Royal Forestry Department and forestry policy in Thailand, please see Royal Forestry Department (1971), Anchalee (1988), Filipchuk (1991), and Saneh and Yos (1993); for a comparative study of local and scientific concepts of forest classification, see Santita (1996).

3. There is without a doubt a basic contradiction in terms in the state policies at work here. On the one hand, Thai society was basically an agrarian society. In the past, when forests were abundant, local people farmed on forestland that they cleared off to make their living. The state then encouraged and provided support to such practices by granting them land rights and land titles. Even after the opening up of the Thai economy to the world market over a hundred years ago, the state continued to support farmers to turn more forestland into farmland in order to produce surplus agricultural products for exports, and the revenue generated was spent on financing the modernization programs. On the other hand, the RFD repeatedly made accusations that forest farmers were encroaching on the forest reserves. Such official attitudes and practices of the RFD totally disregarded the long-established local tradition and the fact that land clearance by local farmers had in fact been in response to government policies. His majesty the king once said, "In forests designated and delineated by the authorities as reserved or restricted, there were people there already at the time of the delineation. It seems rather odd for us to enforce the reserved forest law on the people in the forest which became reserved only subsequently by the mere drawing of lines on pieces of paper. The problem arises in as much as, with the delineation done, these people became violators of the law. From the viewpoint of law, it is a violation, because the law was duly enacted; but according to natural law the violator of the law is he who drew

the lines, because the people who had been in the forest previously possessed the rights of man, meaning that the authorities had encroached upon individuals and not individuals transgressing the law of the land" (Local Development Institute 1992, 22–23).

References

Anan, Ganjanapan. 1998. The politics of conservation and the complexity of local control of forests in the northern Thai highlands. *Mountain Research and Development* 18 (1): 71–82.

Anchalee, Jengjalern. 1988. Forestry for community: An analysis of forest policy in Thailand. Unpublished PhD thesis, College of Environmental Science and Forestry, State University of New York.

Bourdieu, P. 1990. *The logic of practice*. Stanford, CA: Stanford University Press.

———. 1991. Language and symbolic power. Trans. Gino Raymond and Matthew Adamson. Cambridge, MA.: Harvard University Press.

Cholthira Satayawatana. 1987. *Lua Muang Nan* [The Lua of Nan]. Bangkok: Muang Boran Publishers.

Condominas, G. 1990. From Lawa to Mon, from Saa' to Thai: Historical and anthropological aspects of Southeast Asian social spaces. Canberra: An occasional paper of the Department of Anthropology, Research School of Pacific Studies, Australian National University.

Filipchuk, V. R. 1991. Forest management in Northern Thailand: A rural Thai perspective. Unpublished MA thesis, Department of Geography, University of Victoria.

Guha, R. 2000. *Unquiet woods: Ecological change and peasant resistance in the Himalayas.* Berkeley: University of California Press.

Haimendorf, C. V. 1982. *Struggle for survival.* Delhi: Oxford University Press.

Hirsch, P. 1990. Review essay: Marginal people on marginal land. *Bulletin of Concerned Asian Scholars* 22 (4): 55–59.

Kondo, D. 1996. The narrative production of "Home," community and political identity in Asian American theatre. In *Displacement, Diaspora, and Geographies of Identity*, ed. Smardar Lavie and Ted Swedenburg. Durham, NC: Duke University Press.

Kunstadter, P. 1978. Subsistence agricultural economies of Lua' and Karen Hill Farmers, Mae Sariang District, Northwestern Thailand. In *Farmers in the forest: Economic development and marginal agriculture in Northern Thailand*, ed. Peter Kunstadter, E. C. Chapman, and Sanga Sabhasri. Honolulu: University of Hawaii Press.

Local Development Institute. 1992. *Community forestry: Declaration of the customary rights of local communities: Thai democracy at the grassroots.* Bangkok: LDI.

Martin, B., and C. Mohanty. 1986. Feminist politics: What's home got to do with it? In *Feminist studies, critical studies*, ed. Teresa de Lauretis. Bloomington: Indiana University Press.

Miron, L. F. 1999. Postmodernism and the politics of racialized identities. In *Race, Identity, and Citizenship: A Reader*, ed. Rudolfo D. Torres, Louis F. Miron, and Jonathan Xavier Inda. Oxford: Blackwell.

Mohanty, C. T. 1987. Feminist encounters: Locating the politics of experience. In *Destabilizing theory: Contemporary feminist debates*, ed. M. Barrett and A. Phillips. Cambridge: Polity Press.

Pile, S. 1997. Introduction: Opposition, political identities and spaces of resistance. In *Geographies of Resistance*, ed. Steve Pile and Michael Keith. London: Routledge.

Pile, Steve, and Michael Keith, eds. 1997. *Geographies of resistance*. London: Routledge.

Royal Forestry Department. 1971. *History of the Royal Forestry Department B.E. 2439–2514*. Bangkok: Royal Forestry Department (in Thai).

Sahlins, P. 1994. *Forest rites: The war of the Demoiselles in nineteenth-century France*. Cambridge, MA: Harvard University Press.

Saneh, Chamarik, and Yos Santasombat, eds. 1993. Pah Chum Chon Nai Prathet Thai: Naew Tang Karn Pattana [Community forestry in Thailand: Development perspectives]. Bangkok: Local Development Institute.

Santita, Ganjanapan. 1996. A comparative study of indigenous and scientific concepts in land and forest classification in northern Thailand. In *Seeing forests for trees: Environment and environmentalism in Thailand*, Philip Hirsch. Chiang Mai: Silkworm Books.

Scott, J. C. 1976. *The moral economy of the peasant*. New Haven, CT: Yale University Press.

Scott, J. C. 1999. The state and the people who move around: How the valleys make the hills in Southeast Asia. *IIAS Newsletter* 19: 3–4.

Sengupta, N. 1988. Reappraising the tribal movement—II: The economic basis. *Economic and Political Weekly* 23 (8).

Turner, V. 1969. *The ritual process*. Ithaca, NY: Cornell University Press.

Yos Santasombat. 1992. Community-based natural resource management in Thailand. *Asian Review* 6: 78–124.

———. 2001. *Lak Chang: A reconstruction of Tai identity in Daikong*. Canberra: Pandanus Books, Australian National University.

———. 2003. *Biodiversity, local knowledge and sustainable development*. Chiang Mai: Regional Center for Social Sciences and Sustainable Development. Faculty of Social Sciences, Chiang Mai University.

"Beautiful Beasts" and Brave Warriors: The Longevity of a Maasai Stereotype

9

LOTTE HUGHES

I N 1932, THE MAASAI PEOPLE of colonial Kenya (formerly British East Africa) submitted a memorandum to the Kenya Land Commission (KLC) about massive land losses they had suffered at the hands of the British in the 1900s.[1] Through their "chiefs, headmen, and elders," they began by describing their ethnic group. Instead of using their own words, however, they chose to repeat a description of the Maasai made by "eminent Britishers."

> This Nilotic-Hamitic tribe of pastoral nomads in former days overran East Central Africa. They owed their supremacy to their military organization under which the warrior companies or *sirits* lived apart and formed a republic of young men governed solely by ideas of military glory . . . They are a pagan tribe impervious to the efforts of any missionary society. Their bravery is proverbial. The customary diet is meat, milk and blood: any form of agricultural labour is beneath their dignity. The Masai are conservative pagans and so far have shown but little response to administrative effort. (*Kenya Land Commission Evidence and Memoranda* 1934, 1221)

They wished, they said, to "place on record glimpses of our status prior to the British advent as well as the characteristic [*sic*] and our origin as analysed" by supposedly eminent persons. They recited this largely derogatory account, proudly declaring, "We have deserved the special attention of almost all authors who have written books on East and Central Africa," and they gave a list of books that the KLC could consult for further information. This began with *Through Masai Land* by Scottish explorer Joseph Thomson, who is credited with being the first European to cross "Kenyan" Maasailand in the 1880s (Thomson 1885).[2] I shall return to this celebrated travelogue shortly.

More than seventy years later, some Maasai are still describing themselves in remarkably similar terms. (Of course there are many exceptions, and ethnic identity is contested within the community itself, but I wish to discuss what may be termed the more unreconstructed accounts.)[3] In self-essentializing fashion, they emphasize social conservativism, imperviousness to modernity and development, men's activities and manhood, the centrality of warriors (*il-murran*) in Maasai society, military prowess, and the supposedly warlike nature of the community, even though there are no more wars to go to and cattle raiding is banned. In certain texts and orally, people and their practices are frozen in time. The Maasai are "the great warrior people who roam the endless plains" (Olol-Dapash 1997).[4] Pastoralism remains central; there is little or no mention of nonpastoral livelihoods, which ignores the fact that the Maasai economy diversified in the second half of the twentieth century and many people have become urbanized or move to and fro between urban and rural areas. Instead, it is claimed that "[they] still live much as they did thousands of years ago, herding cattle, sheep and goats" (Saitoti 1981, dust-jacket blurb)[5] or that "the Maasai are probably the most purely pastoral peoples of Africa" (Kantai 1971, viii). A classic description of a noble warrior standing on one leg opens the book *Herd & Spear*, coauthored by a former Tanzanian Maasai park conservator (Saibull and Carr 1981). In the first chapter, "Who Are the Maasai?" there is barely any mention of women (other than mythical ones) or nonwarriors; it is as if they don't exist. Throughout, the emphasis is on male roles. The majority of photographs, even in a chapter on women, celebrate warriors. Elsewhere, only Maasai women such as Naomi Kipury have tended to write about women.

To give a more recent example, Kenyan Maasai activist Johnson Ole Kaunga focused largely on young men and warriors in an article on the challenges facing urban-based Maasai in Tanzania. While making important points about the effects of land losses, the marginalization of indigenous peoples in national development processes, and the cultural exploitation of "warriors" in tourism and hairdressing enterprises, it was ahistorical and factually inaccurate in some fundamental respects (Kaunga 2002). He wrote that the "vast majority of men are employed as security guards—a task that is appreciated by most, including the Maasai themselves, as it is a reflection of the role of the traditional Maasai warrior: warlike and fierce." He noted that non-Maasai fear this community because their warriors are reputed to be "strong [men] who can kill a lion." But is it helpful to invoke this stereotype? The majority of male youths (certainly in Kenya, though the picture may be different for Tanzania) no longer choose to be warriors but go to school instead; therefore it is erroneous to make warriorhood and lion killing, as acts of bravura, sound pivotal in Maasai society today. The work that young men do in urban centers is anathema to them, suggested Ole Kaunga, partly because these "once were warriors" are fit only for pastoral life. These jobs are also undoubtedly badly paid, insecure, and demeaning. One could add that the loss of young men to urban centers as well as school has also resulted in a rural labor crisis; male elders are having to do the lion's share of herding, dealing with external livestock raiding, and organizing other defensive measures, all of which were traditionally tasks undertaken by younger men.

However, although the pastoral idyll remains a cultural ideal for Maasai, it is no longer the only reality. The author says he does not know when Maasai first began drifting to towns, but this is evident from the literature on urbanization in East Africa. Maasai were becoming urbanized from the 1890s; there is nothing new about the phenomenon. In fact, one could argue that Maasai adaptability to change, and their ability to enter and exploit new markets, is something to be celebrated rather than abhorred. If Luise White is correct, the earliest "urban pioneers" were African prostitutes, who included Maasai women—not because they had looser morals but because they sought socioeconomic independence from men (White 1990). This may be an unpalatable truth. Ole Kaunga did not refer directly to Maasai women's involvement in urban prostitution today, but he coyly mentioned how women are increasingly visiting towns and leaving their families at home, which "opens up the chances and opportunities for promiscuity and increases the risk of HIV/AIDS infection," as if men do not also indulge in risky sexual behavior.

My full response to this article, submitted to *Indigenous Affairs*, respectfully suggested that indigenous peoples should beware of "buying into" old colonial stereotypes, and urged the journal to check the accuracy of contributors' claims before publishing them. The editors did not reply let alone publish my heretical remarks. But my concerns remain: a very powerful stereotype was created in the mid- to late nineteenth century, largely by European travelers and missionaries, and this is still evident in some self-descriptions of who the Maasai are today, which do not do them any favors. It was subsequently added to and amplified by other writers and producers of images, a process that John Galaty, Neil Sobania, and others have described (Galaty 2002, 347–67; Sobania 2002, 313–46; and other chapters in this volume). It has been internalized to some extent by some Maasai, a point ignored by Galaty. Among non-Maasai, there are countless examples in the public arena (such as coffee-table books, advertising, tourism promotion, and film) and in the private sphere of the longevity of the stereotype. For an example of what people "privately" think, correspondence sent to me by white Kenyans and former British colonial officials regarding my research contains classically derogatory remarks about the Maasai's alleged unbridled aggression, warlike "nature," sexual promiscuity, conservativism, arrogance, backwardness, idleness, waste of good land, and so on.

Where does all this come from? Let us now turn to the fount of the stereotype—Joseph Thomson, a fascinating character whose writings are ripe for deconstruction.

Travelers in Maasailand

Passing through the forest, we soon set our eyes upon the dreaded warriors that had been so long the subject of my waking dreams, and I could not but involuntarily exclaim: "What splendid fellows!"

—THOMSON 1885, 160

The early European explorers of this region damned the Maasai faintly with praise while overemphasizing their ferocity. The ambivalent tone was set here by Thomson, a precocious twenty-five-year-old geologist dispatched by the Royal Geographical Society in 1883 to find a direct route between the coast and Lake Victoria. German naturalist Dr. Gustav Fischer had taken the same route weeks earlier but was forced to turn back at Lake Naivasha by Maasai enraged at his party's behavior. A few other Europeans had already made contact with Maasai groups but had not explored their heartland. Thomson was by then the veteran of a major 1878–1880 expedition to Central Africa, and a smaller one in 1881 (Thomson 1881).[6] In Maasailand, he consciously paved the way for commercial exploitation of the territory; the Imperial British East Africa Company was formed in 1888, and in 1895, the protectorate (precursor to Kenya colony) was founded. Pioneer administrator, naturalist, and traveler Sir Harry Johnston, whose posts included special commissioner to Uganda in the late 1890s, called Thomson "the real originator of British East Africa" (Johnston 1908).

The roots of the colonial relationship between the Maasai and the British were embedded in these nineteenth-century encounters. In their writings, these earliest travelers (who included emissaries of the crown, naturalists, hunters, and missionaries) produced a damagingly stereotypical image of the Maasai that influenced subsequent views and policy toward them. This was so powerful that it shaped early administrative policy and continues to resonate today. A direct line can be drawn from travelers' perceptions (not that these were totally uniform) to those of early administrators and influential settlers, via ethnographers and others. In some cases, ethnographers and administrators were the same people; for example, British officials Hinde, Hobley, Hollis, and the German Merker (in neighboring German East Africa), all combined their duties with amateur ethnography, which served government and facilitated the imperial classification and control of ethnic groups (Hinde and Hinde 1901; Hobley 1910; Hollis 1905, 1909; Merker 1910).

Many of these travel texts had scientific pretensions that overlaid an expansionist colonizing ethos and were written primarily by white middle-class men who came to map and measure "nature." While classifying African fauna and flora, the travelers also spent a great deal of time and energy categorizing "primitive" peoples, defining themselves and the culture they represented in relation to the exotic Other. Although it is dangerous to see everything in starkly dichotomous terms, some of which break down under closer examination, white, civilized, clothed, moral, industrious, and Christian were self-defining qualities counterpointed by the classifications black, wild, naked, immoral, idle, and pagan. Anthropologists broadly followed suit, and the categories hardened as British administration advanced upon the Maasai and adopted the early taxonomies.

Although travelers expressed a wide range of views of the Maasai, the dominant and longest-lasting image was an overwhelmingly derogatory one. I suggest Thomson was primarily responsible for producing this; other scholars have laid the blame elsewhere. This chapter critiques some key travel texts and the novels they inspired, and challenges other scholars' accounts. It will begin by looking at Thomson's work before discussing, in less detail, other travelogues, some of which present alternative views. This does not claim to be an exhaustive trawl of the literature; in particular, it omits German texts that were not translated into English, since my interest is in writings that directly influenced the English-speaking public and the British colonial administration. Neither will it analyze visual portrayal, a story in itself. From the 1890s onward, pictures of "bushmen" and Maasai and Zulu warriors dominated popular representations of African peoples in books, lantern slides, postcards, and colonial exhibitions. The warriors came to represent their respective ethnic groups, powerfully reinforcing the idea in the Western mind that these "tribes" were predominantly martial, and indigenous women played a lesser (usually decorative) role.[7]

The reputation of the Maasai as a bloodthirsty, martial race had prevented European commercial exploitation of upcountry East Africa; this
was a deliberate ploy by coastal slave and ivory traders.[8] Thomson slew the
dragon by proving it was possible to move unscathed through Maasai territory. He set out on this journey in some trepidation, but when he finally
met the Maasai, he was agreeably surprised. He noted their "astonishing
gravity" and "aristocratic dignity." They exhibited a "natural fluency and
grace . . . and a dignity of attitude beyond all praise." He was particularly
struck by their powers of oration (a spokesman addressed him "with all the
ease of the professional speaker") and the absence of "obtrusive, vulgar in-
quisitiveness or aggressive impertinence," which had so vexed him among
other Africans (Thomson 1885, 161–62). Far from being astonished and
curious on seeing a white man, the warriors coolly surveyed him. But two
pages later, they were fighting over gifts Thomson had brought to buy his
way through Maasailand. He likened them to animals: "They rave and tear
like a couple of dogs over a bone. . . . A pack of half-starved wolves suddenly let loose on small animals could not have made a more ferocious and
repulsive exhibition" (170). The "beautiful beasts" tag would remain with
the Maasai forever.

In the meantime, Thomson went happily upon his way. "Greatly struck
by the unusual manners of these savages, so different from the notion we
have formed of them, we move on, not a bit inconvenienced by crowding
or annoyed by rude remarks." He noted with approval the great beauty and
style of both men and women. Some elders dropped into camp, "visiting
us with all the dignity of lords of the creation." He was filled with admiration (Thomson 1885, 168–69, 272).

Thomson had expected to be met with aggression. His fears were
compounded by the news that his rival, Fischer, journeying ahead of him,
had clashed with the Maasai, and at least three of the latter had been shot
dead. It seemed highly likely that the community would take revenge on
the next European to come along. In fact, he found the Maasai in a conciliatory mood. A posse of men came to discuss the deaths and their implications for Thomson's safe passage, and did so in a reportedly calm and
reasonable manner. Agreement was reached, and there was no suggestion
of violence. Later, threats from Maasai still angry about Fischer forced
Thomson to return briefly to the coast for reinforcements, but despite his
worst fears, he was never physically attacked. Yet he ended up damning
them as "ferocious," seeming to forget later in the story just how friendly
he had found them to be. What had happened to change his perception
of events?

One answer lies in Thomson's intent as a writer. The ascendancy of the explorer-writer coincided with the development of print and cheaper mass production. As some of his contemporaries suspected, he sought to spice up the story—the racier the tale, the better its likely reception and the healthier his sales would be. Wild tales of African "savagery" sold well, while gentler stories of amenable indigenes did not, simply because they did not satisfy the public appetite for lurid representations of the Other, now whetted by a series of published travelogues that had brought fame to their authors. These included sagas by James Bruce (1790); Mungo Park (1799); Richard Burton (various from 1856); David Livingstone (1857, 1866, 1874); John Speke (1864); James Grant (1864); and Henry Morton Stanley (1872, 1878). Livingstone and Stanley in particular directly inspired Thomson, and he sought to compete with the heroism of fellow Scotsmen, Bruce, Park, Clapperton, Grant, Livingstone, and Cameron. By the time he began writing, certain norms had been established in travel texts about Africa, which included

> the distinction between "savage Negro" and "civil Mohometan," and the commentaries on the Africans' indolence, their unbridled passions, and their cruelty or mental retardation. . . . They formed part of the series of oppositions and of the levels of classification of humans demanded by the logic of the chain of being and the stages of progress and social development. Explorers just brought new proofs which could explicate "African inferiority." (Mudimbe 1998, 13; also see Brantlinger 1985)

More fundamental reasons for Thomson's change of tack link to power relations and fragile masculinity—his own interior journey. With regard to the first, Thomson expected to be regularly entertained by aboriginal dancers while he played voyeur and demigod, looking down upon the show. The whole circus was horribly reversed among the Maasai. He had made the mistake of inventing a medicine-man act, designed to inspire fear and awe and thus keep the Maasai at a safe distance. When he wanted to demonstrate his powers (particularly to show that he could control the epidemics then decimating Maasailand, for which he feared he might be held accountable), he brewed up Eno's fruit salt, "sang an incantation—generally something about 'Three blue bottles'" and whipped his false teeth in and out. Such antics earned him the title of white *laibon* or prophet/medicine man, and at first, they were well received (Thomson 1885, 286). Anne McClintock has described this as an attempt to "manipulate the other by mimicking what [explorers] took to be the other's specific fetish," and that Thomson's ritual use of gloves, sextant, gun, and

Eno's in fact revealed "his own faith in the power of his fetishes" (Mc-Clintock 1995, 229).

As time passed, Thomson realized his error, as he was constantly made to perform by an audience that was no longer amazed but invasive—not that the coolest of warriors had been particularly impressed before. His personal space was violated. As the distance between "actor" and audience evaporated, so did the initial awe shown by black of white. "They played with us as a cat does with a mouse" (Thomson 1885, 379). He had unwittingly set himself up to be knocked down, becoming indignant as the Maasai showed less and less respect. Worse, he was now the joke and they the jokers—"who laughed at whom? [was] one not insignificant guide to who was in control," writes Philip Morgan of colonial encounters in the South Pacific (Morgan 1999). Complaining about "the atrocious life one is compelled to lead among the Masai savages," Thomson wrote:

> They ordered us about as if we were so many slaves. I had daily to be on exhibition, and perform for their delectation. "Take off your boots." "Show your toes." "Let us see your white skin." "Bless me! what queer hair!" "Good gracious! what funny clothes!" Such were the orders and exclamations (anglicized) which greeted me as they turned me about, felt my hair with their filthy paws. (Thomson 1885, 337)

Only a few miles down the road, yet he had come a long way from this earlier description of receiving a curious warrior into his tent: "After I have exhibited to his untutored gaze all the marvels of my person and tent, he may be cajoled out." Thomson was no longer in control of the exhibition. The "savage gaze" was now tutored, the "savage" voice imperative. By the time Thomson's party had reached Mount Kenya, he said, "The sooner I was clear of the Masai the better. . . . Eno's fruit salt and a couple of artificial teeth were no longer novelties" (Thomson 1885, 304, 388). The lack of distance between self and Other had become dangerous: "I had to sit continually on exhibition." By now, Thomson was not so much afraid of the Maasai as of his own fragility as a theatrical event. Greg Dening notes, "Priests in their rituals cannot afford to be seen as actors. Nor can scientists" (Dening 1996, 113). Thomson was posing both as "priest" and scientist and was, therefore, in double trouble. The theater of awe was reversed, and a welter of confused emotions arose in him:

> We had to eat humble pie to propitiate their lordships . . . and yet, strangely enough, in the midst of it all we made great friends with some of the elders, who delighted to sit and talk with us, showing a frankness and an

absence of suspicion such as I have never seen elsewhere among Africans.
. . . In some respects I began almost to like the Masai (men as well as
women), as I gradually became accustomed to their arrogant ways. . . . The
damsels, of course, would have been without fault, if they had only dis-
carded clay and grease and used Pears' soap. (Thomson 1885, 337–38)

In spite of his qualms, Thomson found discourse easy and enjoyable with
people who were "tremendous talkers as well as fighters." It was all very
confusing. The Maasai were likeable in certain ways, and not so unlike Europeans, while their pubescent girls were surprisingly attractive, apart from
their smell: "They are really the best-looking girls I have ever met with in
Africa" (Thomson 1885, 428). Sexual innuendo runs throughout this text.
Playing the medicine man earned Thomson female approval, which he
clearly relished, and he flirted constantly with Maasai maidens.

Masculinity and Moral Dilemmas

This brings me to the second point: Thomson's fragile masculinity. The inner confusions evident in *Through Masai Land* were more fully aired in a later
work of fiction, *Ulu*, cowritten with former fellow student Miss Harris-
Smith, which is essential reading as a supplement to the travelogue (Thomson and Harris-Smith 1888). This has been overlooked by most scholars and
misread by Thomson's biographer, Rotberg.[9] In the two-volume novel,
Thomson rehashed the expedition story to make his Scottish adventurer hero
Tom Gilmour emerge triumphant from his brush with the Maasai. Most importantly, the barriers to sexual attraction between white and black were
leapt as Gilmour courted Ulu, a beautiful half Chagga, half Maasai girl. The
novel provided Thomson with a license to rove, exploring subjects that were
out of bounds in the travelogue. Gilmour fantasized about marrying Ulu, a
union that would "bring his contempt for society and social frauds to a fitting climax" (Thomson and Harris-Smith 1888, 1:34).

> To marry a negress for the sake of having something to care for besides
> one's self! Plenty of room for self-sacrifice there, I should fancy! I wonder,
> now, if I *could* care for a negress? After all, why not? A man grows fond of
> his dog, and even gets to have a certain feeling of companionship for him;
> I suppose it would be equally possible with an M-Chaga maiden—some
> fresh, budding young child of nature, even though black and barbaric.
> (Thomson and Harris-Smith 1888, 1:36)

Thomson described Gilmour as "passing through some great mental and
moral crisis." It is tempting to see this crisis—also of masculinity and cul-

tural identity—as his own. Brantlinger comments on the "adolescent quality" of this and similar tales, noting that "Africa was a great testing—or teething—ground for moral growth and moral regression; the two processes were often indistinguishable" (Brantlinger 1985, 189–90). While attracted to Ulu, Gilmour admired Kate Kennedy, a virtuous missionary's daughter who was the foil to everything Ulu represented: "To Gilmour Kate was Europe personified." Kate's father chided Gilmour over his marriage plans, asking how he could "reconcile his low opinions of the capabilities of the savage nature with your intention of marrying her [Ulu]?" The answer was that Gilmour had no intention of reconciling them. But he was very taken with the idea of "developing what of good there may be in her." At other times, he questioned the wisdom of "civilising" Africans, arguing with the missionary, "Has it never occurred to you . . . what the true significance of this cry of 'opening up of Africa to civilisation' really is? . . . Do you call old clothes, new diseases, additional vices and drudgery, along with gin, rum and gunpowder, Europe's best and noblest?'" (Thomson and Harris-Smith 1888, 1:122–23, 142, 168, 2:19–22, 32). It is impossible to know how much of this was written by his coauthor, but Gilmour/Thomson swung wildly between the extremes of imperialist triumph and self-reflective guilt. It was an early "development" discourse.

Ulu and other local people mistook Kate for a deity. Gilmour hoped they would also see him as godlike, but he feared he had grown too close to the "natives" for such reverence; Thomson was clearly warning readers against the kind of overfamiliarity that had caused him so much trouble in Maasailand. Kate was kidnapped by Maasai warriors, and Gilmour pursued them, fearing—in so many words—that she might be raped. ("Better death than *that!*") The kidnappers were portrayed as "these licentious, bloodthirsty savages, the indulgence of whose brutal passions was their sole rule in life." Kate was the total antithesis of this; Gilmour caught sight of the Maasai and the virginal girl, "their swarthy figures throwing her white dress into more marked relief." A meat feast was described in the crudest possible way, the captive Kate looking on in horror at warriors gorging on and fighting over raw flesh (Thomson and Harris-Smith 1888, 2:38, 54, 65–66, 71–75). This scene amplified four key stereotypes: violence, unrestrained greed, consumption of raw meat and blood, and beastliness. On another occasion, Ulu was mauled by a lion. In this passage, the authors again bracketed the Maasai with criminals and dangerous animals: "'El-Masai!' 'Robbers!' 'Buffaloes!' 'Lions!' were the terror-striking words that passed from lip to lip" (Thomson and Harris-Smith 1888, 2:2–3).

This novel represents Thomson's wishful rewrite of his own relationship with the Maasai, in which he was restored to his "rightful" place. Yet the subtext—Gilmour's self-disturbing attraction to Ulu and all she represented—renders the story much more complex. Gradually, Gilmour fell in love with Kate and spurned the "savage" child, who died in Kate's arms. Thomson appears in *Ulu* to have faced up to his fear of becoming an "other among others."[10] He crossed the line and embraced the Other openly, pondering what would happen if he totally abandoned his old life and immersed himself in Africa. Ultimately, he chose Europe, and Africa expired.[11]

To return to the travel text, on leaving the Maasai behind, Thomson greeted other Africans with evident relief. The ideal "native" was unsophisticated, polite, and Thomson fearing, and they performed dances on demand. By comparison, he left the reader with an impression of the Maasai as beautiful but beastly, idle occupants of a land too good for them, who existed only to talk, fight, and fornicate—though he did acknowledge their oratorical strengths and suggested that the warriors were reformed by marriage. It was a refrain that was to be repeated often. Furthermore, Thomson is frequently described as having "penetrated" Maasailand (and said so himself), but in fact its inhabitants successfully penetrated his frontline defenses. There are many examples of this in the travel text (such as bodily invasiveness and violations of personal space), but nonphysical forms include intellectual invasion through cross-examination, mockery, and making him the butt of jokes. Public ridicule is a social sanction among Maasai, and Thomson was thereby put in his place.

But in the longer term, he achieved more in Maasailand than he ever intended. His writings helped to spawn the erroneous idea that pastoralists wandered aimlessly, failing to occupy, fully use, or appreciate the land, and therefore they had no claim to it. This would be used by colonial administrators to justify land snatching and forced moves. Most importantly, in emphasizing what he saw as the profound ethnic differences between Maasai and other Africans, and their fierce independence, Thomson helped to create a stereotype that underpinned later development interventions in both Kenyan and Tanzanian Maasailand. It was in the interests of early colonizers to maintain and exploit ethnic difference, but this view changed as administrators began to see it as a barrier to development and modernization. By the 1920s, the Maasai were routinely condemned for their stubborn conservativism and apparent unwillingness to join the twentieth century. Difference had become a danger to the modern state (see Hodgson 2000, 58–78). This language is still used to condemn them today.

Much of what I have said about Thomson is negative. But he was also a talented writer who produced a hugely entertaining page-turner in *Through Masai Land*. Fabian has shown, with reference to the Central African Lakes text, and Simpson with reference both to this and the Maasai text, that Thomson could also be perceptive, culturally sensitive, mature for his age, frank, and self-reflective (Fabian 2000; Simpson 1975, chaps. 12 and 14). Today, the value of these works to scholars lies in their rich historical detail.

Thomson's Influence and Reception

The Maasai travelogue possibly reached millions of readers through being copublished in the United States and translated into German and French. Though Thomson published other accounts of other journeys, this made his name. His influence was not only direct but diffused, threaded as it was through best-selling contemporary fiction.

Western images of Africa were forged by tales of exploration and derring-do, and Rider Haggard (among others) amplified them. He acknowledged Thomson as the inspiration for his fictional hero Allan Quatermain, chief protagonist of the novel of the same name.[12] So far as I am aware, other scholars have not spotted the significant similarities between *Through Masai Land* and this novel. *Allan Quatermain* described the adventures of an Englishman and two friends who set out to find a white race believed to live in the highlands of the African interior. However, its early chapters are dominated by descriptions of European clashes with the Maasai, whose warriors are repeatedly described as "bloodthirsty savages" having "the face of a devil," as "cruel and savage men," and as "rascally," "bloodthirsty villains," a "dog of a black savage," and so on. There is a ludicrous early scene in which the travelers are attacked at night by "swimming Masai" while anchored midstream because they did not consider it safe to sleep ashore after a "ferocious" warrior shook his spear at them. Many rural Maasai cannot swim and detest immersion in water, but according to Haggard, they were in the habit of lurking in lakes and rivers in order to attack passing boatmen. A warrior with a "dim but devilish-looking face appeared to rise out of the water" and knifed an African servant lying asleep in the canoe. Quatermain severed the attacker's hand with a Zulu battle-axe, but "he uttered no sound or cry. Like a ghost he came, and like a ghost he went, leaving behind him a bloody hand still gripping a great knife . . . that was buried in the heart of our poor servant." This is the Maasai as "ghastly apparition," as ghouls who haunt one's waking dreams—a specter raised by Thomson in the first quote of his I cited (Haggard 1887 (1995), 24–29).

The party's next adventure mirrored the trials of Kate Kennedy in *Ulu*, which Haggard must have read in draft form or discussed with Thomson since his plagiarism is obvious. On arrival at a mission run by the Reverend Mackenzie, the travelers meet his small daughter, Miss Flossie, known as "Water-lily" to local Africans and allegedly regarded as a deity because of her white skin and fair hair. Soon afterward, Miss Flossie was captured by Maasai; in a passage strongly redolent of the Kate/warrior imagery, she was riding a white donkey when apprehended by the black "savages." A warrior came to tell Mackenzie that his daughter would die at dawn unless he swapped her for one of Quatermain's companions. Speaking in strangely Shakespearean English, he added, "'If thy answer is late thy little white bud will never grow into a flower . . . for I shall cut it with this' and he touched the spear" planted in the ground beside him. Miss Flossie's virtue was clearly threatened. Slaughter ensued; the white men rescued the girl in a daring dawn raid and gave the Maasai a good hiding. While held captive, Miss Flossie was continually stared at by warriors who had never seen a white person before and "handled her arms and hair with their filthy paws"—exactly Thomson's words (Haggard 1887 (1995), 59, 72–82, 88). Haggard seems to have taken the story of Ulu, interwoven it with scenes from Thomson's travelogue, and created a fantastic concoction that thrilled generations of schoolboys. His stories had an incalculable effect on grown men, too. British administrator Frederick Jackson only went to East Africa after being urged to do so by Haggard, his neighbor in Norfolk.

Leaving aside contemporary press reviews, there has been remarkably little subsequent criticism or attempts to deconstruct his texts. Elspeth Huxley described *Through Masai Land* as "a thrilling tale of adventure . . . a classic among books on Africa." The history of the interior did not start with any certainty, she said, until Livingstone, Speke, Thomson, and other "great Victorians" made their journeys (Huxley 1943, 241, 238). Less predictably, Dr. Norman Leys—left-leaning champion of Maasai land rights in the 1900s—also eulogized Thomson in his preamble to the story of the Maasai moves, calling *Through Masai Land* "one of the best books of exploration in existence" (Leys 1924, 91). Thomson is still written about in glowing and largely uncritical terms. Beachey claims, "He did much to bring the country of the Maasai and the Maasai themselves into clearer perspective, demythicizing [*sic*] much of the lore and nonsense that had been built up around that tribe in the nineteenth century" (Beachey 1996, 99). While the first statement may be true, the second is not; Thomson produced significant quantities of myth and nonsense himself.

Robert Rotberg claims, "Unlike so many other explorers and the men of advancing empires, Thomson ostensibly approached Africa and Africans with methods worthy of admiration" (Rotberg 1970a, preface, 9).[13] Unlike, say, the German explorer Carl Peters, he did not shoot his way through tribal encounters, but this is still too easy an appraisal (Peters 1891). Rotberg concedes that Thomson had his faults, including a tendency to overdramatize, but that we should applaud his courage: "As a dogged personal triumph over adversity and infirmity, it is unsurpassed in the annals of African exploration" (Rotberg 1968, xi–xiii). He mostly fails to look beyond the survivalist and Pax Britannica discourse. (Other scholars' critiques will be covered in the next section.)

Missionaries Krapf and Rebmann

These two Germans, employed by the British Church Missionary Society (CMS), separately explored the Kilimanjaro, Ukambani, and Usambara regions between 1847 and 1852. They first published their travel journals in English in missionary magazines, and these formed the basis of a book by Krapf, published in German in 1858 and in English two years later (Krapf 1860). Since they did not travel as far as the Maasai heartland of the northern Rift Valley, their account of this community borrowed heavily from the perceptions of coastal traders, who had a vested interest in demonizing the Maasai in order to deter other visitors.

Johann Ludwig Krapf was the elder of the two and arrived in East Africa from Ethiopia after abandoning an attempt to convert the Galla (Oromo) people. His most often-quoted observation of the Maasai is, "They are dreaded as warriors, laying all waste with fire and sword, so that the weaker tribes do not venture to resist them in the open field, but leave them in possession of their herds, and seek only to save themselves by the quickest possible flight." He also described them as "these worst of heathen"; "these truculent savages" who "conquer or die, death having no terrors for them"; and said "[they] do not make slaves of their prisoners, but kill men and women alike in cold blood" (Krapf 1860 (1968), 359–60, 365–66). However, like Thomson, he also noted the "wisdom [and] fluency of speech" of the so-called chiefs. His account included descriptions of their beauty, polygyny, and trading patterns with neighboring peoples (which contradicts claims that the Maasai were always on the attack); their diet (said to include game, which was only eaten when people faced severe famine); and their use of land, roaming the great plains in search of water and grass. He noted their "great distaste for agriculture" and their belief that eating cereals enfeebled people. Their perceived arrogance and land greed was plain: they considered themselves "the exclusive possessors of the plains and wildernesses" (Krapf 1860 (1968), 358–59, 362). The picture drawn was of a primarily martial people, greedy for more land than they needed or profitably used.

Knowles and Collett in a 1989 paper, and Collett in a 1987 book chapter, claim that Thomson's was a "reasonably balanced account" of the Maasai, that it was Krapf who emphasized their warlike aspects, and that "Thomson's description of the Maasai was subsequently ignored by most administrators and settlers in Kenya, who instead adopted the imagery of Krapf's description and further elaborated upon it."[14] Collett states that Thomson's account "did not survive the advent of British administration" but quickly gave way "to an ethnocentrically 'British' image of both the Maasai and Maasailand" (Collett 1987, 137). It is not clear what this means; Thomson was also ethnocentrically British. Collett rightly points out that the "fearsome reputation" of the Maasai predated Thomson, but he wrongly says it was "enhanced by the murder of Fischer . . . in 1883" (Collett 1987, 137). He was not killed by the Maasai but returned to Germany to tell the tale of his adventures, dying in Berlin in 1887.[15] (He is possibly confusing Fischer with German murder victim Dr. Albert Röscher.)[16]

Collett suggests that administrator Lord Lugard, in remarks made in 1893 about Maasai diet and failure to cultivate fertile land, was responsible for creating "the most prevalent stereotype" and introduced the idea that the Maasai were not fully utilizing the land (Lugard 1893, 417). Though important, this is arguably not the most prevalent one. Also, Thomson had previously suggested that Laikipia was empty and was therefore available to European settlers, which is a different concept. Collett claims that it was "Lugard's emphasis on the warlike nature of the Maasai" that was used to justify British annexation of their land, but Krapf, Thomson, and minor travelers such as Hildebrandt clearly got in first; Lugard was merely repeating what had been said many years before (Collett 1987, 138; Hildebrandt 1877).

Knowles and Collett rightly state that "the reaction of the early Europeans to the Maasai . . . is important because the images that are adopted by the Europeans play a central role in subsequent events" (Knowles and Collett 1989, 433). But to call Thomson's text "reasonably balanced" does not suggest a close reading. Thomson, they say, painted a much more complex picture both of the internal workings of Maasai society and its relations with neighboring agriculturalists, largely because he had firsthand experience that Krapf lacked. Agreed, this is what sets the two texts apart.

But Krapf devoted relatively little space to the Maasai in proportion to his description of other peoples—nine pages, plus short references—whereas Thomson devoted the best part of a lengthy book to them and their habitat. It is also simply not common sense to suppose that Krapf, a German, had the greater impact on British perceptions and administrative policy, particularly when one takes into account the fictionalized repetition and amplification of Thomson's Maasai stereotypes in *Ulu* and *Allan Quatermain*, which I have covered in some detail because they are important and hitherto overlooked adjuncts to the travel text. Krapf inspired later missionary activity and possibly played a part in attracting European settlers. But it was Thomson who reveled in wild imagery of unreasoning "savages" who settled scores through violence, which was not justified by his experiences. And by describing rich pastures, forests, game, water sources, and other environmental delights in a climatically healthy, apparently underpopulated place, he played a key role in attracting European farmer-settlers, who also loved shooting, to the highlands of Kenya.[17]

Largely based on Krapf, these authors reduce early myths about the Maasai to two: their warlike tendencies and their dietary preferences, linked to a loathing of cultivation. They say British administrators then used the latter to develop further myths about land use (the Maasai failed to reap the maximum economic benefit from land by farming it) and emphasized Maasai use of raw foods (milk, honey, blood) and meat in order to "remove them from the category of cultured human and place them in the category of natural man" (Knowles and Collett 1989, 441). Also, in seeing the Maasai as purely pastoral, "this eliminated the need to understand how a 'predatory' group could simultaneously terrorise and trade with neighboring peoples" (Collett 1987, 138). There were undoubtedly contradictions embedded in these representations. But colonial official Harry Johnston understood that pastoral women and older men bartered with other communities for vegetable food, and he devoted almost as much space to the habits of agricultural Maa speakers as he did to the pastoral sections, certainly in *The Uganda Protectorate* (1902).[18] His was a highly influential and important voice, central to the "scramble" for East Africa, who barely appears in Knowles and Collett's references.[19] In a particularly influential 1908 article, which recommended concentrating the Maasai in one reserve, Johnston accused Boer farmers, not the Maasai, of failing to develop the highlands (Johnston 1908). Though much of what they say is valuable, I suggest that Knowles and Collett make too much of "the dietary myth" at the expense of other important and interconnected misrepresentations such as immorality, idleness, and land greed. Collett in particular devotes disproportionate space to Lugard's views, virtually ignoring Johnston.

Other Dissenting Voices

Reading the remarks of some of Thomson's contemporaries, one wonders if they were writing about the same people. (In one sense, they were not: some of these travelers explored present-day Tanzania and met different groups of Maa speakers such as the Ilparakuyu, not necessarily the northern sections described by Thomson.) "The Masai were very kind in their manner to me wherever I met them," wrote missionary J. T. Last of a journey made in November 1882, though he realized this was linked to expectations of gifts. He spoke of "hours of pleasant conversation" with elders (Last 1883, 522–23, 527). Medical missionary Dr. Baxter, "having made friends with the Masai . . . found them most kind and hospitable." Archbishop Farler "found them a very peaceful people."[20]

Hungarian Count Teleki's "adventures among the Masai" in 1887 and 1888 were told in two volumes by his companion Ludwig von Höhnel (1894). Hunting tales were interwoven with amateur ethnography and fulsome descriptions of landscape, fauna, and flora. The Maasai, with one or two exceptions, were found to be friendly, peaceable, charming, and helpful. The visitors' early fear of "the dreaded inhabitants of these districts" gave way, on closer acquaintance, to admiration. They were greeted at first with presents of oxen, not demands for gifts. Höhnel declared, "We had no reason to complain of the behaviour of the natives" and called them "the noble race of the Masai . . . by far the most interesting and most powerful people with whom we came in contact." Warriors joined Teleki in a buffalo hunt, while other Maasai traded cattle, donkeys, leather, and fuel with the visitors. Women and children brought firewood to their camp, and children made themselves useful by fetching water, while "old men squatted down round the fires to chat with our men." There was no suggestion of the mutual "ethnic" hostility emphasized by Thomson between the Maasai and coastal porters. The author remarked upon the Maasai love of "talking and listening" as much as cattle raiding, their "great command of dialectics," and the "parliamentary etiquette" evident in debates (Von Höhnel 1894, 83, 131, 132–33, 242). When it finally came to distributing presents, Höhnel refuted Thomson's account and put the record straight:

> Remembering Thomson's description . . . [of the violence which greeted his distribution of gifts], we expected a fight to ensue for the spoil, and we awaited the onslaught with bated breath; but nothing of the kind occurred,

and it seemed as if the warriors knew that for us the dark cloud of terror enveloping them had rolled away. If I did not explain further, these remarks might very easily be misunderstood, so I will add how it was that, even before we had seen any of them, we had decided that the Masai were an unusually brave, but at the same time a bloodthirsty and covetous, people. We had had no need to refer to old accounts and rumours, but had got our information from the reports of Dr. Fischer and Joseph Thomson. . . . Thomson describes the Masai in very much the same style as the ivory traders, but does not give any instances of bad treatment at their hands, and further acquaintance with these much-dreaded warriors convinced us that travelling amongst them was not fraught with any special danger. (Höhnel 1894, 132–33)

Höhnel had virtually accused Thomson of lying. He also believed the Scot had said rather too much about licentiousness—the "free love" prevailing in the warrior camps—since many warriors actually stayed true to one sweetheart. Among the numerous insightful observations in Höhnel's text are those about women, notably references to a "clever" old woman called Nakairo, whom the travelers hired as their go-between with the Maasai and the Kikuyu (Von Höhnel 1894, 292, 295).

In 1891, J. R. L. Macdonald led a preliminary survey for the Uganda Railway, which brought him into frequent contact with Maasai (Macdonald 1897). He noted how friendly they were toward his colleague James Martin (Thomson's deputy on the Maasailand expedition), despite being refused gifts: "In fact, the Masai became so friendly that, when one of his Indians went astray, they fed the wanderer like a fighting-cock, and three days later brought him back to the depot." With few exceptions, civility and peacefulness characterized all exchanges. Warriors approached the party with the point of their spears covered with balls of cotton wool, a sign of peace. All they wanted to do was shake hands, to such an extent that the gesture became very tiring. The warriors were asked to back off and became annoyed, and their leader lectured Macdonald on the need for Europeans to tolerate Maasai customs if they wanted to visit Maasailand. Peace was agreed. Later, "the Masai loyally adhered to their word, and, though next day we marched northward amidst hundreds of them, we had absolutely nothing to complain of, and at each successive kraal were hailed with cheery greetings." A couple of near altercations were averted through diplomacy. On the final leg of his journey, Macdonald reported "nothing more eventful to chronicle than peaceful meetings with Masai and a hostile encounter with a troop of lions" (Macdonald 1897 (1973), 61, 68–71, 100, 102, 321). The supposed threat of Maasai aggression toward travelers on the railway, and Europeans living nearby, was to be one of the major reasons for their forced removal from the Rift in 1904–05, but there is little evidence for such claims in this text.

The Views of Early Administrators

First, I shall examine remarks made by administrators who were relatively admiring of the Maasai, before turning to those who were most condemnatory. Sir Gerald Portal worked with Macdonald in Uganda. He was "Commissioner for the British sphere on the mainland" and agent and consul-general at Zanzibar when he traveled to Uganda in 1893 to investigate what was happening there. In his account of this journey, but before he had met the Maasai personally, Portal retold a "tale of a thrilling nature" about an alleged Maasai attack on a caravan of coastal traders who had passed the same way four months earlier. This passage is redolent of Thomson and Haggard and illustrates how the Maasai stereotype was being adopted and amplified. The traders had set up camp and were sleeping confidently in the open when

> they were rudely awakened by a din as of the infernal regions. By the fitful firelight, as they started up, they caught a vision of immense weird forms, apparently above the height of men, towering above whose heads were strange shapes and devices—horns of antelopes and of cows, crowns or halos of long eagle-feathers, the skins and grinning heads of monkeys, of leopards, and of cats, and as they moved there was a clash of many bells attached to their thighs, knees, and ankles; like demons these huge forms flitted and bounded about between the fires, while the light glanced from their strange head-gear, their garters and anklets of bells, from great shields painted with patterns of red, black, and white, and above all, from mighty spears seven feet high. . . . Barely had [the traders] time to realise that these tall and active forms were not ghosts . . . but veritable Masai warriors in all their war dress . . . when the ghoulish, triumphant laughter which burst from the leaping warriors was mingled with more than one despairing shriek. (Portal 1894, 65–67)

When Portal actually met some Maasai near Lake Naivasha, he was as smitten with the warriors as Thomson had been. Again, they were "splendid fellows." Portal was particularly taken with the heraldic motifs painted on each warrior shield—the coat of arms of fellow aristocrats. Ambivalence was in the air again.[21] He could not disguise his admiration for what he saw as the raw physical and intellectual superiority of the Maasai, especially when contrasted with the despised figure of the "semicivilized native" represented by his Zanzibari porters. Portal exhibited a typically European love of the African in his raw state (whatever that was imagined to be), which went hand in hand with contempt for the half-educated pretender. He soon contradicted his earlier tale, declaring that future travelers need not fear the "dreaded, all-conquering, and triumphant 'bogie' of ten years ago." Their glory had declined since they had lost so many cattle to disease. However, he still considered them a great curse because their raiding and reputation checked the development of neighboring "tribes" and had cleared populations from large areas.

Like Höhnel, Frederick Jackson, who served in British East Africa before becoming governor and commander in chief of Uganda (1911–1917), refuted Thomson's scaremongering. He felt it was part of a deliberate ploy by traders. He wrote, "There is a point in Thomson's book that I have never been able to account for, unless it was part of the scheme of the traders to choke off other Europeans, and that is his account of the insolent and overbearing manner of the moran [warriors], and the gross indignities to which he was subjected by them." Given the number of guns his party carried and the fact that he was regarded as a great white medicine man, "Why, then, did he submit to such indignities?" Jackson concluded that "the terrors and dangers of entering Masailand were very grossly and purposely exaggerated by a small clique of traders" in order to "keep the door closed as long as possible and their happy hunting-grounds free of poachers" (Jackson 1930, 190–91). To illustrate the saying "give a dog a bad name" and show the damage done by imagination and rumor, he described how a mild disagreement between him and some warriors was "converted into a desperate fight" by a couple of porters who took the embroidered story back to the coast. Jackson's direct experience of the Maasai was "a complete revelation to me. It was an experience so totally different from anything I had expected. No one could have been more friendly than they were, from start to finish" (Jackson 1930, 132).

Johnston veered more erratically than Jackson between praise and condemnation of the Maasai, indicating in his writings that he had read both Thomson and Krapf (Johnston 1910). In a quasi-ethnographic survey, he placed "the Apollo-like Masai" high up the scale of "types" of Africans (Johnston 1902, 1:vi; 1910, 822). Though the pastoral sections had had "a devotion to cattle which caused them to raid and ravish in all directions," this was now diminished, while the so-called agricultural Maasai lived in peaceful, permanent villages and grew large crops. He denied that they still posed a military threat, noting that commerce was "slowly but surely humanizing" them; the majority now preferred trading to fighting. He refuted the idea that they were work shy, saying, "All Masai men are adept at milking both cows and goats, for which reason they are much in request as herdsmen in the employ of Europeans." As for diet, only the warriors ate nothing but milk, blood, and meat (Johnston 1886, 537; 1902, 789, 803, 810, 812–13, 818–19, 834).

Sidney Hinde, collector of Masailand, was based at Machakos Fort from 1886, where he employed local warriors to mount punitive raids on other "tribes." With his wife, Hildegarde, he wrote *The Last of the Masai*. This title was not meant to sound a death knell for the whole race, but only those dwindling persons of "pure blood" who remained culturally "uncontaminated by admixture with Bantu elements and contact with civilisation." The Hindes chronicled the supposedly pure elements of this culture, lamenting the fact that the Maasai in their unadulterated state were fated to disappear. Their book was a hymn to waning virility; under European rule, they said, Maasai raiding could no longer be tolerated, but at the same time, "the destruction of so virile a race would, nevertheless, be a permanent loss to East Africa." They commended the Maasai for their dignity, their "undoubted gift of oratory," their "keen perception of justice," and their "considerable reasoning faculties." Like Thomson, the Hindes emphasized the profound differences between the Maasai and neighboring peoples. All little girls were "prostitutes." Echoing Thomson and Haggard, the ghostly Maasai were said to "haunt certain districts"; while this can simply mean to frequent a place, its other connotation is more sinister. Sir Charles Eliot, second commissioner of British East Africa, also used the term (Hinde and Hinde 1901, xiii, 33–36, 72, 91, 109; Eliot 1905, 134).

The Routledges devoted a chapter to denigrating the Maasai in *With a Prehistoric People*, a tribute to the Kikuyu as the progressive African of tomorrow. (Huxley repeated this juxtaposition three decades later when using large photographs of a naked warrior, captioned "A Young Masai Warrior—The Old Africa," and a Kikuyu clad in European clothing complete with felt hat, "Kikuyu Man—The New Africa," on facing pages of a guide to East Africa [Huxley 1943, 244–45].) They wheeled out every stereotype, from moral depravity to unadaptability and a propensity for mindless violence, concluding, "The Masai is by nature greed personified—sulky, morose and vindictive; a born thief, an arch liar. . . . For any form of manual labour he is mentally disinclined and physically unfit. He is material that civilisation cannot grind up in her mill" (Routledge and Routledge 1910). Now the categories were hardening as administration advanced, and attempts to control and develop the Maasai were seen to be failing.

In Charles Hobley's memoirs, published nearly two decades later, one can clearly see the Thomson and Krapf refrains woven through a textbook guide to "native" ways and colonial remedies. He referred to Maasai blood-thirstiness and the risk that they would, if unchecked by the British, have swept the country and trampled upon the "wretched cultivators." According to this view, shared by Portal, not only were the Maasai not amenable to development, but they also threatened the development of others. However, he was by no means entirely unsympathetic, believing that Maa-sai herds were potentially great assets to the country and that their owners could become "very useful members of the community" (Hobley 1929, 59–61). In 1904, when assistant deputy commissioner for the protectorate, he had spoken up for Maasai land rights in the Rift Valley in correspondence with the colonial office.

It was Charles Eliot who did most to employ the early stereotypes in the course of administering the Maasai, and it is his views that have been most frequently quoted long after all these other individuals have been for-gotten. In 1904, he wrote an erudite introduction to Hollis's work on Maa-sai language and folklore, in which he acknowledged that his information about the Maasai was drawn from Thomson, Krapf, Johnston, and Merker. He repeated some of Thomson's condemnatory remarks and added several of his own. He emphasized Maasai military organization, said their men did little else but fight and tend cattle, and viewed the disasters of the 1890s (famine and epidemic disease) as just desserts for a community that had grown prosperous through plunder. In other writings, he declared,

> The future of these people is not an easy problem. They resemble the lion and the leopard, strong and beautiful beasts of prey, that please the artistic sense, but are never of any use, and often a very serious danger. Even so the manly virtues, fine carriage and often handsome features of the Masai arouse a certain sympathy; but it can hardly be denied that they have hith-erto done no good in the world that any one knows of; they have lived by robbery and devastation, and made no use themselves of what they have taken from others. (Eliot 1905, 143)[22]

In a 1903 memorandum, he claimed, "The customs of the Masai may be interesting to anthropologists, but morally and economically they seem to me to be all bad, and it is our duty, as it will also be to our advantage, to change them as soon as it is practicable" (Eliot 1903, 12). These views were shared by leading settler Lord Cranworth:

> Here we have a people who, beautiful to look at and in some ways attractive in character, have as far as we know never been of any use to any living soul.

Like ravening beasts, they have lived on the weakness of their neighbours, amongst whom they were classed with pestilence, famine, and disease. Have this people any inherent right to be conserved in this condition? Have we not rather a duty to execute by leading them, or forcing them, to be of some economic use, or perish? (Cranworth 1912, 37)

Many times, Eliot damned the immorality that allegedly accompanied Maasai militarism, and he urged officials not to tolerate the "free love" practiced by warriors and unmarried girls. This was a vision of vice and idleness intertwined, a theme later picked up with enthusiasm by Rupert Hemsted, officer-in-charge of the Southern Maasai Reserve, who wrote in 1921, "The Masai are a decadent race, and have only survived through being brought under the protection of British rule. . . . They remain primitive savages who have never evolved and who under present conditions, in all probability, never can evolve. Their environment is fatal. They live under conditions of indescribable filth in an atmosphere of moral, physical, and mental degeneration" (*Masai Annual Report* 1921–1922, 9).

Finally, George Sandford regurgitated and concretized the stereotypes in his administrative history of the Maasai. Now they officially existed. Having explained their (logical) aversion to wage labor—they found manual work degrading, did not need cash because they had very few personal needs, and enjoyed enormous wealth in livestock—he damned the "unemployed" warriors who refused to work for Europeans. In the reserve, they were able to remain idle in a state of "opulent apathy" that was leading to unhealthiness and degeneration, both physical and mental. Military qualities were no longer required, and with it, the warriors' raison d'être had disappeared (Sandford 1919, 2, 4, 7). Their supposed degeneracy and enfeeblement were then used to justify oppressive controls.

Persistent Paradigms

There are echoes of the earliest negative imagery in later perceptions of Maasai deviance from a colonial and postcolonial norm. The Maasai largely defied attempts to harness them to the colonial economy. With some exceptions (warrior mercenaries on punitive expeditions, caravan guides, mail runners, herders, and even stokers on the Uganda Railway),[23] they refused in the early days of contact to engage in wage labor for Europeans, though this changed over time. Not being peasant cultivators but proud and self-sufficient stockmen, the Maasai did not fit the lord-peasant model that underpinned early white settlement. Africans who would not work for the state were deemed to be against it. In order to justify coercive and ultimately repressive measures against the Maasai, the British had to relegate them to the level of inherent deviants requiring correction. The twin poles of their perceived deviance were economic backwardness and moral depravity, sometimes used almost interchangeably. These can be further broken down:

- Economically, they had allegedly failed to evolve from herders to cultivators in the linear progression by which civilization was measured.
- While "rudimentary capitalists," they allegedly refused to sell surplus cattle for cash (Spencer 1984, 67).
- They largely refused to sell labor surplus to their own requirements. Their young men, a potential workforce, were seen to be idle and therefore both useless and menacing.
- Their mobility rendered them less controllable than settled communities. Without actively doing anything to harm the state, they were nevertheless seen to be out of control.
- They were beautiful beasts, physically of an "ideal type," but predatory of others. Again, this rendered them useless—except as raw material to anthropologists.
- They were morally depraved because they had "stolen" land and practiced polygyny and "free love." Their male dress was indecent, and they had foul eating (and other) habits. Perceived sexual greed paralleled their alleged land greed.

In current tourism promotion of Kenya and Tanzania, in which the Maasai reluctantly feature, some of these supposed characteristics are used to market them as national symbols. (Also, as Sobania [2002] notes, cattle rarely appear in these and earlier images; visually, at least, the Maasai have finally been destocked, a long-term aim of British officials who accused this community of overstocking.) They are the face of "old Africa," portrayed as persistent primitives whose beautiful beastliness and aristocracy—implying "pure blood," a total fiction—are a major draw for foreign visitors seeking the titillation of tribal contact. A priority for wildlife tourists has always been to get close to large, dangerous animals in the wild; now the trend is toward offering close encounters of a tribal kind.[24] In both tourism promotion and glossy fashion magazines (which frequently use tribal people as fashion accessories in order to suggest wildness, authenticity, and sexual frisson between white female models and black youths), those perceived to be the most beautiful, noble, martial, endangered, and animal-like repeatedly feature.[25] Educated Maasai in particular are uncomfortable with such portrayals, but since many communities gain financially from tourism (and fashion teams often stay at community-managed lodges like Shompole, a David Bailey favorite in Kenyan Maasai territory), they risk shooting themselves in the foot by challenging this. They share a conundrum facing many indigenous communities around the world: how does one take one's fair share of tourist dollars without compromising dignity, exposing private culture and sacred sites to public scrutiny, and allowing intellectual and cultural property to be ripped off? The situation is not helped by the activities of certain self-appointed "cultural ambassadors" abroad; middle-aged men who dress up as warriors in order to tout "Maasai-ness," they arguably promote a false image to the U.S. public and media in particular. Community activist Daniel Salau expresses skepticism: "They have no mandate at all from the community, are commercially driven by self interest, and only serve to further the Kenyan government's objective of using the Maasai as objects of charity" (personal communication).

The traditional defensive role of the warriors has now fallen to young, politically charged activists, which is maybe why people still cling to the warrior ideal: they see themselves as defending and safeguarding the community in the widest sense. "Militarism" is one response to environmental and political pressures. Since the summer of 2004, Kenyan Maasai are again publicly redefining who they are, in relation both to the former colonial power and the independent nation state, in order to call for reparations and land restitution.[26] A divided community is presenting itself as united, although splits are sorely apparent. In memoranda presented to the British and Kenyan governments, activists are again quoting derogatory remarks about the Maasai from colonial documents, but this time around, these are loudly condemned. However, the warrior past is being invoked in erroneous claims that hundreds of warriors bravely fought and died in defense of their motherland, when in fact the Maasai did not violently resist colonial intrusion. This historical revisionism reflects a failure to accept that an earlier generation of warriors did not prevent the British from taking their land. As a consequence of land losses and the supposed disappearance of social structures, it is claimed "the Maasai are losing their identity" (Simel 2003).[27] That is highly doubtful, if not impossible. It has always been fluid and continues to evolve in response to internal and external factors.

Notes

1. *Maasai* is the correct spelling, but *Masai* will be used when citing colonial-era records. The KLC was a government-appointed commission of inquiry into African land issues. The forced moves were the subject of my doctoral thesis, "Moving the Maasai: A Colonial Misadventure" (University of Oxford, 2002). A revised version was published by Palgrave Macmillan in 2006.

2. There were numerous reprints All quotes are from the first.

3. For one example of an exception, Daniel Salau of SIMOO (Simba Maasai Outreach Organisation) urges the Maasai to engage with the globalization process in a 2002 paper for *Civicus*. There is no mention of warriors or of celebrations of supposedly timeless traditions; it only urges the Maasai to safeguard their culture while simultaneously embracing the modern world, www.globalpolicy.org/globaliz/cultural/2002/0920masaai.htm.

4. Viewable at www.montelis.com/satya/backissues/dec97/maasai.html. This credits Thomson with the "discovery" of Maasailand.

5. He may not have written this, but he would presumably have approved it.

6. A paper on the 1881 journey is in *Proceedings of the RGS* (1882). See Rotberg's introduction to the 1968 edition of Thomson's *Through Masai Land*; Rotberg 1970a; Fabian 2000.

7. Besides Sobania (2002) and Galaty (2002), see Landau and Kaspin (2002); Stevenson and Graham-Stewart (2001).

8. This is not a contradiction of the claim that Thomson was primarily responsible for producing the derogatory image. The crucial difference was that he disseminated it in printed, mass-produced form.

9. Brantlinger (1985) calls it an "African Pygmalion story" (189). Rotberg (1970a) rightly says *Ulu* "provided a superb outlet for many of Thomson's fantasies," but claims, "The setting is true, the action—except for the denouement—reasonably plausible, and the dialogue acceptable if occasionally stilted" (239). Elsewhere (1970b), he writes that it was only in *Ulu* that Thomson fully expressed how Africa "satisfied a deep streak of romance" in him—a gross understatement (304).

10. "When we discover that there are several cultures instead of just one, and consequently at the same time, when we acknowledge the end of a sort of cultural monopoly, be it illusory or real, we are threatened with destruction by our own discovery. Suddenly it becomes possible that there are just *others*, that we ourselves are an 'other' among others" (Paul Ricoueur 1955).

11. Naudé (2003) discusses other colonial texts that flirt with cross-racial sex, including William Plomer's *Turbott Wolfe* (1926), Haggard's *King Solomon's Mines* (1885), and *She* (1887). In Haggard's texts, white men have brief affairs with African women who die before the affair is consummated. Says Naudé, "It is not unusual for the white male explorer-heroes of colonial literature to admit to their being sexually attracted to the female inhabitants of the explored (and ultimately

conquered) territory—yet without fail the plot prevents the physical culmination of said attraction, frequently through the convenient death of the black woman." Brantlinger makes a similar observation regarding *King Solomon's Mines* and links the fates of the African women Foulata and Ulu. "Like aristocrats in Renaissance pastoral, [Haggard's white heroes] cleave to their own kind and return to the light" (192).

12. "Authorities," a postscript to Haggard (1995 edn.). Allan Quatermain and friends also feature in *King Solomon's Mines*, but this plot does not so obviously mirror Thomson's story.

13. Thomson's brother also wrote a biography, published 1896.

14. Quotes are Collett in Anderson and Grove (1987), 137; Knowles and Collett 1989, 434.

15. "He brought home the first news about the Masai" (Schnee 1920 1:627–28). Fischer wrote *Das Masai-land* and *Mehr Licht im dunkeln Weltteil* (both published in Hamburg, 1885).

16. Röscher was murdered by members of "Wahiao tribe" near the coast in March 1860. *Proceedings of the RGS*, new series (1881), 3:686; Schnee 1920, 3:182.

17. This is enlarged upon in a chapter on imperial travellers in Beinart and Hughes, forthcoming 2006.

18. The Maasai are divided into socio-territorial sections called *il-oshon*. Some have disappeared, or been absorbed into other sections, since the nineteenth century. Members of certain 'defunct' sections, such as the Il-Aikipiak, are currently re-asserting their ethnic identity.

19. There are two brief references in Collett (1987, 138, 140) regarding wild animals Maasai allegedly killed for food and the creation of game reserves respectively. There are none in Knowles and Collett (1987).

20. Baxter and Farler took part in a discussion at the RGS following Last's paper (1883, 539, 540).

21. British ambivalence toward, and admiration for, the "aristocratic" qualities of the Maasai are explored by Tidrick (1990, chap. 5).

22. Excerpt quoted in Collett (1987, 139), who also points out Eliot's use of stereotypical images.

23. Eliot (1905) said Maasai were employed as stokers, work "which they do not consider as derogatory to a warrior, possibly being analogous to tending cattle" (100).

24. This is not new, except in the way that such encounters are expressly marketed today by tourism promoters. For a colonial example, David Bunn has written of early tourism in South Africa's Kruger National Park: "In many English tourist accounts it is clear that the experience of proximity to 'raw natives,' as they were called, was a crucial aspect of enjoyment for whites" (Bunn 2003).

25. For example, see "Big Game," a fashion shoot by David Bailey at Shompole, Kenya, in British *Vogue*, January 2004.

26. The history of these claims is more fully discussed in Lotte Hughes (2005).

27. A memorandum presented by Maasai representatives to the British and Kenyan governments in August 2004 was partly based on this earlier paper but did not repeat this phrase.

References

Beachey, R. W. 1996. *A history of East Africa 1592–1902*. London: I. B. Tauris.

Beinart, W., and L. Hughes. Forthcoming, 2006. *Environment and empire*. Oxford: Oxford University Press.

Beinart, W., and J. McGregor, eds. 2003. *Social history and African environments*. Oxford: James Currey.

Brantlinger, Patrick. 1985. Victorians and Africans: The genealogy of the myth of the dark continent. *Critical Inquiry* 12 (1), 'Race', writing and difference. Chicago: University of Chicago Press, 166–203.

Bunn, David. 2003. An unnatural state: Tourism, water and wildlife photography in the early Kruger National Park. In *Social history and African environments*, ed. W. Beinart and J. McGregor. Oxford: James Currey.

Collett, David. 1987. Pastoralists and wildlife: Image and reality in Kenya Maasailand. In *Conservation in Africa: People, policies and practice*, ed. David M. Anderson and Richard Grove. Cambridge: Cambridge University Press.

Cranworth, Lord. 1912. *A colony in the making*. London: Macmillan.

Dening, Greg. 1996. *Performances*. Chicago: University of Chicago Press.

Eliot, Charles. 1903. Memorandum on native rights in the Naivasha Province. Published in *Africa* 8 (1904). London: HMSO.

———. 1905. *The East Africa protectorate*. London: Edward Arnold.

Fabian, Johannes. 2000. *Out of our minds: Reason and madness in the exploration of Central Africa*. Berkeley: University of California Press.

Fischer, G. 1884. Dr Fischer's journey in the Masai country. *Proceedings of the Royal Geographical Society* 6 (2).

Galaty, John G. 2002. How visual figures speak: Narrative inventions of "the pastoralist" in East Africa. *Visual Anthropology* 15 (3–4).

Haggard, H. Rider. 1887. *Allan Quatermain*. London: Penguin Popular Classics, 1995.

Hildebrandt, J. M. 1877. J. M. Hildebrandt on his travels in East Africa. *Proceedings of the Royal Geographical Society* 22 (2).

Hinde, H., and S. L. Hinde. 1901. *The last of the Masai*. London: Heinemann.

Hobley, C. W. 1910. *Ethnology of Akamba and other East African tribes*. Cambridge: Cambridge University Press.

———. 1929. *Kenya: From chartered company to crown colony: Thirty years of exploration and administration in British East Africa*. London: H. F. & G. Witherby.

Hodgson, Dorothy L. 2000. Taking stock: State control, ethnic identity and pastoralist development in Tanganyika, 1948–1958. *Journal of African History* 41 (1).

Hollis, A. C. 1905. *The Masai: Their language and folklore*. Oxford: Clarendon Press.

———. 1909. *The Nandi: Their language and folklore*. Oxford: Clarendon Press.

Hughes, Lotte. 2005. Malice in Maasailand: The historical roots of current political struggles. *African Affairs* 104/415 (April): 207–24.

Huxley, Elspeth. 1943. Chapter 2 in *The British Commonwealth and Empire*, ed. W. J. Turner. London: William Collins.

Jackson, F. J. 1930. *Early days in East Africa*. London: Edward Arnold.

Johnston, H. H. 1886. *The Kilima-Njaro expedition: A record of scientific exploration in Eastern Equatorial Africa*. London: Kegan Paul, Trench & Co.

———. 1902. *The Uganda Protectorate*. London: Hutchinson.

———. 1908. The East African Problem. In *The Nineteenth Century and After*, no. 380, October.

———. 1910. *Britain across the Seas: Africa. A history and description of the British Empire in Africa*. London: National Society's Depository.

Kantai, B. Ole. 1971. Foreword to *The Maasai*, by S. S. Sankan. Nairobi: East African Literature Bureau.

Kaunga, Johnson Ole. 2002. The living and working conditions of urban-based indigenous peoples: The case of the Maasai of Tanzania. *Indigenous Affairs* 3–4. Copenhagen: IWGIA.

Kenya Land Commission Evidence and Memoranda. 1934. Vol. 2. London: HMSO.

Knowles, Joan N., and D. P. Collett. 1989. Nature as myth, symbol and action: Towards a historical understanding of development and conservation in Kenyan Maasailand. *Africa* 59 (4).

Krapf, J. L. 1860. *Travels, researches and missionary labours during an 18 years' residence in Eastern Africa*. London: Trübner & Co. Repr., London: Frank Cass, 1968.

Landau, Paul S., and Deborah Kaspin, eds. 2002. *Images and empires: Visuality in colonial and post-colonial Africa*. Berkeley: University of California Press.

Last, J. T. 1883. A visit to the Masai people living beyond the borders of the Nguru country. *Proceedings of the Royal Geographical Society*, vol. 5, new series, June.

Leys, Norman. 1924. *Kenya*. London: Hogarth Press.

Lugard, F. D. 1893. *The rise of our East African empire*. vol. 1. London: Blackwood. Quoted in Collet 1987.

Macdonald, R. L. 1897. *Soldiering and surveying in British East Africa 1891–1894*. London: Dawsons. Repr., Folkestone, England: Dawsons of Pall Mall, 1973. All quotes are from the 1973 edition.

Masai Annual Report 1921–22. Kenya National Archives.

McClintock, Anne. 1995. *Imperial leather: Race, gender and sexuality in the colonial context*. New York: Routledge.

Merker, M. 1910. *Die Masai*. Berlin: Dietrich Reimer.

Morgan, Philip. 1999. Encounters between British and "indigenous" peoples, c1500–1800. In *Empire and others: British encounters with indigenous peoples, 1600–1850*, ed. M. J. Daunton and R. Halpern. London: University of California Press.

Mudimbe, V. Y. 1988. *The invention of Africa: Gnosis, philosophy and the order of knowledge*. Oxford: James Currey; Bloomington: Indiana University Press.

Naudé, Stephen. 2003. "A very bitter love-making": Women as points of cross-cultural encounter in William Plomer's *Turbott Wolfe*. Paper presented at the conference The Unifying Aspects of Cultures, Vienna, November 2003. www.inst .at/trans/15Nr/04_07/naude15.htm (accessed January 13, 2006).

Oliver, Roland. 1957. *Sir Harry Johnston and the scramble for Africa*. London: Chatto & Windus.

Olol-Dapash, Meitamei. 1997. The future of the Maasai people and wildlife. *Satya* magazine, December.

Peters, Carl. 1891. *New light on dark Africa: Being the narrative of the German Emin Pasha expedition*. London: Ward, Lock, & Co.

Portal, Gerald. 1894. *The British mission to Uganda in 1893*. London: Edward Arnold.

Ricoueur, Paul. 1955. *Histoire et vérité*. Paris: Seuil. Quoted in Mudimbe 1988, 20–21.

Rotberg, Robert. 1968. Introduction to the new edition of Thomson, J. *Through Masai Land*. London: Frank Cass.

———. 1970a. *Joseph Thomson and the exploration of Africa*. London: Chatto & Windus.

———, ed. 1970b. *Africa and its explorers: Motives, methods and impact*. Cambridge, MA: Harvard University Press.

Routledge, W. S., and K. P. Routledge. 1910. *With a prehistoric people: The Akikuyu of British East Africa*. London: Edward Arnold.

Ryan, James. 1997. *Picturing empire: Photography and the visualization of the British Empire*. London: Reaktion Books.

Saibull, Solomon Ole, and Rachel Carr. 1981. *Herd & spear: The Maasai of East Africa*. London: Collins & Harvill Press.

Saitoti, Tepilet Ole. 1980. *Maasai*. London: Elm Tree Books.

Salau, Daniel. 2002. Globalization entrenches itself on the Maasai. *Civicus*. www .globalpolicy.org/globaliz/cultural/2002/0920masaai.htm (accessed January 13, 2006).

Sandford, G. R. 1919. *An administrative and political history of the Masai reserve*. London: Waterlow & Sons.

Schnee, Heinrich, ed. 1920. *Deutsches Kolonial-lexikon*, vol. 1. Leipzig: Quelle & Meyer.

Simel, Joseph Ole. 2003. The Anglo-Maasai Agreements/Treaties: A case of historical injustice. Unpublished paper presented to a seminar organized by the Office of the UN High Commissioner for Human Rights, Geneva, December.

Simpson, Donald. 1975. *Dark companions: The African contribution to the European exploration of East Africa*. London: Paul Elek.

Sobania, Neil. 2002. But where are the cattle? Popular images of Maasai and Zulu across the twentieth century. *Visual Anthropology* 15 (3–4): 313–46.

Spencer, Paul. 1984. Pastoralists and the ghost of capitalism. *Production pastorale et société* 15.

Stevenson, M., and M. Graham-Stewart. 2001. *Surviving the lens: Photographic studies of South and East African people, 1870–1920*. Vlaeberg, South Africa: Fernwood Press.

Thomson, Joseph. 1881. *To the Central African lakes and back: The narrative of the Royal Geographical Society's East Central African Expedition, 1878–80*. London: Sampson Low, Marston, Searle & Rivington.

———. 1882, 1883, 1884. Papers in *Proceedings of the Royal Geographical Society*, vols. 4, 5, and 6 (2), new series.

———. 1885. *Through Masai land: A journey of exploration among the snowclad volcanic mountains and strange tribes of eastern equatorial Africa*. London: Sampson Low, Marston & Co.

Thomson, Joseph, and E. Harris-Smith. 1888. *Ulu: An African romance*. 2 vols. London: Sampson Low, Marston, Searle & Rivington.

Tidrick, Kathryn. 1990. *Empire and the English character*. London: I. B. Tauris.

Von Höhnel, Ludwig. 1894. *Discovery of lakes Rudolf and Stefanie: A narrative of Count Samuel Teleki's exploring and hunting expedition in eastern equatorial Africa in 1887 and 1888*. London: Longmans, Green.

White, Luise. 1990. *The comforts of home: Prostitution in colonial Nairobi*. Chicago: University of Chicago Press.

Becoming Rom: Ethnic Development among Roma Communities in Bulgaria and Macedonia

10

ANDREA BOSCOBOINIK

"GYPSIES/ROMS ARE A SPECIFIC ETHNIC COMMUNITY, an 'inter-group ethnic community' which has no analog in the other nations of Europe" (Marushiakova et al. 2001, 25). The complex features of these groups along with the recent political transformations in Eastern Europe probably explain the fact that they began to be in the limelight since the last twenty years. At the present time, Roma issues stir political concerns as well as academic research, and "gypsy" movies and music are considered "trendy." This new focus is evidenced in a variety of research documents, journal articles, newspapers, and Internet sites dedicated to Roma subjects.

There is a growing focus on Roma communities and Roma-related groups since these are now seen as more than simply a colorful and rather exotic group. The lives of Roma and related groups in post-Communist East European countries have worsened in many ways, more so than in other countries. They face violence and discrimination in education, employment, health care, housing, public places, and law enforcement, and they are ill equipped to compete in the new market economies.

Affirming that the Roma and Roma-related groups nowadays are the most disadvantaged population in Europe according to all the major indicators—education, opportunity, income, and employment—is no overstatement. In addition, they are often scapegoats for society's ills and are subject to violent attacks. As victims of this miserable situation and of racist attacks (from skinheads, but also from the police), they seek to migrate to the West, and in the last years, hundreds of Roma have sought asylum in Western countries.

Besides the intention of understanding and divulging its marginal situation in society, the importance of grasping Roma issues was from the beginning a practical one. The European Union was concerned about the situation of Roma in the applicant countries, and, as a membership requisite for countries applying for membership, the EU has stipulated that social and economic situations of the Roma be improved. Thus, the new European Union members have had to submit models of integration of minorities.

The interest in Roma and Roma-related-group minorities also means that they are no longer an Eastern European peculiarity but a collective and general European concern. With the recent integration of ten East European countries into the EU, and when the aspiration of countries such as Romania and Bulgaria to EU membership becomes a reality, Roma will represent the largest minority in Europe. Until recently, they were only marginally taken into account. Based on qualitative research on perceptions of others and of the self within Roma communities in Bulgaria and Macedonia, our focus will be on the microsocial, as opposed to the macrosocial point of view hitherto devoted to considering Roma political and economic issues.

The qualitative methodology of this research, organized by Ethnobarometer, constitutes a particular and new approach to Romani issues. Self-perceptions of ordinary Roma appeared to be absent in most publications. Interviews based on life histories were conducted in Bulgaria and in the Republic of Macedonia with people who define themselves as belonging to any Roma group. These interviews cover a wide range of geographical areas and informants' characteristics (age, gender, occupation, level of education, and social and economic levels). A wide representation of Roma people were asked to talk about their opinions, their perceptions, their lives and experiences, and others' views of them. Focusing on an inside view of Roma with the necessary scientific distance (i.e., we did not become "Gypsy activists") allowed us to have firsthand opinions from Romani sources. In this manner, it was possible to analyze ethnic identity developing in Roma communities and Roma-related groups in Eastern Europe.

What's in a Name?

To name is to impose an identity on something or somebody. A name allows people to know what or whom one is talking about. Naming is essential for our study because it defines our subject. The first obstacle we meet and the first evidence that something must be clarified is the very naming of the population. In ethnological studies, when dealing with a well-defined population, the appellation chosen by its members is preferred to an external one; that is, the interest is in how individuals and groups want to be identified. However, in this case, there is no common agreement on a general self-appellation. This lack allows all sorts of external appellations, often with negative connotations and associations with negative stereotypes, and these allow and influence perceptions of self and other. Therefore, our first question is what to call this population, a labeling with which they can identify and that does not bear a negative connotation.

Gypsy is an English term denoting groups considered to have emigrated from India since the tenth century, in waves and to different regions. The term *Gypsy* and several European variants such as *Tsiganes*, *Zigeuner*, and *Gitanos* are considered pejorative by many. Others, however, find that *Gypsy* is a cover term that includes all group subdivisions (Marushiakova and Popov 1997). Roma is only one of such communities in Eastern Europe. *Romani* is in general used as an adjective. *Rom* refers to a member of the group, and *Roma* refers to a plurality of members and to the group as a whole. However, some authors prefer to use the plural following English grammar—that is, *Roms*, not *Roma*—and find it less connotative than *Gypsies*. Still others write *Gypsies/Roms* or even use both terms interchangeably, as though they were synonyms. Needless to say, some scholars emphasize the difference connoted by the various names.

The absence of agreement about how to identify this particular population is true not only among scholars or official bodies; it is also problematic for the surrounding population. For instance, twenty years ago, nobody in Bulgaria called the Roma by this name. One of the reasons could be that they were probably considered insignificant and were therefore ignored. Besides, during the socialist period, an assimilation policy strove to eradicate all minority groups. Moreover, different names were (and still are) applied when speaking of Roma, generally pejorative, as for instance *mangal*, meaning "black," with reference to skin color. This lack of agreement between official bodies, authors, and the surrounding population mirrors the lack of agreement in the community itself in recognizing a general appellation, although the reasons are obviously different.

Almost every document, book, or article dealing with Roma indicates that this is not a unified homogeneous community. Instead, what we call "Roma community" is in fact composed by a multiplicity of heterogeneous groups that may have very little in common and whose ties are very fragile. This particularity explains the fact that many members of this social group do not recognize themselves under the general appellation

Roma. Instead, they identify themselves rather with a restricted group (for instance, in Bulgaria, with the Eerli, Koshnichari, Kovachi, Zhorevtsi, Wallachian, etc., and in Macedonia, with the Barutchi, Konopari, Dzambazi, Topaanli, Magjuri, Gilanlji, Gavutne, Kurtofi, Cergari, etc.), demonstrating that the inner group of belonging is a stronger identity element. "Outlining a positive image of 'us'—the group with whom the speaker directly identifies himself—is much more convincing than the identification with 'all the Roma,' which is doomed to failure against the background of the group stereotypes" (Benovska 2003, 61). The differences between the groups are based not only on language, religion, or way of living, but also on the level of education and wealth. There are some extremely rich Roma who have nothing (and do not want to have anything) in common with the majority extremely poor Roma. The international distribution of Roma intensifies the differences between all the groups gathered under a same name. Actually, there is no social, economic, or cultural cohesion between the Roma living in different countries.

Thus, the members of this population do not always agree on the labeling for their identification. For some, *Roma* is denigrating; for others, *Gypsy* is deprecating. Still for others, it is not just a question of simply changing the old known word *Gypsy* for the more politically correct *Rom* without any other identity or cultural consideration. Such change of designation is considered only a euphemism. The word *Gypsy* may be used with pride, as if it were a challenge to the non-Gypsy. It can be hidden or denied for the discriminatory view it conveys. Moreover, a term may be acceptable if used by a Rom, but obviously not when used by a stranger (a *Gadjo*). Hence, terms may be understood as pejorative or complimentary according to the context.

Besides, many Roma-related groups such as Travelers, Sinti, Kale, Balkano-Egyptians, Ashkali, Beas, Yenisches, and so on, do not want to be labeled as Roma, simply because they consider themselves a distinct group. Moreover, this may create tensions among the groups that feel assimilated to another. As revealed in a seminar organized by the Council of Europe in September 2003, there is no consensus among the variety of Roma and Roma-related groups about a common denomination in which all groups might recognize themselves and that could be then used at an international level. Therefore, besides the symbolic dimension of a naming, the lack of a common name is rather practical, as for instance when considering social policies intended to cover some needs of these groups.

Taking into account that there is no accordance in choosing or accepting a category name, they will hereafter be called "Roma and related groups," so as to indicate their composite character. *Roma* is chosen because it corresponds to the more numerous group living in Eastern Europe, and with whom most interviews were made in Bulgaria and Macedonia. Nevertheless, this initial difficulty in naming a group (or a group of groups) proves that there is something to investigate concerning its very existence, its identity, and its self-perception. Moreover, while some representatives of these groups defend the differences between them, others (Roma and non-Roma) search to establish and show a common identity, and this will be our focus here.

Are Roma an *Ethnie*?

According to Anthony Smith (1987), a common proper name to identify and express the essence of the community is one of the features presented by an *ethnie*. The other main features he mentions are a myth of common ancestry; shared historical memories, including heroes, events, and their commemoration; one or more elements of common culture, which normally include religion, customs, or language; a link with a homeland, not necessarily its physical occupation by the *ethnie*, but its symbolic attachment to the ancestral land; and a sense of solidarity. As mentioned in the previous section, the first element is not present among Roma and related groups. Their lack of a common name reflects an insufficiently developed collective identity. "Until a collective cultural identity receives a proper name, it lacks, in an important sense, a recognizable sense of community (both by members and outsiders)" (Smith 1993, 29).

The other five dimensions are also not strongly represented among Roma and related groups. The different groups share few cultural elements, no common religion, no exclusive language, and no exclusive customs. Some groups are nomads, or, having been nomads in the past, they do not present a symbolic attachment with a specific common territory. For groups of nomads and travelers, territory is not a relevant element. Moreover, given their scattered geographic distribution, they might feel a link within each country they have inhabited over the centuries rather than with a mythical ancestry land. The sixth point mentioned by Smith is that people have to think of themselves as a group in order to constitute an ethnic community; this condition is not present in the different Roma-related groups. These groups are not aware of a common identity. Without shared myths and memories and a sense of solidarity that these engender, we would be speaking of an ethnic category rather than a community. An ethnic category represents the loosest level of incorporation, where there is simply a perceived cultural difference between the group and outsiders, and a sense of the boundary between them (Hutchinson and Smith 1996, 6). Actually, Roma and related groups perceive a difference between themselves and other majority and minority groups inhabiting the same country.

One factor that must be taken into account is the difference between the ethnicity claimed by the people themselves and that attributed to them by others. There is also the possibility that the claimed or felt ethnicity of group members may be shaped by what is attributed to them by others (Guibernau and Rex 1997, 8). From Fredrik Barth (1969), we have learned that ethnic identity is influenced from both sides of the boundary and that ethnic groups both achieve their identity and have it ascribed to them from outside. Moreover, different criteria may be applied in classifying themselves and in classifying the others.

According to our informants, the awareness of a Roma ethnic belonging comes "only" from the outside, that is, from the other ethnic groups. In this sense, it was outsiders who began categorizing them as members of a particular community. "What is clearly confirmed by the survey is that self-identification is weaker than the identification coming from outside the Roma community, from the other ethnic groups who perceive the Roma as a homogeneous group distinct from them, and often isolated deeply by them" (Kostova 2003, 52).

The research in Bulgaria confirms the idea that individuals considered by others as belonging to Roma communities do not recognize themselves or fully accept the Roma identity. One informant said in an interview, "We have never considered ourselves Gypsies; they consider us Gypsies." In contrast, the interviews conducted in Macedonia show that several people acknowledged being Roma, even if they could hardly say why. The answers ranged from "a feeling" and "speaking a Romani language" to "respect the customs and traditions." However, it is clear that in any interaction there is a manipulation of identity, which, as a dynamic process, is composed of several aspects. Moreover, identity is contextual; each person may identify him/herself in various ways according to circumstances and the person to whom he/she speaks (in our case, the interviewer). Different affiliations of an individual are invoked for different purposes and on different occasions. Following an attitude of the "expected answer," a person may play with the different facets of his/her identity, not to deceive the other, but rather to keep a pleasant dialogue and perhaps even to gain some advantages.

There are many possible reasons for rejecting or ignoring an identity that is negatively stereotyped, as it is for the Roma. We propose that other possible reasons explaining why individuals considered by others as belonging to Roma communities do not recognize themselves as such or fully accept the Roma identity might be the following.

A general category of Roma does not mean much when considering the heterogeneous reality. For one thing, as we have said, Roma communities are divided into different groups based on historical lifestyle (sedentary or nomadic), religion (Christian or Muslim), traditional occupations, language, and other cultural distinctions. The different groups or metagroups are hierarchically organized and do not intermingle. Each group considers itself as being "the purest, the best, the highest ranked" (Marushiakova and Popov 1997, 55). Groups considered "Gypsy" in the past have automatically been integrated under the label *Roma* lately in official documents. However, these groups defend their specificity and distinction from Roma. Thus, an individual conceives him/herself first as a member of his/her group or metagroup and does not appreciate being linked or confused with other persons with whom he/she does not identify at all.

Although nearly all of those interviewed knew which "subgroup" of Roma they belonged to and had opinions and value judgments about "their" group in relation to other "groups," there are other "subgroups," beyond an ethnographic definition, that are equally important for the people concerned. Economic status, educational level, and religious affiliation also heavily influence Romani internal means of self-identification and relating to others. As indicated by intellectuals interviewed in Macedonia, very little attention has been paid to viewing Roma as belonging to different social groups as opposed to a unified, and isolated, cultural entity (Plaut and Memedova 2005, 37).

Because of the group's low social status, some Rom may feel embarrassed to be identified with it and may prefer to identify with other social groups. This is commonly known as the phenomenon of preferred self-identity (Marushiakova and Popov 1997; Benovska 2003). However, some individuals will accept belonging to this group if they can find some advantage or profit. On the other hand, if a person has acquired a certain social level, he/she might possibly not want to acknowledge his/her Roma origin, as it could be perceived as a degrading loss of "prestige." In this case, the person would prefer to hide his/her origin if possible (Kostova 2003, 49). For some, the very general appellation, either *Gypsy* or *Roma*, based on ethnic origin, is rejected as highly offensive. Those affected interpret it as negative labeling, a reference to someone dirty, impolite, and lazy.

Poor Roma may feel indifferent about identity and cultural questions, as they need to solve more pressing daily problems such as basic physical survival. One informant said to our interviewer in Bulgaria, "Do you know that 99 percent of the Gypsies can no longer think because of hunger?" Obviously in such extreme cases, who cares about identity or ethnic belonging?

The emergence of evangelist churches and their strong aspiration to become the first reference for their members could be another reason for modifying identity perception. These churches have had a significant impact on Roma communities, and for those whose commitment is stronger, the church has become their first identification. Another consequence of joining these churches is the detachment from Roma rituals and traditions and their rejection as pagan.

The Process of Ethnicization

Because of the aforementioned, it is uncertain whether we should consider Roma and related groups as an ethnic group, at least considered from the point of view of self-awareness. However, they are increasingly considered as such by some specific intellectual and political groups. Moreover, we think that there exists an intention of "creating" a general category for an ethnic group to be labeled *Roma*. This trend of reinforcing a common consciousness or creating a shared identity between different groups implies that there is a process of what could be called the "ethnicization" of Roma communities and related groups (or might we say an "ethnicization" of problems?).

There is as much argumentation about the theory of ethnicity as there is about the constitution of such groups. In fact, we need not accept, as the theory of primordiality would suggest, that they are simply given. Rather, we can consider that an ethnic group could be constituted to serve particular purposes. The first question arising then is, who promotes ethnicity? And the second is, why?

As Christian Giordano put it, "L'ethnicité est-elle portée par un mouvement social ou de managers d'identité? Dans le premier cas, elle provient d'une frustration ou d'une colère spontanées, issues d'un mouvement de bas en haut, face aux prétentions destructives d'une culture étrangère dominante. Dans le second cas, en revanche, l'ethnicité doit être interprétée comme le produit de managers d'identité, issu d'une élite et instauré par en haut" (Giordano 1997, 166–67). The developing sense of community for all Roma groups is motivated by a group of intellectuals rather than being a mass ideology or social movement. It does not come from bottom to top; it is proposed by identity managers, political entrepreneurs, or even strangers to the groups—that is, from top to bottom.

Furthermore, there is the distinction between the categorization of groups by others, which can serve to reify and distill a sense of ethnicity, and the self-willed adoption of a collective ethnic identity by the group itself (Banks 1996, 131). As Richard Jenkins points out (1986, 177), the majority group categorizes a minority and hence reifies its very existence as a group. Thus, external ascription can act to bring "groups" into being. This is also the mechanism developed between established and outsider groups analyzed by Norbert Elias. The higher cohesion rate of one group contributes to a power inequality, leading it to a dominant position that allows its members to stigmatize outsiders, relinquish them into another group, and often exclude them (Elias 1994, xviii–xix). As a matter of fact, Roma and non-Roma are outsiders to each other. This is true especially for Roma activists and leaders who have a sense of belonging to a group and categorize the rest of the world as Gadje. Whereas non-Roma categorize a group of people as being Roma, not all Roma, as not all Gadje, recognize this labeling as pertinent to them. In summary, it is possible to distinguish at least three groups leading the above-mentioned process of ethnicization from different points of view and with different purposes (Boscoboinik and Giordano 2005).

Roma Elite Groups

Roma elite is of a rather recent origin, and it has been encouraged, often by external organizations, to better represent and defend the interests of the Roma communities vis-à-vis the majority. Roma elite groups have shown an increased concern in their community's culture and organization. Contrary to the attitude of rejection mentioned in the previous paragraph, Roma elite members are proud of being Roma. They promote a sense of common belonging to a minority group, seeking to develop a shared consciousness. In this sense, there is an identity management of Roma communities, culturally and financially administered by the elites.

The Surrounding Population

Social and economic crises favor the "demonization" of the Roma population, thereby turning them into scapegoats. There are sectors of society in which a serious economic crisis instigates feelings of fear and hatred toward a particular Other and spurs victimization of this group. The perennial struggle for scarce resources exacerbates cultural differences. In Bulgaria nowadays, there is economic rivalry among the fragmented population. The competition for jobs reinforces negative attitudes toward the Roma communities, which are then gathered into a homogeneous enemy group based on ethnic characteristics. In Macedonia, the presence of a larger number of other cultural, linguistic, and religious groups (besides Macedonians, there are Albanians, Turkish, Roma, Serbs, and Vlaches) dilutes this stigmatizing process based on cultural difference.

From the Exterior

Finally, even scholars and activists, sometimes unwillingly, also help in the development of an ethnic group. The many research projects, publications, and organizations that poured from the last wave of interest in these communities focalized attention on them as a distinctive group, favoring the emergence of an ethnicization process. However, it must be noted that authors working on the ethnicity concept have hardly ever made reference to the Roma. This is clearly seen in handbooks and readers on ethnicity, where these groups have almost always been absent. In academic books and research programs, Roma have been considered either a minority or a social or political problem, but rarely an ethnic group.

The first two groups show the two poles of this ethnicization process: a positive ethnicization when it is referred to one's own group, and a negative ethnicization when it constructs the Other. The first refers to positive values as identity, culture, and language, while the second one evokes negative social behaviors.

Purposes and Consequences of the Ethnicization Process

There are different reasons to which ethnic bonding might be applied. We focus on the ethnicization process encouraged by elites. The fact that identity may be manipulated for adaptive purposes and to obtain certain benefits is a process largely known not only in the long history of Roma groups but also in other communities. Another goal of encouraging a common identity awareness is to reach a political unification of the Roma and even to create a transnational nonterritorial nation. For Ilona Tomova, members of the Roma intelligentsia "are trying to establish political unity for the Roma in the country in order to allow them to take part successfully in putting forward and solving the serious socio-economic problems of this section of the population of Bulgaria" (Tomova 1995, 22). Therefore, it is possible to affirm that this identity management is directed toward pragmatic ends and toward obtaining practical benefits. However, besides the political and organizational aspect, there is also a symbolic dimension of this ethnicization process.

The segregation to which Roma communities are confined and the negative attitudes they have to endure bolster the idea in Roma intellectuals that unification is essential to create a common feeling that could better defend general Roma interests. Besides, they are convinced that the separated Roma communities would gain in force and confidence if they should feel they are sharing a common identity. Indeed, for some Roma leaders, if Roma were accepted as a nonterritorial nation, this fact would lend greater international legitimacy to the advocacy of their individual and collective human rights, consequently improving their general living conditions as a people.

Hence, efforts are made by elites, intellectuals, and political party leaders to bring Roma together in order to show a common interest, a "common battle." However, there is a conspicuous division and a remarkable divergence of relationships between this feeble "leadership" and its "rank and file." To consider the existence of a Roma mass mobilization in view of the creation of their own nation would thus be premature (Barany 2002, 202ff). Barany aptly speaks about the weakness of an ethno-national feeling of belonging. Based on data regarding the Czech Republic, he stresses that only a few people with a relatively high social status who aspire to a political career, or a group with a particularly low status who hope for higher social benefits, show any interest in or express the desire for a Roma identity (Barany 2002, 203). Despite the specificity of the context, this observation certainly holds true for other countries like Bulgaria.

Although the intentions of some Roma political leaders might be honest and noble, some others resemble a description of "political entrepreneurs" (Barth 1995). Considered in a general context, he characterizes them as politicians who use the politics of cultural difference to further their ambitions for leadership. "Leaders seek these constituencies and mobilize them by making select, contrastive cultural differences more salient, and preferably by linking them to grievances and injustices, whether in the past or escalating in the present" (Barth 1995). They search to mobilize such constituencies in dissatisfaction so that they can lead them to a promised satisfaction. However, as it will be discussed later, such discourses have not yet convinced the widespread ordinary Roma people.

From all these above-mentioned processes, it becomes clear that the political conditions and organization of Roma have improved to some extent, whereas their socioeconomic situation has deteriorated in the post-Communist countries. However, Barany's clear analysis shows that Roma attributes for political action are extremely poor by virtually all criteria of successful ethnic mobilization (Barany 2002, 77ff). He evokes that there is no single unifying element among Roma, no unique religious affiliation, no gathering political party, no common language, and so on. Barany also mentions the weak Roma identity, the lack of past mobilization experience, the absence of gathering symbols or leaders, and the poor financial resources, among other elements. In the 1970s, Thomas Acton wrote that the Roma are a "most disunited and ill-defined people, possessing a continuity rather than a community of culture. Individuals sharing the ancestry and reputation of 'the gypsy' may have almost nothing in common in their way of life and their visible or linguistic culture" (Acton 1974, 54).

Since detecting and grouping elements that could clearly target the heterogeneous Roma subgroups and related groups is not easy, the search is directed into the past—that is, into a common origin. The subjective belief that may unite different Roma groups is not so much a shared culture but a unity of descent and a kind of common destiny. What is important is a myth through which they can all be recognized and recognize themselves. Actually, a common origin and the fact that they face discrimination is what is mostly heard when they are asked about the common elements between Roma and its related groups. Tales and myths about the origin of Roma were cited in the interviews with Bulgarian Roma leaders and intellectuals. The link with the ancient India homeland explains the current cases of imitation and adoption of Indian cultural practices. The reverse side of the coin is that the Indian origin is also applied by racist slogans that demand, "Gypsies, go back to India!" In any case, due to the lack of their own written historical tradition, Roma nationalists may feel forced to develop "invented traditions" (Hobsbawm 1983) linking old and modern practices, easily acceptable and recognized by all groups.

The proliferation of Roma organizations is one of the most tangible consequences of this attention to ethnic awareness urged by Roma elites. Foundation data, programs, and main objectives differ from one Roma organization to another, as does their geographical reach. According to their coverage, the local, national, and international associations have different ambitions. For instance, international Roma organizations advocate principally for collective rights as a people and the unification of all Roma transnational groups. Their activism is growing, and their avowed intention is to protect Roma cultural, economic, linguistic, and educational rights within the states where the Roma live. Many also strive for the recognition of Roma as a nation. Local Roma organizations in Bulgaria, however, are more modest. They work primarily at a neighborhood level by trying to solve some of the problems the community faces (Chanteraud 2003). Also, in Macedonia, the majority of the Roma NGOs' activities are focused on the community and family level. They have grown since the mid-1990s, and in summer 2004, there were 120 registered Roma NGOs in Macedonia, 30 of which are considered active (Plaut and Memedova 2005, 29).

However, Roma individuals are rather skeptical toward any kind of group associations whose final goals are probably not understood or are doubted. This attitude could be explained by a lack of feeling of belonging to a general community; hence, they might be indifferent toward an organization in which they do not feel represented. The same was found in the interviews in Macedonia concerning the Romani political parties. Not one of those interviewed trusted the Romani political parties or the politicians who were representing, but not addressing, the needs of the Romani population in Macedonia. As a middle-aged Romani woman stated, "They are only after their positions and functions and they would leave us poor people to die" (Plaut and Memedova 2005, 36).

Lack of political experience might be another explanation for the distrust toward Roma or Roma-related organizations and political parties. Traditionally, Roma have never been involved in any kind of social or political management beyond the inner group. Moreover, the Roma elite group is still extremely small, and a large proportion of educated Roma choose not to be involved in Gypsy affairs (Barany 2002, 204). Also, the fact that some leaders are not willing to share power causes the organization's disintegration or separation into split groups. The accelerated rhythm of organizations' openings and closings nourishes the feelings of distrust.

Certainly, these processes are not a Bulgarian or Macedonian peculiarity. Roma organizations have developed and declined for similar reasons in all Eastern European countries since 1989. Undoubtedly, Bulgarian and Macedonian Roma organizations have not until now achieved the exploits of evangelist churches. The incorporation in a given religious community grants illusions and expectations; principally, they bestow a true sense of belonging when all other references are missing. In our opinion, this is the key to the attractiveness of these new religious movements.

Conclusion

Stating that these groups do not have a common fully accepted name and that their members do not recognize themselves as belonging to a general category—that is, that there is a weak feeling of a uniform Roma self-perception—does not mean that the groups do not exist. However, a distinction must be noted on three levels: cultural, ethnic, and socioeconomic. Roma and related groups maintain a feeling of difference vis-à-vis the surrounding majority population. This feeling has been reinforced by the discrimination they have faced since their arrival in Europe and are still facing. Thus, the Roma consciousness as a separate group is constantly reaffirmed from the outside.

Even when there is an "ethnic" manipulation creating a social category, it is not less true that these groups, considered at a socioeconomic level, have an undeniable problem of poverty and discrimination. One cannot deny the vulnerability, prejudice, and negative stereotypes they endure in everyday life. This social group, consisting of several subgroups and meta-groups, exists and needs attention. However, it is doubtful that socioeconomic solutions come from an ethnicization of the groups and their problems.

An improvement of the Roma's socioeconomic situation does not necessarily presuppose the creation of their own nation (even without their own state or territory, as some would like). Actually, this project appears anachronistic since it refers to eighteenth-century development models, which, at the time, were certainly successful. However, it is questionable whether these strategies are still appropriate and worthwhile (Giordano and Boscoboinik 2003, 26). Moreover, due to severe internal divisions based essentially on sociocultural differences, Roma and related groups are not very willing to identify with a social configuration resembling what is defined as a nation or to perceive themselves as a united group with an ethnic connotation. Following Barany, this holds true for Roma in the whole European context, as the personal and cultural feeling of belonging to a nation is precisely what most Roma do not share at this time (Barany 2002, 78).

An unfortunate consequence, contrary to the expectations of Roma leaders and intellectuals, is that the process of strengthening an ethnic consciousness might finally deepen the differences between the educated and noneducated Roma. In fact, as we have already said, the poverty of the latter hinders any other engagement than that of securing a daily living, and they express no interest in any identity question. Barany points out that the "enormous cultural distance between the tiny Romani intelligentsia and the masses of undereducated and often apathetic ordinary Gypsies, contributes to poor political communication in the Romani community and to the fact that Gypsy politics is, more than anything, elite politics. It is dominated by a handful of Gypsy activists and leaders who desperately (but usually without success) try to prove that they do represent 'their people' and that they do have a constituency" (Barany 2002, 204).

The problems that Roma communities are facing are essentially those of many other Bulgarians, Macedonians, and other ethnic groups. Therefore, finding solutions for the social and economic problems not only of Roma communities is crucial, particularly without forcing an ethnic status. In fact, in other Balkan countries, we have witnessed that stressing an ethnic belonging has led to nationalistic conflicts. This does not mean supporting a movement toward assimilation of Roma communities into the majority. A socioeconomic integration does not mean a cultural assimilation. Yet the need for equal access to economic development must be achieved by means other than stressing belonging to an ethnic minority in order to prevent ethnic conflicts in Eastern Europe. Better conditions for Roma are expected to come from a recognition of the value of human diversity.

References

Acton, Thomas. 1974. *Gypsy politics and social change*. London: Routledge & Kegan Paul.

Banks, Marcus. 1996. *Ethnicity: Anthropological constructions*. London: Routledge.

Barany, Zoltan. 2002. *The East European gypsies. Regime change, marginality and ethnopolitics*. Cambridge: Cambridge University Press.

Barth, Fredrik. 1969. *Ethnic groups and boundaries: The social organization of culture difference*. London: George Allen & Unwin.

———. 1995. Ethnicity and the concept of culture. Paper presented to the conference Rethinking Culture, Harvard 1995. www.wcfia.harvard.edu/ponsacs/seminars/Synopses/s95barth.htm.

Benovska, Milena. 2003. "I am a pure Gypsy..." The Roma individuality in the distorted mirror of group stereotypes. In *Roma's identities in Southeast Europe: Bulgaria*. Working paper, no. 8. Rome: Ethnobarometer, June.

Boscoboinik, Andrea, and Christian Giordano. 2005. Roma's identity and the political arena. In *Roma's identities in Southeast Europe: Macedonia*. Working paper 9. Rome: Ethnobarometer, May.

Chanteraud, Annabel. 2003. Le rôle des ONG dans la reconnaissance des minorités: Le cas des Roms en Bulgarie. In *Roma's identities in Southeast Europe: Bulgaria*. Working paper 8. Rome: Ethnobarometer, June.

Elias, Norbert, and John L. Scotson. 1994. *The established and the outsiders: A sociological enquiry into community problems*. 2nd ed. London: Sage Publications.

Giordano, Christian. 1997. L'ethnicité et l'espace monoethnique en Europe centrale et orientale. In *Dire les autres: Réflexions et pratiques ethnologiques*, ed. Jacques Hainard and Roland Kaehr. Lausanne: Editions Payot.

Giordano, Christian, and Andrea Boscoboinik. 2003. Introd. to *Roma's identities in Southeast Europe: Bulgaria*. Working paper 8. Rome: Ethnobarometer, June.

Guibernau, Montserrat, and John Rex, eds. 1997. *The ethnicity reader: Nationalism, multiculturalism, and migration*. Cambridge: Polity Press.

Hobsbawm, Eric, and Terence Ranger, eds. 1983. *The invention of tradition*. Cambridge: Cambridge University Press.

Hutchinson, John, and Anthony Smith, eds. 1996. *Ethnicity*. Oxford: Oxford University Press.

Jenkins, Richard. 1986. Social anthropological models of inter-ethnic relations. In *Theories of race and ethnic relations*, ed. John Rex and David Mason. Cambridge: Cambridge University Press.

Kostova, Dobrinka. 2003. The perceptions and self-perceptions of Roma: Individual and Community Crisis. In *Roma's identities in Southeast Europe: Bulgaria*. Working paper 8. Rome: Ethnobarometer, June.

Marushiakova, Elena, et al. 2001. *Identity formation among minorities in the Balkans: The cases of Roms, Egyptians and Ashkali in Kosovo*. Sofia, Bulgaria: Minority Studies Society Studii Romani.

Marushiakova, Elena, and Vesselin Popov. 1997. *Gypsies (Roma) in Bulgaria*. Frankfurt am Main: Peter Lang.

Plaut, Shayna, and Azbija Memedova. 2005. Blank face, private strength: Romani identity as represented in the public and private sphere. In *Roma's identities in Southeast Europe: Macedonia*. Working paper 9. Rome: Ethnobarometer, May.

Smith, Anthony. 1987. *The ethnic origin of nations*. Oxford: Blackwell.

———. 1993. The ethnic sources of nationalism. In *Ethnic conflict and international security*, ed. Michael E. Brown. Princeton, NJ: Princeton University Press.

Tomova, Ilona. 1995. *The gypsies in the transition period*. Sofia: International Center for Minority Studies and Intercultural Relations.

Subtle "Primitives": Ethnic Formation among the Central Yaka of Zaire

11

EUGEEN ROOSENS

THIS IS ETHNOGRAPHY FROM THE PAST. The case study illustrates that some very isolated African populations that, some thirty years ago, had been barely in touch with the urbanized world showed mechanisms of ethnic formation that come close to processes found in contemporary urban America, in what is called "symbolic ethnicity" (Wright 1994).

The Luunda, Suku, and Yaka of central Kwaango in southwest Zaire, whose culture I studied between 1961 and 1965, had all been colonized by Belgium (Roosens 1971). The Baluunda, Basuku, and Bayaka—names used by the local population—were generally amalgamated as the "Yaka" or "Bayaka" in the ethnographic literature. This "tribe" or "people" was, in fact, a set of merged populations of diverse ethnic origin. At least the three ethnic categories mentioned above could be distinguished in the population of central Kwaango. All were, within the traditional system, subjects of one king or ruler, the *kyaambvu* of Kasongo-Luunda, who presented himself as Luunda and traced his origins via his ancestors and predecessors back to Koola (a region in Shaba, Zaire), the country of the *mwaata yaambvu*, the prince of the Luunda kingdom.

The Luunda, in all probability, conquered the area in the seventeenth century. Using a strong assimilation and intensive intermarriage policy, they merged with the existing ethnic groups to the extent that the opposition of Luunda versus non-Luunda only survived in certain facets of the sociocultural reality, primarily in the opposition between the categories of "political chief" and "landowner" and in the ideology and rites expressing this political duality. A great deal of importance was attached to the latter political structure by the parties involved. The institution was

311

clearly African and had survived throughout the colonial and postcolonial periods.

Like many populations of the south, the Yaka were oriented toward economic development and acquisition of "modern civilization," albeit in a rather passive way. The Yaka of Muningulu I studied were separated from what is now Kinshasa by hundreds of miles of savanna path, and they had little or no acquaintance with the West, let alone with the broader world system.

In Kinshasa, where a large number of Yaka, mostly men, had settled as immigrants in squatting zones, and where in the 1960s they formed a socioeconomic underclass, both the Luunda and the non-Luunda hailing from central Kwaango tried to disappear ethnically. They were hiding their origin and only used Lingala, a local contact language, in public places.

"Primitive" Conditions?

The Yaka of central Kwaango are a group that current stereotypes, even in 1995, would depict as belonging to the "best-conserved" peoples of Africa. In the 1960s, the Yaka were often cited as an unknown, very primitive, and isolated group.

In professional circles, of course, there has long been awareness of how deceptive the word *primitive* is. But if it simply means very different from the West, which is often the case, or if it means having changed relatively little under the influence of external factors, then this hardly scientific concept is indeed applicable to the Yaka of the 1960s. For this reason, they are suitable for reflection on ethnic formation in an isolated region with a very low degree of technological development, especially as it is often suggested that the present ethnic phenomenon is a kind of return to the preindustrial past. Some even see it as a dangerous and unproductive regression to something that should be gone for good, like religion (Patterson 1977).

The term *tribalism* is often used with pejorative connotations, implying a reversion to an earlier period in the evolution of humankind. Considered within this frame of reference, the Yaka should have provided a clear example of what a monolithic, seamless tribe looks like. The facts, however, were totally different. Ethnic formation among the Yaka appeared to be a subtle and complex process. In order to be able to work with firsthand data that I collected over several years of field research, I will limit the scope of this article to the Muningulu region, located in the central part of the Kwaango region.

Ethnic Structure: A Subtle Layering

Well before the 1960s, a few missionaries who were interested in the culture and the history of the people with whom they lived had wondered about the origins of the Yaka, but they found no clear answer to their questions. One thing emerged with relative certainty, however; the population that the colonial and missionary organizations called the "Bayaka" was composed of different groups: the Luunda, the Yaka, the Suku, and probably other peoples. A colleague-anthropologist, who had done a great deal of work among the Suku, was, after a short visit to the eastern Yaka region, convinced that the so-called Yaka of the eastern zone of the Kwaango region were not at all Yaka "by origin" but were genuine Suku. In other words, among the interested Europeans, the respective ethnic identities remained unclear and opinions divided. This division of the experts reflected, at first sight, a confused situation within the local populations themselves.

A closer look, however, revealed that this confusion only resulted from the way the Europeans formulated the problem. Europeans realized that some people from this region were identified as Luunda, others as Yaka, and still others as Suku, whereas in Kinshasa, all were indistinctly labeled "Bayaka" by members of other ethnic groups or categories. The assumption was that a given group of people had to be either Yaka, Luunda, or Suku by origin and filiation. It was not noticed, though, that mostly *the same people* identified themselves as Yaka under certain circumstances and called themselves Suku or Luunda in another context, whereas a small number of other inhabitants of the same region vehemently rejected the name Bayaka or Basuku and called themselves Baluunda only.

The older men and notables from the Muningulu region—actually the only ones who had the right to discuss the subject in the presence of an outsider—stated that the important people of the region were all Luunda. The political chiefs and their family members called themselves Baluunda, not Bayaka. They used Muyaka (singular) as an abusive word for the least respected of their subjects. They said that their ancestors came from Koola, from the court of the *mwaata yaambyu* of Koola, a region of present-day Shaba. I was able to note the following, rather stereotypical texts about these origins.

The first text presents the arrival of the Luunda as a kind of idyllic event: a young woman, a sister of the *mwaata yaambvu*, went on a journey with her retinue to the region of the Kwaango River, where she met a native hunter who soon became her husband. She gave him the power of Koola, and their descendants became the rulers of the region.

The Origin of Us, the
Luunda of Kasongo-Luunda

We, we are descendants of Luunda, of Mwaadi Kamoonga, a sister of Koola. She requested permission to go on a journey from her brother, the Mwaata Yaambvu of Koola.

She said, "I want to go on a journey. I am going to visit our vassals so that they will pay us the tribute of Luunda."

Her brother answered her: "It is fitting that you, my sister, lay out the fields (metaphor for "tend to the affairs of the kingdom"); afterward, come back where I, your brother, reside."

She took her brother Kihuunda Mangaanda with her and gave him the dancing drum, the signal drum, the *bisaandzi* (singular: *kisaandzi*, a kind of instrument with tuned strips of iron), and the rattles.

Kihuunda Mangaanda was like someone who suffers from the neck disease. Kihuunda Mangaanda went always further along very bad roads.

Phaangwa Mataku Mansandzi Kamoonga Lukawasa went along the road of Kwaango. She was in the midst of singers in order to sing with the *bisaandzi* of Luunda.

There was a hunter who always killed wild animals. His name was Muta Kateela Khaandza Mudimi Kadimina Ndzala ("who shoots [hunting] shoots out of need [for meat]; who works the field, works it from hunger"). He observed that smoke from a fire began to rise.

Arriving, he saw a house surrounded with shrubs, as a plot for a house generally appears. He came with the spoils of his hunt, laid them on the ground, and bowed to the earth to greet the queen.

He said, "Greetings, Deputy."

Kamoongo Luwakasa replied, "Greetings."

After they had acted thus, Kamoonga Luwakasa took her water pipe and brought out tobacco and hemp. She smoked; a part of it she gave to him, Muta Kateela Khaandza Mudimi Kadimina Ndzala.

Muta Kateela Khaandza gave some of his game to Kamoonga Luwakasa. In the evening he left and went hunting again.

He came again, again with game. Another day he appeared again with more spoils.

He came to Mwaadi Kamoonga Luwakasa. He said, "Queen, today I sleep here because I am very tired from hunting."

Mwaadi Kamoonga Luwakasa said, "Very good."

When night fell, this man, Muta Kateela Khaandza Mudimi Kadimina Ndzala spoke: "Queen, I am your vassal. It would be good if I were also your husband."

Mwaadi Kamoonga said, "I, I may not marry you. If you want me to be your wife, let us then first send the matter to the residence of my brother, the Kyaambvu of Koola."

Muta Kateela said, "Very good, Queen Kamoonga,"

Mwaadi Kamoonga sent a message to the Mwaata Yaambvu of Koola. He answered, "If you, my sister, have found a man that suits you, there is no objection. I send you a Luunda knife, a drinking cup from the chief, and a lion skin on which your husband, Muta Kateela Khaandza, can be enthroned. Let him live with you, our sister from Koola."

She gave birth to their first child. They named him Pfumusaangu Mwaaku Kambumba Maafu Kambadika Thiinu Mudimi Ndzala.

Then they lived many years the hunter and his sister [of the Mwaata Yaambvu]. When Kihuunda Mangaanda heard "Your sister, Kamoonga Luwakasa, has married a man," and when she already had given birth to two children and he saw her again, he asked, "What is this, my sister? You marry without informing me?"

Mwaadi Kamoonga said, "You, my brother, have acted badly. You went wandering and left me behind alone. As matters now stand, my brother Kihuunda Mangaanda, it is no longer possible to grant you the investiture because I have given the power to my husband from Koola, Muta Kateela Khaandza Mudimi Kadimina Ndzala, and not to you, Kihuunda Mangaanda."

Kihuunda began to wail, but in vain, since all questions about the power had already been settled.

When Chief Khaandza died, he appointed his son, Pfumusaangu Mwaaku Kambamba Maafu Kambadika Thiinu Mudimini Kadimini Ndzala from Luunda, from Koola (here usually follow the names of the *byaambvu* [plural of *kyaambvu*] who succeeded each other).

Another text, which is performed as a kind of song at feasts in the presence of the traditional political Luunda rulers and their suite and relatives, presents the dominance of the Luunda with much more cruelty.

Great King, who draws all human life force to himself, who has masses of people destroyed.

Muni Phutu Mangaanda, Mwaata Yaambvu [names of prominent historical kings].

Who walks on palavers [is master over], who walks on disputes.

Everywhere you take what you want.

Who shall curse you [kill you]?

N-syeenini phoombo [a kind of large tree], that one cannot climb.

Descendant of Kamoonga Luwakasa [sister of the Mwaata Yaambvu, who came from Koola; see previous text], who holds in his possession the foot ring of the chiefs, the foot ring of the Kyaambvu [note: ankle ring (*kazekele*) of the *kyaambvu*; whoever succeeds in stealing it has the power].

Who keeps watch over the maize, who supervises the wealth of people.

The second wife is charged with the cooking; the first wife takes care of
the *myoombo* [sacred trees].

Who loves the *matuumba* drum [a double drum carried around the
neck], who loves the rattles [note: these musical instruments are said to
have been imported from Koola].

Washing out of the road [who channels the rainwater; figuratively, the
chief who organizes everything], who lets the fog rise [who is the origin
of all sorts of mysterious events, such as the death of particular people].

The others sleep next to fire of dead wood; you sleep on the bones of
sons of men. [Note: formerly, the body of the *kyaambvu* was lowered into
his grave on the arms of two men who were forced to sit down in the
grave with their wrists tied together.]

The older informants from the region explained the historical events in
the line of these texts: the Luunda were conquerors who came to rule the
people already settled in the Kwaango region. They came from the king-⊁
dom of the great *mwaata yaambvu* of Koola. Hence, the supreme authority
of the Yaka, the *kyaambvu*, who lives near Kasongo-Luunda, considers
himself the younger brother of the *mwaata yaambvu*, a metaphorical kinship term. This also explains that, up to the middle of this century, a kind
of *missus dominicus* was sent on foot every year from the court of the
mwaata yaambvu to the court of the *kyaambvu*. He reenacted the historical
journey of the forefathers and would be welcomed enthusiastically everywhere on his route to the capital of the Luunda of Kwaango.

It was self-evident for the local population that the political chiefs were
Luunda. The territory of the approximately three hundred thousand Yaka
was divided into about ninety regions. Each region was governed by a political chief who regularly paid tribute to the *kyaambvu* and offered hom-
age to this supreme authority in his residence near Kasongo-Luunda a few
times a year. At the same time, all the informants agreed that the Luunda,
who came from Koola centuries ago, married native women from the
Kwaango region, generally daughters of the autochthon chiefs, and that
this practice had been continued by their descendants.

Ethnic Descent: A Symbolic Construction

Whoever conceives ethnic belonging as a pure, monolithic reality faces a
major difficulty, for it ought to be clear to everyone, and for the local population, that the descendants of the above-mentioned "mixed" marriages
could at most be half-Luunda. Everyone realized that a kind of mixing
had taken place, and this for generations. The informants even stressed the

point; the Luunda had been using marriage as a kind of strategy, and they still did. A political chief of a region was generally polygamous and married women from several of his villages. Muningulu, for example, the chief of the Muningulu region, had in the early 1960s about twenty wives, among whom many were from various villages of his region. The children of these marriages, in turn, married young people from still other villages so that the political chief developed a very wide network of married relatives and descendants that made him a kinsman throughout his entire fief. In this way, Chief Muningulu was not only the lord of his region but also a relative in each of the village communities. At the same time, he was able to collect accurate information on his region and on the loyalty of his subjects.

Moreover, it was clear from the more than seven hundred family genealogies I recorded (Roosens 1971) that the Luunda of the 1960s related genealogically and biologically to the original Luunda immigrants from Koola only in the same "diluted" way as many Native Americans relate to their pre-Columbian ancestors.

When the aforementioned situation is analyzed in terms of the following theoretical assumptions, the questions of ethnic formation and structure become quite clear: (1) ethnic identity is an ongoing process in which a feeling of belonging and continuity-in-being (staying the same person[s] through time) is generated and kept alive, resulting from an act of self-ascription, and/or ascription by others, to a group of people who claim both common ancestry and a common cultural tradition (De Vos and Romanucci-Ross 1983; Hutnik 1991; Roosens 1994), and (2) in ethnic formation, reference to the "ancestors" (De Vos and Romanucci-Ross 1983)—the family metaphor—is at least as important as the maintenance of sociocultural distinctions—the boundary metaphor (Barth 1969; Roosens 1989).

Among the Yaka of Muningulu, descent was reckoned in a double-patrilineal manner: a person belonged at the same time to the patrilineage of his father and to the patrilineage of his mother. The paternal side did have a certain predominance, however. A man or woman who had a Luunda father and a non-Luunda mother could readily call himself or herself Luunda and leave the other half of his or her ancestors in the background. Someone with a Luunda mother and a non-Luunda father could do the same.

Whoever was able to do so displayed the Luunda aspect of his or her ancestry, but not everyone with any Luunda ancestors was allowed to identify as a Luunda. A limited number of people of the region were constrained by the political system to display their non-Luunda origin, even if they had Luunda political chiefs among their direct ancestors. The people who were forced to identify as non-Luunda—as Suku or Yaka—were the *tulaamba* (plural of *kalaamba*), the so-called landowners of the region. According to the collective representations of the Yaka, the Luunda chiefs were the most important men of the region, but they owned no land. The land was kept under the collective ownership of the ancestors of the *tulaamba*, the people who already lived in the region when the Luunda arrived. In the local ideology, these ancestors of the *tulaamba* formed a kind of absolute beginning; they were seen as the original and genuine owners of the land. Nobody could encroach on this collective ownership without compromising the fertility and the survival of the region. Should the political chiefs have passed themselves off as landowners, the population would have been afflicted by infertility and all kinds of other disasters. Thus, even the *kyaambvu*, in the conversations I had with him, stressed that he was not the owner of the land but that he did rule over the people, including the *tulaamba*.

One day, an argument developed in my hut between the Luunda subchief of the region (at the same time, chief of the village) and one of the landowners of the region. The political chief called the *kalaamba* his slave (*mpika*). The latter replied that the Luunda would fare like the Belgians at the time of independence; the Luunda, too, would have to return to where they came from. This *kalaamba* who was called a slave in my presence was the grandson of a political regional Luunda chief, but this aspect of his ancestry was totally ignored in the context of the discussion.

The opposition between the two functionaries—the political chief and the landowner—who each embodied a people, was thus given form by their respective ancestry and by a few cultural traits. The distinction between the two figures and the differences between the rites they carried out were considered essential for the survival of the entire population. A binary opposition had developed in the Kwaango region between Luunda and non-Luunda. Both categories were eminently incarnated by particular figures who had a public function: the Luunda by the *pfiimu mbeele*, or the political chief, and the non-Luunda (e.g., the Suku) by the *kalaamba*.

A Luunda chief was eligible for appointment to a political office by descent in the male line; the landowner inherited his office via matrilineal calculation, from a maternal uncle or from a maternal uncle of a maternal uncle. The "original" autochthons were thus placed in opposition to the Luunda by complementary functions that are occupied by virtue of a distinct ethnic belonging. The ethnic belonging of the functionaries, however, was presented as an intrinsic quality flowing from "pure," "full-blooded" descent, while every adult knew that pure, unmixed filiation on either side was out of the question. But this reality was simply not taken into account.

Those who were neither political chief nor landowner usually stressed their Luunda descent, displaying their belonging to the higher layers of the society. Almost everyone, except the landowners, could have ascribed themselves to the "better people." This explains that the above-discussed interpretation of the past and the legitimation of the political structure by the ruling Luunda were accepted by virtually everyone. That the inhabi-✶ tants of central Kwaango identified themselves as Luunda whenever possible was undoubtedly due to the relative prestige associated with this social identity within Yaka society. Moreover, the relationship and the historical bond with the *mwaata yaambvu* were felt to be a source of prestige, even to outsiders. Many residents of the region could just as well have identified themselves as Suku or Yaka, but they did not do so because it was contrary to their interest. As one can see, the social determination of ethnic identity can be far removed from the actual biological basis, even though this biological distance is publicly known.

Only in a few villages on the periphery of the eastern central area did the inhabitants mention to inquiring outsiders that they were, in fact, Basuku. In doing so, they presented themselves, at least verbally, as being independent vis-à-vis the ruling Luunda chief. But they did not display or instantiate this position in daily routines, and they did not attempt to secede. Their ethnic self-definition reflecting the antagonism between the political Luunda chief and the descendants of the former original autochthon rulers only emerged in particular circumstances (e.g., when questions of ethnic origin were formally discussed with outsiders).

Becoming Invisible in City Life

Anyone from central Kwaango who moved into Kinshasa in the 1960s was classified by city dwellers as a Muyaka. In Kinshasa, the term *Muyaka* sounded like an insult; it carried the connotation of being underdeveloped, a peasant, a rural primitive, and so on. In the city, the Yaka had long been known as still untouched by modern times, as people who were willing to take care of the heavy, dirty, unskilled jobs for very low wages. The urban population did not make the subtle distinction between Luunda and non-Luunda. The Luunda of Kwaango had no status in the modern city and were even unheard of. Apparently, their status of conquerors coming from Koola was a local phenomenon, acknowledged only in the rural area of the

Kwaango. In the city, Bayaka were only Bayaka—backward people from the wilderness.

In the city, most Yaka tried to remain ethnically invisible outside their familiar surroundings. When they visited bars, markets, or stores, they spoke a version of vernacular Lingala, even among themselves. And many children of immigrants from the Kwaango did not learn the Yaka language, Kiyaka.

The ethnic identity of the Yaka was not a kind of tribalistic straitjacket. Neither was their ethnic group a seamless social texture left over from an original, primitive past.

References

Barth, P., ed. 1969. *Ethnic groups and boundaries*. Boston: Little, Brown.

De Vos, George A., and Lola Romanucci-Ross, eds. 1975. *Ethnic identity: Cultural continuities and change*. Palo Alto: Mayfield.

Hutnik, M. 1991. *Ethnic minority identity: A social psychological perspective*. Oxford: Clarendon Press.

Patterson, O. 1977. *Ethnic chauvinism: The reactionary impulse*. New York: Stein & Day.

Roosens, Eugeen. 1971. *Socio-culturele verandering in Midden-Afrika: De Yaka van Kwaango*. Antwerp-Utrecht: Standaard Wetenschappelijke Uitgeverij.

———. 1989. *Creating ethnicity: The process of ethnogenesis*. Newbury Park: Sage Publications.

———. 1994. The primordial nature of origins in migrant ethnicity. In *The Anthropology of Ethnicity: Beyond "Ethnic Groups and Boundaries*," ed. H. Vermeulen and C. Covers, 81–104. Amsterdam: Het Spinhuis.

Wright, L. 1994. One drop of blood. *New Yorker*, July 25, 46–55.

SHIFTING ETHNIC IDENTITIES: IV
THE *REALPOLITIK* OF
CULTURAL CONTROL

FOR MANY EUROPEAN COUNTRIES, the mid-1600s through the 1700s was the Age of Discovery, when Europeans began establishing and developing trade in their newly discovered areas. This colonization soon became recognized as "colonialism," a fitting term implying ideological components for acculturation enforced from the top down. With superior weapons for death and destruction and the other accoutrements of advanced material cultures, the occupiers often began with the introduction of systems of classification (e.g., skin color), useful for assigning resettlement. Also, in addition to classifying "discovered" lands as their own, the colonizing powers forced the indigenous peoples to reevaluate who they were. Acceptance of these definitions of the self became a necessary survival strategy.

The exemplar we present is the region of South Africa, which was "discovered and settled" by the Dutch, quite early in the period of European expansion. Other Europeans were performing parallel acts in many other parts of Africa, but we look at South Africa as perhaps the most characteristic, the most literal in its ideological intentions, and therefore the most resistant to revoking acts which ensured that the usufructs of colonialism (land grabs, forced resettlement, and apartheid) were protected. This they did with the fervor of true believers in their mission. Of course, one should not consider the takeover of the African continent without including the slave trade (i.e., the kidnapping and selling of human beings in many parts of Africa), since a case can be made that this has very important implications for identity, both ethnic and personal. However, we do not consider that issue in this section, since the literal definition of it would place slavery in the past. Yet one sees elements of it lingering in assigned roles suggesting that the self belongs to the Other (the dominant cultural group).

Freedberg's "The End of 'Whiteness': The Transformation of White Identity in South Africa" describes the plight of Afrikaners in their struggle to maintain a white ethnic identity as they worked mightily, but failed, to stave off the end of apartheid. Politico-social dominance now lost, unlike the English in South Africa who maintained a relationship with their country of origin, these Afrikaners could not "go home again." Their system for controlling "their" Africans featured classifying "subjects" as white, black, or coloured, the latter referring to a person of Asian or Indian descent or a mix of black, white, or other combinations. Strategies for resettlement were based on this taxonomy. (This was not unlike the case of "resettling" the Native American Indian by American whites; this was done by forced marches from their millennial econiches to sections of the country where, even if they survived the transport, they would not easily adapt to drastically different climates, flora, and fauna. Few did, and that, of course, was the point.) Interestingly, the older generation of Afrikaners are now being critiqued in confrontational dialogue by their young progeny, who ask their parents and grandparents, in word, print, and theater, how they could possibly have dreamt up "the wildly impractical and immoral" system of apartheid. These young white Afrikaners now eat African foods, learn African languages, and do not disapprove of interracial marriages. Freedberg, an accomplished journalist and newspaper editor, provides insightful analyses along with well-informed and well-documented views on the many political readjustments in this country.

Scheper-Hughes, in her chapter, "Mixed Feelings: Spoiled Identities in the New South Africa," takes the reader into the field of her ongoing study of violence and the transition to democracy in Cape Town and a nearby village. Presented are samples from her collection of personal narratives of marginality and suffering as experienced and expressed by coloured people, many of whom feel the irony that they are offspring of male Afrikaners and Hottentots (and therefore they are often disparagingly referred to as "Hot-Nots"). Their classifiers often thought of them as nonpersons, with no identity because they are neither black nor white.

Scheper-Hughes is intrigued by the concept of the nonclassifiable and in her analyses finds some comparisons with Mary Douglas's view that unclassifiables come to be viewed as impure and polluting, and therefore dangerous and punishable. Coloureds try to pass as whites if they can (which could be viewed as both polluting and dangerous by the ruling class). They voted heavily for white supremacy in the elections, for fear the blacks would do nothing for them if they gained power, or perhaps even punish them for being part white, as well as for their efforts to pass for white. Coloureds consider their lot the most miserable of all. Scheper-Hughes demonstrates in her fieldwork and her exposition, as she did in her study of the poorest in Brazil, that it is possible for the researcher to be the objective, observing anthropologist and at the same time be passionately involved in expressing a need for change in a social system. Her approach is reminiscent of the arguments for and against relativism in anthropology's past. Those who argued against the relativists maintained that a social system may be culturally integrated, logical, and well functioning as a system, yet not be considered either ethical or moral in the course of human events. What is the researcher to present, and indeed, what is she or he to do "in the field" in the face of monstrous inequities? The chapters in this section provide information from different types of research; this allows the reader to approach this important issue not only from the standpoint of historical cultural change, but also from the perspective of the anthropologist who has studied the culture over a long period of time. These investigators isolate those features of identity stress deemed of supreme relevance in the complexity of contemporary "globalization."

Lola Romanucci-Ross

The End of "Whiteness": The Transformation of White Identity in South Africa

12

LOUIS FREEDBERG

> *The unity in a racial group can only develop among its own people, separated from the others. The only national unity for whites is unity amongst the whites.*

—ELECTION STATEMENT, PRIME MINISTER H. F. VERWOERD, 1961,
QUOTED IN THOMPSON 1985, 44

A S A RESULT OF ONE of the more remarkable political transformations of the twentieth century, the challenge for white South Africans is how to maintain a sense of ethnic identity now that their identity constructed during the apartheid era has been stripped of its central component of political and social dominance. The experience of white South Africans—indeed of whites in most parts of Africa—illuminates the view that ethnic identity is not a permanent construct. Rather, as De Vos notes, "Ethnic identity is a continually evolving process, sometimes occurring within a single generation" (Romanucci-Ross and De Vos 1995, 17). In the case of South Africa, after over three hundred years of racial rule, the adaptations forced on whites came relatively abruptly. How they have adapted presents a case study of the degree to which ethnic minorities can adapt to extreme changes in their status in a society.

Whites in South Africa, who make up just under 10 percent of a population of 45 million, constitute by far the largest concentration of whites anywhere on the continent.[1] Despite half a millennium of European presence on the continent, whites as a group do not represent a significant political or cultural force anywhere else other than in South Africa. In Zimbabwe, where they once totaled some 250,000, or one-sixteenth of the total population, they are a dwindling presence, as they are in other former British colonies like Malawi, Zambia, Uganda, and Kenya. They have almost completely disappeared in the former Portuguese colonies of Mozambique and Angola. The white population in Algeria is similarly depleted. In the wake of the Algerian civil war, by 1961, over 800,000 French nationals—the overwhelming majority of Algerians of French descent—had left the country. Even in Kenya, where some 50,000 whites decided to stay after independence, according to Francesca Marciano, author of the Kenyan-based novel *Rules of the Wild*, they have become a marginal group.

> It's not as if whites have any power in Kenya. I mean, Kenya is run by Africans. The government is African, as are the big businessmen. It's an African run country. So who are these white people? They're almost a lost tribe, obsolete. They're not really part of the social grain and so, in a way, they're free to have this easier life. No one really pays any attention. (Marciano 1998)

In South Africa, the end of apartheid points to the end of "whiteness" in Africa, in the sense of an identifiable white minority with a distinct identity and a disproportionate hold on political and economic power.

White South Africans are, in effect, experiencing a kind of "identity shock." Identity, as De Vos has argued, is made up of key elements such as a language that sets a people apart from the rest of society and provides a sense of racial uniqueness, a tradition of territorial or political independence, a sound economic base, aesthetic cultural patterns, and a set of religious beliefs built around their origins and past tribulations (Romanucci-Ross and De Vos 1995, 18–23). In South Africa today, whites can no longer claim to have permanent control of the country and its land. The movement of blacks into former white towns and neighborhoods also poses a threat to whites' once-secure sense of territorial control. Their language has been tainted by its association with the apartheid state and has been downgraded as a result. Their cultural patterns have been superseded as the norm by those of black majority. The heroes of Afrikaner history have been deposed from their exalted status, their names and statues removed from streets, towns, buildings, and airports. The Dutch Reformed Church, which provided with such certainty the moral and religious foundations for apartheid, is now far less sure of itself. In other words, central elements of white identity have been stripped away.

The central question explored in this chapter is the extent to which whites will attempt to hold on to a distinct "white identity" in a post-apartheid South Africa, or whether a new, more Africanized identity will emerge. Will whites become marginalized and isolated as they have almost everywhere else in Africa? Or will they become full participants in South Africa's evolving democracy? How they adapt psychologically and socially to the new order—and how the new order responds to them—will be crucial factors in the evolution of this still-emerging identity.

In the last decade, a series of studies of the construction of "whiteness" in the United States has pointed to the mostly un-self-conscious nature of white identity in countries where whites are in the majority and have a disproportionate share of political and economic power (Roediger 1991; Jacobson 1998). In those societies, whites tend to take their identity for granted and don't see their positions of relative privilege as necessarily related to the color of their skin. "Whites as the privileged group take their identity as the norm and the standard by which other groups are measured, and this identity is therefore invisible, even to the extent that many whites do not consciously think about the profound effect being white has on their everyday lives" (Martin et al. 1996). Ethnic minorities, almost by definition, are the groups that are noticed and studied, which, as Dyer (1988, 44) has argued, has "had the effect of reproducing the sense of oddness, differentness and exceptionality of these groups." Meanwhile, he explained, "the norm has carried on as if it is the natural, inevitable, ordinary way of being human." The rise of multiculturalism and the celebration of the ethnic identity and customs of racial "minorities" has made whites more visible and has forced at least some to explore their roots in their ancestral countries of origin, even in societies where whites are in the majority. But for most, whiteness remains an un-self-conscious, unexamined experience.

By contrast, there has been nothing un-self-conscious or invisible about whiteness in South Africa. Almost by definition, by being a highly visible minority in a largely black society, whites had to justify to themselves, and to the outside world, how and why they could maintain their position of dominance over the majority of the population. Over time, the white minority, and especially the government it elected, became pariahs in the international community. Rather than traditional ethnic minorities, it was they who, in Dyer's terms, were "odd, different and exceptional." "In contrast to the American experience of whiteness, which emanates securely from the position of the invisible norm, buoyed up by demographic, economic, and political advantage, the more-threatened whites in South Africa have always been highly conscious of their whiteness. They knew that this entailed privilege and that their whiteness was indeed the most salient factor in influencing all aspects of their lives" (Steyn 1997, 9).

This chapter also points to how the experience of white South Africans can provide lessons for whites in countries where they are the dominant racial group. In many countries, including the United States, white majorities are being reduced through increased immigration and higher-birth-rate population growth among some minority groups. In an era of global trade, more open markets, television broadcasting, and ease of travel, whites increasingly have no choice but to embrace a diverse world in which they don't necessarily dominate. While the adaptations being required of whites in the United States are not nearly as extreme as those demanded of whites in South Africa, the two societies may learn from each other as they come to terms with a central challenge of the twenty-first century: how to preserve a distinct, affirming identity in societies marked by greater diversity and migration, as well as growing empowerment of previously disenfranchised minority groups.

White Identity in a Segregated South Africa

White settlers came to South Africa beginning in 1652, when Jan Van Riebeeck and a band of Dutch colonists hired by the Dutch East India Company landed at the Cape of Good Hope. The purpose was not to stay there permanently but to establish a "refreshment station" to cultivate vegetables and rear cattle to supply ships when they sailed around the cape on their way to the company's main settlement in Batavia in Java.

The relationship between the white colonists and the indigenous population was a tense one from the start. Van Riebeeck was himself a reluctant participant in the company's venture, described by Frank Welsh as a "short, fiery pragmatist, who endured ten years of service in a place he detested, among people he disliked, always yearning to return to the East Indies," where he had previously been posted (Welsh 1999, 21). From the outset, there was conflict between the colonists and the local indigenous Khoi Khoi inhabitants over pasture lands, especially those in the valley behind Table Bay.

So began an era of white colonization that eventually encompassed virtually the entire continent. The independence movement of the 1960s shattered whatever degree of coexistence that might have been achieved. Suddenly, whites no longer were assured of being the dominant group. Some were gently pushed aside by the arrival of democratic rule. Some fled in the face of hostile military dictatorships. Some chose to stay, even though they were no longer automatically a member of the ruling elite.

To assume a privileged place within the white minority in South Africa, a basic requirement was that one had to *look* white. The *appearance* of whiteness was paramount. Many "whites" who had mixed racial backgrounds managed to pass as white even though they had racially mixed backgrounds. During the apartheid era, a Race Classification Board would consider applications from individuals who wanted to be "reclassified" as belonging to eight different racial groups: African (still the term used to describe blacks), Malay, Griqua, Cape Coloured, Indian, Chinese, and white. Most of the applications came from so-called coloureds wanting to be reclassified as white.[2]

But although it had a racial foundation, white identity was reinforced by deeply held religious and cultural beliefs, especially among Afrikaners. A series of bloody events—most notably the defeat of the Zulus on December 16, 1938—convinced Afrikaners that they represented a superior civilizing force blessed by God. So, for example, D. F. Malan, an ordained minister in the Dutch Reformed Church who became the first prime minister of the apartheid state when the National Party took power in 1948, said,

> The last 100 years have witnessed a miracle behind which must lie a divine plan. Indeed, the history of the Afrikaner reveals a will and a determination which makes one feel that Afrikanerdom is not the work of men but the creation of God. (Moodie 1977, 1)

The apartheid state eventually enshrined its religious beliefs in what it called Christian National Education, which permeated the curriculum taught in public schools serving children of all racial groups.

The Afrikaans language—descended from Dutch but resembling Flemish more closely—was also a key component of Afrikaner identity, even though it only emerged as a distinct language in the early part of the twentieth century and only became one of South Africa's two official languages in 1925 (the other was English).

During the apartheid years, white identity was strengthened by the apartheid state, whose major purpose was to accrue most of the country's land and resources for the benefit of whites. The vast majority of whites supported the National Party and its policies. White cohesion was maintained through residential segregation, which meant that, other than domestic servants and other lower-status blacks, most whites had little contact with the majority of the black population. It was possible to live as a white South African without any real sense that whites were in fact a small minority.

Black migration to the cities was strictly controlled through a series of apartheid-era laws. Within cities, blacks were forced to live in distant townships that whites had little reason to visit. In cities and rural towns known as *dorps*, restaurants, movie theaters, hotels, parks, beaches, and other places where whites would congregate were all strictly segregated. School children attended schools that were segregated by law, and college students enrolled in mostly segregated universities.[3]

The apartheid state also created a labor market based on "job reservation," a complex set of laws that reserved certain jobs for whites, and others for blacks, coloureds, and Indians. Many whites may have had considerable contact with blacks and other "nonwhites" in the workplace, but those contacts were almost always with blacks whom they supervised or who did low-status, low-paying work.

When in 1948 the National Party scored an upset victory over the United Party headed by then Prime Minister J. C. Smuts, Afrikaners for the first time had reached the pinnacle of power in a country where their ancestors had settled almost exactly three centuries before. It was a heady time. The National Party moved at breakneck speed to consolidate their power and to codify and entrench racial rule. The party became the vehicle for the expression of Afrikaner nationalism in a virulent, ethnocentric form. English-speaking whites for the most part were not a part of the movement, and they were not sought after to participate in it. Throughout its forty-six years in power, there was never an English-speaking leader of the National Party. Only a handful of English-speaking whites ever represented the National Party in Parliament.

At the same time that it was building the apartheid edifice, the National Party, with equal zeal, promoted the economic empowerment of Afrikaners. Within two decades, Afrikaners were dominant players in the country's leading financial institutions—institutions they had been excluded from until the National Party came to power.

Afrikaans was entrenched as one of the two official languages. Even black school children were required to learn it, many unhappily. The student uprisings in Soweto that began in 1976, marking the beginning of the era of protest that eventually led to a negotiated settlement of the conflict, were triggered by the refusal of students to be taught in Afrikaans, which they despised as the "language of the oppressor."

During the forty-six years it was in power, the National Party played a key role in shaping and reinforcing Afrikaner identity. During that time, it was never once even remotely challenged by any other white political party. English-speaking whites tended to be in the opposition, initially supporting the United Party, which disbanded in 1977 because of dwindling support, and in far smaller numbers the liberal Progressive Party. Election results during the apartheid era indicate that most English-speaking whites either voted directly for the National Party or for political parties that embraced some form of racial rule in South Africa. Even English-speaking whites, who tended to have more liberal views than Afrikaners, never supported a party that espoused basic democratic principles like "one man one vote." The notion of extending full democratic rights to blacks was viewed by most whites as a radical, even revolutionary slogan that would, if enacted, bring chaos and destruction to South Africa.

During the years the National Party was in power, Afrikaner identity, argue Heribert Adam and Hermann Giolomee, encompassed much more than the Afrikaans language, culture, and race. "It is in fact a political code word that relates to the status which accompanies political domination, and to the range of ethnic interests, privileges and spoils, of which crucial ones, such as career chances in the civil service and public corporations depend on political control and the policy of separate development, which ensures Afrikaner hegemony" (Adam and Giliomee 1979, 122).

What also united whites—and distinguished them from other settler or colonial groups in Africa—was that almost all viewed South Africa as their permanent home. Afrikaners had no links to their countries of origin, which their ancestors typically had left centuries earlier. Some English-speaking whites still had links to the United Kingdom and claims to citizenship there. But that was not the case with the majority of English-speaking whites who also had nowhere else to go. Although periods of conflict (such as after the Sharpeville massacre of 1960 and the Soweto uprisings in 1976) invariably triggered a surge of out migration, there was never a period of significant mass migration of whites from South Africa. Even for whites who did have the ability to get visas to other countries, the dilemma was that they would almost certainly have to accept a lower standard of living abroad. That reality also was a powerful incentive for whites to stay.

Jews occupied a special place within the white ethnic framework. At their peak, the Jewish population consisted of only 150,000 Jews, never constituting more than 5 percent of the white population. But they were influential in academic and business circles. Early on, the National Party made a deal with the Jewish leadership: in return for acquiescence in the apartheid state, Jews would be allowed to raise funds for the State of Israel, which came into being the same year the National Party came to power. Jewish organizations like the Bnoth Zion were allowed to bypass currency control regulations which prohibited the transmittal of South African currency abroad. Thus most Jewish activism was focused on Zionist causes. For some Jews, their Jewish identity superseded their South African identity, and for decades many Jews left South Africa to go on aliyah to Israel, initially settling on kibbutzim there. But the majority of Jews, like other whites, chose to stay in South Africa.

Some whites, of course, did oppose the apartheid state, to varying degrees. A small number left South Africa to join the African National Congress (ANC) in exile. Most came from the ranks of English-speaking whites, although a small number of them were Afrikaans speaking. Whites who opposed apartheid, especially those who joined the ANC, were seen as traitors to their race. For Afrikaner antiapartheid activists, this was especially the case. Many whites could understand why blacks would join the liberation movements, but for a white Afrikaner to do so was seen as a betrayal, not only of the other whites but of the Afrikaner "volk," an almost mystical notion with racial, cultural, and nationalistic connotations.

So, for example, in 1983, Carl Niehaus and his wife Jansie, at the ages of twenty-three and twenty-two respectively, were charged with treason after he was found to have surveyed several sites as potential targets for sabotage by the ANC. As Allister Sparks describes, "Both were Afrikaners from deeply rooted Afrikaner families and they had been studying at the politically select Rand Afrikaans University, but they had joined the ANC which made them ethnic traitors as well as subversive activists" (Sparks 2003, 141). Carl Niehaus was sentenced to fifteen years imprisonment, and his wife Jansie received a four-year sentence. Carl Niehaus was only released in 1991, a year after Nelson Mandela was freed from prison.

In the last years of apartheid rule, a small number of Afrikaner intellectuals began to challenge the apartheid state more directly. Frederik van Zyl Slabbert, an Afrikaner sociologist at the University of Cape Town, was elected leader of the liberal, antiapartheid Progressive Party, and convened the first above-ground meeting of Afrikaners and the African National Congress in 1987 in Dakar, Senegal, in clear violation of the law. That sensational meeting was a key event in the forces that led to the release of Nelson Mandela and the subsequent unraveling of the apartheid state.

But even whites opposed to apartheid and who remained in South Africa were not forced to relinquish the privileges that came with being white. They continued to live in white neighborhoods, patronizing segregated restaurants, movie theaters, and other segregated facilities. Almost none lived in the black townships. A small number lived in residential areas known as "gray areas," like Woodstock in Cape Town. These tended to be working-class neighborhoods where interracial couples had found places to live, or where low-income whites had been able to find relatively low-cost housing. So, by the time apartheid ended, most whites had had relatively little meaningful contact with blacks who constituted the majority of the population.

Assaults on White Identity in the Postapartheid Era

The fall of apartheid represented a shattering assault on white identity in South Africa. Just as many in black Africa underwent a process of detribalization during the postcolonial period (Uchendu 1995, 131), white South Africans had to undergo their own unique form of "detribalization."

The psychological adaptation forced on most whites has few historical parallels. Their ties to their mother countries had long been severed, and they regarded themselves as permanent inhabitants on the most southerly region of the continent. When Nelson Mandela became president on May 11, 1994, over 350 years of racial rule in South Africa came to an end. Unlike whites in other parts of Africa, they had nowhere else to go. They could either actively resist the new order, or they could try to adapt to it.

Whites did have several years to prepare themselves for the official end of white minority rule. The seminal moment occurred on February 2, 1990, when President F. W. de Klerk announced at the opening of Parliament in Cape Town that the African National Congress, for over three decades a banned organization whose members the Pretoria regime had labeled as terrorists and systematically harassed, jailed, or assassinated, would be legalized, and Nelson Mandela would be released from jail.

Following Mandela's release on February 11, 1990, Mandela spearheaded four years of negotiations with the Afrikaner minority. Whites became familiar with Mandela, whose stature grew rapidly and whom most whites soon came to accept as their best hope to avoid a bloody civil war. Most importantly, they viewed him as someone who could tamp down any impulse for revenge or retribution on the part of aggrieved blacks.

But despite these events preceding the official end of white minority rule on May 11, 1994, when Mandela was inaugurated as president on the grounds of the Union Buildings in Pretoria, the change in the status of whites occurred extraordinarily rapidly when measured against the long sweep of racial rule in South Africa. Even after negotiations had begun with the ANC in 1990, the government's negotiators were still presenting "power sharing" schemes in the mistaken belief that they could come up with a resolution that would avert black majority rule. The very concept of a black president was a radical one even at that late stage.

In some ways, whites have adapted remarkably well to the changes. There has not been a mass migration of whites out of the country. There has been no serious attempt by the most conservative whites to destabilize the new government. There has not been a surge of racial conflicts or hate crimes.

A small group of neo-Nazi whites, led by the Afrikaner Weerstand Beweging's Eugene Terreblanche, did attempt armed resistance during negotiations leading to the democratic elections in 1994, but they were easily crushed and isolated. Separatist Afrikaners established the all-white community of Orania, now with a population of five hundred residents, located in an isolated rural area. Not even black workers are allowed to set foot in the privately owned community. "The difference between the Afrikaners who are European descendants is so much from the African tradition that it's really two worlds. It's two kinds of identity and two kinds of culture. So bring them together like one community, I don't think it's acceptable," explained seventy-six-year-old Carl Boshoff, who is married to the daughter of former prime minister Hendrik Verwoerd, often referred to as the "architect of apartheid" (Morin 2004). But Orania and the views expressed publicly by its leaders are an anomaly on the South African landscape, an almost quaint artifact rather than a threat to the new democratic state.

That is not to say that whites are overwhelmingly positive about the transformations they are experiencing. A 2004 survey conducted jointly by the *Washington Post*, the Kaiser Family Foundation, and Harvard University, ten years after the end of white minority rule, showed that whites are conflicted and even confused about the changes they are experiencing.

The survey reveals a vast attitudinal divide between blacks and whites. Fifty-eight percent of whites felt the country was going in the wrong direction, compared to 34 percent of blacks. Seventy percent of whites said the quality of both education and health care was worse than under apartheid, while 81 percent of blacks said the quality of education had improved during the postapartheid period, and 70 percent also said health care had improved.

At the same time, the majority of whites—58 percent—said that "democracy has been a good thing for South Africa," compared to 83 percent of blacks. Remarkably, when asked whether, "considering everything, would you go back to apartheid?" 76 percent of whites answered that they would not, and close to the 86 percent of blacks who answered the same way. Forty-seven percent of whites said they were optimistic about the future, compared to 43 percent who said they were not. By contrast, 70 percent of blacks said they were optimistic about the future.

In light of the bitter conflict that many predicted the end of apartheid would bring, these attitudes signify that whites on the whole have responded positively to the extraordinary transformation of their society.

There have been practical reasons for this positive adaptation. First, the central theme of Nelson Mandela's five-year term as president was racial reconciliation, and as a result there have been few overt racial attacks by blacks against whites. Second, the ANC's economic policies have not included seizure of white assets. In contrast to Zimbabwe's land reform debacle, the Mandela government established a Land Claims Court along with well-defined procedures for claiming land appropriated by the apartheid regime.

In fact, most whites have continued to live just as they had before, still enjoying a relatively high standard of living, at least compared to most blacks. Third, the spatial arrangements created by apartheid rule have not changed dramatically; most blacks still live in outlying townships, and most white neighborhoods have remained largely white. Fourth, most whites have nowhere else to go. Most do not have family ties or ancestry that would entitle them to a visa in the United Kingdom, the United States, Canada, or Australia, to name just four of the most favored emigration destinations. Fifth, most whites took a wait-and-see attitude after the election of Mandela. Even though they might not have embraced the transition to majority rule, their attitude was to give the new government a chance to show that it could rule successfully. Sixth, the fact that whites were in the minority—and a shrinking minority at that—presented a demographic reality that they could no longer escape. It was a case, as P. W. Botha not so subtly described it a decade earlier, of "adapt or die"(Schrire 1991).

Democracy and the Erosion of White Identity

Nonetheless, the transition from apartheid rule has challenged white identity in multiple ways. Laws like the Group Areas Act, which barred blacks from living in most white neighborhoods, disappeared immediately on Mandela's taking power. Over the past decade, wealthier blacks have moved into white neighborhoods, and many whites have had to accept integrated residential neighborhoods in a way they never had to prior to 1994. Similarly, all forms of what was called "petty" apartheid—segregation in restaurants, hotels, beaches, and so on—also became unlawful, so whites had increased contacts with blacks, reinforcing the message that the days of white privilege were over. For example, in the affluent section of Cape Town known as Sea Point, which resembles Miami Beach, whites living in luxury high-rises along the seafront were accustomed to having a wide promenade along the oceanfront to themselves, ironically with a clear view of Robben Island, where Nelson Mandela was incarcerated. After 1994, blacks in large numbers would travel to Sea Point from the townships, especially on weekends, much to the unhappiness of the white residents. Ten years later, however, the number of visiting blacks has declined, and those that do visit seem to coexist peacefully with the still predominantly white population.

In an unthinkable reversal of social relationships under apartheid rule, whites are being forced to go out of their way to treat blacks courteously. In some cases, blacks get preferred treatment over whites in restaurants and other service industries. That's because white business owners are acutely sensitive to being labeled as "racist" by customers and clients, which would in turn invite attention and perhaps criticism from government officials. Beyond that, there is a practical reason to want to please black customers: blacks are in the majority, and it is in the interest of the corporate sector to reach out to the black community in the most cordial way possible.

The most direct way whites have been affected by the transition has been by the government's aggressive affirmative-action policies, which are entrenched in the new constitution, effectively turning the apartheid era's policies of job reservation for whites on its head.[4] Companies who want government contracts are expected to have blacks represented at the highest levels of management. Key sectors of the economy have been pressured to draw up "charters" in which they pledge to meet certain affirmative-action goals within a specified period of time. "Black Economic Empowerment," or BEE, has become a part of postapartheid discourse and has been used to justify transfers of wealth to a small but growing elite of black entrepreneurs.

As part of the negotiations that led to majority rule, the ANC agreed that the existing civil service would be protected for the first five years of democratic rule, a period that also coincided with Mandela's term in office. But even during the period that they were supposedly protected, affirmative-action pressures limited the kinds of government jobs whites could get, as well as their opportunities for promotion.

In an interview with the author, Andy Miller, a white Afrikaner who was a regional director of the South African Police Union, representing mostly white police officers, reacted angrily to former members of the ANC being given top positions in the police force:

People with no education, no normal qualifications, and with no police history in the police force have come out of the bush, and the government says, "Thank you. You are now a major or a colonel." . . . These are political appointments. That is not affirmative action. We are going to draw a line here and take a strong stand, and if we have to take action on this point, then that is what we are going to do. (Freedberg 1995)

But blacks in leadership positions are unapologetic about the need to replace whites with blacks at senior levels of the labor market. Makisizwe Mandela, one of Nelson Mandela's four children, was affirmative-action officer at the University of Witwatersrand. In a 1996 interview, she said,

Whites have to realize they are in Africa, and blacks are not prepared to abide by the past. Black people are not prepared to accept the status quo any longer. They want to see change, they want to see visible change, not tomorrow, not in 20 years, they want to see visible change now. (Freedberg 1995)

The impact of these aggressive affirmative-action programs on whites is that many feel there is no longer a secure place for them in the postapartheid economy. Beyond that, they are aware that they will have to compete with blacks for jobs, and in most instances blacks will be favored over them. Among all the changes wrought by the end of apartheid rule, this is the arena that has caused the most bitterness and resentment.

For Afrikaners, the end of apartheid has been especially cataclysmic. Key institutions that were central to the maintenance of Afrikaner identity have essentially collapsed. One notable example is the demise of the National Party that for decades played a central role in the political socialization of most Afrikaners. The party easily won every election from 1948 to 1990, almost always by an overwhelming margin. So, for example, in the general elections held in November 1977, the National Party won 82 percent of the vote (South African Institute of Race Relations 1977, 21). In the first nonracial elections, held in 1994, the National Party only won 20.4 percent of the vote. Reconstituted as the New National Party, in the 1996 municipal elections, it won 18.4 percent of the vote, 7 percent in the 1999 general elections, and a paltry 1.7 percent in the June 2004 general elections, with only seven seats in the four-hundred-member Parliament (Sparks 2003, 133). After that last crushing defeat, on August 4, 2004, the party closed its doors altogether. Its leader, Marthinus Van Schalkwyk, was given a post in President Thabo Mbeki's cabinet (as minister of environmental affairs and tourism) and remarkably encouraged its members to join the ANC—the former "terrorist organization" the National Party had sought for decades to crush.

Thus, within a decade of the end of white minority rule, Afrikaner nationalism—a key element in shaping and sustaining white Afrikaner identity—was a spent force on the South African landscape.

White identity was battered from other directions as well. Beginning in 1995, the Truth and Reconciliation Commission, or TRC, helped to demolish some of the mythologies about apartheid that most whites had readily embraced. During the apartheid era, many whites were convinced that apartheid was not as oppressive as its critics claimed. Any complaints about abuses at the hands of the apartheid regime were glibly written off as foreign, Communist-inspired propaganda. Many whites convinced themselves that the system was a benevolent autocracy that benefited blacks far more than would have been the case if a black government were in power. Frequently during the apartheid years, the conditions of South African blacks were favorably compared with those of blacks elsewhere in Africa on government-controlled radio and television. The goal of government propaganda was to convince whites as well as blacks that, thanks to apartheid, South African blacks were actually better off than their African counterparts.

The TRC challenged the myth of apartheid as a system from which everyone benefited, both blacks and whites. Many whites, of course, dismissed the commission as simply an attempt to divide the white community and as unfairly weighted to embarrass and expose the previous regime. But the preponderance of evidence and the harrowing public hearings—many carried live on television and radio—forced many whites to accept that apartheid had been a far crueler system than they had believed, or wanted to believe.

In the postapartheid period, Afrikaners also had to deal with threats to their language, which not only was a key element in sustaining their identity as white South Africans but was also closely identified with the apartheid state. Pieter Dirk Uys, the brilliant South African satirist, would joke in his shows that Afrikaners had become best known around the world for one word: apartheid. For some, the identification of Afrikaans with the apartheid state was a painful reality they had to confront. Thus the Afrikaner poet Antjie Krog, who covered the TRC for the South African Broadcasting Corporation, reflected,

> Was Apartheid the product of some horrific shortcoming in Afrikaner culture? Could one find the key to this in Afrikaner songs and literature, in beer and braaivleis?[5] How do I live with the fact that all the words used to

humiliate, all the orders given to kill, belonged to the language of my heart? At the hearings many of the victims faithfully reproduced those parts of their stories in Afrikaans as proof of the bloody fingerprints on them. (Krog 2000)

As part of the negotiated settlement with Nelson Mandela, the ANC agreed that Afrikaans would remain an official language, but it would be only one of eleven official languages (the others being English, Ndebele, Xhosa, Zulu, Sepedi, Sesotho, Setswana, Swati, Venda, and Tsonga). The government set up "national lexicography units" as well as "national language bodies" for each of the eleven languages. Television and radio programs were supposed to be presented in different languages according to a strict percentage of each hour. The system has been extremely cumbersome, and to no one's surprise, English has become the most widely used language, including in official government circles. Within the Afrikaner community, there is still great anxiety about the future of Afrikaans, and there has been a great deal of organizing to ensure its survival. Groep van 63 (Group of 63), consisting of Afrikaner academics and authors, was formed in 2000. Established in the same year was the Afrikaanse Aksiegroep, or PRAAG (meaning "pride" in Afrikaans). Dan Roodt, its forty-seven-year-old founder, says the group seeks "cultural autonomy" for Afrikaans speakers. "Once at the center of South African identity, Afrikaners now find themselves at the scrap heap, and prone to the same old identity crisis that used to haunt them through the 19th century under British rule, and which was only resolved by the suffering of the Anglo-Boer war," Roodt (2002) wrote polemically. "What nation building really means in South Africa is the complete destruction of Afrikaans culture and Afrikaner identity."

Another challenge to Afrikaner identity comes from younger Afrikaners who are questioning the fact that their parents and grandparents could have been so misguided as to dream up an idea as wildly impractical and immoral as the apartheid state. They are undergoing a period of soul-searching and are demanding answers from their elders. This intergenerational tension sprang to the surface in a rancorous public debate sparked by a book published in 2000 by Willem de Klerk, a former editor of the Afrikaans newspaper *Rapport* and brother of former president F. W. de Klerk. As Allister Sparks has cogently described, de Klerk enumerated the numerous assaults on Afrikaner identity experienced since the toppling of the apartheid state.

Loss of power. Loss of influence. Loss of prestige. Loss of security. Loss of language. We are suffering from a poverty of political, religious and cultural leadership. (Sparks 2003, 135)

He went on to criticize young Afrikaners who are attempting to cast off their Afrikaner identities:

> The following argument can be heard, with variations among thousands of modern young Afrikaners: we are just a collection of materialistic or fugitive Europeans and degenerate adventurers. Actually a bunch of immigrants who through the centuries of colonialism, seized South Africa and looted it. We speak a European dialect. Our history consists mainly of a series of military and strategic incidents in the plundering of the San, the Khoi, and the Africans. We have no clear profile of a binding self existence, and therefore we can hardly be called a people. The notion of an Afrikaner is a lie. The sooner we throw it in the rubbish bin the better. (de Klerk 2000, 9, translated by Sparks)

But de Klerk rejected such a pessimistic view, arguing that the way to reshape a reborn Afrikaner identity was to acknowledge the injustices inflicted in the name of Afrikaners and enter into a partnership with the formerly disenfranchised groups.

> The concept of being part of a rainbow nation is essential. To be a South African, white Afrikaner, mainly of European descent and an African, is the right formulation. The one does not exclude the other. (de Klerk 2000, 57, translated by Sparks)

But instead of being a rallying cry that united Afrikaners, de Klerk's appeal inflamed younger Afrikaners. Chris Louw, a journalist who once worked for de Klerk, wrote a lengthy and angry response in *Die Beeld*, an Afrikaans-language newspaper in Johannesburg. In it he accused de Klerk of being part of the problem, of being a leading member of the only generation of Afrikaners not to have fought in a war, but which willingly sent their children to fight in wars to defend apartheid (under the apartheid state, there was a mandatory draft). Despite all the bravado, Louw wrote, when it came time to negotiate the transition, the leaders among de Klerk's generation meekly handed over power to the black majority.

> Where were the boasts, the threats, the fiery speeches, the pledges? I was there. It was a pathetic sight to behold as your arguments—your delusions— were ripped out from under you. (Die Beeld, in Sparks 2003, 139)

Louw's missive triggered an outpouring from other Afrikaners, in a cascade of additional letters to Die Beeld and in other forums. A conference chaired by Frederik van Zyl Slabbert was held in Potchefsroom and brought together many of the letter writers to vent their feelings. And

Louw's letter morphed into a well-received play, *Boetman is die Bliksem in,* which toured throughout South Africa.

The soul-searching continues among Afrikaners today. Among younger Afrikaners, some are embracing identities that were off-limits during the apartheid years. There is a vibrant gay Afrikaner culture. And instead of apologizing for their Afrikaner roots, they are embracing them. So, for example, restaurants specializing in traditional Afrikaner foods associated with the old South Africa—like *koeksisters* and *melkterts, waterblommetjie bredie,* and *biltong*—have sprung up throughout the country, often run by young hip Afrikaners.

At the same time, whites cannot avoid the reality that they were on the losing side of the struggle and that if they are to secure a place in the new South Africa, they will have to abandon the old trappings of whiteness. Increasing numbers of whites are embracing interracial relationships. They cannot continue to "act white" without being relegated to the margins of the society. New laws allow victims of hate speech or racial slurs to bring charges against perpetrators. The old swagger of the white minority— embodied in the apartheid era of *baasskap* (bossism)—is gone.

After the collapse of the Soviet Union, few Russians would admit that they had been Communists. A similar phenomenon has occurred in South Africa. These days, it is hard to find a white person who acknowledges having supported apartheid. Invariably, they confide that during the apartheid years, they were working from "inside the system" to effect change, pressing officials to release Mandela, and so on. It is now common for Afrikaners to join the ANC. While some are genuine converts, for many, joining the ANC is but a device to improve their employment or business prospects.

It is difficult to predict how exactly white identity will evolve over time. Will whites retain a separate, heavily race-based identity? Will intermarriage dissipate the white population as an easily identifiable ethnic group? Will they leave South Africa before that happens? Will they be able to? The challenge will be to maintain their ethnic identity in a culture that doesn't value it, in a society where "whiteness" was closely identified with one of the most explicitly abusive systems of racial oppression of the twentieth century.

Also unclear is whether whites will be a positive force for change in a democratic South Africa, or whether they will be become a sullen, marginalized minority burdened by, and blamed for, South Africa's apartheid past.

When racial segregation was dismantled in the American South, there were great hopes that whites, shaped by what C. Vann Woodward described as "the burden of Southern history," would become a positive force for change (Woodward 1993). "What the Southern experience provided—or could have provided—was a wisdom, born of failure, defeat and the realization of human fallibility," writes the historian George Fredrickson. Instead, Southern whites attempted to hold on to their privileged status, even in the face of court rulings and government orders to the contrary. "The end of legalized segregation did not mean the end of race based politics in the South" (Fredrickson 2004).

White reaction to a desegregated South Africa has been markedly different, in large part because whites in South Africa are a minority, and a shrinking one at that. They cannot hold on to their old values and identity without risking their own economic survival and their participation in mainstream South Africa. Those whites, especially older ones, who came of age during the apartheid era will obviously be the slowest to adapt. But South African whites will be unable to appeal to the state, as Southern whites did before and after *Brown v. Board of Education*, to retain racially segregated schools or to resist by force the attempts by the national government to impose integration. Instead, they will feel great governmental pressures to integrate schools, to impose affirmative-action programs, and to end racial biases in hiring and promotion.

All this has caused whites, Steyn (2001) argues, to experience "a loss of sense of relevance, a loss of guaranteed legitimacy, a loss of honor and a loss of face."

> "Feelings of anomie, disorientation, grief, nostalgia, excitement, freedom, vertigo—the range of feelings that accompany the failure of a belief system, the demise of "certain certainties"—these are feelings that are likely to be part of the experience of being white in South Africa for some time." (Steyn 2001, 161)

Going forward, white identity will be shaped as much by how they respond as by how the government and blacks in general respond to them. So far, the government has taken a two-pronged approach, allowing whites to retain their wealth and property while making it clear that whites have to make way for black aspirations. That means that no matter how willing whites might be to embrace the new order, they may still find themselves marginalized and isolated. A controversy at the end of 2004 over the failure of the government to appoint Geoff Budlender, among the country's leading civil-rights lawyers, to a judgeship in the Cape Provincial Court illustrates the drawbacks of being white—no matter how progressive one might be—in the postapartheid period. Budlender was a leading student activist in the 1960s. As an attorney, and later as director of the Legal Resources Center, he won numerous key cases against the Pretoria regime, especially in the arena of land reform. However, in the postapartheid period, he continued to press the new government on land reform and AIDS, winning two key lawsuits in each arena. He applied three times for a judgeship and was thrice rejected, sending a depressing message to whites worried about whether a place exists for them in a new South Africa. If even a leading and respected progressive is denied positions for which he is eminently qualified, then there is little hope for those with far less sterling credentials.

These fears aside—which is admittedly a big aside—being white in Africa may also offer extraordinary opportunities for whites to shed their old racially based "whiteness" and to assume a whiteness that draws from the African landscape, context, and culture. Goldberg (1993) says whites should "think the unthinkable," that they should allow themselves "to be intellectually and culturally influenced by thoughts of black people, that whites and blacks think through the conditions of possibility for whites to be black" (218).

But there may be a middle ground short of whites trying to become "black." Some South Africans have long called themselves white Africans. That is a nomenclature that most whites would have rejected completely in the past. But it may well be the construct that will serve them best in the new South Africa.

In some ways, white Afrikaners may be better poised to make the transition to a postapartheid society than English-speaking whites. Afrikaners were far more likely to view themselves as "African" than English-speaking whites, in part because they did not have the same facility with the English language. Afrikaans is a language spoken nowhere else but Namibia, and that fact alone has done much to keep Afrikaners tied to South Africa more intimately than English-speaking whites, who can more easily move to any number of countries where English is spoken.

"Whiteness," as it evolved and was expressed during South Africa's segregationist past, no longer exists. Instead, white ethnicity is becoming more "African," perhaps for the first time since whites first came to Africa over four hundred years ago. Younger whites are increasingly learning indigenous African languages, eating traditional African food at African restaurants, and embracing interracial relationships. They are being forced to acknowledge the black majority as well as the realities of their minority status. But tragically, this belated embrace of their African environment comes at a time when it is least likely to be accepted by the black majority.

Notes

1. According to the South African census, in October 2001, there were 44,819,778 people in South Africa. Of those, 70 percent classified themselves as black or African, 9.6 percent as white, 8.9 percent as "coloured," and 2.56 percent as Indian or Asian. See South Africa Yearbook, 2003–2004.

2. In 1985, for example, 1,167 race "reclassifications" took place when 702 coloureds became white, 249 Africans became coloured, 43 coloureds became Indian, and so on. See 1985 Survey of Race Relations in South Africa, SA Institute of Race Relations, Johannesburg, 3–4.

3. It is one of the ironies of white identity in South Africa that Jews were especially prominent among whites who opposed the apartheid state. Many assumed prominent positions in the African National Congress (ANC), most notably Joe Slovo, who rose to head the military wing of the ANC. Inside South Africa, Helen Suzman was the sole representative of the Progressive Party for many years in the all-white Parliament, elected year after year from her largely Jewish suburb of Houghton in Johannesburg.

4. Article 9 of the Bill of Rights in the South African Constitution reads, "To promote the achievement of equality, legislative and other measures designed to protect or advance persons or categories of persons, disadvantaged by unfair discrimination may be taken."

5. A *braaivleis* is the Afrikaans word for barbecue. During the Truth and Reconciliation Commission hearings, the *braaivleis*—typically a benign social gathering—became a metaphor for some of the worst abuses under apartheid. At one especially gruesome TRC hearing, one former member of the security police described how he and his fellow officers had burned bodies of their black victims over a fire for hours while they enjoyed a *braaivleis* nearby.

References

Adam, Heribert, and Hermann Giliomee. 1979. *The Rise and Crisis of Afrikaner Power*. Cape Town: David Phillip.

De Klerk, Willem. 2000. *Afrikaners: Kroes, Kras, Kordaat*. Cape Town: Human & Rousseau.

Dyer, R. 1988. White. *Screen* 29:44–65.

Fredrickson, George. 1981. *White supremacy: A comparative study in American and South African history*. New York: Oxford University Press.

———. 2004. Is there hope for the South? *New York Review of Books*, Oct. 2, 2004.

Freedberg, Louis. 1995. Affirmative action in South Africa. Report on *All Things Considered*, National Public Radio, September 5, 1995.

Goldberg, D. T. 1993. *Racist culture: Philosophy and the politics of meaning*. Oxford: Blackwell.

Jacobson, Matthew Frye. 1998. *Whiteness of a different color: European immigrants and the alchemy of race*. Cambridge, MA: Harvard University of Press.

Krog, Antjie. 2000. *Country of my skull: Guilt, sorrow and the limits of forgiveness in the New South Africa*. New York: Three Rivers Press.

Marciano, Francesca. 1998. Interview in Salon.com with Don George, Oct. 9.

Martin, J. N., R. L. Krizek, T. N. Nakayama, and L. Bradford. 1996. Exploring whiteness: A study of self labels for white Americans. *Communication Quarterly* 44 (2): 125–44.

Moodie, T. Dunbar. 1975. *The Rise of Afrikanerdom: Power, Apartheid and the Afrikaner Civil Religion*. Berkeley: University of California Press.

Morin, Richard. 2004. A world apart: A decade after the fall of apartheid in South Africa: An isolated white community clings to its past. *Washington Post*, March 31.

Roediger, David R. 1991. The wages of whiteness. London: Verso.

Romanucci-Ross, Lola, and George De Vos, eds. 1995. *Ethnic identity: Creation, conflict and accommodation*. Walnut Creek, CA: AltaMira Press.

Roodt, Dan. 2002. Old split over Afrikaner identity fuels new terror. *Business Day*, Nov. 28.

Schrire, Robert. 1991. *Adapt or Die: The End of White Politics in South Africa*. New York: Ford Foundation.

South African Institute of Race Relations. 1977. S.A. race relations survey.

Sparks, Allister. 2003. *Beyond the miracle: Inside the new South Africa*. Johannesburg: Jonathan Ball Publishers.

Steyn, Melissa. 1997. New shades of "whiteness": "White" identity in the New South Africa. Paper presented at Multicultural Citizenship in the New South Africa, Cape Town, Institute for a Democratic South Africa, Dec. 15–17.

———. 2001. *"Whiteness just isn't what it used to be": White identity in a changing South Africa*. New York: SUNY Press.

Thompson, Leonard. 1985. *The political mythology of apartheid*. New Haven, CT: Yale University Press.

Uchendu, Victor. 1995. The dilemma of ethnicity and polity primacy in Black Africa. In *Ethnic Identity*, ed. Lola Romanucci-Ross and George De Vos. Walnut Creek, CA: AltaMira Press.

Washington Post, Kaiser Family Foundation, Harvard University. 2004. *Survey of South Africans at ten years of democracy*. Menlo Park, CA: Kaiser Family Foundation.

Welsh, Frank. 1999. *South Africa: A narrative history*. New York: Kodansha International.

Woodward, C. Vann. 1993. *The burden of southern history*. 3rd ed. New Orleans: Louisiana State University Press.

Mixed Feelings: Spoiled Identities in the New South Africa

13

NANCY SCHEPER-HUGHES

Still Waiting

THIS CHAPTER IS PART of a larger, ongoing study of violence and the "democratic transition"[1] in Cape Town and in the small village of Franschhoek, a politically conservative (*verkrumpte*) fruit-and-wine-producing community that is dominated to this day (politically and economically) by a white farm-owning class of conservative Dutch Reform Church Afrikaners. Franschhoek (under the pseudonym "Wyndahl") was the site of Vincent Crapanzano's research in the early 1980s, which resulted in his controversial book *Waiting: The Whites of South Africa* (1985). Crapanzano portrayed the whites of Franschhoek/Wyndahl as comfortable, socially isolated, and self-absorbed "racists" who were trapped in a passive state of suspended animation, "waiting" (as it were) for the future to go away and leave them alone.

I was interested in learning something about the "other" waiting residents of Franschhoek—the "coloured" workers and newly arrived black squatters—in order to understand what the "democratic transition" meant in this small and tense community. To this end, I conducted episodic research in greater Cape Town and in Franschhoek between 1993 and 1994 (when I joined the Department of Social Anthropology at the University of Cape Town) and in 1996, 1997, and 1999. In the mid-1990s, some 1,300 whites lived in Franschhoek. The larger population, however, consisted of the more than 3,000 "coloured" farm workers, the descendants of Dutch, French, and English settlers and their covert and still-unacknowledged carnal relations with indigenous Khoisan herders (so-called Bushmen and Hottentots), Malay slaves, and Bantu (mostly Xhosa) peasants. For generations, the Cape Coloured provided farm labor to whites in the Boland (farm country of the Western Cape). With the end of apartheid, a new population of South African blacks, disproportionately young, single, and male, left the old rural homelands and came to work, some to settle in beautiful Franschhoek. By 1999, the time of my last research trip, the new black residents of Chris Hani squatter camp on the outskirts of Franschhoek numbered almost 2,000 and had begun to replace the coloured farmworkers on the surrounding vineyards and farms.

My research in the coloured communities of the Cape concerned the political debates and struggles of the day over access to land, schooling, housing, and reparations for the suffering afflicted on black and coloured South Africans under apartheid. A fierce competition between the still largely (de facto) segregated black and coloured communities over basic amenities has thwarted the ANC government's dream of building a race-blind rainbow nation. As the new black squatters began to "jump the waiting lists" in the mid-1990s to occupy housing sites that had been long promised and designated for coloureds, the coloured community of Franschhoek, led by local activist women, retaliated by moving a few hundred mixed-race farmworkers along with the elderly, sick, unemployed, and homeless onto a strip of public land bordering the main street of Franschhoek, where they formed Vietnam Bos (Vietnam Woods) squatter camp. The war analogy was intentional, one of the activists, Minnie Peterson, told me: "We are declaring war on the Black squatters of Chris Hani camp." Similar tensions marked postapartheid relations between South African blacks and coloureds in the multiethnic neighborhoods of Cape Town (Mowbray to Salt River) and in the townships of the Cape Flats.

Despite the years of the antiapartheid struggle, "race" remains a salient category in the new South Africa, a bitter and seemingly intractable legacy of the postcolonial condition. In this chapter, I explore relations between the apartheid state's official construction of "coloured" as a demographic category of indeterminacy; the personal narratives of exclusion, marginality, suffering, and spoiled identity expressed by coloured people in the transitional democratic state; and the temporary resolution of the social and psychological conflicts in a paradoxical reassertion of coloured identity in the first democratic elections (1994) as these were played out in the Western Cape. In the end, the coloured population of the Western Cape seemed to have no choice but to cast their lots with the National Party (NP, the party of apartheid), which had, paradoxically, given the group a cultural and political identity and therefore something of a stake in the new postapartheid, multicultural, democratic state.

Exiles from Eden:
A Brief Social History of the Cape

We have been planted here, we believe, with a destiny . . . for the evolution of Africa and the advancement of Christianity.

—HENDRIK FRENSCH VERWOERD, 1966

The Cape of Good Hope figured in the Dutch colonial imagination as a "*lui-lekker* land," a place of natural beauty, ease, and plenty, where even "the savages" seemed hardly to labor to feed and decorate bodies described by the first European visitors as healthy, supple, and full bodied. When Jan Van Riebeeck, the head merchant for the Dutch East India Company, and his men arrived and established the first European settlement in the Cape in the mid-seventeenth century, they had no intention of exploring the vast interior of the peninsula, which the colonizers described as a sandy, barren, and inhospitable desert. Van Riebeeck wished to contain the first European settlement to the cultivation of a network of coastal gardens to serve as a supply station for ships en route between Europe and the East.

Many other European ships, particularly from England and Portugal, sailed into the Cape in the late seventeenth century, and they competed with the Dutch in establishing their own provisioning outposts there. But the Dutch remained dominant in the Cape for the first four decades of the European presence. They were the early "Dutch Masters" of the world traffic in rich trade goods—gold, ivory, sugar, tobacco, dyewood, and slaves—and it was the Dutch mercantilists who brought Europe, Africa, and South America into the same economic and cultural orbit. Central to the Dutch mercantile hegemony was their dominance in the slave trade. Early conquests in Northeast Brazil, West Africa, and Angola allowed the famous trade triangle to flourish, whereby European trade goods were exchanged for slaves in West Africa, who were then transported to Northeast Brazil to work on sugar plantations. The sugar was to be sold in Europe to satisfy a voracious new taste, a craving really, for sweetness that was intentionally cultivated in urban workers (see Mintz 1985; Wolf 1982).

Van Riebeeck was under strict "company" orders to keep peace with the indigenous herding people—the Khoikhoi as they called themselves, or Hottentots as the Dutch called them—to trade with them for sheep and cattle, but *not* to enslave them. The first slaves were introduced to the Cape from elsewhere—Angola, Guinea, Bengal, and Madagascar. In the end, it was Dutch, rather than Portuguese or English, that became the language spoken (in a patois) between master and slave in the Cape and that evolved into the Afrikaans language.

The colonial myth of the discovery of a lost Garden of Eden and a state of primordial innocence was a recurring subtext in the European narratives of conquest in the New World and Africa among English, Spanish, and Portuguese colonizers, as well as the Dutch. However, the interpretations of this biblical image differed in Catholic and Calvinist contexts. Pedro Vaz de Caminha, the Portuguese scribe who sailed with Pedro Alvares Cabral in 1500, described the discovery of Brazil as "an earthly paradise, a kind of tropical Eden" and a place where "sin [or at least colonial guilt] did not exist" (Parker 1993, 9). Colonial Brazil was imagined by the Portuguese as a land free of interdiction, where an infantile polymorphous perversity and sensual gratification could reign freely. Native women were portrayed as alluring, sensual, and, above all, available. Gilberto Freyre, Brazil's first national anthropologist, fell readily into the colonial myth of Eden when he described the coastal Indians of Pernambuco as "the first to offer themselves to the whites, the more ardent ones going to rub themselves against the legs of these beings whom they supposed to be gods" (Freyre 1956, 85).

Unlike the Portuguese, the Dutch Calvinist colonizers armed and defended themselves against the threat of sensuality attributed by them to the "naked" savages. The Dutch who landed in the Cape tried to seal off their community from the Hottentots. Contributing to the early segregative impulse was the extraordinary natural beauty, the sublime natural landscape of the Cape Peninsula. On seeing the view from the National Botanical Gardens at Kirstenbosch in the southern suburbs of Cape Town, the early nineteenth-century British botanist William Burchell was moved to write of the almost indescribable and incomparable beauty of the area:

> The view from this spot . . . is one of the most picturesque of any I have seen. . . . The beauties here displayed to the eye could scarcely be represented by the most skilful [sic] pencil. . . . To the left the noble Table Mountain rose in all its grandeur. . . . The last beams of the sun, gleaming over the rich, varied, and extensive prospect, laid on the warm finishing lights, in masterly and inimitable touches. (cited by Coetzee 1988, 36–37)

The colonizers justified the right to seize and domesticate all this beauty in the name of the Dutch East India Company by means of two contradictory colonial narratives. The first represented the Cape Peninsula as uninhabited virgin territory, as empty space there for the taking. This narrative suggested that the indigenous population of seminomadic Khoikhoi herders did not live in the Cape year round but merely returned there each spring to water and rest their cattle and sheep.

A later version of the "empty land" myth was the story that the Dutch settlers arrived in Table Bay at roughly the same time that African Bantu speakers (mainly Xhosas and Zulus) traveled south and crossed the Limpopo River into what is today Transkei, South Africa. In this narrative, both black Africans and white Afrikaners were fairly recent "settlers" in South Africa, a story that is still told in some parts of the country. There is, however, abundant archaeological evidence of Bantu-speaking peoples living in the South African Transvaal as early as the fifth century AD, and of Bantu speakers settled along the Transkei coast long before the sixteenth century (Wilson and Thomas 1969, 138).

The alternative (and contradictory) colonial narrative acknowledged the presence of indigenous people in the Cape but denied them a fully human status and hence their right to ownership of the lands on which they were settled. Absolute distance with the Khoisan peoples of the Cape was established through a relentless cataloging of the native peoples' physical and cognitive differences. J. M. Coetzee (1988, 13) notes the repetition in colonial memoirs of stereotypic descriptions of the Khoisan peoples, especially their implosive "pseudospeech" (often described as "turkey gobbling"), their diet of unwashed intestines, their use of animal fat for cosmetic purposes, the "peculiarities" of the pudenda of their women (the so-called the Hottentot apron), and, above all, their incorrigible indolence.

In his 1686 work, *Short Account of the Cape of Good Hope and of the Hottentots Who Inhabit That Region*, William Ten Rhyne, physician for the East India Company, wrote,

> All the Hottentots have slender and finely-knit bodies. . . . Their noses are snub, their foreheads low; they are thick-lipped, and have curly woolen hair, shaved into various patterns. . . . The women are distinguished from the men by their ugliness. And they have the peculiarity . . . of dactyliform appendages, always two in number, hanging down from their pudenda. . . . If one should happen to enter a hut full of women . . . then with much gesticulation and raising their leather aprons, they offer these appendages to view. (cited by Oakes 1989, 103)

In all, the Hottentots were described as ugly, unwashed, and smelly, their food unclean, their meat consumed nearly raw, their clothing unelaborated animal skins, their habitation the meanest of huts, and their speech (full of clicks) the "language of monkeys," not humans. What kept the Hottentots in their backward evolutionary state was, above all, their "idleness," meaning their refusal to work for Dutch wages. The specter of Hottentot (later of coloured) idleness haunts the colonial and postcolonial history of the Western Cape.

If the natural beauty of the coastal Cape Peninsula was legendary, then the city that the Dutch built overlooking Table Bay was known more for its ugliness. Obsessed with hierarchy, rank, order, and all the insignias of privilege, the Dutch colonial engineers applied basic geometric grid forms to convert the spectacular landscape into rigidly organized and uninteresting towns with grid street plans that were interspersed with forts. Dutch colonial town plans reflected an obsession with order born of desperation (Hall 1991, 46) as colonial authorities struggled to control the chaotic growth of the city and the unruliness of those whose lands were being colonized. Tucked away within the well-ordered townhouses of Cape Town Dutch colonists were slaves living in attics, kitchens, and basements, turning affluent homes into prisons. And behind these stately homes were "warrens of side streets and alleyways where a large underclass of poor whites, artisans, mixed race coloureds, free blacks, and slaves lived" (Hall 1991, 52).

It came as a shock to the Victorian English novelist Anthony Trollope to discover during his visit to South Africa in 1877 that the city of Cape Town was neither beautiful nor white. Trollope went to South Africa expecting to find in Cape Town a charming and civilized outpost of Europe. Instead, he found a city that struck him as "a poor, niggery, yellow-faced, half-bred sort of place, with an ugly Dutch flavour about it" (1878/1973, 4–5). English-speaking Capetonians were not, Trollope discovered, the primary population at all:

> A walk through the streets of Cape Town is sufficient to show the stranger that he has reached a place not inhabited by white men. . . . The gentry no doubt are white and speak English . . . but they are not the population [which primarily comprises] Coloured persons, Malays, Mahommidans flaunting about the town in their turbans and flowing robes. . . . And there is a Hottentot admixture, a sprinkling of the Guinea-coast Negro, and a small Kafir [Bantu] element mixed within a preponderance of Dutch blood. (1878/1973, 78)

Although hardly a radical, Trollope heaped scorn on the conventional colonial trope of the lazy coloured:

> The stranger in South Africa will constantly be told that the coloured man will not work. . . . It will be the first word whispered in his ear when he arrives, and the last assurance hurled after him as he leaves the coast. And

yet during his whole sojourn in the country he will see all the work of the world around him done by the hands of coloured people. It will be so in Cape Town far away from the Kafirs. It will be so on the homesteads of the Dutch in the western Province. . . . And yet he will be told, "the nigger will not work." (1878/1973, 458)

Dispossession

From the mid-seventeenth century to the end of the twentieth century, African farmers and herders, black and coloured laborers, and farmworkers were gradually but thoroughly dispossessed. Until the mid-nineteenth century, the majority of Bantu-speaking Africans in Southern Africa lived in independent chiefdoms. Following the Xhosa wars in the mid-nineteenth century and the Zulu War in 1879, which signaled the fall of the last black empire in South Africa (see Edgerton 1988), the final onslaught on the land and its people began in the early twentieth century via the bureaucratic violence of government-sponsored social engineering.

The Land Act of 1913 reduced African ownership to 7 percent of the land, although black South Africans constituted 80 percent of the population. The black "reserves," styled after North American Indian reservations, were a scattered patchwork of barren and unproductive lands that consigned black South Africans to penury and hunger. But the final coup came decades later, beginning in 1948, with the Afrikaner National Party's policy of apartheid. A centerpiece of this policy was the national government's forced removals of more than 3.5 million black South Africans from white and urban areas to what were now called "Bantustans" or "self-governing homelands." These "homelands" were a pretext for what were really concentrated labor reserves designed to service white-owned agricultural estates and the mines in the East and West Rands.

The language and policies of race segregation were periodically "modernized" and sanitized (see Boonzaier and Sharp's 1989 introduction). By the time of Prime Minister Hendrik Verwoerd's "scientific" approach to apartheid (apartness/separateness), the dispossession was concealed within a modernist discourse on cultural "self-determination" and city and regional planning. Thus, the most brutal mass relocations of black and brown people on the entire African continent were passed off as urban planning in the interests of promoting the growth of orderly, self-contained "model cities" and towns; preserving greenways and open spaces; and preventing the kind of chaotic urbanization that was occurring throughout much of the Third World at roughly this same time.

What white South Africans seemed to fear most was the threat of de-mographic "swamping" by nonwhite populations, black and coloured. Consequently, the modern history of South Africa was one of increasing restriction and interdiction against the presence of black bodies, which were seen as contaminating, violating, and unaesthetic "foreign objects." In the bureaucratic language of apartheid, African people were described as "influx" and "overflow," and as "black spots" to be "removed." Like stub-born stains, their presence needed to be "rubbed out." Like feces, their bodies and possessions were to be "evacuated." Like cancelled checks, black and brown women and children were to be "endorsed out." The subse-quent attacks on and violent destruction of older urban black communi-ties, settlements, and squatter camps served both antiblack and anti-urban-white South African agendas. Slum removal simply meant black removal.

Still, these same dark-skinned bodies were needed for labor. A series of "pass laws" (though *impasse laws* might better describe them) controlled the movement of black South Africans into cities and towns, where they were temporarily housed in worker hostels (see Ramphele 1994) as "guest work-ers" carrying approved travel permits. Following the post–World War II in-dustrial expansion of Cape Town, the pass laws were overlooked for a time so that by 1948—when the National Party came into power—there were an estimated 150,000 nonwhite squatters in Cape Town. Among the first actions taken by the new apartheid government was a brutal crackdown on the black South African population in greater Cape Town. This was fol-lowed, two decades later, by a similar crackdown on Cape Town's even larger mixed-race coloured population, those who dared to think that their cultural and linguistic kinship with white Afrikaners might allow them to escape the worst ravages of the apartheid madness.

The Murder of District Six

At the turn of the century, Cape Town was, as Anthony Trollope (1878/ 1973) noted, a predominantly working-class, mixed-race community of small shopkeepers, artisans, laborers, and dock workers. At the heart of Cape Town, and walking distance from the old city center, was the sprawl-ing, boisterous, congested neighborhood officially named "District Six" (though called *Kanaladorp* by its coloured residents). District Six was just the kind of mixed community one would expect to find in a port city that was a stopping-off point between nations and continents. The neighbor-hood brought together immigrants from Britain and Australia, Jews from

Tsarist Russia and later from Soviet Lithuania, Indians from Durban, Portuguese from all over, and a smaller number of Chinese. These newer arrivals mixed with the earlier residents of the Cape—the mixed-race Cape Coloured, Malay Muslims, and Black South Africans.

Even more threatening to the social engineers of apartheid than residential integration was the tolerance of racially mixed marriages characteristic of District Six. It was a place where a person might be the son of a West Indian seaman and a coloured seamstress from the rural Western Cape, or the offspring of a female migrant from St. Helena and a Lithuanian Jewish cabinetmaker. Another person's father might be a Tamil Indian migrant from Natal and her mother a Muslim woman from a Kalk Bay fishing family with an unmistakably Portuguese surname.

In District Six, people of different "colors" attended the same schools, belonged to the same trade unions, shopped in the same markets, drank in the same bars and canteens, and enjoyed themselves in the same movie houses. District Six was famous for its gambling and its gangsters, and for its vibrant street life dominated by hawkers and pushcarts. With the possible exception of the Indian market in Durban, there was nothing else quite like District Six in the rest of South Africa. The neighborhood represented a plausible if imperfect model of racial integration, and for that reason alone it was marked for demolition by "the Nats" (National Party) as an unacceptable "black spot," a blight on the urban landscape of Cape Town. District Six was the National Party's worst nightmare, a vision of the inevitable "browning" and "Africanization" of South Africa.

Thus District Six was simply ripped out of the city by the "urban renewal" bulldozers of apartheid in 1965. The forced removals of more than 60,000 people were carried out with the precision of a military operation; trucks arrived to remove, forcibly when necessary, the residents of the neighborhood and their possessions.[2] The exiles, some of whose ancestors had lived in central Cape Town since the days of the Dutch East India Company, were relocated by color, following the criteria of the Group Areas Act. "Blacks" were driven out to informal settlements in Kensington, Ndabeni, and Langa. "Coloureds" were sent to ugly new settlements carved out of the barren, sandy lots of the Cape Flats. Apartheid race classifications tore families and neighbors apart when the classifications were designated to different "group areas." As so, for a brief and terrifying period of South African history, Cape Town was definitively (if not permanently) claimed for whites alone.

With the destruction of District Six, the heart and soul of Cape Town was destroyed. Without the teeming and lively population of District Six to fill its streets, the downtown area quickly became a vacant, spooky, and ghostlike complex of gloomy concrete-and-glass office buildings. The white colonizers had finally realized their dreamscape of an "empty land" in the Cape. What was once the "Grand Parade," the central square of Cape Town, remained grand in name only. In its place was a bleak and windy car park for white civil servants who worked in the Civic Center building. In the late 1970s, a large underground shopping mall was built on the site of the old railroad station. Indeed, life in general had gone underground.

To this day, District Six is a scar-faced zone of social abandonment, to appropriate a term used by Joao Bielh (2005) in an entirely different context. Few people of any race live there. Here and there one encounters a few inhabited flats with children playing skip rope in front of a stoop, and there are a few places of uncertain commerce along with one or two churches, which the pious Dutch Reform practitioners of apartheid were afraid to raze. These churches stand alone surrounded by ruins and open lots filled with weeds, broken glass, chipped bricks, and rusted tin. But for the most part, District Six is dead. There was a certain poetic justice in the Anglican Church's choosing to locate its celebrated Trauma Center for the Victims of Political Violence and Torture on a deserted and gutted-out side street of District Six, where it functioned for the early years of the democratic transition from 1994 to 1997.

Because of the enormous social and symbolic significance of District Six for the coloured population of the Western Cape, it has left a profound sense of loss, resentment, and betrayal that has never been adequately recognized by the formal institutions of social repair in the new South Africa, such as the Truth and Reconciliation Commission. Its presence is an open wound that contributes to a sense of victimhood among the coloured population of Cape Town, who all too often turn their misplaced rage against the new ANC government. Adam Small, for example, a noted coloured intellectual of the Western Cape, expressed a sentiment (personal communication; see also Small 1971) that was widespread in the mixed-race community of the Western Cape when he said, "The history of coloured people is the *most* tragic one you have in South Africa."

Apartheid and the Construction of Coloured Identity

The existence of ambiguously "raced" people (i.e., coloureds) was a wild card (the Joker) in the system and ideology of strict race segregation on which modern South African apartheid was built. The origins of the popular view of "coloureds" as a residual or leftover category was inscribed in the apartheid laws that defined South African citizenship in terms of a system of racist population classifications (see West 1989). Apartheid was implemented through the hated Population Registration Act of 1950 (which was amended no fewer than fifteen times between 1956 and 1986).

Under apartheid (1948–1994), racial segregation and classification were used to separate people into absolute categories of difference. One's racial classification then determined every aspect of one's life—where and with whom one lived, where and how one worked, how one traveled, how one was educated, and even the quality of food one ate. The key metaphors that were mobilized in maintaining apartheid were spatial: fears of physical contact, of mixing, of spillage, and of leakage. The solution was separation, exclusion, and containment.

The apartheid state constructed and enforced—often with violence—a system of group identities. Over time, the state revised its official categories and modernized its arguments to marshal national and international support for its racist policies. The apartheid police state controlled the ideological content of education, television, and radio. It used censorship to control the press. Consequently, these crucial institutions were corrupted, and they reproduced the official apartheid discourses about race, nationhood, citizenship, racial violence, and public security that played a role in defining the South African social and political reality as a constant state of siege. Ultimately, apartheid shaped individual and group subjectivities and social self-perception.

Section 1 of the apartheid state's Population and Registration Act identified three basic racial classifications: black, coloured, and white. A black person (sometimes classified as native or Bantu) was defined as one "who is, or who is generally accepted as, a member of any aboriginal race or tribe of Africa." A White person was defined (in extremely hedged-in and nutty language) as "a person who is (a) in appearance obviously a White person, and who is not generally accepted as a Coloured person; or (b) is generally accepted as a White person and is not in appearance obviously not a White person." Finally, a white person excluded "those who were once classified as White but who voluntarily confess that they are by descent a Black or a Coloured person, unless it is proven that this admission is patently false."

Coloureds were defined under apartheid as the racial population formed by the historical mixing of the indigenous Khoi-san peoples and the early European settlers: the Dutch, but also the English, Portuguese, and Germans. Later, the coloureds mixed with African Bantu groups and

Malay peoples who were brought to the Cape Colony as slaves. But the official legal definition of "Coloured" in the Population Registration Act was simply a residual category. A coloured person was defined as a "person who is *not* a White person or a *Black*."

This empty definition led to many absurdities. In a famous and often-cited press interview given by Mrs. de Klerk in the early 1990s, the wife of the last white president of South Africa described the coloured population as follows:

> You know, *they* [coloured people] are a negative group. The definition of a coloured person in the population register is someone that is not white and not black, and is also not an Indian, in other words a non-person. . . . They are left overs, the people that were left over after the other racial nations were sorted out. They are the rest. . . . The coloureds were always under the wing of the whites. They have never been on their own. They have no history of governing themselves. . . . They must be supervised.

The de Klerks prevented their own son from marrying a young coloured woman to whom he was engaged, which caused a deep rift in the family. Several years later, F. W. de Klerk made a public apology to his estranged son and to the Cape coloured community.

Section 5(1) of the Population Registration Act later subdivided coloureds into seven "ethnic" groups: Cape Coloured (the largest and most definitive of the category), Malay, Griqua, Chinese, Indian, other Asiatic, and "other coloured." Despite these subgroups, the South African government continued to use the term *nonwhite* to describe all those who were either African blacks or coloureds.

Over time, the Registration Act added further bureaucratic clarifications (often to the point of absurdity) in order to assist civil servants in the time-consuming task of classifying people who did not fit neatly into the ordained categories. Eventually, cultural "traits," language, and "habits," were added as markers of racial and ethnic identity, in addition to "appearance" and "general acceptance as such." Finally, section 5(5) was added, which stressed the importance of "descent" over "appearance" or popular consensus. Under this section, a person was classified as white if both natural parents were so classified. Thus, a person was classified as coloured if both natural parents were so classified, or if one parent was classified white and the other classified as coloured. Where a person was the child of one black and one coloured parent, classification followed that of the father.

As the antiapartheid struggle grew during the 1980s, many South Africans did begin to resist the invidious race-caste system. Although it was almost suicidal for White South Africans to do so, some secretly married blacks and coloureds. If they were reported by neighbors, the white spouse was reclassified to the race of the nonwhite spouse, creating a small population of phenotypically white people officially classified as "blacks" or "Bantus." But meanwhile a great many mixed-race coloureds continued to pass as whites. A much smaller population of politicized coloureds did self-identify during the antiapartheid struggle as blacks, refusing the intermediate category that had traditionally allowed them more privileges under apartheid.

In all, the apartheid system of race classification was a hodgepodge of contentious and problematic indicators, further complicated by the possibility of formal reclassification through appeal to the government bureaucracy, the despised Race Classification Board. Each year, the board sat and reviewed the cases of all those who believed they had been wrongly classified. In 1986, 1,624 South Africans sought reclassification, and of these, 1,102 were successful. About half the petitioners were Cape Coloureds seeking reclassification as whites, and half were blacks seeking reclassification as coloureds. Those requesting reclassification were subject to humiliating physical "tests," such as whether a pencil inserted into the hair would stay in place or fall to the ground.

Neither Black Nor White

Brazil, South Africa, and the United States share certain similarities in that the population of each nation is to a large extent the product of racial and ethnic mixing in a context of European colonialism and African slavery (see Degler 1971; Marx 1998). However, the race-caste or race-class system that arose in each case gave very different social positions and value to the mixed person.

In Brazil, an ideology of "racial democracy" invented the "mulatto" as an ideal social type so that to be Brazilian meant to celebrate and to lay claim to a universal sense of "brownness." However, in practice, Brazil is a deeply racist country, although one in which the existence of a multitude of socially ranked racial distinctions (which refer both to appearance and to class-linked behavior) means that racial identity is in part ascribed and in part achieved. Brazilians are not so concerned with the genetic background of a person as they are with physical features—hair, cheekbones, lips, and color of eyes and shade of skin—and with social comportment and family name. Brazil could be described as a kind of racial free market in which people actively trade in racial identities. The rules of the game are to try to disidentify with the lower and darker designations such as "*preto*," "*moreno*," or "*pardo*," and to be included in one of the "whiter" and higher-status groups ("*galego*," "*loiro*," or "*branco de terra*"). Education, professional achievement, and money "lighten" the skin. In Brazil, passing is not viewed negatively but is recognized as a fairly universal social strategy. Within this system, the mulatto is valued not only as a national prototype but also as an available "escape hatch" for the black person who can, with hard work, eventually attain that status. Mostly class barriers restrict the racial mobility of blacks ("*os negros*") in Brazil.

In contrast to Brazil, where there is a spectrum or a continuum of race- and class-linked ethnicities, in the United States, a rigid race-caste system emerged around two "absolute" qualities: black and white. North Americans (with the exception of Louisiana) never developed an intermediate category in which to locate biracial people. The operating principle behind American apartheid was that each group could remain "pure" because any biological degree of blackness (i.e., "black blood") made that person completely black, while whites were defined as those without any trace of black ancestry. Historically, the U.S. race-caste system (see Berreman 1972) allowed no place in the American social imagination for ambiguity or for mixed people. Today, the cultural-identity revolutions that began in the 1960s, and the new biotechnologies of DNA testing, have challenged the way black, white, and bi- or multiracial Americans understand their social and racial histories.

In South Africa, the social construction of the mixed person passed through various phases, at times (exemplified by District Six) resembling the Brazilian racial continuum, and at other times (under apartheid) resembling the American system of absolute racialization. One experiences considerable cognitive dissonance as one moves among the three systems. American blacks visiting South Africa often refuse to see coloureds as anything other than black. Coloured South Africans visiting America often express strong racial prejudice toward African Americans. Conversely, the South African classification of "coloured" is like the Brazilian notion of, well, a Brazilian! A visiting journalist from Rio de Janeiro described to me his shock when he was taken to a "coloured" township in the Cape Flats: "It was as if the South African government took all of Brazil and gave it a single 'racial' classification and then banished it to a segregated ghetto." He toyed with the idea of writing a piece entitled "Brazil in a Township" as a way of explaining the South African notion of coloureds to Brazilians.

Spoiled Identities

> *And that, my friend, is why I ran away. I ran away because I*
> *was scared of the coming changes, and scared of the consequences*
> *of not changing. I ran because I wouldn't carry a gun for*
> *apartheid, and because I wouldn't carry a gun against it. I ran*
> *away because I hated Afrikaners [white Afrikaans speakers] and*
> *loved blacks. I ran away because I was an Afrikaner and feared*
> *blacks. You could say, I suppose, that I ran away from the*
> *paradox.*
>
> —RIAN MALAN, MY TRAITOR'S HEART.

Apartheid not only shaped social self-identities in South Africa, but it spoiled those identities, filling people of all races with feelings of disgust and self-loathing, even long after the antiapartheid struggle had begun. Father Michael Lapsley, a naturalized South African from New Zealand and wounded chaplain to the ANC, thought about his "whiteness" for the first time when he arrived as a young Anglican priest to South Africa and experienced his white skin (in the context of white oppression of African blacks) as a mark of Cain, a stigma. In an interview with him in 1994, he told me, "Whiteness for me became like leprosy, something that would not wash off. Although I knew a lot about apartheid beforehand, I never really understood what it would mean structurally to be an oppressor . . . so my decision to join the struggle for liberation was also a struggle for the recovery of my own humanity" (see also Worsnip 1996).

Indeed, there is no easy way to be "white" in South Africa, even in the new, nonracial South Africa. Nor is there is any easy way to be "brown" or "black" when this is tied to a specific ethnic identity, whether "Hottentot" (Khoi), Zulu, Xhosa, or "Cape Coloured." Even the simple questions "Where are you from?" or "Where were you born?" can be seen in some South African circles as an attempt to peg a person to a particular ethnic group and are therefore a lapse in social etiquette.

Erving Goffman (1963) identified the social dynamics of "spoiled identity" resulting from the stigmas of physical difference, ethnicity, and "tribe," and the stigmas of behavior and morality, to which I would now add the stigmas of history and of place. A continuing dilemma of the nonracial South Africa is the legacy of apartheid that has spoiled all cultural and ethnic identities, although some are more spoiled than others: Zulu (because of its identification with the right-wing Inkatha Freedom Party); Afrikaner (because of its political history of institutionalized racism); and coloured (because it is seen as a fictive category, a "pure invention" of apartheid) are perhaps the most spoiled identities today.

Zulus and Afrikaners have developed a strong oppositional identity (and accompanying political organizations) to reassert ethnic and national pride. During the politically volatile period leading up to the first democratic elections, Zulus marched proudly and defiantly in the streets of Durban wearing leopard skins and carrying "tribal" weapons (sticks or, lacking these, golf clubs will do), while Boer civil servants flaunted their language, their "backkies" (large tanklike trucks), their backyard *braais* (the traditional Afrikaner barbecue), their semiliteracy, and their white tribal dreams. Like angry township youth (once dubbed "the lost generation"), Zulus and Boers were seen as dangerous and thus were respected as well as ridiculed. In recent years, both groups have ingeniously invented and reinvented their ethnic "histories" (Sharp 1994; see also Berreman 1971 for a comparative example of the struggle to escape from stigmatized ethnic identity).

Cape Coloureds, however, are without either the cultural panache or the symbolic capital of South African Zulus and Boers. South African intellectuals and progressives discredit coloured identity as a legal fiction, a bureaucratic invention, one of the many nightmares of apartheid. Meanwhile, the mother tongue of the coloureds, Afrikaans, is perceived by all as the language of their oppressor, the white Dutch settler, the hated Boer, the sly and absent "fathers" who "spawned" but never claimed their mixed-race offspring. Thus, to this day, South African coloureds are still generally viewed by other South Africans and even by themselves in the same way that Robert Redfield described peasants—that is, as "part-people with part-cultures" (see Foster 1967). Coloured social self-identity and self-esteem suffer accordingly.

The Dilemma of Coloured Identity

Because they stand in between what was arguably an essentially bipolar race model (black/white), South African coloureds are social liminals, the halfway mark between whites and blacks. They are a marginal and therefore dangerous category; in Mary Douglas's (1970) terms, coloureds are anomalous, "out of place," and "out of set." Consequently, South African coloureds were often viewed with suspicion, mistrust, and even hate by other social groups. The in-betweenness of South African coloureds and other marginals (such as South African blacks who speak only Afrikaans and interracial couples of all kinds) is as pernicious as the subalterity of other oppressed groups.

During the apartheid era, black South Africans expressed little solidarity with the coloured population, sometimes describing them as "part settlers," "half whites," or (most damningly) as "brown Afrikaners" (that is, brown Boers). Coloureds were seen as a "remnant" and a reminder of the first-vanquished black tribes of the Cape Colony: the Khoi (Hottentots) and the native San (the Bushmen). Racist whites (and some blacks) in the rural Western Cape still refer to coloureds by the hated terms *Hot-nots*, *Bushmen*, and *Basters* (bastards).

To white South African racists, coloureds are a perennial reminder of the failure to maintain white purity and separateness under colonialism and apartheid. In the village of Franchhoek, conservative white farmers told me with a straight face that the large coloured population there had "arrived by boat from other countries." They could not, even in the late 1990s, accept their social and biological ties with the "inferior" race.

Even the educated classes share some of these same toxic stereotypes. A professor of physics at the University of Cape Town reminisced about his boyhood school days in liberal Cape Town: "I always felt sorry for the coloureds. We said the worst things about them. We said that coloureds had no backbone, that they were lazy, they had no loyalty, and that their mothers were loose. The worst insult you could throw at a school chum was to say, 'Your mother didn't love you, and your father was a coloured!' I had a coloured friend once who told me, 'David, you don't know how lucky you are. You're English and you're white. Even the kafir boy [i.e., the "nigger"] knows that he's black. But we coloured people, we're just a mess.'"

Cape Coloureds refer to themselves as *gekleurdes*—that is, coloureds—but in their Afrikaans dialect, the term carries a positive sense of being a "colorful" people. Many others simply refer to themselves as *bruinmense*, or "brown people," and leave it at that. But none are immune to the negative ways that black, white, and even indigenous South Africans view their social group.

Indeed, when a small group of self-identified San "Bushmen" (now residing in the Kagga-Kama nature reserve of the Northern Cape) emphasized *their* racial distinctiveness and distance from the mixed-race Cape Coloureds, I began to understand the pervasiveness of the dilemma of coloured identity. Coloureds seemed to represent the one ethnic group from which every other group wished to disidentify. They were/are the generative scapegoats of the pre- and postapartheid era. One could say that they were the only "race" abandoned by the antiracial, antiapartheid struggle. Dawie, the leader of the Kagga-Kama San band, explained to me his disdain for the Cape Coloured:

> Bushman and "Baster" [i.e., the coloured] don't live together because the Bushmen came here first and the Baster came last. . . . The Bushmen was here first and then Jan van Riebeck came [the Dutch colonizer] here . . . and he was a white man and he came to a Bushman's woman and from there on came all this mixing. The last was the Baster. . . . I believe it when they say "Baster," but not when they say coloured, because the Baster, he's got no color; he's a mix-up. He's just a mongrel.

During my visit with this small (indeed residual) band of Kagga-Kama San, which took place immediately following the democratic elections in 1994, Dawie expressed his fear that the new South Africa might force even more race mixing. He emphasized the necessity of marrying in to preserve Bushman bodies and all their physically defining characteristics. Dawie said, "We are afraid to marry other kinds, for then surely we will disappear. We want each baby to come out looking like a Bushman, with the same little ears [pointing to a baby in one of his wives' arms], the same round little head, the same cheekbones. Everything must be just so, perfect. We must not marry with blacks for then we will become kafirs [a derogatory term for Black South Africans] . . . and we must not marry with coloureds or we will become Basters. *When that happens it will be our end.*"

The sense of in-betweenness, of having no clear identity, was articulated in many different ways by my coloured informants and friends in Franschhoek. The following statements taken from the life histories of coloured farmworkers illustrate the dilemma:

> Nellie Prince (sixty-plus years): "I don't see myself attracted to Blacks. The coloured people are more conservative. And I don't see myself cozying up with the whites either. I am coloured. I was born coloured, and coloured I will die."
>
> "What does it mean to be coloured?"
>
> "I . . . I . . . don't know, really."
>
> Minnie Peterson (thirty-seven years): "As a coloured person in South Africa, I don't really know where I stand. I don't know whether to trust the whites or the blacks. I don't even know what it means to be coloured. We don't really have a culture. We don't have our own language. We speak Afrikaans, the language of the Boer. Whatever languages we had in the beginning—Malay and Khoi—a few words got mixed up with Afrikaans . . . but that's all that's left."

Myra Braderman (thirty-five years): "What does it mean to be a Xhosa [a Black African]? That's easy. They dress differently. Some wear large earrings. When the boys are fifteen or sixteen, they are taken up to a mountain for initiation so they can become men. They are cut. Colored boys are not circumcised except for some Muslims."

"And what does it mean to be coloured?"

"To be coloured? Wait . . . wait . . . wait [her hand is on her head]. Oh, this is difficult. Just give me some time to collect my thoughts."

"Dress?" I ask, trying to be helpful.

"No, it's nothing of ours in particular."

"Language?"

"No, that's not ours."

"Food?"

"Yes! We like our *bredei*. It's a kind of Irish stew made with carrots, beans, and mutton. We like pasta, potatoes, and meal. Coloured people don't fancy vegetables unless they're flavored with meal. We like carrots cooked with sugar and a little custard."

"Religion?"

"No, no different, unless you are a Muslim. But when I say coloured, I mean us, the 'Afrikaner coloured,' the 'half settlers,' the 'half Hottentots' that we are, for better or worse."

Jana October echoed the same in saying, "We can call ourselves black, but to the blacks, we will always be yellow-skinned Hot-Nots."

Although few coloured farmworkers could identify any salient social or cultural features distinguishing them as a social group, the one festival clearly identified with Cape Coloureds, the Coon Carnival celebrated in Cape Town on New Year's Day, filled them with embarrassment. Considered the poor coloured man's holiday, the Coon Carnival reveals all the contradictions of colored identity and status. Imitating the black minstrel tradition of the American South, the "coons" lampblack their faces and parade under such self-deprecatory names as the "Mississippi Nigger Minstrels." Strumming their banjos and singing inane ditties like "Playing with My Ding-a-ling," the coons act out white stereotypes of coloreds as happy-go-lucky, shiftless, witless ne'er do wells.

An egregiously racist entry on the Coon Carnival in the *Standard Encyclopedia of Southern Africa* (1972, 336) referred to coloured peoples' "zest for life" and their "animated dancing and prancing" on the main parade of Cape Town. It concluded, "The Cape would be much the poorer without its Yankee Doodle Dandy Darkies" (336). The Coon Carnival reproduces the mimetic quality that haunts South African coloured identity, labeling it as childish, imitative, and farcical.

As is true of carnival play the world over, the playful mockery, ridicule, and defiance—in this case of pernicious racial stereotypes—can backfire and reinforce the negative images. Politically aware coloured people reject the Coon Carnival as a ritual of self-loathing. An anthropologist colleague from the University of Cape Town (personal communication) recalled a poignant scene at a Coon Carnival in the early 1990s (when American identity politics began to enter South Africa and collide with the decidedly anti-identity politics of the ANC and the South African Communist Party). A coon minstrel, his face painted and ready to perform, jumped to his feet and loudly proclaimed: "I'm coloured, I'm coloured. I have no identity!"

Arthur Mac-William Smith, the then "progressive" ANC-aligned white mayor of Franschhoek, interpreted the local coloured "culture" of his farm region in terms of Oscar Lewis's culture of poverty:

> "Our" coloured is very much like your Negro population. He is of a lower economic group. He tends toward a matriarchal society. You get more drunkenness, more drugs, not because he's coloured but as a consequence of the slum culture in which he lives. Despite his slum culture, the coloured shares the same church (Dutch Reform), the same language (Afrikaans) and the same western values as the Afrikaner. The coloured is not an African in the true sense of the word. He is African the way whites here are African . . . as an outsider. Our coloured man is like your American Negro. He is an American (or South African) in all respects except for his color and his lower social class. Your red Indian is more like our Black African, except that our indigenous cultures are very strong and populous here.

"How do you know the difference between coloured and black?" I asked the mayor in one of our early interviews. His answer reveals some of the tensions and contradictions still surrounding the idea of race and ethnicity as simultaneously existentialist and manipulated categories in South Africa. He replied, "Black is . . . well, coloureds are always mixed bloods . . . and you know them by their language and by their looks."

"Umm . . . but some Blacks are 'mixed' too," I replied.

"Er, yes, but . . . not really. They may be mixed with other black 'tribes,' but they are not mixed with whites, because if they were mixed with white they would be classified as 'coloured.'"

"That would have been taken care of in years past through the Population Registration Act?"

"Yes, quite so, and up until now, a person with any mixed blood would certainly 'go' for the coloured classification. It would be impossible for him to pass as white, and there would be no reason to try and pass as black, because being colored naturally gave a person more opportunities—better schooling, better housing, social mobility . . . all those material benefits. But there are also *real* differences in culture between the two groups."

Resistance

The antiapartheid struggle sought to free all South Africans from racist and merely racialist thinking and to construct alternative collective identities in terms of political commitment and "the struggle." Race was a disallowed discourse to be stamped under the feet of revolutionary *toyi-toyi* dancers. Meanwhile, progressive academics, anthropologists foremost among them (see Boonzaier and Sharp 1989), pursued cultural-critique discourses in an attempt to problematize and destabilize "race," "colour," "tribe," "ethnicity," and "culture" as these were co-opted by the state to implement apartheid. Today, South Africans of good will have their hands raised and their fingers curled, ready to supply scare quotes that throw into question the social fictions that the apartheid state presented as hard facts and as reality. However, the necessary attacks on biological and cultural essentialisms (the apartheid state often used "culture" as a surrogate for "race") seemed to leave no space for positive assertions of cultural and ethnic identity, even when viewed simply as a shared history. This was especially true for the coloured population.

Thus, despite the dismantling of official apartheid, psychological apartheid remains strongly entrenched in South Africa, and coloured identity remains ambiguous and problematic. A recent pamphlet written by a respected coloured scholar (Van der Ross 1993) entitled "100 Questions about Colored South Africans" leaves the reader more confused than enlightened. The question of coloured "identity" is given considerable attention:

What is our identity?

Because we are the result of so much mixing, it is difficult, indeed impossible, to define our limits. . . . This is why, of all South Africans today, we have the least sense of identity. But a person's identity is largely what a person considers it to be! (1993, 5)

Do the Coloured people have an identity?

The fact that people refer to the 'coloured people' means that there is a certain identity as a population group. But as we have said it is hard to define the Coloured people in exact terms. When people refer to themselves as 'we, the coloured people' or as 'Bruinmense,' they are using a term of identity just as when people refer to themselves as 'we Xhosas.' . . . Yes, we have an identity; if we don't wish to accept or admit or agree to it, we must find some other way of identifying ourselves." (14)

Other questions treated the issue of whether to keep the apartheid term *coloured* or to create a new term. Van der Ross stresses the historical fluidity of ethnic terms, which can pass from stigmatized to valued in a short period of time, pointing to the shift in the United States from *black* as a derogatory term to *black* as a valued term of self-identity. And he notes that the largest black American organization in the United States is still called the NAACP, the National Association for the Advancement of Colored People.

During the struggle years (late 1970s and 1980s), some progressive coloureds identified themselves socially and politically as "blacks." It was part of a grand and ultimately successful strategy for building a broad base of unity among all South Africa's disenfranchised. However, beginning in 1990 with the first phase in the transition to democracy, coloured peoples' identification with blacks again became problematic. Black identity is no longer seen as the best strategy for advancing the political and material circumstances of South African coloureds. A new discourse on differences between black and coloured has reasserted itself. It emphasizes the considerable competition between the interests of the two groups. In its vulgar form, the new discourse has fed old racist stereotypes that try to advance coloured status by denigrating black status in a neo–social evolutionary model that plays to fears of black violence and primitivity.

Mixed Feelings: The Coloured Vote in the April 1994 Elections

The democratic elections of 1994 were accompanied by a strong reassertion of coloured identity that was expressed in a resounding "coloured" vote for the new National Party, the "reformed" party of apartheid. The vote registered coloured peoples' keen "opposition" to black leadership and dominance under the ANC. One of the great ironies of the democratic elections that brought Mandela and the ANC into power was the near unanimous support by coloureds in the Western Cape for "Papa" de Klerk, the last white president of South Africa. The absentee Afrikaner father was claimed in the end.

In the months and weeks prior to South Africa's first democratic elections, I tried to engage coloured farmworkers in political conversations. What one heard throughout the Cape was that the "coloureds" would be responsible for "selling out" to the racist National Party, and that in the end, the coloureds would forget their oppression at the hands of the Boers who gave them "preferential" employment over the blacks, who paid them in brandy and in wine (through the "dop system"), and who bribed them with food baskets and secondhand, castaway clothes.

What the coloureds of the Western Cape said themselves in the weeks preceding the elections and in the midst of campaign fever was that they felt squeezed out, superfluous, "in the way," because the real contest in South African politics was being played out in shades of black and white. Either one joined the ANC and *toyi-toyi*ed with the blacks, or one joined the Nats and waltzed with the Boer—but in each case, one was dancing with the enemy, maybe even dancing with the devil, and as Minnie Peterson of Vietnam Bos (coloured) squatter camp summed up the situation,

> As a coloured voter you are caught in the middle. You don't have anything that is your own. You don't have a language, and you don't have a political party. The ANC is the party of the blacks (no matter what they say or would like us to believe). The National Party is for the Boer. So, as a coloured person, where do I stand? The *toyi-toyi* is not our dance, and though we sometimes *toyi-toyi* with the blacks, we do it with mixed feelings. I can't vote for the ANC because I do not believe—with all the problems the black people have in this country—that the ANC will be able to take care of us too. So, in the end, I will have to side with the Nats, but I'll vote for them with mixed feelings. For generations, we were used by the Boer, but now I want to believe that things are changing and at the end of the day, the Boer will recognize us as his [*sic*] kin.

If the search for paternity, legitimacy, and kinship with the primordial Boer father-ancestor—and hence the search for personal identity—underlies part of the farm-laborer coloured vote for the local white National Party (as I believe it did), fears of retaliatory black violence were the most commonly articulated reason for casting their lots with the National Party given by coloured voters as they arrived by busloads to attend the final NP rally at the Good Hope Center in Cape Town and to catch a glimpse of "Papa de Klerk" himself.

As I stood in my academic robes along with a few dozen religiously affiliated mixed-race Christian and Muslim faculty from the universities of Cape Town and Western Cape in a silent protest against the blatantly racist NP campaign against Mandela and the ANC, in front of the Good Hope Center where de Klerk and Hemus Kriel were about to address thousands of coloured voters who were bussed in from the Cape Flats and from the surrounding rural farm country, we were verbally assaulted by the workers (some of them already quite drunk before midday). They called us "kafir-lovers" and "coloured traitors" and tossed beer cans and other debris at us.

The South African Police (SAP) threatened to arrest us because (they said) they feared a mob scene following the rally, and they could not guarantee our "protection" from the "angry mobs" as they poured out of the Good Hope Center. As we waited outside, loudspeakers broadcast the messages of de Klerk and Kriel to the coloured voters. Kriel, in particular, traded in racist imagery, speaking in Afrikaans, and made many references to the black so-called "Station Strangler," a serial killer who preyed on young coloured boys in the Cape Flats, and praised the NP Afrikaner police chief who had apprehended a major suspect and thereby allowed coloured parents to sleep more easily. But even de Klerk was not above making pointed references to the "necklace" (the burning of suspected police and other "collaborators" by putting a burning tire around their necks) as a key ANC political strategy.

The message obviously reached home, for on that and subsequent days leading up to April 27 and 28, similar sentiments were cast by coloured voters, even as they waited on the long, snaking queue in front and around polling stations in the Western Cape. The following comments were tape-recorded on the election days in the coloured township attached to Franschhoek, in mixed-race Mowbray and in Mitchell's Plein:

"Look at how the blacks kill their own people. They are a race of killers. When the ANC comes into power, we all had better go out and buy ourselves a coffin. Some of the coloured are so stupid. They go to ANC rallies, and before you know it they are jumping up and down saying, "Viva Mandela! Viva Mandela!" And I think, "Yeah, long live Mandela and death to the rest of us! Toyi-Toyi for Jesus, not for Mandela!"

"We [coloured people] can't vote for Mandela. He was in prison, man. Ah, he is a criminal! Who wants a criminal for President?"

"We can't have a kafir-man [a nigger] for President!"

"Natives can't lead us. What do they know about anything? Shame, they will send us all back to the stone age."

"Wherever the *swarts* [blacks] go, there is violence, bloodshed, and burning tires. Look at the rest of Africa: Burundi and Somalia. When the ANC had its rally in Athlone [a coloured community in the Cape Flats], three children were trampled to death. When the National Party held their rally in the Good Hope Center, no one died. Everything was peaceful. The coloured people are tired of violence."

"But wasn't it the NP that took away coloured peoples' homes and forced them to live in the Cape Flats?" I asked.

"Not here in Mitchell's Plein," denied the woman. "That was over in Mannenberg where the people from District Six were forced to move. We ourselves 'chose' to come here. And we always had our food under the Nats. We kept our jobs, even if the pay wasn't so good. There was no equal pension, but . . . we didn't really suffer."

After elections, the coloured mood was more subdued. The "Kaffir Man" (Mandela) was now their president, while the local prime minister of the Western Cape, following the strong coloured regional vote, was the ex-chief of police, Hemus Kriel. Now they would have to live with him and his initial (and of course ultimately failed) attempts to create a separatist Western Cape designed to keep black migrants out of the "homelands" in search of jobs and homes. But even more curious, the Afrikaner Hemus Kriel and the local "white old boys" of the "New" National Party (NNP) would have to learn to live with coloured voters who had become their main constituency.

In a way, political events had come full circle. Originally, in the Western Cape, the social identity "Afrikaners" was applied to the "half-bred, half-caste offspring of slaves" (*Cape Times* 1877). The colonial administration used the term to refer to the new population of "mixed descent" born in the Cape Colony (Gilomee 1994, 8). Then the term was used by Dutch speakers to refer to all colonists with some Dutch European ancestry, to both white and brown "Afrikaners." Soon after, the term Afrikaners took on its ideological and political connotations and was adopted as a term of self-reference by Dutch-speaking colonists who held white supremacist convictions. An early history published in 1898 defined the Afrikaner as "a person of Dutch extraction, who believed in the advancement of the brandy market, protections for the common farmer, and the repression of the Black native" (cited by Gilomee 1994). Throughout this historical process, the intermediate population of brown Afrikaners in the Western Cape was at times included in Afrikaner identity and politics and at times excluded. The Cape Coloured—like blacks in the American South—had the voting franchise for a period and then lost it and had to fight to regain it. Hermann Gilomee, a progressive Afrikaner political scientist at the University of Cape Town, has stressed the political dimensions of the contraction and expansion of Afrikaner identity in the history of modern South Africa. He notes that in the elections of 1920, the National Party, as the main vehicle of Afrikaner nationalism, competed with some success for the coloured vote. But when in the elections of 1929 the

National Party got only 10 percent of the coloured vote, the National Party dropped the coloureds and adopted the divisive ideology and strategy of apartheid. In the early 1990s, with the goals of the antiapartheid struggle finally in sight, and in light of an expanded franchise, the National Party was again forced to redefine Afrikaners to include the interests of the coloured voters (who were again being courted as "Brown Afrikaners") with considerable success.

Thus, the same party—the National Party, or the "Nats"—that was responsible for the segregation and forced removals of the coloured population in the Western Cape was transformed in the mid-1990s into the official party of Cape Coloureds. Consequently, in the Western Cape, the National Party had to be accountable to their coloured constituency, for better or worse, as the party's fragile political future rested with them and not with South African whites. By the 1999 general elections, the New National Party was wiped out as a national force but maintained some vestigial strength in the Western Cape and among the Cape Coloured population. By the 2004 general elections, the majority of the party deserted per force to the ANC, and the NNP Federal Council voted to disband on April 9, 2005.

Consequently, a pervasive doubt about the legitimacy of their history, their social and political identities, and their uncertain "ethnicity" is a continuing and painful theme among the coloured people of the Western Cape. Of course, nothing is ever stable or predictable in politics or in personal or cultural identity. The jury is not yet out, and it remains to be seen what the Cape Coloured population will ultimately make of its new franchise and ultimately of themselves and their place in the New South Africa.

Notes

The fieldwork for this chapter was supported by a faculty research grant from the University of Cape Town, South Africa (1993–1994) and by a Harry Frank Guggenheim grant (1997). An earlier version of this chapter was presented at the National Humanities Center Conference on "Identities: Personal, Cultural, and National," Chinese University of Hong Kong, June 2–4, 1994, and a revised and expanded version of that paper was published in the *Kroeber Anthropological Society Papers*, vols. 89–90, 2003. I owe many intellectual and personal debts to my former colleagues at the University of Cape Town, most especially to Wilmot James, former chair of the Department of Sociology and former director of IDASA, the Institute for the Study of Democratic Alternatives in South Africa. Emile Boonzaier and John Sharp's South African Keywords project introduced me to the contradictions and intricacies of the South African apartheid race-caste system. Conversations with Charles Hale at the School for American Research during the summer of 2003 challenged me to "refuse the dichotomy" between assimilationism and neoliberal state-endorsed "multiculturalism" as the only possible alternatives to social self-identity.

1. See Scheper-Hughes 1994, 1995, 1998, 2000a, 2000b.

2. This story was told to me by many friends and informants in the Western Cape. My son-in-law, Santos Roman, was a primary-school child when his family was forced to leave District Six and made to reside in one of the ugly sand-trap townships of the Cape Flats. His father, Michael Roman, who had worked for many years as a librarian's assistant at the University of Cape Town, never recovered from that forced removal.

References

Berreman, Gerald. 1971. Self, situation, and escape from stigmatized ethnic identity. In *1971 Yearbook of the Ethnographic Museum*, University of Oslo, 11–25. Oslo: Universitetsforlager.

———. 1972. Race, caste and other invidious distinctions in social stratification. Theme issue, *Race* 23 (4): 385–414.

Bielh, Joao. 2005. *Vita: Life in a zone of social abandonment*. Berkeley: University of California Press.

Boonzaier, Emile, and John Sharp, eds. 1989. *South African keywords*. Cape Town: David Philips.

Cape Times. 1877. Editorial. May 5.

Coetzee, John M. 1988. *White writing: On the culture of letters in South Africa*. New Haven, CT: Yale University Press.

Crapanzano, Vincent. 1985. *Waiting: The whites of South Africa*. New York: Vintage.

Degler, Carl N. 1971. *Neither black nor white: Slavery and race relations in Brazil and the U.S.* New York: Macmillan.

Douglas, Mary. 1970. *Purity and danger*. London: Routledge & Kegan Paul.

Edgerton, Robert B. 1988. *Like lions they fought: The Zulu war and the last black empire in South Africa*. Berkeley: University of California Press.

Foster, George M. 1967. What is a peasant? In *Peasant Society*, ed. Jack Potter, George Foster, and May Diaz, 5–13. Boston: Little, Brown.

Freyre, Gilberto. 1956. *Masters and the slaves*. Berkeley: University of California Press.

Gilomee, Hermann. 1994. Afrikaner identity and franchise contraction and expansion in South Africa. Paper presented at the International Conference on Democracy and Difference, University of Cape Town, May 5–7.

Goffman, Erving. 1963. *Stigma: Notes on the management of spoiled identity*. New York: Hall, Martin.

Hale, Charles R. 2002. Does multiculturalism menace? Governance, cultural rights and the politics of identity in Guatemala. *Journal of Latin American Studies* 34:485–524.

Hall, Martin. 1991. High and low in the townscapes of Dutch South America and South Africa: The dialectics of material culture. *Social Dynamics* 17 (2): 41–75.

Malan, Rian. 1990. *My traitor's heart: A South African exile returns to face his country, his tribe, and his conscience.* New York: Atlantic Monthly Press.

Marx, Anthony W. 1998. *Making race and nation: A comparison of the U.S., South Africa, and Brazil.* Cambridge: Cambridge University Press.

Mintz, Sidney. 1985. *Sweetness and power: The place of sugar in modern history.* New York: Penguin.

Oakes, Dougie, ed. 1989. *Illustrated history of South Africa.* Cape Town: Reader's Digest Association, South Africa.

Parker, Richard. 1993. *Bodies, pleasures and passions.* Boston: Beacon Press.

Powedermaker, Hortense. 1993. *After freedom: A cultural study of the deep south.* Madison: University of Wisconsin Press.

Ramphele, Mampela. 1994. *A bed called home.* Cape Town: David Phillips.

Scheper-Hughes, Nancy. 1994. The last white Christmas: The Heidleberg Pub massacre (South Africa). *American Anthropologist* 96 (4): 1–28.

———. 1995. Who's the killer? Popular justice and human rights in a South African squatter camp. *Social Justice* 22 (3): 143–64.

———. 1998. Un-doing: Social suffering & the politics of remorse in the new South Africa. *Social Justice* 25 (4): 114–42.

———. 2000a. Sacred wounds: Writing with the body. In *Soft vengeance of a freedom fighter*, by Albie Sachs, xi–xxiv. Berkeley: University of California Press.

———. 2000b. After the war is over. *Peace Review* 12 (3): 423–29.

———. Forthcoming. Anatomy of a quilt: The Gees Bend Freedom Quilting Bee. *Anthropology Today.*

Sharp, John. 1994. Should we condemn all primordial discourses? A comparative perspective on a South African dilemma. Paper presented at the Department of Social Anthropology, University of Cape Town, December 3.

Small, Adam. 1971. A brown Afrikaner speaks: A coloured poet and philosopher looks ahead. Munger Africana Library Notes, no. 8, October.

Standard Encyclopedia of Southern Africa. 1972. Cape Town: Nasou Limited.

Trollope, Anthony. 1878/1973. *South Africa.* Cape Town: A. A. Balkema.

Van der Ross, Andrew. 1993. 100 questions about colored South Africans. University of the Western Cape (Xerox copy).

Vatuk, Ved Prakash. 1979. Forward to *Caste and other inequities: Essays in inequality*, by Gerald Berreman, vii–ix. Meerut, India: Folklore Institute (Distributor: Manohar Book Service, New Delhi).

Verwoerd, Hendrik Frensch. 1966. *Verwoerd Speaks: Speeches 1948–1966.* Ed. A. N. Pelzer. Johannesburg: APB Publishers.

West, Martin. 1989. Confusing categories: Population groups, national states and citizenship. In *South African keywords*, ed. Emile Boonzaier and John Sharp, 100–110. Cape Town: David Philips.

Wilson, Monica, and Leonard Thomas. 1969/1971. *The Oxford history of South Africa*. New York: Oxford University Press.

Wolf, Eric. 1982. *Europe and the people without history*. Berkeley: University of California Press.

Worsnip, Michael. 1996. *Michael Lapsley: Priest and Partisan*. Melbourne: Ocean Press.

Conclusion
Ethnic Identity:
A Psychocultural Perspective

GEORGE A. DE VOS AND LOLA ROMANUCCI-ROSS

I N CONCLUSION, WE RECAPITULATE and integrate a number of themes and theoretical arguments presented in the foregoing chapters.

Most observers of ethnicity today are not only interested in how ethnicity still totally defines citizenship in national states, but rather in how it remains a question of *relative* acceptance or derogation among those of separate origins who have technically become citizens in a multiethnic modern state. Historically, the question is sometimes who is actually included in the majority and which groups are constrained to be minorities in a composite national entity.

Where Are We From?
Causality and Continuity

As discussed in chapter 1, ethnic identity is in essence a *past-oriented* form of identity, embedded in the presumed cultural heritage of the individual or group. This form of social self-identity contrasts with a sense of belonging linked with citizenship within a political state, or *present-oriented* affiliations to specific groups demanding professional, occupational, or class loyalties. It also contrasts with those identities that reject both past and present in favor of a *future-oriented* ideological commitment to a realizable future social goal.

To know one's *origin* is to have not only a sense of provenience, but perhaps more importantly, a sense of *continuity* in which one finds the personal and social *meaning* of human existence to some degree. It is to know *why* one behaves and acts in accordance with custom. To be without a sense of continuity is to be faced with one's own death.

Extinction of a group occurs when, as a California Indian once remarked to anthropologist Alfred Kroeber, "the bowl of custom is broken and we can no longer drink of life." Ethnicity can most readily be *symbolically represented contrastively.* It may involve self-consciously perceived variations in *language* and *customs* from others. It may be symbolized in affirmative *ritual practices* such as dramatic symbolic representations recalling past collective ordeals or days of heroic triumph. Ethnicity is explained by *religious myth,* since religious beliefs or myths are, in effect, very often attempts to explain group origin and group continuity.

Two alternate forms of myth occur as widespread explanations of origin among peoples of the world. These are autochthonous myths of human origin from a given sacred place and, alternatively, religious myths that dramatize "the journey"—an event buried in the distant past. Myths explaining origin buttress a conviction that one's group arrived "here" from elsewhere. Origin, in this sense, has a spatial, territorial dimension. One's idea of social meaning is also temporal. A feeling of social belonging also obtains from moving through time or territory, both as an individual and as a member of a group and a culture. Traditions characteristically present a script for group continuity from the past into the future, carefully perpetuating factual fictions or fictional facts as links that bind generations.

Concern with origins is a concern with *parentage.* To know who they are, individuals and groups look back genealogically to their progenitors and possibly eponymous ancestors. Some mythologies explain how men and women descended from a primordial mating event; others explain group diversity as totemic, where human subgroups are descended from different animals or plants.

In Judeo-Christian mythology, the Tower of Babel marks the origin of linguistic diversification by punitively dividing groups from each other for their presumption to wish to reach up to the heavenly creator. Mythological explanations of origin help explain present differences between groups as well as providing the rationale for such differences.

Curiously, a number of mythological traditions indirectly reveal the converse. They are attempts by a cultural group, for the sake of present cohesion, to deny previous diversity of origin by disguising evidence of past amalgams that occurred through conquest. Greek myths excel in disguising past conflicts, including changes from matrilineal to patrilineal descent as a result of conquest, into an organized Olympic Pantheon. The book of Genesis in the Hebrew Bible, according to Freud, disguises the several separate tribal origins of Jews with different gods who were united in monotheistic allegiance. Genesis gives internal evidence suggesting that there occurred a blending of two or more deities (Elohim) into one Yahweh. Similarly, the Japanese mythology preserved in the Kojiki and Nihongi gives ancient and internal evidence that prior political conflicts were resolved religiously by producing a more unified, accommodatively organized pantheon of deities. Religion is regulation. It is purpose. It is destiny. It maintains order and prevents an entropic reversion to primal chaos. An ethnic identity exists in a moral universe.

What Must We Do?
Moral Control and Ethnic Belonging

Origin myths establish who one is, and, because of one's progenitors, with which group one has rights and obligations. Such knowledge helps individuals resolve priorities of loyalty and allegiance in terms of a *past* frame of reference. It helps to integrate and regulate one's behavior. It defines the classes of persons to whom one can express affection or vent aggression. It indicates those who deserve respect and those who are to be derogated. The sense of history is celebrated in collective ritual. Ritual acts are also expressions of commitment, be it to a religion, to a nation of loyal citizens, or to an ethnic group. Such acts are a collective experience that teaches those who participate who they are. The redundancy of ritual goes beyond verbal expression, reinforcing emotional response and allowing participants to identify with one another in sharing an explicit sense of purpose. Rituals of belonging can be dramatizations of ancestral suffering and triumph, out of which future purpose is born and sustained. For example, for the Jews, the sacred holidays commemorate historical occurrences that reaffirm reasons for continuity. The communion ritual for Christians (ingesting the body of Christ from a common vessel) represents both the historical fact of the beginning of Christianity and the sense of belonging to a group that moves forward with a purpose to the Last Judgment.

In modern societies, as in folk cultures, the reasons for *present* rules can be explained by *past* mythology. Taboos of food and other constraints on behavior are explained in terms of past occurrences, usually a specific mythologized event. It seems that humans always have to know *why* something is or is not done, and mythology provides the explanations that justify required behavior. Many of the historical occurrences that are ritualized or become legend tend to be symbolic victories of survival or attempts at revival. In Native American history, the Ghost Dance was the revivalist ritual of a defeated people. Today the massacre at Wounded Knee and the long bloody forced marches of Native American families from their eastern homes into western reservations are tales of ordeal that stimulate a need for survival by the maintenance of group consciousness.

Revivalist movements and legends of ordeal are affirmations of the state of affairs that existed before a traumatic defeat that has marked a people, symbolizing a temporal extension backward to a time of group strength that existed before defeat. As we indicated in the introduction, the contemporary militant black movement among African Americans in the United States contains an explicit and an implicit affirmation of a dignified and respected African identity as a point of origin.

In rituals of affirmation that reinforce ethnic identity, there is often reference to a mythical golden age before the fall. Fascist Italy returned to Roman military insignias and titles in an attempt to reestablish continuity with the past Roman Empire. Thus, some Italians sought symbolically to wipe out millennia of fragmentation, foreign conquest, and subjugation. For authentic Fascists (and there were some), this was an affirmation of pan-Italianism, as was their attempt to purge the Italian language of foreign idioms. In their zeal to eradicate borrowed impurities, some Japanese even became anti-Buddhist, since it was a "foreign" religion that had invaded Japan thirteen centuries earlier. Some French groups, alarmed by the threat of "Franglais," are attempting to keep the French language "pure."

Ethnic identity can be a positive affirmation containing a negative potential for exhibiting a hysterical or paranoid defense. As in all forms of belonging, it can be used to express one's humanness, or to deny the humanness of others; its use depends on collective and individual mental health. It also depends on an agreed-upon reality of external pressure and oppression. In addition to creating a sense of common origin, ethnic identity also defines the rules of comportment. The essential correctness of one's own behavior and the behavior of one's group may or may not be contrasted with the behavior of outsiders.

Groups differ greatly in the degree to which contrastive criteria are used. Social behavior in conformity to group expectation cannot be completely regulated through socialization, and therefore no culture can afford the absence of "reinforcers" of desired behavior. These are understood by all group members as having an inviolability even stronger than formal law. Punishment is meted out to those who break the covenant of belonging through incorrect behavior, thereby destroying group cohesion and threatening group survival. Belonging to a group, then, means being aware of group expectations and group regulations—we know who we are through learning what we are expected to do and what not to do. Embodiment of group identity may be found in periodic ritual religious acts, as discussed by Durkheim in *The Elementary Forms of Religious Life* (1947). It may also be embodied in a written tradition that is, at the same time, a body of laws, such as the Christian and Jewish bible or the Islamic Koran.

The need to follow unique rules may permit a given people to maintain their identity despite their *present* proximity to others. Indeed, such awareness of proximity and difference may cause the differences to be amplified and to become emblematic. Jews are a well-known case in point. They have kept their integrity by following their tribal regulations throughout their history. The Batak in Sumatra, by maintaining their *adat* (law), create an illusion of cultural continuity that enables them to move easily into culturally heterogeneous modern cities (Bruner 1976). Objectively (i.e., as seen by the outsider), their law changes, but those who identify themselves as Batak perceive no change in their law. Belief in the continuity of law keeps them identified as Batak.

In some ethnic groups, recruitment is possible; candidates with no "birthright" may be asked to experience a rebirth ritual signifying that they will henceforth recognize and obey the laws joyfully. Such emphasis on *law* is characteristic of the boundary area between ethnic identity and citizenship. As more emphasis is placed on the political dimension of belonging, a *present* orientation begins to supplant the *past* in the sense of social identity. There is a variety of differences of emphasis between a *present* commitment to a state and to an ethnic group. In a pluralistic society, a major sanctioning force of an ethnic group is ostracism. But in commitment to the state, one accedes to submission to law and, by force if necessary, to the political authority that is rationalized by all as necessary to survival.

It is possible to be simultaneously a loyal *citizen* of the state, a part of the superordinate political unit, and a member of an ethnic minority. Problems arise only if the rules are mutually antagonistic. When Jesus was asked about the coin of the Roman realm, he resolved what was supposed to be a conflict over Caesar's and God's possessions by giving each his own. Many Christians were later persecuted because they insisted on mixing logical levels (to paraphrase Bertrand Russell and Gregory Bateson) and created a dialectic that the Romans took up in a gleeful collusion to send them on their journey to Paradise. Actually, the Romans expected and accepted ethnic and religious diversity, but they would not brook the lack of respect implicit in repudiating the necessary symbolic acts of allegiance to the then-current Roman hegemony.

Like other forms of loyalty, ethnic identity is experienced as a moral commitment, making rejection of conflicting moral and legal commitments mandatory. When commitment becomes *future* oriented and therefore ideological or politicized, there is less necessity for maintaining an ethnic *past* concern with parentage and origin. The initiation ritual seems to suffice, a ritual in which the rebirth usually symbolizes rejection of actual ancestry and a pledge of allegiance to shared future goals of the new group. Allegiance shifted from past-oriented Roman *gentes* (origin of the word *gentiles* in the New Testament) to a future-oriented Christian church. Later, Marx and Trotsky repudiated Judaism in envisioning a new Communist future.

How Are We Different?

One's primary reference group is the audience observing one's behavior, and indeed some groups do not pay too much attention to outsiders in trying to define who they are. Other groups create their image at the expense of outsiders. Depending on the individual, as well as on group traditions, inclusiveness or exclusiveness may be important. Most often, a person's expected behavior tells one who one is; that is, it defines the reference group of primary belonging. Others who behave differently are not part of our group, and we come to know who we are by knowing who we are not. Of course, contrastive representations mark sex, age, and class differences.

The use of contrast is not so much dictated by geographic proximity as by the nature of the contact with another group. In identity maintenance, one has to assess the nature of the possible threat that close contact with an alien group implies. In a modern pluralistic society, where contact is intense and unavoidable, certain minor symbolic emblematic measures remain vital to maintaining psychological distance from those outside one's group. In constructing any theory of ethnic identity, it is necessary to consider how external or social-distance factors are related to internal or psychological-distance factors in identity boundary maintenance. Any or all cultural features can be used emblematically for contrastive purposes, including the prescribed and the tabooed, special foods, social rituals, ideals of physical beauty, and phonemic styles.

Many cultural effects become self-consciously contrastive only when contact with strangers suggests alternatives. Foods have seemed naturally edible or inedible, phonemic sequences natural and logical, and standards of beauty divinely decreed. The manner and degree of reaction to newly discovered differences depends on the social or physiological threat posed by the contrastively perceived behavior. There are tolerable and intolerable differences within what is recognized as behavioral contrast. Others doing what is rigidly tabooed by one's own group will be most disturbing.

Romanucci-Ross was told by Sori islanders of an event that took place between themselves and Harenggan islanders (an Admiralty Island of the Bismarck Archipelago) a long time before culture contact with the West. The Sori were received with all due hospitality and given women, which the Sori thought was very nice indeed.

But how horrendously crude of the Harenggan men to expect the Sori to lend Sori women when the Harenggan paid them a reciprocal visit! The Sori were so offended they broke off all diplomatic and trade relations with the Harenggan up to at least 1967 (Romanucci-Ross 1985). Projection of negative traits on an alien group is widespread. What is socially disavowed within one's own group is projected as prevalent among outsiders. In the Admiralties, one group will often refer to the customs of other New Guinea groups by saying, "as in the manner of pigs and dogs" (Romanucci-Ross 1985).

Contrasts may be viewed on a vertical or a horizontal dimension. Some contrasts neither elevate nor degrade outsiders. In other circumstances, a particular pattern of behavior may be seem within a vertical framework of superiority-inferiority. For example, in noting racial differences, Europeans respond differently depending on whether the subject is African or Chinese. Before the nineteenth century, Europeans were quite impressed by the achievements of the Chinese. They made invidious comparisons between the Chinese and Africans, whom they found primitive, since they understood nothing of the unperceivable (to them) complexities of some African cultures. Europeans have only recently begun to learn to appreciate the aesthetics of African art as a highly developed alternative to the naturalist traditions that persisted until the end of the nineteenth century in Europe.

In maintaining ethnic boundaries, some groups are more insistent on contrastive exclusiveness. Others are more open and inclusive, that is, apt to bring in individuals to become part of the group rather than continue to emphasize differences. Polynesians, for example, exhibit an easy sense of inclusiveness, and Melanesians are acutely sensitive to differences. Melanesian cultures amplify all possible differences in continually creating new ethnic distinctions.

Similarly, white American attitudes have dictated that anyone with a black ancestor, no matter how remote, could not be considered white. Contrastive racial distinctions have been an obvious part of the dilemma of

American identity. One factor determining criteria for exclusion or inclusion is reckoning of descent, whether lineage is traced bilaterally or unilaterally. Among Jews, for example, group belonging hinges on whether the mother is a group member, since, according to some scholars, the mother is considered the major disciplinary socializing influence assuring that the child recognizes and adheres to the law through his or her formative years. One might easily reason, however, that matrilineal societies, though patronymic, appear to care very much about the bloodline of the mother. In certain primitive societies, ownership of material and nonmaterial cultural elements demands certainty as to who the *real* bloodline progenitor is. Motherhood is resistant to impeachment on this issue.

At times, a contrastive sense of ethnic identity actually came about through conflict. In Melanesia, the cargo cult phenomenon, according to Schwartz (1995), depended on the believers *and* on the nonbelievers, who provided the dynamic contrastive tensions necessary for the movement to sustain itself. The sense of one's existence in such a culture depends upon a continual rivalry and confrontation within the system.

The internal or external sense of contrast in a culture may, as noted above, be emphasized in either a vertical or a horizontal direction. Contrastive ethnic feelings can be directed toward individuals considered equal antagonists, or the sense of ethnic separateness may be based on viewing another group as inferior. In time, such a disparaged group may indeed come to view themselves as inferior. They exhibit, in Kardiner's terms (Lee and De Vos 1981), some internalized "mark of oppression" in their self-concepts.

It is psychologically difficult for groups whose self-esteem has been based on physical prowess to avoid interpreting military and political defeat as proof of personal worthlessness. An unhappy history of ethnic identity is exemplified by some Native Americans. Some groups, as a defeated warrior people forced to live with their conquerors, have not as yet devised a satisfactory collective means of escaping the psychological effects of the destruction of their own cultural identity in the course of the past century. Jews, on the other hand, defeated and dispersed, nevertheless sustained pride in the relative invulnerability of their intellectual religious attainments that buffered the effects of political annihilation. Scots, ambivalent as they have remained over their forced political union with the English, have found compensatory ethnic pride in commercial enterprise, with the added advantage of permitted regional self-sustenance.

Finally, the study of contrast in ethnic identity leads us back to the discussions in chapter 1 of stratification in systems of ethnic pluralism. It also relates further to a topic not considered in this volume, namely, the entire question of regional national *ethnic ascendancy* as it influences the political interaction of supposedly independent national states. For example, viewing European history in ethnically interactive terms as patterns of emulation, one notes the gradual cultural ascendancy of the French in Europe from the reign of Louis XIV and continuing into the twentieth century. The ascendant French in Europe developed nonreciprocal relations with others, as the French language became dominant internationally. Throughout Europe, it became the language of the nobility. Intermarrying nobility (and royalty) transcended specific ethnic loyalties. The language of the Polish and Russian courts, for example, became French. Today, American commercial ascendancy is met with ambivalence with respect to its effects on ethnic identity. The language of international trade, commerce, and transportation has become English. The French are resisting, as best they can, the commercial success of the American film industry and popular music in an attempt to maintain French "culture" as still psychologically equal if not ascendant.

Ethnic Leadership

Leadership in shaping ethnic history is a topic merely broached in this book. We need further exploration of the psychocultural characteristics of legendary heroes as well as the actual leaders of ethnic movements. How does their behavior, real or mythical, actual or imputed, correspond to the central social issues of highly desirable group traits? When examined carefully, we would probably find that minority-group leaders personify some of the complexities of divided ethnic loyalties or contrastive heroic assertions against another group's possible ascendancy. "Stagalie," a folk legend of black Americans, is a heroic figure capable of exercising exaggerated violence with bravado and dominance. Such prowess is deemed necessary for survival in the harsh underworld of black counterculture, a culture developed partially as a result of the denial to blacks of access to the majority society. Clever, cunning, and cruel, rogue and outlaw, Stagalie is the symmetrical inversion of the traditional, acceptable "Black Sambo," who symbolized to whites the subordinate status of blacks.

Native Americans have a store of heroes ranging from the elusive Apache Geronimo to the religious leader Handsome Lake. All are symbols of resistance or some form of religious revival that might allow one to avoid acknowledging final defeat. In modern times, Charles de Gaulle represented a final attempt at ethnic ascendancy by France, the final resistance to becoming a coequal rather than a dominant partner in forming a European multiethnic community. For Turks, Kamal Ataturk has been a symbol of modern rebirth, a figure of transition, through which to be Turkish could also mean to be modern.

Curiously, in numerous instances, the leader who personifies an ethnic group is an outsider. Such a leader often vehemently affirms his allegiance as the means of overcoming his questionable legitimacy of belonging. Ataturk was of Anatolian ancestry, a minority group within the old Turkish Empire. Hitler was an Austrian, perhaps of Jewish descent. Napoleon was a Corsican of possible Italian origin. De Gaulle's ancestors were Flemings from what became northwest France from the time of Louis XIV, who had taken on a new, more French-sounding name to emphasize their loyalty to France. Malcolm X, a leader of the black movement in the United States, was all the more motivated toward a black identity by the previous excruciating ambivalence he experienced when he once attempted to identify strongly with the majority whites (Haley 1966). The reaffirmation of his black identity was a positive resolution of a deep psychological stress—internal tensions were transmuted by a strong need to affirm the black man's right to dignity. The autobiography of Valiers (1968), a French-Canadian ethnic leader, is a highly poignant parallel to that of Malcolm X. It demonstrates the functional similarity between racially or culturally mixed inheritances in producing a divided self, a problem that for some people can be resolved only by an exemplary affirmation that may result in the appearance of a group hero.

A potential sense of alienation in many members of a minority group can be overcome by witnessing how the hero behaves in order to become a "true" person. Such a person can bend events to a realization of common purpose. Ethnic-identity movements, therefore, are usually led by individuals who, at given points in their careers, manifest some resolution of previously disturbing internal states, which are also experienced by many other members of the group at large. Such movements are also collective alternatives to isolated individual attempts at passing or guarding one's ethnic feelings in silence.

If we describe leaders, we must also have an idea of characteristics of followers. Many cultures prepare the individual for loneliness, alienation, or isolation. In some simpler societies, it is in solitude that one encounters the sacred. Among the Plains Indians, death and rebirth occurred during the Sun Dance, in which the flesh is punctured deeply beyond the muscle layer (pain is sustained alone), or during the (lonely) Vision Quest. For Amerindian missionaries, as well as those from Tibet and Siberia, only solitude in the wilderness could open doors in the human mind—doors that could, for example, make of one a healer or a great leader. "To learn and to see," said a Mexican Huichol Shaman, "one must go many times to the mountain alone."

But individuals in complex societies, where value is placed on highly narrow intentional fields, seek meaning in a leader—even in cyberspace, if necessary. (No one wants to be outside the information highway, regardless of how trivial or banal the information.) If one's fundamental belief is in science, technology, and progress, then solitude as a subjective state is to be feared and shunned. One seeks the reassurance of the leader and the comfort of an approving surrounding mass of others just like oneself.

Ethnicity and Healing:
A Medical Dimension

The relevance of ethnic belonging has come to be recognized by researchers in medical anthropology. Romanucci-Ross found a hierarchy of resort within curative practices. Specific "native diseases" required specific native remedies, whereas one went to the white man's hospital for white man's diseases. Furthermore, native diseases also had points of origin in other native ethnic groups, and one had to go to *their* healers, and one had to practice preventive medicine against such foreign witchcraft. If cures appeared elusive, a local group would declare loyalty to their own diseases (Romanucci-Ross 1977). Crandon-Malamud found diversity in ethnicity and class as determining choices in a medically pluralistic society in Bolivia. She noted that groups negotiated the meanings of their ethnic affiliations through "medical dialogue," with resulting political and economic (and ethnic) implications in diagnosis and cure (1991).

The breakdown of the Soviet Union has provided fertile ground for the reemergence of shamanism, which had been targeted for extinction by the former Soviet central government (Balzer 1991). Official government vehicles brought modern Western medicine to rural villages as local shamans were derided or even incarcerated as drunks and charlatans (Balzer 1993a). But now shamanic curing and healing are dramatically on the rise in such places, even in some urban areas (Balzer 1993b).

The shaman, in his role as technician of ecstasy and healing, traditionally created a culturally shared "inner space" in which the healing of the body and the body politic occurred. Healer and poet, a shaman was the keeper and interpreter of symbols that were cultural instruments to perceive and arrange reality. A shaman wielded and maintained for the group the generators and stylizers of forces that compelled mind and experience. One could return to a shaman for identity surrounded by a world in disarray or in ruins (Romanucci-Ross 1989).

Contextual Changes in the Individual Expression of Ethnic Identity

Society in general expects the individual to maintain some behavioral consistency. One must remain recognizable, or social interaction is impossible. In moral terms, an individual is supposed to maintain "integrity." Ethnic identity, like any form of identity, is not only a question of knowing who one is subjectively, but of knowing how one is seen from the outside. Ethnic identity requires the maintenance of sufficiently consistent behavior so that others can place an individual or a group in some given social category, thus permitting appropriate interactive behavior.

Extremes of mobility—social, geographic, or ethnic—are socially disruptive. Society needs consistency in attribution for interpersonal functioning. In other words, identity involves some internally socialized consistency with respect to behavioral norms so that the individual and those with whom one is in contact know what to expect in interpersonal relationships. It is uncomfortable to be part of a social scene or watch a dramatic presentation in which the players change their designated parts in an inconsistent fashion. To some degree, people must be able to relate in terms of approximations or stereotypic expectations. Complete unpredictability in another's behavior makes social communication impossible. Internally, an individual also has to maintain a sense of self by certain patterns of consistency. The work of George Herbert Mead describes how a "generalized other" is internalized in the composition of a consistent sense of self.

Self-consistency within given cultures is related to the periodic use of altered states of consciousness that allow a person to overcome limitations imposed by conscious control of a consistent self. Individuals in trance, for example, can act out roles that are too inconsistent with the usual self to be tolerated in an ordinary state of consciousness. A striking example of this is found in the documentary film by Jean Rouch, *Les Maitres Fous*. On their weekends, natives of Ghana who are working in modern industrialized factories participate in a new religion, which consists of a communal feast. A live dog is dismembered. The individuals in trance eat and share this "communion." In their trance state, they become white colonial officials, exemplifying social power and prestige. Such behavior was impossible for these people to assume in their ordinary state of consciousness. In trance, however, they could emulate the members of the then-dominant Western white culture, strutting and assuming other postures of self-importance. The internal structure of these assumed roles, of course, remained a foreign mystery to the participants of the feast. Edward Sapir (1968) talked about cultures as "genuine" or "spurious," stating that a person is only "natural" in one language. A second acquired language never takes on the internal natural emotional richness of one's language of nativity or childhood.

Changes of ethnic identity, therefore, may seem somewhat artificial and external if the changes are assumed after personality structure has rigidified into the consistent pattern of an adult. To be subjectively genuine, changes in identity must start sufficiently early to make the assumption of a particular behavior feel internally natural to the individual. A sense of identity is, by definition and by implication, a conscious part of the self rather than the operation of unperceived automatic mechanisms. It is a conscious awareness of what and who one is in relation to a social group. An ethnic identity is developed through time and takes on various meanings in the course of one's life experience, as one contrasts one's social group in some measure against the dominant culture and against other groups within it.

In chapter 1, Romanucci-Ross discussed briefly the continuing internal and external feedback in identity affirmation that is received and acted upon. Primary family and face-to-face identity are influenced in modern society by the multitudinous recordings of experience received through print and other message media. There is a continual onslaught of socially perceived information and continual editorializing about it, keeping a person in touch with the past history of one's group and its present circumstances. The reverberations of such experiences may not be immediate but become particularly significant at crisis periods in the trajectory of a lifetime. The social feedback mechanisms that establish, develop, and maintain an ethnic identity have immediate and delayed effects that may only become manifest much later in the life cycle.

For some, crises in consistency occur at points of challenge or choice; for others, choice or commitment is gradual or cumulative. These points of choice may be imperceptible or highly dramatic. Individuals can identify by gradually taking on a certain way of behaving, but by doing so they eliminate the possibility of alternate ways of behaving. The process need not be painful, though it often is when one cannot consciously resolve inconsistent and conflictual modes of behavior.

Identity theory, therefore, must be related to some concepts of a continuing need for closure, for self-consistency, that embodies both the cognitive and the affective. Some individuals learn to live with ambiguity and dissonance (and, as a matter of fact, it is not unknown for this to eventually become a survival tactic or a means of manipulating others). These internal inconsistencies may find expression in collective social movements and in complex forms of individual adjustment or maladjustment.

Choice points are not only related to alternatives between two models of behavior; they are also related to the levels of inclusiveness to which the individual refers his or her behavior. The individual may learn to identify with expanding circles of inclusiveness. One's first level of inclusiveness is with self alone, the next perhaps with family and other face-to-face relationships in the community. One may transcend a community by identifying with a professional world. The psychological investment in each of these widening or segmenting circles will vary in strength.

Our focus in this volume is on the level of belonging related to ethnicity as we have defined it—levels and modes of cultural separateness in one's sense of self. We cannot, therefore, consider the other realms of identity except insofar as they reflect our particular concern. For black Africans, there are several alternative levels of belonging in modern societies. One goes from the community or so-called tribal group into a broader identity with a nation-state, or a group of similar nations (all of black Africa, for example), or even with an entire continent (the African continent as a whole in contrast with Europe, Asia, or the Americas). Usually, an individual can move from one such realm of identity to another without conflict, for one of these identities can be contained within the other. In the case of mutually exclusive ethnic identities, however, there can be crises in which the behavior demanded on one level is inconsistent with the behavior expected on another. It may be that the individual can find no stable position from which to resolve the resulting tensions.

In some societies, there are tragic representations of conflict related to priority of parental loyalty. Ancient Greek culture produced tragic myths concerning dilemmas of loyalty. For example, the tragedy of Orestes as presented in the Greek play grows out of the conflict produced by the competing claims of his mother and father for his loyalty. This tragedy embodies a residual problem of Greek cultural history in which patrilineal invaders overran ethnic groups with matrilineal descent. In killing his mother to avenge his father, Orestes is affirming his ultimate ethnic membership in the newly established patrilineal system. Symbolically, in the modern age we find tragic dilemmas of belonging related to social, racial, or ethnic marginality, such as the dilemma of the Eurasian in *Love Is a Many Splendored Thing*. There are many heartbreaking instances of various Eastern European family members deciding to be loyal to one or another of the political divisions into which subordinate ethnic groups were arbitrarily divided. The chapters of Milosz and Gilliland offer brief glimpses into this aspect of highly complex histories of ethnic conflict.

The mestizo in Mexico is often seen as an individual who is caught between an Indian and Spanish sense of belonging. In Mexico, the condition of being a mestizo in culture and in personality is complex. Physical appearance is important but not conclusive. Mexicans rank themselves according to skin color and physical types: at the pinnacle are the most Caucasian, the most Spanish looking; at the bottom are the most Indian looking. In between, there are various degrees of Indianness in skin color and comportment (Romanucci-Ross 1983). These racial and behavioral-cultural traits are almost always correlated with socioeconomic status. In Mexico, as elsewhere, there is a positive correlation between being darker and being poorer. In this context in Mexico, a sufficient amount of money or power can compensate for skin color. Questions arise as to how external social ascriptions fit or do not fit the inner identity of the person who is accorded or denied status by the ascribing group, for the social power of ascription in Mexico is quite evident (Romanucci-Ross 1983).

The present situation in the United States is more confused. There are so many standards and so much flux with regard to ethnic pluralism that individuals can transmit and receive many false signals. Passing is widespread. Names are changed. Modern plastic surgery even allows one to pick out a new physiognomy in an attempt to change one's social acceptability.

Where there are two or more rigidly defined lifestyles, as in the Indian and the Spanish-Mexican, the force of group ascription may make almost irrelevant the subjective experience of the individual who is being defined. In situations where external standards are themselves in transition or lack universality, a sense of inner conflict arises out of the greater measure of choice placed on the individual self. One is constrained to define as best one can where he or she fits in, or who one is. Thus, there are probably differences from one culture to another in the degree to which subjective conflict will have as much force in determining behavior or attempted behavior as will the external force of ascription exercised by the society.

In some circumstances, a dual or combined identity is not denied but encouraged. In Hawaii, for example, individuals of mixed Hawaiian and Chinese ancestry make a point of affirming themselves as a group, differing from either the pure Chinese or Hawaiian, just as mestizos in Mexico are a recognized ethnic group even though members are graded according to the degree of racial mixture and to the degree of Spanish or Indian cultural behavior. In a strong resurgence of ethnic specificity among the students at the University of California, a group of Eurasian students who had never united with others on the basis of their mixed ancestry found it expedient to come together as a small group to self-consciously discuss whether they identified more strongly with the heritage of their Caucasian parent or with that of their Asian parent. This type of identity decision concerns the issues raised about a contemporary democratic sense of integrity reflected in a felt necessity to affirm rather than deny the less prestigious segment of one's ancestry. This sense of integrity runs counter to previous patterns that emphasized identification with one's more socially elevated ancestors, a common mode of tracing genealogies practiced in aristocratically oriented societies.

Instrumental and Expressive Uses of Ethnicity[2]

Lastly, the social meaning of ethnicity is *both* rational-instrumental and deeply emotional and expressive. Instrumental interpersonal behavior is principally goal oriented; what one does or what one is concerned with is seen as a means to an end. It is behavior guided by some form of rationality. Expressive behavior, by contrast, is an end in itself, a result of a prior affective arousal or emotional need. Causal or rational or expediential concerns are secondary to feeling states.

Instrumental Behavior and Ethnic Identity

ACHIEVEMENT. Social definitions of success or achievement are found in every society. In a pluralistic society, personal success in one's endeavors may require one to emphasize ethnic belonging or to disguise it. In chapter 1, we discussed passing at some length, including situations in which a person changes behavior or appearance to attain what is socially defined as success. We have also mentioned how minority status can, in some instances, stimulate compensatory striving. Many Japanese Americans were so motivated by their immigrant parents (De Vos 1973c). In other instances, as in the situation that Ogbu (1978) discusses in understanding the poor school performance of many American black children, a defensive minority identity can prevent an individual from trying to succeed.

Crises in identity maintenance occur when one must choose between conflicting group loyalties, such as between the demands of ethnic-group membership and professional integrity. In the United States as elsewhere, there are continuing dilemmas over taking care of members of one's own ethnic group versus a priority of responsibility to inculcated professional standards. In Nigeria, the Thos did so well professionally and economically that the other major ethnic groups finally responded by driving them out of non-Tho regions of Nigeria. Many other examples of the forceful suppression of too-successful ethnic minorities can be easily recalled.

The ethnic composition of various professions and trades in the United States has changed over the years. Some, however, continue to manifest ethnic differences due to earlier patterns of exclusion. The exclusion-inclusion process in trades and professions begins with admittance or nonadmittance to training programs. Patterns of ethnic prejudice, though, may readily shift to more subtle forms of recognition or nonrecognition through appointments.

Advancement related to "quality in professional performance" can be and often is ethnically controlled. The pure notion of professional integrity is somehow lost in a labyrinth of multiple causal loops, and the achievement process over time will display many of the characteristics of a self-fulfilling prophecy. Opportunities will be better used by those whose personalities have been cultivated to understand and exploit ethnically biased opportunities to maximal advantage.

COMPETENCE. Ethnic identity may determine one's confidence in one's capacities to take on socially acceptable goal-oriented activities. Expectations of self are shaped by capacities or incapacities attributed by others to one's ethnic group. As part of one's ethnic identity, one may face many situations that demonstrate personal inadequacy rather than increasing confidence. In other instances, an inherited high social status is, at the same time, an avowal of one's potential capacity. It is thus psychologically easier for members of certain groups to move up to expectations of group competence if there is a collective confidence shared by the group. In such a group, the social self is developed around supportive attitudes. It is more difficult for an individual to assert his or her competence when one is a member of a group with no such supportive tradition. That individual has to depend more on independent capacities for status than do members inheriting such psychological support.

RESPONSIBILITY. As we have indicated, being a member of a group is partially defined by feeling compelled to obey the group's moral codes. Individuals who identify ethnically with a group also identify ethically with it. They may feel guilt or remorse for acts of omission or commission that are related to the well-being of their group. Not only responsibilities, but what is irresponsible and reprehensible is defined in group terms. As in the case of the Italians already cited, some groups have as part of their traditions both positive definitions of expectations and fears of how individuals, characteristically for the group, fail in meeting responsibilities. The dilemma of identity within many groups is this awareness of traditional avoidance of duty, as well as the heroic representations of what one should do to be truly moral.

Defined in ethnic terms, responsibility in all groups has an internalized moral dimension. Some who seek to escape ethnicity do so because they judge that the negative social and personal features of their inheritance far outweigh the positive. In times of crisis, however, they find themselves vulnerable to falling into a negative destiny. They may come to define their own moral failings as culturally inherited traits. In other instances, the positive expectations of what it is to be a member of a group are considered a burden to be avoided. One seeks to identify with a less demanding subgroup as a way out of the constraints of one's own tradition. But George Santayana, in his brilliant novel *The Last Puritan* (1936), suggests that a conscious disavowal of a tradition does not erase deeper layers of socialization. De Vos (1973a), describing "psychological lag" in Japanese arranged marriages, points out how conscious avowals of a right to "free marriage" do not result in any great decrease in arranged marriages in Japan. Many Japanese do not feel morally right about a free marriage for themselves, although they consider it acceptable intellectually for other Japanese.

In an ethnically pluralistic society, an individual may wish to take on a minority identity to take advantage of the seemingly freer pattern enjoyed by members of another group. Such individuals may attempt to take part in minority-group activities, but they are usually not accepted and remain outsiders. They are not considered to have the necessary "soul" to be included. In short, one's sense of ethnic identity invariably implies some assumption or avoidance of responsibility and guilt. A minority group member, by introjecting a negative ethnic self-image, may take on an internal conflict about ethical standards. Some, therefore, seek to avoid an ethnic identity as morally distasteful or burdensome and use it as an external explanation for personal failings.

CONTROL OR SOCIAL DOMINANCE. We have indicated how ethnicity is related to concepts of social and political power. One tends to assess oneself, as well as one's group, as being placed by society in a superordinate or subordinate position with respect to other groups. If placed in a superordinate status, an individual can view as legitimate the authority wielded in assuming dominance over members of other groups. Such individuals may experience some social insecurities related to an inculcated need to maintain control over others. A sense of emphasis on group ascendancy can be used to hide individual impotence. When the dominant group feels its authority threatened, the subordinate-but-feared group may be pressured to show symbolic signals of its continuing subordination. The more insecure, the more the need to manifest symbolically one's dominance and the more the need to receive symbolic gestures of submission from members of subordinate groups. The emphasis on German superiority in Nazism, for example, followed past defeats, including the social and economic impotence of the lower-middle-class Germans during the economic chaos of the last Weimar Republic. These groups found some psychological and social assuagement in the ideology advocated by Hitler: German ethnicity imparted a right to feel powerful and dominant, and it relieved the individual of his or her own sense of weakness. Belonging to a "superior" group helps resolve questions of individual assertion.

To espouse an ethnic identity, a person of subordinate status may have to assume a moral imperative to seek liberation and autonomy and to reassert a necessary independence of oneself and one's group from the oppressor. Negatively, there may be ambivalence over rebellion. One may feel impelled to rebel, and at the same time, one senses the rebellion to be an illegitimate act of infantile origin. The psychodynamics of submission, rebellion, or autonomy are complex. The same social acts may spring from different levels of maturity; submission, for example, may be an instrumental, mature decision to survive, or it may be an infantile form of dependency uncalled for and not easily reducible to a simple psychological explanation. An individual, as part of a tradition, may inherit modes of social trickery used by subordinates in somehow maintaining themselves vis-à-vis individuals of superior status (e.g., the "laughing barrel" of American blacks). There may also be ambivalence about social submission and compliance that an individual may project outward as a problem of group identity. The relation of ethnic identity to power and exploitation is a large topic that needs no further illustration to indicate its relevance.

MUTUALITY. Ethnic or subcultural traditions define modes of competition as well as modes of cooperation expected of the individual by one's group. Competitive activity may be deemphasized within the group at the same time that competition with individuals outside the group is encouraged. For example, among the Burakumin, minority outcastes of Japan, competitive activities or expressions of aggression among children

are discouraged within the group but are implicitly and explicitly encouraged toward the majority children.

Standards of ethical competition within a group are often quite different from those permitted when the individual is dealing with people outside the group. Very often, within-group activities of an instrumental
nature emphasize the need for concerted behavior and mutual trust in acting together toward the realization of goals. At the same time, some groups
realize that they may be betrayed from within. This makes it difficult for
the group to unite to attain political or social goals. Mexican Americans,
for example, have shown continual distrust of their leaders.

With respect to each of these dimensions of instrumental activity, the
individual may be faced with a dilemma of identity, since maintaining oneself within one's own group may be a disadvantage when one is seeking to
realize personal goals. One must then decide whether it is worthwhile to
give up group identity or to maintain it and seek to realize goals despite the
inconveniences of one's ethnic status. In some cases, conversely, allegiance
to a group is reinforced because group membership affords support in the
cooperative or competitive realization of goals.

Expressive Behavior and Ethnic Identity

Maintenance of one's ethnic loyalty always involves expressive, emotional
needs. The psychological rewards of remaining a minority outweigh the instrumental advantages of leaving or changing behavior to gain occupational
or social advantage. Such decisions are very complex. In each instance, one
must assess the relative strength of a variety of expressive vectors in understanding behavior related to group affiliation. The following are some fragments of topics that deserve more than the cursory comments we summarize.
A fuller exposition of a psychocultural theory of ethnic identity would explore these motivational features in greater depth (Lee and De Vos 1981).

HARMONY. A universal need of group living is some kind of peacefulness
or harmony within one's group relationships. Feelings of conflict and contention are muted within the group; whenever possible, hostilities are displaced onto individuals not belonging to the group. Many groups,
however, unfortunately also embody in their traditions of membership
forms of discord, hostility, and resentment that are directed more internally
than externally.

Social movements arising from within minority groups are often attempts to unite the group to achieve a new sense of harmony. The most

expedient mechanism for effecting internal harmony is to find a way of deflecting socially disruptive behavior onto outside individuals. Thus, considerable emotional benefits can be gained by certain church memberships, such as the Black Muslims. Membership permits a new conceptualization of one's ethnic self in such a way that internal kinship is reinforced while at the same time the individual is given a means of deflecting one's aggressive needs onto legitimately hated outsiders. Most groups use mechanisms of this type in one way or another to maintain their continuance. By so doing, one reaches for a greater sense of peacefulness and ease within the group. Consequently, there is an increase in uneasiness, wariness, and suspicion regarding given outsiders who are cast in the role of enemy. Scapegoating is a well-established mechanism central to any social psychological study of prejudice and ethnocentrism. It is a characteristic both of majority and minority groups in plural societies.

AFFILIATION. The sense of affiliative belonging involved in ethnicity has been discussed throughout this volume. Social isolation is an intolerable state for most humans. The threat of separation from the group is one of the most stringent of human sanctions. An ethnic group can provide for a mutual sense of contact possible only in some areas of communication to those sharing common past experiences. In this regard, a generalized ethnic identity may in some instances supplant more direct personally intimate one-to-one relationships.

There can arise a generation gap in ethnic identity. An individual may find satisfying if not intimate companionship more readily with peers of similar ethnic origin than in contacts with primary family members of a different generation. For many Mexican American youth, an ethnic peer group quickly replaces the primary family as the primary reference group.

Problems of ethnic identity can arise if self-affirmation signals that one is leaving one's group. This, in turn, can lead to rejection by, and enforced isolation from, others of one's group. A choice to go it alone involves severe psychological strain. In *Japan's Invisible Race* (1969), De Vos and Wagatsuma cite examples of Japanese outcastes who tried to pass for some time but finally returned to their own group, giving up promising professional careers bought at the cost of social estrangement. The whole topic of individualism and alienation related to problems over a sense of group belonging deserves more exposition than can be given here. De Vos has covered some of these features with Hiroshi Wagatsuma in exploring alienation and suicide among Japanese (De Vos 1973b).

NURTURANCE. Nurturance is the transmission of care from the older to the younger generations. The sense of nurturance may not extend beyond ethnic boundaries. The parental attitude, if genuine, assumes the younger individual needs *temporary* assistance, not that he or she is permanently incapable of taking care of him- or herself. This attitude between groups may slip over into one of a permanent paternalism that is psychologically damaging to the recipients. The dependent role of wards that the government forced upon Native Americans has helped perpetuate chronic identity problems that have been socially debilitating for the groups that they were supposedly designed to aid.

Ethnic relationships are often expected to supply care, help, and comfort in times of need. For some, ethnic membership provides a field for expressing benevolence. Many find within themselves a need to care for others, to care for the more helpless of one's own kind. Conversely, members of an ethnic group not only expect sociability or alliance, but they expect to be able to express dependency needs to other members.

Whereas individuals expect nurturance and care from their group and often feel responsible for caring for others in their own group, they may find themselves relatively deprived personally, socially, or economically within the larger society, because of their minority or ethnic-group status. Many ethnic groups in plural societies set up special benevolent societies to take care of distressed members. American Jews have been pioneers in professional welfare agencies in the United States.

A major problem of public welfare programs has been the incapacity of professionally trained workers to reach people across ethnic barriers. Similar problems arise in public health programs. The recent interest in medical anthropology arises from recognition that ethnic identity and differences in cultural traditions are important social factors in reaching and aiding the disadvantaged.

Members of one's own ethnic group, when professionally trained, have the advantage of reaching people who need help. Both psychiatry and medicine require mutual trust and mutual belief; it is psychologically difficult to become dependent on an outsider. Finally, in some groups, one might find that there is the unhappy perception that members are mutually depriving one another. This may not be overtly stated to outsiders but a felt experience that adds to ambivalence about maintaining group membership.

APPRECIATION. Ethnic identity is related basically to pride in a positive way, or to shame and degradation in a negative way. Each group seeks to create for itself a sense of humanity, dignity, self-respect, and proper status. Any human being resents the possibility of being neglected, ignored, or unappreciated, or worse, actively degraded, disparaged, debased, and depreciated. Ethnic identity often involves vulnerable feelings about self-respect or a potential sense of worthlessness. Some groups are particularly sensitive to the opinions of others, to their public image. Other groups are more self-sufficient. Perhaps the English and the Japanese are extremes of this continuum. English self-sufficiency is related to a need for appreciation limited to those within their class system. In both the English and Japanese, a deep sense of shame may be aroused by improper behavior on the part of a member of one's own group. A readiness to take on external values often crucially curtails the self-sufficiency of Japanese. As a nation, they are particularly vulnerable to external criticism or inadvertent disparagement.

Expressive feelings concerned with appreciation are central to understanding many difficulties that arise in intragroup and intergroup relationships. Culture traits cannot help but be evaluated. What is seen in highly positive terms within a group may, with alien contact, lose its value as soon as it is perceived by others in a devalued way.

Theodore Schwartz has discussed the origin and development of cargo cults, not as a reaction to an external dominance of Western culture, but much more directly related to the devaluation of what was of value in Melanesia in their economic interaction. That is, the Melanesians could no longer believe in their symbols of economic worth when they were faced with the knowledge of a much superior technology producing goods of greater worth than they could possibly imagine within their traditional culture.

Resultant crises in the sense of self felt acutely by Melanesians led to the development of the cargo-cult preoccupation, in which they hoped for the arrival of superior cargo from some supernatural source. Without extreme self-devaluation, they could not countenance the idea that these superior material artifacts were simply the products of people like themselves.

One of the great problems of culture contact is such crises of self-assessment. These occur when a group is forced to recognize the relative merits and sometimes the superior technology of an alien group. Within pluralistic societies, there is constant mutual evaluation. Such collective evaluative comparisons can add to or detract from the individual's appraisal of personal worth as a member of a group.

PLEASURE AND SUFFERING. Ethnic identity is ultimately related to questions about the satisfaction afforded by social life and to the problem of arriving at a mature capacity to tolerate the suffering and death that is the destiny of all. As in the metaphor of the California Indian sadly commenting on the death of his culture, ethnic identity is found in the "cup of custom" passed on by one's parents, from which one drinks the meaning of existence. Once the cup is broken, one can no longer taste of life. It is a light-scattering prism through which one views life with a sense of curiosity and creativity. It is both a means and an end, insofar as one develops a capacity to enjoy. An ethnic identity gives savor, the taste of one's past. The tastelessness of instant artifice is what the younger generation today describes as "plastic"; it is the opposite of the sense of past accumulations, of meanings husbanded and passed on to a new generation. Stripped of these, individuals face indifference, boredom, and a sense of normlessness or anomie. This is the result not only of a lack of regulation governing life but of the lack of savor and seasoning that occurs with the heedless casting out of past custom. Ultimately, ethnic identity is the unexpressed meaning of anthropology. Anthropologists intellectualize about human culture, yet they try to preserve in their own modes of pursuing knowledge the value of the human past, to assert that without consciousness of the past, the present becomes devoid of meaning.

In ethnic identity, there is a commitment to endure suffering. In the Christian context, to change the Indian metaphor, one's culture is also the common chalice in which suffering blood becomes redemptive wine. To some few, identity can be a commitment to masochism, but to most, it is simply a necessary stigmatic emblem one must learn to carry without disguise. Each group perhaps thinks that in maintaining itself it has to undergo certain forms of unique suffering not experienced by others. It may be reassuring to some and perhaps deflating to others to recognize that consciousness of suffering is not unique to any one group but is the destiny of our common humanity, whatever our separate cultural origins.

Notes

1. See Erik Erikson, *Identity, Youth and Crisis* (1968).

2. A scheme of instrumental-expressive social interactional concerns has been used by George A. De Vos in his previous work in understanding social role behavior in Japan (1973c). It is a conceptual framework that has evolved out of analyses of the Thematic Apperception Test in different cultural settings. It is discussed at length in the recent volumes by De Vos and De Vos, *The Basic Dimensions in Conscious Thought* (2004a) and *Cross Cultural Dimensions in Conscious Thought* (2004). This scheme has also been applied to analyze the persistence of a Korean ethnic identity within a Japanese society that had at one time sought to obliterate

any separate identity on the part of subjects of Korean ancestry residing in Japan (Lee and De Vos 1981).

References

Balzer, Marjorie Mandelstam. 1991. Doctors or deceivers? The Siberian Khanty shaman and Soviet medicine. In *The Anthropology of Medicine: From Culture to Method*, ed. Lola Romanucci-Ross, Daniel E. Moerman, and Laurence Tancredi, 56-84. South Hadley, MA: Bergin & Garvey.

———. 1993a. Shamanism and the politics of culture: An anthropological view of the 1992 International Conference on Shamanism, Yakutsk, the Sakha Republic. *Shaman* 1 (1): 71-96.

———. 1993b. Two urban shamans: Unmasking leadership in fin de-Soviet Siberia. In *Perilous states: Conversations on culture, politics, and nation*, ed. George E. Marcus, 131–64. Chicago: University of Chicago Press.

Bruner, Edward. 1976. Some observations on cultural change and psychological stress in Indonesia. In *Responses to change: Society, culture and personality*, ed. George A. De Vos, 234–52. New York: D. Van Nostrand Company.

Crandon-Malamud, Libbet. 1991. Phantoms and physicians: Social change through medical pluralism. In *The anthropology of medicine: From culture to method*, ed. Lola Romanucci-Ross, Daniel E. Moerman, and Laurence Tancredi, 56-84. South Hadley, MA: Bergin & Garvey.

De Vos, George A. 1973a. Some observations of guilt in relation to achievement and arranged marriage in the Japanese. In *Socialization for achievement: The cultural psychology of the Japanese*, ed. George A. De Vos, 144–46. Berkeley: University of California Press.

———. 1973b. Role narcissism and the etiology of Japanese suicide. In *Socialization for achievement: The cultural psychology of the Japanese*, ed. George A. De Vos, 438–85. Berkeley: University of California Press.

———. 1973c. *Socialization for achievement: The cultural psychology of the Japanese*. Berkeley: University of California Press.

De Vos, George A., and Eric S. De Vos. 2004a. *Basic dimensions in conscious thought*. Boulder, CO: Rowman & Littlefield.

———. 2004b. *Cross cultural dimensions in conscious thought*. Boulder, CO: Rowman & Littlefield.

De Vos, George A., and Hiroshi Wagatsuma. 1966. *Japan's invisible race*. Berkeley: University of California Press.

Durkheim, Emile. 1947. *The elementary forms of religious life*. Trans. W. Swain. Glencoe, IL: Free Press.

Erikson, Erik. 1968. *Identity, youth and crisis*. New York: Norton.

Haley, Alex. 1966. *The autobiography of Malcolm X*. New York: Grove Press.

Kardiner, Abram, and Lionel Ovesey. 1962. *The mark of oppression*. Cleveland: World Publishing.

Lee, Changsoo, and George A. De Vos. 1981. *Koreans in Japan: Ethnic Conflict and Accommodation*. Berkeley: University of California Press.

Ogbu, John. 1978. Minority education and caste: The American system in cross-cultural perspective. New York: Academic Press.

Romanucci-Ross, Lola. 1966. Conflits Fonciers a Mokerang village Matankor des iles de l'Amiraute. *L'Homme* 6 (2): 32-52.

———. 1977. Hierarchy of resort in curative practices. In *Culture, disease and healing*, ed. David Landy, 481–87. New York: Macmillan.

———. 1983. *Conflict, violence, and morality in a Mexican village*. Chicago: University of Chicago Press.

———. 1985. *Mead's other Manus; Phenomenology of the encounter*. South Hadley, MA: Bergin & Garvey.

———. 1989. The impassioned cogito: Shaman and anthropologist. In *Shamanism: Past and present*, ed. M. Hoppal and von Sadovsky, 35–42. Budapest: Istor Books.

Santayana, George. 1936. *The last Puritan*. New York: Scribner.

Sapir, Edward. 1968. Contributions to cultural anthropology. *International Encyclopedia of the Social Sciences*. New York: MacMillan.

Schwartz, Theodore. 1995. Cultural totemism. In *Ethnic Identity*, ed. Lola Romanucci-Ross and George A. De Vos, 3rd ed. Walnut Creek, CA: AltaMira Press.

Valiers, Pierre. 1968. *Negres Blancs d'Amerique: Autobiographies Precoce d'un "Terroriste" Quebecois*. Montreal: Parti Tris.

Index

Note: Page numbers in *italic* indicate figures.

Africa, 329; in the United States, 23–24
Pearson, Drew, 27
peer groups: identity formation and, 24–25; language use and, 24–25, 28
Peters, Carl, 277
Peterson, Minnie, 347
phenomenon of preferred self-identity, 301
Piccioni, Giovanni, 51
Piceno, Italy: aesthetics of ethnic identity in, 59–60; brigandage in, 51–52; child development in, 60–62; community in, 57–59, 62–64; family in, 53–55; formation of identity in, 66; language in, 52–53; people of, 47–50; religion in, 55–56; time in, 56–57
Pirandello, Luigi, 65
pleasure, ethnic identity and, 397–98
Plejic, Irena, 106
plural societies, 2
Poland, Jews in, 80–81
Poles, and Lithuanians, 72–79, 86–87
politics of location, 243
Population Registration Act (South Africa, 1950), 356–57
Portal, Gerald, 282–83
Portes, Alejandro, 177
professional identity, 13
public welfare programs, 396

Quintana, 62

race, ethnicity and, 5
racialization: essentialization and, 227–28; Japanese Brazilians in Brazil, 210–20; Japanese Brazilians in Japan, 220–26
racism, immigrants and, 167–69
Rama V, King of Thailand, 252
Redfield, Robert, 361
relativism, 323

religion: ethnicity and, 7–9; family character of, in Italy, 55–56; identity offered through, 12; in Lithuania, 74, 76–79, 82, 84–85; Moroccan immigrants and, 200
responsibility, ethnic identity and, 391–92
Rhitman-Augustin, Dunja, 90
rice, 248
Rita da Cascia, Santa, 55–56
rites of passage, 20
rituals, 377–80
Roma, 295–309; background on, 236–37; consequences of ethnicizing, 306–7; definition of, 296–99; disadvantages of, 295; elite among, 303; ethnic identity of, 299–302; ethnicization of, 302–4; as European concern, 296; origins of, 306; purposes of ethnicizing, 304–5; scapegoating of, 303–4; statehood for, 308; subgroups of, 297–98, 301
Roodt, Dan, 339
Röscher, Albert, 278
Rotberg, Robert, 272, 277
Rouch, Jean, 386
Routledge, K. P., 284
Routledge, W. S., 284

Sacchi, Arrigo, 63
Salau, Daniel, 288
samba, 225–26
Sandford, George, 286
Santayana, George, 392
Sapir, Edward, 387
scapegoating, 142, 303–4, 395
Schama, Simon, 10
Schwartz, Theodore, 397
"Sciabolone," 51
Seikyosha (Society for Political Education), 125
Serafino, Saint, 56

About the Contributors

Andrea Boscoboinik is a research assistant at the Institute of Social and Cultural Anthropology at the University of Fribourg, Switzerland. She is the scientific coordinator of the project "Perceptions, Self-Perceptions and Social Organization of Roma in Central and East European Countries" organized by Ethnobarometer (Italy). Her main topics of research include ethnic minorities and the social impact of catastrophes. She is the coeditor (with Christian Giordano) of the book *Constructing Risk, Threat, Catastrophe: Anthropological Perspectives* (2002), edited by University Press, Fribourg, Switzerland.

George A. De Vos, a psychologist and anthropologist, is emeritus professor of anthropology, University of California at Berkeley. He is the author of twenty books and 180 articles documenting his over fifty years of cross-cultural field experience and research in the United States, East Asia, and Western Europe. He has been a National Institute of Mental Health research fellow at the National Institute for Training and Research on Delinquency (France), a senior fellow of the American National Science Foundation, University of Rome, and the United Nations Social Defense Research Institute in Italy, and a research associate at the Centre Charles Richet d'Etudes des Dysfonctions de l'Adaptation, Ecole des Hautes Etudes en Sciences Sociales, University of Paris. Several times he has been an exchange professor: in 1978, exchange professor, University of Paris; 1980, exchange professor, Ecole des Hautes Etudes en Sciences Sociales, Paris; 1980, visiting professor, Katholicke Universiteit te Leuven, Leuven, Belgium; 1989, exchange professor, Katholicke Universiteit te Leuven,

Leuven, Belgium; 1990, exchange professor, Leningrad University (now St. Petersburg); 1992, visiting professor, University of Barcelona; and 1996, visiting professor, University of Padua, Italy. He has written extensively on Japanese cultural psychology (*Socialization for Achievement* 1973); on religion (*Religion and the Family in East Asia* 1986); on social problems, like delinquency (*Heritage of Endurance: Family Patterns and Delinquency Formation in Urban Japan* 1984) and minority-group issues (*Japan's Invisible Race* 1966, *Koreans in Japan* 1981, *Social Cohesion and Alienation* 1991); and the use of psychological tests cross-culturally (*Oasis and Casbah: Algerian Culture and Personality in Change* 1960, *Symbolic Analysis Cross Culturally: The Rorschach Test* 1989). More generally, he has written and edited *Ethnic Identity* (1975, 1982, 1995); *Responses to Change: Society, Culture and Personality* (1976); *Culture and Self: Asian and Western Perspectives* (1985); *Status Inequality: The Self in Culture* (1990); and *Social Cohesion and Alienation: Minorities in the United States and Japan* (1992).

Fabienne Doucet is assistant professor of human development and family studies at the University of Connecticut. She has a PhD in human development and family studies from the University of North Carolina at Greensboro. A scholar of immigration, her current work focuses on Haitian youth, and her research interests include parenting values and beliefs, parent-child relationships, culturally diverse families, racial and ethnic identity, the construction of social class, racial socialization, gender socialization, and qualitative methodology. From 2000 to 2002, she was a National Science Foundation minority postdoctoral fellow at the Harvard Graduate School of Education, where she conducted a study of the way values and beliefs about academic achievement are communicated between Haitian immigrant parents and children and how this process impacts upon children's academic· engagement. In 2003, she was awarded a National Academy of Education/Spencer fellowship to work on a book manuscript based on this research. Related areas of interest include racial and ethnic identity, gender, and social class issues as they pertain to the schooling and life experiences of immigrants. Dr. Doucet's previous work has examined African American preschoolers' engagement in academically relevant activities, as well as African American parents' and caregivers' beliefs, values, and practices surrounding the preparation of preschool children for the transition to school.

Louis Freedberg is an editorial writer at the *San Francisco Chronicle*. Born and raised in South Africa, he has a BA in psychology from Yale and a PhD in anthropology from the University of California at Berkeley. For several years, Freedberg ran programs in the San Francisco Bay Area for young people on the margins of the public school system. During the antiapartheid era, he founded the Institute for a New South Africa, which established links between black communities in South Africa threatened with removal at the hands of the Pretoria regime and communities in the United States. As a reporter, he wrote extensively about the antiapartheid movement and the postapartheid period beginning with the release of Nelson Mandela in 1990. He has written for a range of publications, including the *New York Times*, the *Washington Post*, *Washington Monthly*, and the *Nation* magazine. He was the recipient of the John S. Knight Journalism Fellowship at Stanford University, where he examined race relations within the youth culture. He was also awarded an Alicia Patterson Journalism Fellowship when he wrote about the unintended consequences of U.S. immigration policies. During his fellowship year, he was based at the Urban Institute in Washington, D.C.

Mary Kay Gilliland is on the anthropology faculty at the University of Arizona, Tucson, and at Pima Community College, Tucson, where she has also served as chair of social sciences for ten years. She has done fieldwork in Yugoslavia, Croatia, and Bosnia for more than twenty years, and recently with Bosnian refugees in Tucson. Proficient in Croatian, Serbian, and Bosnian (or what was Serbo-Croatian), her research interests include family, gender, marriage, the cultural construction of identity, refugees and migration, and ethnogenesis in the Balkans, focusing on what she calls "reclaimed lives" in this region. Her writings include articles on pre- and postwar Yugoslavia and Croatia, and Bosnian refugees.

Philip Hermans is associate professor of educational anthropology at the University of Groningen in the Netherlands. He studied psychology and anthropology and took his PhD in anthropology from the University of Leuven, Belgium. He has been a guest scholar at the University of California, USA; visiting researcher at the University of Durban-Westville, South Africa; and visiting professor at the universities of Leuven, Belgium, and El Jadida, Morocco. He has done research and published on Moroccan culture, Moroccan Islamic folk medicine, ethnicity, and the integration and education of ethnic minority children.

Lotte Hughes is a former journalist, now an historian of Africa. After spending three years as a postdoctoral researcher and junior fellow at St.

Antony's College, University of Oxford, she has recently been appointed to a lectureship in African Arts and Cultures at the Open University, Milton Keynes, UK. She received her MA in area studies (Africa) at the School of Oriental and African Studies, University of London (1988), and her doctorate in modern history at the University of Oxford (2002). Her doctoral dissertation examined Maasai land losses and forced moves in colonial Kenya. A book based on this—*Moving the Maasai: A Colonial Misadventure*—will be published in 2006 by Palgrave Macmillan. A commissioned history of environment and empire, coauthored with William Beinart, will be published by Oxford University Press. Her first book was nonacademic, *A No-Nonsense Guide to Indigenous Peoples* (Verso 2003).

Czeslaw Milosz was a member of the American Academy of Arts and Letters. He won the Nobel Prize for Literature in 1980. His books of poetry in English include *Bells in Winter*, *The Separate Notebooks*, *Unattainable Earth*, *The Collected Poems: 1931–1987*, and *Provinces*.

Lola Romanucci-Ross, a cultural and medical anthropologist and professor in the School of Medicine, University of California, San Diego, spent several postdoctoral years in Paris studying with Claude Levi-Strauss. Research on the Native American Indian began as part of her graduate studies at the University of Minnesota and the University of Chicago. Each of her ensuing research projects lasted over a number of years in each field site: Mexico, in a study for and with Erich Fromm, New Guinea in the South Pacific with Margaret Mead and Ted Schwartz for the American Museum of Natural History, and Italy in a long-term project that was done in parts over a nineteen-year period. She has published numerous articles in professional journals on aspects of her research. Among her published books are *Conflict, Violence and Morality in a Mexican Village* (1973, 1986); *Mead's other Manus: Phenomenology of the Encounter* (1985); *The Anthropology of Medicine: from Culture to Method* (1983, 1989; in Japan, 1991, 1997); *One Hundred Towers: An Italian Odyssey of Cultural Survival* (1991); and *Ethnic Identity* (with George de Vos, 1975, 1982, 1995); her most recent book, *When Law and Medicine Meet: A Cultural View* (2004), is based on her interest in American culture, researching what happens when scientific evidence in a courtroom brings together two systems exemplifying diverse epistemic principles, science and the law.

Eugeen Roosens was professor and head of the Department of Anthropology at the Katholieke Universiteit of Leuven, Belgium, and also taught at universities in the United States, Canada, and Zaire. He was P. P. Rubens Professor at the University of California (1989–1990). Roosens did fieldwork among the Yaka in Zaire; with the Huron Indians in Quebec; and in Geel, Belgium. He also directed the project, "The Cultural Identity of Ethnic Minorities," a long-term fieldwork project by a team of scholars that operates in five continents. He directed the anthropology team for the Geel project, which concerned community placement of the mentally ill in a Belgium town. His book on Geel has been translated into English, French, German, and Japanese. Roosens has written half a dozen other books on Africa, ethnicity, and immigration.

Yos Santasombat is professor of anthropology at Chiang Mai University. He obtained his PhD from the University of California at Berkeley. He has carried out extensive fieldwork in northern Thailand and in Daikong, northwestern Yunnan, China. He has published over a dozen books and research manuscripts, including *Lak Chang: A Reconstruction of Tai Identity in Daikong* (Pandanus Books, The Australian National University, 2001) and *Biodiversity, Local Knowledge and Sustainable Development* (Regional Center for Sustainable Development, Chiang Mai University, 2003).

Nancy Scheper-Hughes is professor of medical anthropology at the University of California at Berkeley, where she directs the doctoral program in Critical Studies in Medicine, Science, and the Body. Scheper-Hughes's lifework concerns the violence of everyday life examined from a radical existentialist and politically engaged perspective. Her work ranges from AIDS and human rights in Cuba; death squads and the extermination of street kids in Brazil; and the Catholic Church, clerical celibacy, and child sex abuse, to the repatriation of the brain of a famous Yahi Indian, Ishi (kept as a specimen in the Smithsonian Institution) to the Pit River people of Northern California. Her most recent research is a multisited ethnographic study of the global traffic in humans for their organs, which she interprets as a form of invisible and sacrificial violence. She is perhaps best known for her books on schizophrenia among bachelor farmers in County Kerry (*Saints, Scholars and Schizophrenics: Mental Illness in Rural Ireland*) and on the madness of hunger, maternal thinking, and infant mortality in Brazil (*Death Without Weeping: The Violence of Everyday Life in Brazil*). In 1994–1995, Scheper-Hughes moved to South Africa to take up a temporary post as chair of anthropology at the Department of Social Anthropology at the University of Cape Town during the political transition. While there, she began an ongoing ethnographic study of the role of political and everyday violence in the pre- and posttransition periods. She has written a series of essays to be published under the title *Undoing: The Politics of the Impossible in the New South Africa*. Her most recent books are *Commodifying Bodies* (coedited with Loic Waquant; the Theory, Culture and Society series; London: Sage, 2002) and *Violence in War and Peace: An Anthology* (coedited with Philippe Bourgois; London: Basil Blackwell, 2003.

Carola Suárez-Orozco is associate professor of applied psychology and teaching and learning at New York University's Steinhardt School of Education and codirector of Immigration Studies at NYU. Prior to moving to NYU, Dr. Suárez-Orozco was the codirector of the Harvard Immigration Longitudinal Immigrant Student Adaptation Study (LISA). This interdisciplinary research project examined the adaptations of Central American, Chinese, Dominican, Haitian, and Mexican immigrant adolescents to American schools and society longitudinally. Her research focus in recent years has been on the intersection of cultural and psychological factors in the adaptation of immigrant and ethnic-minority youth. She publishes widely in the areas of cultural psychology, academic engagement, immigrant youth, and identity formation. She is the author of *Children of Immigration* (with Marcelo Suárez-Orozco, Harvard University Press, 2001) and *Transformations: Migration, Family Life, and Achievement Motivation among Latino Adolescents* (with Marcelo Suárez-Orozco, Stanford University Press, 1995). They are also the coeditors of the six-volume series entitled *Interdisciplinary Perspectives on the New Immigration* (with Desirée Qin-Hillard, Routledge Press, 2001). She has published a number of articles and chapters on such topics as academic engagement, the role of the "social mirror" in identity formation, immigrant family separations, the role of mentors in facilitating positive development in immigrant youth, and the gendered experiences of immigrant youth, among many others.

Takeyuki (Gaku) Tsuda is associate director of the Center for Comparative Immigration Studies at the University of California at San Diego. After receiving his PhD in anthropology in 1997 from the University of California at Berkeley, he taught for three years as a collegiate assistant professor at the University of Chicago. His primary academic interests include international migration, diasporas, ethnic and national identity, transnationalism and globalization, contemporary Japanese society and the Japanese diaspora, and Brazil. For his dissertation research, he studied the return migration of Japanese Brazilians to Japan as unskilled foreign workers and conducted close to two years of fieldwork in both Japan and Brazil. In addition, he has written on immigration and immigrants in Japan, comparative immigration and immigrant policies, and ethnicity and migration. He has begun fieldwork on a new project on the Japanese diaspora that will compare the Japanese Americans and Japanese Brazilians in the ethnoracial contexts of the United States and Brazil and their experiences when they "return" migrate to their ethnic homeland of Japan. He has taught classes on international migration, social theory, and Japan at both the University of Chicago and University of California at San Diego. His publications include numerous articles in anthropological and interdisciplinary journals as well as a book entitled *Strangers in the Ethnic Homeland: Japanese Brazilian Return Migration in Transnational Perspective* (Columbia University Press, 2003). He is also the editor of *Local Citizenship in Recent Countries of Immigration: Japan in Comparative Perspective* (Lexington Books, forthcoming) and coeditor of *Controlling Immigration: A Global Perspective* (second edition, Stanford University Press, 2004).

Hiroshi Wagatsuma was a psychological anthropologist, known to every student of Japanese cultural psychology. He was the author or coauthor of many memorable books and articles in English and Japanese on Japan's social, ethnic, and national minorities, especially outcastes, mixed bloods, and Koreans. He wrote, with George De Vos, of *Japan's Invisible Race: Caste in Culture and Personality* (Berkeley: University of California Press, 1966). The UCLA Center for Pacific Rim Studies administers the Hiroshi Wagatsuma Memorial Fund to support cross-cultural research between Asian and North American societies.